The Grapevine of
the Black South

SERIES EDITORS

Sarah E. Gardner, Mercer University

Jonathan Daniel Wells, University of Michigan

Print Culture in the South addresses the region's
literary and historical past from the colonial era to
the near present. Rooted in archival research, series
monographs embrace a wide range of analyses that,
at their core, address engagement and interaction
with print. Topics center on format/genre—novels,
pamphlets, periodicals, broadsides, and illustrations;
institutions such as libraries, literary societies, small
presses, and the book industry; and/or habits and
practices of readership and writing.

The Grapevine of the Black South

The Scott Newspaper Syndicate in the Generation before the Civil Rights Movement

Thomas Aiello

The University of Georgia Press
Athens

Portions of chapter 2 appeared, in somewhat different form, as "The Malevolent Gods of Hatred: Race, Representation, and the Puryear Ax Murders," in *Tennessee Historical Quarterly*. Portions of chapter 3 appeared, in somewhat different form, as "'The Shot That Was Heard in Nearly Two Million Negro Homes': The 1934 Murder of William Alexander Scott," in *Georgia Historical Quarterly* 100, no. 4 (2016): 366–403, copyright 2016 by the Georgia Historical Society. Portions of chapter 4 appeared, in somewhat different form, as "'Do We Have Any Men to Follow in Her Footsteps?': The Black Southern Press and the Fight for Teacher Salary Equalization," in *History of Education Quarterly* 58, no. 1 (2018): 94–121. Portions of chapter 6 appeared, in somewhat different form, as "Violently Amorous: The *Jackson Advocate*, the *Atlanta Daily World*, and the Limits Of Syndication," in *Journal of Mississippi History* 76 (Fall/Winter 2014): 183–201. Portions of chapter 7 appeared, in somewhat different form, as "Editing a Paper in Hell: Davis Lee and the Exigencies of Smalltime Black Journalism," in *American Journalism* 33, no. 2 (2016): 144–168.

Most University of Georgia Press titles are available from popular e-book vendors.

Printed digitally

Library of Congress Cataloging-in-Publication Data
Names: Aiello, Thomas, 1977– author.
Title: The grapevine of the black South : The Scott Newspaper
     Syndicate in the generation before the civil rights movement /
     Thomas Aiello.
Other titles: Print culture in the South.
Description: Athens : The University of Georgia Press, [2018] |
     Series: Print culture in the South | Includes bibliographical
     references and index.
Identifiers: LCCN 2018019211 | ISBN 9780820354460 (hardback :
     alk. paper) | ISBN 9780820354453 (pbk. : alk. paper) | ISBN
     9780820354477 (ebook)
Subjects, LCSH: Scott Newspaper Syndicate—History—20th
     century. | African American newspapers—Southern States—
     History—20th century. | African American newspapers—
     History—20th century. | Syndicates (Journalism)—Southern
     States—History—20th century. | Syndicates (Journalism)—United
     States—History—20th century.
Classification: LCC PN4882.5 .A44 2018 | DDC 071.308996073—
     dc23 LC record available at https://lccn.loc.gov/2018019211

In memory of Fuzzy B.

The writing of the Afro-American is the stain in the literature of this country which seriously challenges the myth of American perfection. . . . It is a literature of oppression, it is a cry from the soul of oppressed people. It is also a literature of protest, a cry for redress.

—Richard A. Long and Eugenia W. Collier, *Afro-American Writing: An Anthology of Prose and Poetry*

Northern Negroes (including those who packed their handbags down in Dixie and got that way) may pass up the Northern Negro papers because white dailies print Negro news, or because they feel a certain guilt in reading [a] Negro medium. But the Southern Negro pores over Southern Newspaper Syndicate presentations. . . . While his northern brother is busily engaged in "getting white" and ruining racial consciousness, the Southerner has become more closely knit. The SNS goes into thousands of homes and carries unaltered facts with it. In view of this fact the SNS is forever expanding, pioneering, and improving these presentations which suddenly have aroused race consciousness.

—*Atlanta World*, 1932

Contents

Acknowledgments

There are so many people and institutions that deserve my gratitude for all of their help to make this book happen. It has been years in the making, with dozens of universities, archives, conferences, and colleagues helping to make it possible. There are far too many to name, but I should give special recognition to my school, Valdosta State University, for giving me a grant to travel to fourteen of those archives in one monumental road trip. I would also like to thank Emory University, keeper of the *Atlanta Daily World*'s papers, an archive that I relied on heavily, on which much of this research was built. The librarians of what is now known as the Rose Library were always gracious and helpful, as were those at the University of Memphis, the Birmingham Public Library, the Birmingham Civil Rights Museum, the *Baltimore Afro-American*, the New York Public Library, the Newark Public Library, the State Library of West Virginia, the Tennessee State Library and Archives, the Briscoe Center for History at the University of Texas, the Houston Public Library, Louisiana State University's Hill Memorial Library, the Mississippi Department of Archives and History, the Department of Special and Area Studies Collections at the University of Florida, the South Caroliniana Library at the University of South Carolina, and the Atlanta University Center's Robert W. Woodruff Library. My colleagues in the VSU History Department offered support and advice, as did my friends at the Georgia Association of Historians and the Louisiana Historical Association. My friend Shannon Frystak let me crash at her house in Bethlehem, Pennsylvania, during a research trip, and my friend Mary Farmer-Kaiser read an early treatment of the book's plan more than a decade ago and encouraged the idea. My research assistant Jenny Smith was an invaluable help during one semester. I would also like to thank the *Tennessee Historical Quarterly*, the *Georgia Historical Quarterly*, the *Journal of Mississippi History*, *American Journalism*, and the *History of Education Quarterly*. To these institutions and individuals and to the many others not included in this abbreviated list, I owe my great devotion for their help in what has been a long but rewarding process.

Finally, I would like to thank my family for their love and support; those living: Sooie, Pickle, Madison, Mom, Cards, Ollie, Hank, Willow, Oliver, Templeton, Grey, Funny Feet, Prince Puma, and Backpack; and those no longer with us: Bacon, Tyrone, Fuzzy B., and Splinter.

The Grapevine of
the Black South

Introduction

In the summer of 1928, William Alexander Scott began a small four-page weekly with the help of his brother Cornelius. In 1930, his *Atlanta World* became a semiweekly, and the following year, W. A. began to implement his vision for a massive newspaper chain based out of Atlanta, the Southern Newspaper Syndicate. Advertisements proclaimed "Negroes Are Different in Dixie." In April 1931, the *World* became a triweekly along with several of the Syndicate's companion papers, among them the *Birmingham World* and *Memphis World*. Finally, in March 1932, the *Atlanta World* became a daily. When the Syndicate's reach began drifting beyond the bounds of the South in 1933, Scott changed its name to the Scott Newspaper Syndicate (SNS).

In the generation that followed, the Syndicate helped formalize knowledge among the African American population in the South. It gave black readers in Atlanta, for example, much the same news that it gave readers in New Orleans. When the civil rights movement exploded throughout the region, black southerners would find a collective identity in that struggle. This collective identity did not come solely from skin color or resentment of Jim Crow. The relative uniformity in post-*Brown* activism in the South was built in part on the commonality of the news and the subsequent interpretation of that news. Or as Gunnar Myrdal explains, the press was "the chief agency of group control. It [told] the individual how he should think and feel as an American Negro and create[d] a tremendous power of suggestion by implying that all other Negroes think and feel in this manner."[1] The opinions of individual editors about syndicated news were by no means monolithic, so southern newspaper syndication didn't create complete homogeneity in black southern thinking, but it did give thinkers a similar set of tools from which to draw.

Civil rights activism in the South, after all, looked fundamentally different from that in the Northeast, Midwest, or far West. Urbanization and the effects of the extended Great Migration certainly influenced those differences, as did the resulting residential segregation and the varied presentation of northern racism. Still, such an interpretation has its limitations, as those effects had a relative regional uniformity despite the fact that urbanization and residential segregation took different forms in each northern urban hub. When that paradigm is used to analyze the South, similar breakdowns occur. Life in South Carolina was dramatically different from that in Arkansas, and yet there existed a relative uniformity in the first wave of post-*Brown* activism throughout the South. The commonality that existed among the regions of the South—and that was simultaneously unavailable in other national regions—was the news. Black southern newspaper reporting, despite variances in the subsequent interpretation of that news, was largely the same. "The Negro Press," sociologist Lincoln Blakeney explains, "is the foundation of the Negro citizen's social thinking."[2]

The only way to understand that thinking is to first understand the systematic dissemination of information through the region, and that dissemination was principally the project of the SNS. From March 1931 to March 1955, no fewer than 241 newspapers were associated with the Syndicate. Because so many of its newspapers were small, or didn't last long, or weren't saved, or didn't leave behind business records, the Scott Newspaper Syndicate has often been given short shrift in discussions of the black press, virtually ignored in the historical literature on the development of black media. The syndicates associated with the *Pittsburgh Courier* and *Baltimore Afro-American* hold sway. Stories abound of Pullman porters toting copies of the *Chicago Defender* down South to provide black southerners with information they otherwise wouldn't have had. Northern and eastern syndicates were incredibly influential. But such examinations of more widely available black newspapers neglect the existence of a legitimate and flourishing group of black newspapers throughout the South. This book analyzes that network and its relationship to the black South in the generation before the civil rights movement.

The network, to be sure, had a long legacy. Kinship networks were palpable influences on black radicalism, argues Steven Hahn, as enslaved people developed communication networks across multiple plantations in the antebellum era. These kinship connections acted as cultural unifiers, but they also facilitated the spread of news, rumors, and religion. These networks didn't free people in any way—the power of slavery always trumped kinship—but those relationships would form the bedrock of black action once slavery was no longer in place. During the Civil War, enslaved people drew on the information traveling along those networks to flee their plantations and, often, the South itself. Hahn describes this as both "individual and collective intelligence." The South (particularly the lower South) conscripted black workers into forced labor on abandoned lands. Others stayed on plantations in slavery. But both groups demonstrated a new leverage in the war-torn South, based largely on those kinship networks. Black southerners demonstrated a new ability to organize and a new discipline. When these combined with the wartime needs of white masters, black people were able "to redefine the rules and rights of wartime labor."[3]

The black southern press in the post–World War I period became the modern version of those kinship networks. They looked much the same and served similar ends. Syndicate newspapers dominated in the small towns of the southern countryside. Calls for land reform were replaced with calls for voting rights, but the authors of the new network had learned from earlier racial crackdowns. In a pragmatic effort to avoid confrontation developing from white fear, newspaper editors developed a practical radicalism that argued on the fringes of white hegemony, picking their spots, urging local compromise, and saving their loudest vitriol for tyranny that wasn't local, thus leaving no stake in the game for would-be white saboteurs. "To be black and Southern in those perilous times, and to stake out a position at variance with the canons of segregation and white supremacy," explains historian John Egerton, "required a mixture of conservatism and tactful independence that few non-Southerners could understand or appreciate. Patience and diplomacy and flank-covering caution were essential to survival."[4]

Practical radicalism here bears an affinity to Tomiko Brown-Nagin's "pragmatic civil rights," a term she has used to describe Atlanta leaders' efforts to "preserve the economic self-sufficiency that black elites had achieved under Jim Crow, expand black political influence, and preserve personal autonomy." Litigation for civil rights was a last resort, and integration was not necessarily a measure of equality. In her evaluation of the legal fight for civil rights in Atlanta, Brown-Nagin argues that local communities were the locus of functional change. Community members were "law shapers, law interpreters, and even law makers," and thus the story of the fight for rights in the United States expands by uncovering "the agency of local people."[5] The law shapers and law interpreters in local communities throughout the South and the nation, most of them much smaller than Atlanta, were often the small black newspapers facilitated by the Scott Newspaper Syndicate.

While those small black newspapers were the heirs of early kinship networks, they were more immediately the heirs of the early development of the black press. On March 16, 1827, John Russwurm's *Freedom's Journal* argued that "we wish to plead our own cause. Too long have others spoken for us. Too long has the public been deceived by misrepresentations." Russwurm, the first African American to earn a bachelor's degree, founded the country's first black newspaper with Samuel Cornish. Two years later, his frustration was such that he emigrated to Liberia. (There, in 1830, he created the *Liberia Herald*.) Nell Irvin Painter has argued that the two characteristics of that early black press that most clearly define the difference between it and its white counterpart are a "racial orientation" (as opposed to a "partisan orientation") and "a sense of a supranational racial identity." As sociologist Charlotte O'Kelly points out, during Reconstruction, black newspapers emphasized "the Horatio Alger–type story of individual achievement against great odds," while pushing for "equal citizenship rights and better economic and educational opportunities for blacks." It was a formula the Scotts and many of their member newspapers would later embody. Indeed, as historian Martin E. Dann noted in the 1970s, the nineteenth-century black press "was the focal point of every controversy and every concern of black people representing as it did the strengths and re-inforcements which united the black community."[6]

The twentieth-century press continued that trend. There was, at the onset of World War I, a push for assimilation by the newspapers, prompted by an effort to support the war, but the broader concern of race papers remained race itself and the injustices committed because of it. They covered political disputes between black activists like Marcus Garvey, A. Philip Randolph, and W. E. B. Du Bois, and at times they did take sides, but Frederick Detweiler and others have concluded that coverage by the black press led to greater understanding of those issues and unity around the cause of equality, despite disagreements on the substantive issues of how to achieve it. After World War I, a new radicalism, including Garveyism, emerged in response to blacks' poor wartime treatment. Most of the black press was against Garvey, however, and the *Chicago Defender* aided in bringing about his arrest and eventual deportation. The press, as O'Kelly has demonstrated, "served to solidify in the black person's mind concepts of race and racial struggle." The interwar period saw the black newspaper at its most radical, and that militancy grew its audience and made it nationally relevant, a "much greater intermediary link and integrative force for the black population" than it had been before. It was, in the words of sociologist Guy Johnson, "almost as if all the rancor, all the resentment and brooding, all the inhibited impulses to retaliate for discrimination and injustice were brought together and let loose every week in the two hundred or more Negro newspapers" of the 1930s.[7]

According to a 1932 study of "Negro nationalism," the black press reflected the full range of opinions that a group might have, from radicalism to accommodation. "As a whole, however, it is a decidedly potent influence in wielding those divergent attitudes into something of a more homogeneous character," O'Kelly explains. That homogeneity was necessary during the Depression. African American urban unemployment rose to 50 percent by 1932, making the maintenance of a black business—newspaper or otherwise—a tenuous prospect at best. In 1929, the estimated national income had been $83 billion. In 1932, it was $39 billion. In 1929, average per capita income had been $1,475. In 1932, it was $1,119. There were 1.6 million people—3 percent of the labor force—unemployed in 1929. By 1933, that number had grown to 12.8 million, a full 25 percent of workers. Throughout the first decade of the Depression, one-fourth of all southerners were tenants or sharecroppers, as were half of all southern farmers. By June 1932, farm prices had dropped to 52 percent of the 1909–1914 average.[8]

The black press pushed through the economic crisis with surprising success given the vulnerability of its audience. In 1931, there were 228 black newspapers in the country, up from 130 in 1884. The Depression, however, took its toll, and by 1936 the total number of papers was 115. In 1936, the reported black newspaper circulation was 1,120,198. The following year it was over 1.2 million. "Most significant and heartening," announced the NAACP's *Crisis*, "has been the advance in circulation, advertising revenues, payrolls and equipment of the Negro newspaper during the depression period of the thirties."[9] The business grew throughout the Depression years.

The smaller southern newspapers of the SNS were relatively conservative in their stance on racial activism, particularly compared to northern papers like the *Chicago Defender, Pittsburgh Courier*, and *New York Amsterdam News*. That reputation didn't come from nowhere. After World War I, several white businesses had pulled advertisements from the *Houston Informer* because the companies' owners didn't like the paper's coverage of race rights. In 1921, the paper's offices were raided, and subscriber and advertiser lists were stolen. That same year, the *Dallas Express* received threats from the Ku Klux Klan promising "a Negro massacre" if the paper maintained a radical rights position.[10] In addition, many Syndicate papers were in areas without the strong black middle class that made it possible to fund the organization from a solely African American base. Thus some of those papers had to balance their activist stances between the dual realities of needing white advertising and dealing with stifling Jim Crow laws. Even those like the *Atlanta Daily World*, which had sufficient advertising revenue, and others that relied on the Syndicate for such matters still had to navigate the realities and consequences of white supremacy. The product of those balancing acts in the decades prior to World War II, however, and their outgrowth in the thought of the first wave of civil rights activism were not fundamentally conservative. The southern newspapers of the SNS instead demonstrated a practical radicalism that attacked discrimination in nuanced ways that allowed editors and publishers to critique the Jim Crow system without making themselves targets for white retribution.

Some southern newspapers that were part of the Syndicate were less subtle and more radical than many of their counterparts, demonstrating the regional, economic, and demographic variances that shaped the opportunities for editors. During the early 1930s, for example, black southerners were, to use Sid Bedingfield's words, "trapped in a morass of economic exploitation and political hopelessness." But things were beginning to change. Bedingfield notes in his study of South Carolina journalism that NAACP membership in the state rose from less than eight hundred in the mid-1930s to more than fourteen thousand following World War II. A new Progressive Democratic Party rose to challenge the hegemony of the white Democrats, and by the end of the 1940s, more than seventy thousand black South Carolinians were registered to vote. The linchpin of much of that success was John H. McCray, publisher of the state's most prominent black newspaper, the *Lighthouse and Informer*. The *Lighthouse and Informer* was a Deep South black newspaper that not only was willing to challenge Jim Crow in all of its facets but formed key alliances with leaders like Modjeska Simkins and local activist groups like the NAACP, using journalism to advocate for and coordinate the rights efforts in the state and making "strategic use of society's symbolic codes concerning freedom, justice, and equality to rally the black community and to elicit empathy from potential allies."[11] And it did so with great success, helping achieve equal pay for South Carolina teachers, securing black voting rights in Democratic primaries, and initiating the lawsuit that would ultimately become part of the *Brown v. Board of Education* decision. Throughout the 1940s, the *Lighthouse and Informer* was part of the Scott Newspaper Syndicate.

Of course, the SNS papers had competition. Stories abound concerning the infiltration of northern newspapers into the black South through the railroads, which sent both news and radicalism back home. The messages that papers like the *Courier* and *Defender* carried most certainly helped codify black southern dissatisfaction with Jim Crow—but they were the exception rather than the rule. Those papers have survived, and much of the southern black press has not, and therefore newspapers like the *Defender* get pride of place in southern historiography partly because of their easy availability and partly because of their unequivocal stances. The southern black press, however, dominated the region and actively encouraged its readers to avoid northern papers. The northern papers were, the *Atlanta Daily World* argued, inauthentically black. "Negroes," it reminded readers, "are different in Dixie."[12]

The Scotts were adamant on the point. "Northern Negroes (including those who packed their handbags down in Dixie and got that way) may pass up the Northern Negro papers because white dailies print Negro news, or because they feel a certain guilt in reading [a] Negro medium. But the Southern Negro pores over Southern Newspaper Syndicate presentations," explained one advertisement. "While his northern brother is busily engaged in 'getting white' and ruining racial consciousness, the Southerner has become more closely knit. The SNS goes into thousands of homes and carries unaltered facts with it. In view of this fact the SNS is forever expanding, pioneering, and improving these presentations which suddenly have aroused race consciousness."[13]

The Syndicate sought arrangements with prospective publishers in the towns and cities of the South, all of whom came from different backgrounds and had different levels of experience with publishing. Each of the SNS papers published syndicated editorial content along with more straightforward news coverage, but the publishers' papers remained their own, and the willingness to engage in race rights issues varied from newspaper to newspaper, reflecting the individual concerns of local editors. The relative uniformity of later southern civil rights activism and the widespread devastation of the Great Depression and Jim Crow often give historical depictions of the South an ideological consistency that didn't always exist. Bigotry looked different in Atlanta, for example, where a strong black middle class hovered between white business leaders and the bulk of the city's poor black residents, than it did in Florence, South

Carolina, where black influence was decidedly less palpable, where work opportunities were less available and race relations were more fraught, and where average education and literacy rates were lower than in the big city. Such variances ensured that each of the papers of the Scott Syndicate had its own unique identity, but the consistency bred by uniformity of the news helped serve as a tie that bound classes and regions among black southerners, rural and urban, west of the Atlantic Ocean and west of the Mississippi River.

Despite the real presence of such southern ties, many of the Syndicate papers were outside the South. In July 1932, less than a year and a half after its March 1931 founding, the Southern Newspaper Syndicate added the *St. Louis Argus* (Missouri). It wouldn't stretch the imagination, of course, to classify St. Louis as a southern city, but the following month the Syndicate added the *Indianapolis Recorder*, the *Gary American* (Indiana), the *Newark Herald* (New Jersey), the *Columbus Voice* (Ohio), and the *Detroit Independent* (Michigan). That month the SNS comprised twenty-six newspapers, including the *Atlanta Daily World*, by far its most prolific month to date (the previous high was eight), and either five or six of them, depending on your definition of the relationship of St. Louis to the South, around 20 percent, were in the Northeast and Midwest. That the spread of the SNS would mirror the spread of the black population during the Great Migration is not surprising. But an interesting fact about the spread is that a company that originally sold itself as uniquely and fundamentally southern—in order to compete with more radical northern competitors like the *Chicago Defender* sending editions to the South—would in relatively short order move outside those bounds in order to compete with the established northern syndicates emanating from Chicago, Pittsburgh, Baltimore, and New York. Although the Scott Syndicate receives far less historical treatment than the larger, more activist papers to the north, it spent much of its time and resources in the generation before the civil rights movement in areas outside of its traditionally understood region.

The Great Migration was beneficial to many people escaping poverty and Jim Crow, and it did provide new opportunities for better jobs and higher wages. But it could be a daunting journey. There were glass ceilings, new kinds of race fights, housing and employment discrimination, and even, as one economic analysis has demonstrated, higher death rates.[14] There was also a fundamental separation from the communities and mores of the region those migrants left, making the connective tissue of information all the more important. The establishment of a new grapevine was a necessity as the population was spread thin in new territory that was more welcoming in some ways and less welcoming in others.

Newspapers served as that connective tissue because they played to all classes, unlike monthly magazines. Even when the papers espoused middle-class values, propping up an ideal that wasn't always attainable for many of their readers, the low cost of black weeklies, the sensationalism that dominated their front pages, and the aspirational society news and sports and entertainment coverage ensured that inclusion cut across all class lines. In the early twentieth century, monthly magazines like the *Colored American*, *Voice of the Negro*, *Horizon*, *Opportunity*, the *Messenger*, and *Crisis* addressed a decidedly middle-class professional group, and as historian Michael Fultz has explained, "the opinions projected by these periodicals were articulated largely by the numerically small, but socially influential African-American middle-class and professional group who were coming into their own around the turn of the century."[15] It was a class-based discourse combined with a more expensive publication and long-form content that gave such periodicals their particular character.

The urban middle class was still there at the onset of the Great Depression, but it was numerically even smaller, making black newspapers, although presenting middle-class aspirational values, the voice of the underclass as well as the voice of the race. And in the South, blackness and underclassness went hand in hand. Or, as Gunnar Myrdal famously explained, the principal reason for "why the Negro press exaggerates the American pattern of sensational journalism is, of course, that the Negro community, compared with the white world, is so predominantly lower class." At the same time, the black press was controlled by "the upper and middle classes of the Negro community," who resented racial slights just as their working-class counterparts did, even though "caste barriers serve partly as a protection to give them special opportunities and status."[16] The black press occupied an important liminal space, particularly in the South.

But not only in the South. The *Chicago Defender* was one of the staunchest advocates for black migration out of the South, but as Mark Dolan has demonstrated, in the 1920s it also featured hundreds of advertisements for race records that fetishized the South, its culture, and its benefits, demonstrating that those moving north still maintained ties with the region above and beyond family connections. Migrants' relationships with the South were complex and varied, but most seemed to interpret the region as a meaningful genesis point that was still very much a part of their lives: in music, in foodways, in religion, in manners, in folklore. These cultural bonds strengthened the roots of the grapevine that would maintain such connections through the press, sometimes moving back south through northern nationals like the *Defender*, but more regularly following the vines of the migration north through the papers of the Scott Newspaper Syndicate.[17]

The *Defender*'s subscriber list shows the paper in every remote corner of the South, with estimates that each edition sent to the region was read by five people. The *Defender* had encouraged migration beginning in 1916 and thus helped lead the exodus out of the South. One historian even describes Robert Abbott, the paper's founder, as the "black Joshua" who led the race out of the region.[18] Certainly, the paper had a real and important impact on the South, and it absolutely played a role in convincing southerners to move north. But that narrative rests largely on the easy availability of the *Defender* and the testimony of those who escaped. The *Defender* and other papers like it, however, were supplements to the southern newspapers that provided the news from home, offering a distinct interpretation of events that was decidedly southern and decidedly different from that of papers like the *Defender*. This is evident in the hundreds of newspapers that black southerners created. The Scott Newspaper Syndicate demonstrates an evolution that followed the migration northward. Its development was not about existing newspapers sending copies of editions to a new region. It was about scores of newspapers created along the route north. The roots of this grapevine grew up, not down.

Newspapers were one venue where, as literary historian C. K. Doreski has explained, "the discourses of what we conventionally label 'news,' 'history,' and 'literature' coalesce into an African-American narrative of history and nation." Black newspapers helped mold a racial memory and thus "a racially charged national identity." While this book does not employ a comparative approach to find affinities between the black southern press's editorial politics and the black literature being produced about the region from the distance of the Great Migration, it is important to note that such could be done: a regional identity combining with a race identity to create a specific version of nationhood. "Narrative," Doreski notes, "is the basis of individual and community conceptions of national identity."[19] And while black southern readers had less access to many of the literatures of history and fiction—logistically, financially, educationally—it helps to understand that while "Negroes Are Different in Dixie" emphasized the presses' editorial positions as they related to their readers, they had important dialogues with the other literatures of the Great Migration produced in the generation from the Great Depression to *Brown v. Board* that have yet to be explored.

The newspapers also had dialogues—or, perhaps, monologues—with their white counterparts. Chapter 1 describes the creation of that dialogue in Atlanta, home of the SNS, and the development of a space for it to happen in the pages of a viable southern black press. As chapter 2 demonstrates, the black southern press played a vital role in supplementing stories that were wrongly reported, underreported, or ignored by the local white press, creating a situation where an incident or news item could look completely different depending on whether a reader subscribed to a black or white paper. For black southerners beset by countless forms of othering and innumerable lies about their capacities and social status, an alternative news source that compensated for that othering and prioritized black news locally and nationally was vital to the development of African America and the stability of the black South.

Chapter 3 describes the murder of W. A. Scott and its aftermath and uses the case to examine the politics of the black business class of Atlanta. In chapter 4, the black press takes on the fight for teacher salary equalization in the late 1930s and early 1940s. It was a fight that experienced successes and failures, and it was a fight that the black southern press was uniquely suited to cover. Those newspapers were in the communities where the strikes and lawsuits commenced. They too were struggling for equality in a business that was fundamentally dependent on segregation. They were also entities dominated by men who were advocating for salary equalization in a profession dominated by women. Chapter 5 tracks the Syndicate's spread beyond the South and its reaction to World War II, while chapter 6 uses a 1940s libel case to draw the contours of the syndication relationship between the Atlanta headquarters and the Syndicate's member newspapers. Chapter 7 uses the strange case of Davis Lee to demonstrate the trials of small-time publishers trying to survive in the perilous world of black journalism by relying on services like the Scott Syndicate. Finally, chapter 8 describes the *Atlanta Daily World* and the Syndicate in the years following World War II. While the *World* would survive the century, the SNS would face its demise in 1955.

The number of individuals reached by the Scott Syndicate totaled in the millions, despite the economic rigors of the Great Depression. Though it was southern, the scope of its influence for much of the generation prior to the civil rights movement included a significant presence in the

Midwest, following the trajectory of the Great Migration. Newspapers in smaller communities had less stability than those in larger cities. Most of the papers mentioned in this book and listed in the appendix have left only the sparsest historical traces of their existence. But they did exist, and the formalized information created by syndication helped propagate knowledge in their regions during the period of the most oppressive Jim Crow segregation. An accurate portrait of these newspapers is a necessary first step in the much larger process of using the extant information the Syndicate disseminated to understand the black mind-set from the 1930s to the 1950s.

Such is the project of this book. It necessarily responds to the literature about the subject and the period in the generation before World War II. It engages, for example, with John Egerton's *Speak Now against the Day: The Generation before the Civil Rights Movement in the South* (1995). It also fills in major historical and argumentative gaps (at least for the temporal scope involved) in Henry Lewis Suggs's lesser-known *The Black Press in the South, 1865–1979* (1983) and builds on Patrick Washburn's more recent *The African-American Newspaper: Voice of Freedom* (2006).

Almost every summary account of the black press emphasizes northern papers. Washburn's *African American Newspaper*, for example, almost exclusively deals with northern and western newspapers, rarely venturing below Norfolk, Virginia, and P. B. Young's *Journal and Guide* in its scope. Roland Wolseley's bedrock *Black Press, USA* (1971) does include the *Atlanta Daily World* and *Birmingham World*, along with several other papers from Florida to Texas, but almost all of the southern papers included in the book are from the late 1960s and early 1970s. For all of the important work done by Wolseley, he virtually ignores southern newspapers from the first half of the twentieth century that did not survive into the late civil rights period. Armistead Pride and Clint Wilson's *A History of the Black Press* (1997) does include the black southern press during the nineteenth century, but its coverage of the twentieth century stays decidedly in the Midwest and Northeast. Todd Vogel's 2001 essay collection, *The Black Press*, the first broad account of that topic in the twenty-first century, doesn't include any chapters on the black press in the South. But the bulk of the black population lived in the South, defined itself as southern, and even took hometown southern papers with them after migrating north. This book attempts to remedy these gaps in historical coverage.

The one exception to the general historiographical rule is Sid Bedingfield's *Newspaper Wars* (2017), which examines the role of South Carolina's *Lighthouse and Informer* in conversation with white journalists during the development of a civil rights agenda in the state. While not a summary account like those listed above, its emphasis on a southern state is an important supplement to the growing body of scholarship on the black press. Bedingfield places an example of southern radical journalism and its multifaceted political efforts at the forefront of his historiography, countering the preference for northern newspapers with a longer demographic reach. This book also deals with the activism and legacy of the *Lighthouse and Informer* but places it in a different, region-wide context as part of the Scott Newspaper Syndicate, spreading the focused state-level analysis to the entire region.

This book also has something to say about the Syndicate's role as part of the connective tissue between the white South and the black South. This was another liminal space occupied by the black press: serving as a race conduit just as it served as a class conduit within the race. This is similar to the case of administrators at black universities, for example. They were black, and they were responsible for sustaining a viable black institution, but their dependence on white funding—or, at least, their need to take the attitudes of powerful whites into account—at times made them seem like accommodationists, even though they acted that way in an effort to sustain the institutions that sustained civil rights activism and gave their critics a voice. The same is true for the SNS, which was responsible for sustaining another viable black institution, another theater for learning and a vehicle for race consciousness. And just like administrators at black universities, the editors and publishers of black weeklies (and one black daily) in the South had to sustain the institution of the black press by occasionally depending on white funding—from advertisers rather than legislators—and they always realized the importance of taking the views of powerful whites into account. The small black southern middle class sometimes couldn't provide the sole advertising sustenance of the paper, and the history of the black press in the South had demonstrated that overt attacks on powerful white interests could get you killed. That wasn't accommodationism either. It was practical radicalism.

Thus it was the slightly more conservative Depression-era southern press—including some papers that often wouldn't even support civil rights activism in the post-*Brown* South—that helped create the mind-set for the first wave of southern black activism after World War II. The idea that a syndicate would develop around a large urban newspaper wasn't unusual. The *Defender* and *Courier* both had syndicates at various points in their histories, as did the *Baltimore Afro-American*. But the *Afro-American*'s syndicate numbered twelve papers at its height. The reach of the SNS was simply unparalleled. This book examines that reach, the place of southern newspapers in the historiography of black journalism, and even the ideological underpinnings of the civil rights movement.

Chapter 1

Atlanta, the Scott Family, and the Creation of a Media Empire

W. A. Scott was a simpleton. That's what the veteran journalists all said. He had been a hosiery salesman, a brush salesman, an umbrella salesman. After a stint as a railroad mail clerk, he had tried his hand at publishing city directories in Jacksonville. He had come to Atlanta in 1928 to try it again.

Ric Roberts was one of the veteran journalists, serving as the managing editor and art editor of the Mirror Publishing Company's magazine, which was headquartered, as were so many black businesses, on Auburn Avenue. Roberts was at the soda fountain of the Yates and Milton Drug Store when the young upstart approached him. The normally brooding Scott seemed happy. "Say, Ric," he said. "I'm going to print a newspaper." The dreams of a simpleton. Roberts tried to explain the financial outlay required for such an endeavor, but Scott seemed unfazed. "I don't need a lot of money. It will be a healthier way to start. I won't waste money. I'll use just enough to get going and then I'll work and work and work. See? Now you make me up some headings and things and I'll pay you just as soon as possible." That night, Roberts set the masthead for the *Atlanta World*. Within two weeks, the first edition appeared.[1] The new grapevine of the New South had begun to grow.

The original hub of black journalism in Georgia wasn't Atlanta. It was Savannah. In December 1875, Sol Johnson and John H. Deveaux founded the *Savannah Tribune*, and it became the model for black journalism in the state. The paper vowed to "elevate the masses" and to "be true to the people in every respect." The bulk of the *Tribune*'s coverage emphasized race relations, considering questions of miscegenation, the leadership of Booker T. Washington, and the various stunted attempts to create race congress movements.[2] Washington was always a vexing question for black southerners. The *Tribune*, for example, seemed content with his 1895 Atlanta Compromise speech at the Cotton States Exposition, but when he was quoted in a New York paper two months later discouraging black congressional candidates, the *Tribune* castigated the leader and warned that such pronouncements would lose him the good faith of the people he claimed to represent.[3]

The *Tribune* took an unsurprisingly vigorous stance against lynching and denied the constant claim that black men committing rape was a legitimate reason for such mob "justice." National stories of racial injustice were printed in the paper alongside local stories of similar outrages. Jim Crow segregation laws were problematic, and no black Georgian should support them. Black customers who frequented white drugstores that did not give them full service were part of the problem, abetting such behavior for simple convenience, and at various points in its history the paper called for boycotts of stores and pharmacies that didn't provide equal service.[4]

The *Tribune* also bemoaned the disenfranchisement of black Georgia voters, particularly in Savannah. But in the 1893 city elections, the black vote was courted. "Why such a change?" the paper asked. "There is a division among the whites and all the humbug now practiced by those interested is but the bidding for the Negro vote." The paper was unimpressed. "From past experience we are taught that from neither faction can the Negro expect that recognition to which he is justly entitled." The contradictions for black Savannah seemed limitless. As whites disingenuously courted black votes only when it served their interest, plenty of local black politicians came under the *Tribune*'s fire for selling out to whites. The newspaper sought politicians "who will stand for [their] people at all times and in all places regardless of influences brought to bear and nothing short of this will satisfy us."[5]

In addition, the paper celebrated successful black businesses and railed against how police managed black arrests. The inherent danger in such pronouncements, however, necessarily led to correctives designed to protect the paper. The *Tribune* was situated in a decidedly racist city, and its management understood the advertising imperatives that came with such a reality. In January 1893, for example, the paper published "A Love Letter to Our White Friends Who Are Our Best Friends," calling on the old relationships between white and black, which had been destroyed by the "foreign element" of segregationist politics. Such was the lived reality of the double bind in the black South.[6]

The *Tribune* paid close attention to black education, often touting black colleges as success stories (and in turn finding in them loyal and consistent advertisers for the paper's pages). But the *Tribune* also highlighted primary and secondary education. It ran short stories and black history articles designed to provide a measure of high culture to its readers. But despite such advocacy, as contradictory as some of it might have been, society and crime were always part of the presentation. Religious activities were highlighted, as were accounts of weddings, funerals, and club meetings. Crime stories came with proper Victorian moral denunciations, but the punishment of crime, generally in the form of the chain gang, also came under criticism as a tactic of re-enslavement. There was, to be sure, a fine line to walk.[7]

The *Tribune* dealt with foreign matters with the same complex pragmatism with which it handled everything else. When Henry McNeal Turner's colonization movement spread in the years following Reconstruction, the *Tribune* argued against it, making the case that African Americans were fundamentally American, had played a role in every American success, and could achieve their just aims at home. At the same time, the paper actively stood against the U.S. government when, in 1893, it sought an indemnity from Haiti for the poor treatment of an American in that country.[8] Matters of foreign policy as they pertained to race were nuanced and ever changing, and the *Tribune* carefully maneuvered through them, aiming for what it thought was in the best interests of the black population.

Atlanta's first black newspaper, the *Atlanta Republican*, was founded in 1879, four years after the *Savannah Tribune*, and lasted for eleven years. This was a considerable feat, considering that even white papers in Atlanta had short shelf lives, which led one commentator to refer to the city as the "graveyard of newspapers." In 1900, Atlanta's population was just under ninety thousand, with the black population accounting for 40 percent. By 1920, the population had grown to more than two hundred thousand, but the percentage of black residents had decreased to 31 percent.[9]

Despite that uneven population growth, black Atlanta still needed news. Between 1879 and 1947, forty black newspapers emerged in the city, with an average life span of roughly five years. The early paper that most successfully bucked that trend was the *Atlanta Independent*, owned and operated by Benjamin Jefferson Davis. Davis was born in May 1870, the son of former slaves. He became a teacher in his native Terrell County, Georgia, before taking a job with a white printer in Dawson, the county seat. Though he ran into trouble in Athens (arrested and charged with stealing liquor), the charges were dropped, and Davis remained successful in his hometown. Though he and his family lived in a fifteen-room mansion in

Dawson, Davis knew he couldn't start an influential newspaper in Terrell County, so in 1903, after the birth of his son, Ben Davis Jr., he moved to Atlanta to found the *Independent*.[10]

The paper was a success, and Davis's rise to prominence left him incredibly wealthy, owning, according to Walter White, "one of the first automobiles for either whites or Negroes in Atlanta" and a large house on Martin Avenue. Davis used that wealth in many calculating ways. White described him as having a "kind of ruthlessness." Historian Clarence A. Bacote sees him as "lacking in character," a man who was "treacherous, selfish." In his study of turn-of-the-century black Georgia politics, Bacote argues that Davis "did not have a single prominent friend who at one time or another did not feel the stinging blows from his pen." John Dittmer calls him a "champion mulatto baiter," who "railed against what he perceived as a light-skinned aristocracy."[11]

Davis did his railing in his newspaper. B. F. Cofer, the paper's editor, described his boss as "dominating and very aggressive. He gained control of the Odd Fellows in Georgia through greed, shrewdness and intelligence, and because of his ability to articulate." The *Independent* reported a probably inflated circulation of twenty-seven thousand in 1932. As early as 1904 it had reported a certainly inflated circulation of a hundred thousand. The *Independent* ultimately collapsed in 1933 after the Republican defeat in the 1932 elections and the rise of the paper's more successful counterpart. Davis's paper, recalled his son, was "famous all over Negro America for the fearlessness of its editorial policy," which made it "the most influential Negro weekly in the South." "In many towns in Georgia it was not allowed," he claimed. Historian Robert Brisbane called it "the most militant Negro newspaper in the Deep South." Still, militant or not, every major financial institution in Atlanta advertised in the *Independent*. Its success was based on its editorial page, and the two things Davis pushed more than anything else were the Grand United Order of Odd Fellows and Republican Party politics. Davis had joined the Odd Fellows at age nineteen, well before his arrival in Atlanta. He became very active very early, helping to grow the membership exponentially, and his newspaper was integrally tied to both the organization and the party.[12]

Though he was responsible for the Odd Fellows' growth, he was also at least partially responsible for the group's demise. When he was outmaneuvered for the position of national grand master at the 1912 Odd Fellows convention, he began an open feud with his rivals that split the organization in two, earned him a suspension, and ultimately prompted the removal of his name from the charter. Then he sued for control of the club's assets in a long, bitter court battle that lasted six years and drained the organization of money, resources, and members.[13]

Davis was a devoted and powerful Republican, a leader of the party in Georgia, the president of the Atlanta Board of Trade, and a friend and ally of Booker T. Washington. He served on the platform committee of the 1916 Republican National Convention and as secretary of the executive committee of the Republican Party of Georgia for eighteen years. He was responsible for handing out the patronage in the state during Republican administrations, which put him in a position to serve as gatekeeper for white political hopefuls. That influence, however, didn't last. As white Republicans sought to whiten the party's image, Herbert Hoover and Georgia senator Walter George investigated Davis's patronage program, publicly interrogating him and leading the press to report stories of "a Negro 'humiliating' white men and women who had to come to him for jobs." The scandal dogged Davis's reputation for the rest of his life, but he remained loyal to the party.[14]

Davis had other brushes with power controversies. As historian Donald Lisio notes, "Because Atlanta blacks could vote in municipal elections, Davis had always enjoyed a greater degree of power and independence than most other black politicians in the South." Under Senate investigation, Davis gave many people the impression that he had taken bribes for patronage and misspent campaign funds. It didn't help that one of those patronage appointments, a postmaster named L. F. Peterson, committed a murder-suicide during the investigation. Insinuations swirled that graft paid to Davis had motivated the crime. More graft charges ensued as Senate investigators traveled to Georgia to interview Davis and discover whether he used party money for personal use and took bribes for granting patronage jobs.[15]

These accusations ultimately led to significant attacks, cross burnings, and general threats by the Ku Klux Klan, but Davis was not one to be intimidated. When a bundle of newspapers was returned from Covington with a warning not to return, for example, Davis went to the small town and handed out copies of the *Independent* to roughly 150 black readers while upward of 50 armed whites looked on. This was the kind of resolve that ensured that even though Davis was ousted from his leadership position in the whitening Republican Party, he still worked to maintain his influence in it. His editorials against the Republican lily-whites and his organizing on behalf of black delegates earned him the enmity of many white Georgia Republicans. A Cedartown exporter and Hoover informant, Charles Adamson, called Davis a "grafter" and argued that "the impudence of Ben Davis" was "astonishing." Adamson was certain that "he should be under indictment."[16]

Graft and astonishment were dominant features of the cutthroat business practices of black elites who were able to build empires that fueled rivalries throughout the Auburn Avenue business district. Those practices, however, helped create the new moneyed class in black Atlanta. Matching the growth of that business elite, there were new publishing ventures targeted to the new cultured class. Atlanta, for example, was the home of the *Voice of the Negro*, an important periodical founded in January 1904, which survived roughly four years. Despite its relatively short life and its founding by white publishers, *Voice of the Negro* was a precedent-setting periodical, publishing political content that was rare for black southern ephemera. Jesse Max Barber, one of the magazine's principal editors, was a founding member of the Niagara Movement the year after the periodical's creation. Still, Atlanta in the first decade of the twentieth century was relatively inhospitable. The magazine feuded with Ben Davis's *Atlanta Independent*, and after the Atlanta Riot of 1906, *Voice of the Negro* published its last two years from a Chicago address (though it was still secretly printed in Atlanta).[17] It was not a particularly auspicious omen for the later *World* and Syndicate.

Meanwhile, Ben Davis did have friends in high places. He was a close ally of Samuel Rutherford, founder of the National Benefit Life Insurance Company. In January 1928, for example, Davis assured his readers in a front-page editorial, which read like a laudatory advertisement, that National Benefit was completely solvent after a Memphis bank, the Fraternal and Solvent Savings Bank, failed. Using his connections in the organization, Davis was able to report that the insurance company did have a $100,000 investment in the Memphis bank, but it had weathered the financial storm without any problems. For Davis, National Benefit had only one purpose, "to save the race."[18]

At the same time, Davis was not afraid to use his paper to attack his own race. "The Negro is a child race," he once wrote. "The average Negro leader is as ignorant as a bat." For all of his activism for black rights, John Dittmer points out, "leading Atlanta blacks despised Davis's opportunism and flamboyant lifestyle (the editor had a taste for flashy cars and fast women) and would not permit the *Atlanta Independent* to be read in their homes."[19] They, however, were about to have a new option.

William Alexander Scott Jr. was born on September 1, 1902, in Edwards, Mississippi, the second son of the Reverend William Alexander Scott, a pastor of the Christian church, and his wife, Emmeline. He originally attended Edwards public schools before the family moved to Jackson. His father had relocated to the big city to create the Ferry Street Christian Church, and in 1914, the young W. A. would be the first person baptized in the new venue. Scott completed his secondary education at the high school department of Jackson College when he was seventeen, supplementing his work by becoming the secretary of the school's president, Z. T. Hubert. He showed an early aptitude for music and often accompanied his father to revival meetings around the state, where he would play the organ. After two years at Jackson, W. A. transferred in 1922 to Morehouse, where he was the quarterback of the football team and a star on the debate team. W. A. always had a friendly rivalry with his older brother Aurelius. Aurelius went to Morehouse first, also starring on the football team and debate team. His success is what convinced W. A. to attend as well.[20]

After leaving college, W. A. moved to Birmingham, where he worked sales jobs for the Real Silk Hosiery Company, the Better Brush Company, and Beeler Umbrellas. He was, it seemed to those closest to him, a natural born salesman. He then became a railway mail clerk for the Miami to Jacksonville run, with a home base in Jacksonville. While living in northeastern Florida, he noticed a lack of cohesion among the black entrepreneurs of the city, so he published the *City Business Directory of Negro Enterprises.* His success with that project led him to return to Atlanta to try the same thing. He caught a fortunate break in Atlanta, finding for sale the printing equipment of the Standard Life Insurance Company.[21]

Early in the twentieth century, Heman Perry's Service Printing Company had begun printing materials for local businesses, depending most heavily on the business of the Standard Life Insurance Company. When Standard Life folded, Service Printing tried to stay afloat by securing a loan from Citizens Trust, using its printing equipment as collateral. It turned out not to be enough, however, and Citizens Trust (which Perry had helped to found) foreclosed. In 1925, Standard Life tried to stave off complete collapse by merging with the white Southern Insurance Company, which kept Service Printing doing its work until 1927. The following year, Scott was able to leverage Citizens Trust's desire to unload the equipment it found on its hands and purchased it for what historian Sadie

Mae Oliver calls "a very inconsiderable amount of money with payments most lenient."[22]

This was the situation when Ric Roberts met W. A. Scott at the soda fountain in the summer of 1928. "In this field his alchemy has confused and irritated many of those who considered him an upstart five years ago," said Roberts. With the help of his brother Cornelius, known as C. A., Scott established a printing plant with the Standard Life Insurance equipment and began his four-page weekly. The first issue appeared on August 5, 1928, two short weeks after Roberts first set the masthead. Scott became part of the Associated Negro Press, paying twenty-five dollars for membership and two dollars per month in those early days. He was "trigger-brained, daring, capable and determined," claimed editor Frank Marshall Davis, who also made the case that part of the publisher's motivation stemmed from the success of the black press in Baltimore. Scott had "a burning bitterness toward Carl Murphy of the *Afro-American* newspapers," Davis said. Murphy and Scott were not specific rivals, but the Baltimore publisher had many advantages that Scott never had. Murphy's father had founded the *Afro-American* in 1892, and the son inherited his father's success. He earned degrees from Howard and Harvard and a PhD from Germany. He was an academic who served as chair of Howard's German Department until his father died in 1922, when Murphy took control of the family business. He had, in other words, everything that Scott wanted. "Scott's main ambition was to open a newspaper plant in Washington and publish an afternoon daily for the capital and a morning paper for Baltimore," said Davis, "which would afford him the supreme pleasure of placing a copy each a.m. on the Murphy doorstep."[23]

Formed in 1919 with eighty charter member newspapers, the Associated Negro Press was the original twentieth-century attempt at a grapevine that would bind the new diaspora that had begun to spread throughout the country. It was the *Chicago Defender*, Lawrence Hogan has explained, "along with the possibilities of a national black press it exemplified, that came to serve as the catalyst for the establishment of the Associated Negro Press." Emanating from Chicago under the leadership of its founder, Claude Barnett, the ANP would make the growth of the black press through World War II possible. At the same time, however, that service priced out smaller papers, which could never afford such luxuries. Scott would try to fill that gap by using one ANP subscription for all of the papers he eventually printed, bringing him into regular conflict with Barnett.[24]

Scott took the innovative step upon starting his paper of hiring agents to canvass the black community and solicit subscriptions door to door. It worked, and with a healthy subscription rate and relatively high circulation, Scott then had leverage to sell advertising to a wide swath of clients. "In the beginning, the paper made most of its money through its distribution," Alexis Scott, the third-generation, twenty-first-century president of the paper, explains. "As time went on, advertising became a more critical factor." Davis's *Independent* was there for political reasons. Scott was unconcerned with politics. He wanted to make money, and his aggressive efforts began to bear fruit. "What the *World* contained was of no great interest to him," said Frank Davis, "but how many copies were sold was of primary importance." By 1931, large white-owned corporations like Sears, Roebuck and Rich's department store were advertising in the *World*. "There was clearly a demand," says Alexis Scott, "because the mainstream media did not cover the black community during those days of segregation."[25]

In February 1930, Scott wrote to the Associated Negro Press, explaining that he was planning to publish two days a week instead of one and asking that the service send material by special delivery rather than traditional mail to facilitate a quicker turnaround. "Do not make mention of this as a news item until we get it going," Scott told them. The year after the *World* became a semiweekly, W. A. and his brother Emel visited the office of the *Gary American* in Gary, Indiana, while traveling north. There they met Frank Marshall Davis, to whom W. A. explained his plans for a massive newspaper chain based out of Atlanta: the Southern Newspaper Syndicate, which Scott formed in January 1931. Since he had his own printing equipment and understood that the usual overhead for publishing a newspaper was cost prohibitive—as noted by historian Sadie Mae Oliver, there were "heavy charges for news service; a maintenance staff of local news gatherers and reporters; correspondents at points of pronounced activities; an adequate office force, not excluding the expensive machinery needed in securing the printed sheet"—he developed a plan to foster the ability of entrepreneurs in smaller towns and cities in the South to eliminate some of those expenses. Scott's plant would print local newspapers and supplement local news with other material from the *Atlanta World* and other papers in the system.[26] The Southern Newspaper Syndicate thus created the systematic production of news in the region.

In April 1931, the *World* became a triweekly along with several of the Syndicate companion papers, among them the *Chattanooga Tribune*,

Birmingham World, and *Memphis World*. That summer, the Syndicate began a rotogravure sheet, and Davis moved from Indiana to help run Scott's growing operation. Scott had queried Claude Barnett of the Associated Negro Press about the possibility of a rotogravure section as early as December 1929. The ANP went with a monthly sheet, while Scott had an even larger vision to publish pictures once a week. Many criticized Scott for overreaching, but he responded by reaching further. Finally, on March 13, 1932, the *World* became a daily, adding "News While It Is News" to its masthead in a direct statement of its value over and against black weeklies. "It marked still another epoch in the annals of this race's journalistic endeavors," the paper's first daily edition announced with typical flourish. "The Wiseacres said we were flying High when we conceived The Daily idea and put it to use. They were right. We are flying high. We print more news per week than any other plant in the World—which serves Negroes wholly."[27]

They were flying high. The month following the *World*'s move to a daily, local laborer James Williams insisted that his wife stop reading the paper and go to bed. When she refused, he simply turned out the light so she couldn't see. In the argument that followed, Williams bit his wife's hand and she hit him four times with a hammer, leaving the back of his head severely lacerated. "When I want to read my *Atlanta World*," she told a reporter before her day in court, "I want to read it, and nothing can stop me."[28]

"I have been inclined to question the spreading out process of Mr. W. A. Scott's paper development," observed Jesse O. Thomas, southern field director of the National Urban League, in February 1931. "Upon investigation however I find that it does not represent as great a financial hazard as I had supposed." Thomas realized that all of the Scott papers "carry about the same news except for one or two inside pages" and thus seemed reasonably affordable. "I might add—he is making money," said Thomas. "He has some 1500 subscribers in Columbus and around 2,000 in Birmingham, altho these papers are less than a month old." Thomas's assessment was in aid of convincing Claude Barnett that Scott's planned rotogravure section was worth negotiations. "In the event you go into the proposition with him and find that he is falling down in any way," Thomas assured Barnett, "I think I can whip him into line."[29]

Those negotiations seemed to go well. The Syndicate had enough pictures from its member cities to fill most of the sheet, "but you might have a good picture we might want sometimes," Scott told Barnett. "There will be no overlap of territory covered by your papers and my papers, therefore we can exchange pictures to our mutual advantage."[30]

There were black daily analogues prior to the *World*'s arrival. The first black southern newspaper was *L'Union*, founded in New Orleans in 1862. It stopped publication prior to the close of the Civil War, but with its life began the full flower of black southern presses, which quickly outnumbered their northern counterparts in the decades following the war. The *New Orleans Tribune* became a daily in October 1864. The Baltimore *Daily Evening Chronotype* briefly appeared three years later, and the *Columbus Daily Messenger* appeared in Georgia in 1889. In the 1890s, the *Negro World* was published in Knoxville, Tennessee, and the *Daily American* in Jacksonville, Florida. In the early twentieth century there was the *Muskogee Searchlight* in Oklahoma, the *Benton Watchman* in Louisiana, and the *Waco Observer* in Texas. Several others made brief appearances in the decade following World War I. None of these papers, however, had long shelf lives or large circulations.[31]

The *Atlanta Daily World*, it seemed, was different. It was "the 'ace' accomplishment of the Georgia Negro in the business and service of journalism," according to white commentator Asa Gordon. This isn't to say it was an easy process. The paper struggled financially in its first year, constantly lagging behind in paying its debts to the Associated Negro Press. Overcoming such struggles was an accomplishment made all the greater, Gordon argues, along with other successes like Citizens Trust Bank and Atlanta Life Insurance, because it happened in a period of ugly racial intransigence after World War I and the Depression that followed on its heels, which damaged the prospects for all black businesses in the period. The *World* published six editions per week for six weeks, then began publishing a Saturday paper as well. "When you build something," Scott said, "always build it in such a way that it will not crash if something underneath it should crack." Starting in 1933, in an effort to keep it from cracking, Scott began creating papers outside the South. To accurately reflect his new business model, Scott changed the company's name to the Scott Newspaper Syndicate. "Five years ago he was an obscure hosiery salesman in Atlanta with no experience in or training for the publishing game," wrote the *New York Amsterdam News*'s J. C. Chunn with a fitting sense of wonder. "At the time of his death he was the publisher of the only Negro daily in the country and the head of a syndicate." The SNS owned one daily and two semiweeklies, and it printed more than fifty other weekly papers that blanketed the South and parts of the Midwest.[32]

This was a story of ascension, of linear progress moving a man, a family, and a community forward beyond the bounds set for them by the Jim Crow South. "When the *Atlanta World* first started assailing the Negro newspaper axiom of the age—Negro newspapers cannot be profitably printed more than one time per week—the rest of the newspaper world said the idea was poorly conceived, unthinkable and certain to end its protractors up in a swamp." The *World* "heeded not these warnings," one Syndicate advertisement explained. "It defied time, precedent, advice, and it is moving along nicely with its future almost completely assured." Albert Barnett, writing in 1938, claimed that "the rise of the Scott Newspaper Syndicate" through the most pressing years of the Depression "constitutes an epic in Negro journalism."[33]

Scott's rise, however, also alienated many in the field. "Membership papers are complaining about a practice of the *Atlanta World*," the Associated Negro Press complained. With the frequent publishing schedule of the *World*, the paper was using ANP material before the given release date, allowing Scott to scoop his weekly rivals across the country. The service encouraged the paper in no uncertain terms to cease and desist. Scott, however, was defiant. "I cannot quite see the fairness of our paying extra for fast news service and then being denied the right to use it because our would-be competitors are not in a position to make the same use as we do." It was a good argument. "We pay you for the news while it is news. If we have to hold it for a week after we get it," Scott threatened, the paper could just rewrite the news from other papers "just as the others do and we will not have to pay the five dollars a week." The ANP, however, remained insistent. "The service is designed for the membership and we are compelled to follow those lines which give the greatest good to the greatest number."[34]

The news the *World* was publishing reflected a community in the grips of a stifling Jim Crow. Southern cities stood at the top of the murder lists in the early 1930s, largely due to "lynch law and lawlessness." Birmingham's 54.8 murders per 100,000 people led the nation in 1932, followed by Memphis and Atlanta. Violence enveloped the southern black population, but violence was far from its only worry. "The Negro was born in depression," said Clifford Burke, a community volunteer who described his Depression experience for Studs Terkel. "It only became official when it hit the white man." When it became official, African American urban unemployment rose to 50 percent in the early 1930s. Total black unemployment hovered at twice the national average throughout the decade.

Those who did have jobs were paid substantially less than their white counterparts for the same work. In the North, approximately half of all black families were receiving some form of Depression relief. It was even worse in the South. For example, 65 percent of Atlanta's black families needed aid.[35]

The difficult economic times of the early Depression were such that even white southern newspapers expressed far more radical ideas than they would before or after. The *Baton Rouge Morning Advocate*, for example, argued that capitalism needed to be revised, if not changed altogether. "One thing, at least, the depression has done for us. It has made it possible for us to mention the word revolution without first pulling down the blinds, peeking under the beds and giving the maid the afternoon off."[36] For all of the rhetoric, however, Depression relief was unlikely to go to the maid. Despite the mandates of federal law, aid was not distributed equally. Monthly relief checks in Atlanta, for example, were $32.66 for whites and $19.29 for blacks, with leaders arguing that the discrepancy simply compensated for the typical lower standard of living to which black Georgians were accustomed. The problem was exacerbated in places like Atlanta because, unlike in major northern cities, private charities in the South often excluded aid to indigent African Americans. Into that void went organizations like Lugenia Burns Hope's Atlanta Neighborhood Union, a group of upper- and upper-middle-class black female volunteers who provided social work services for those in need. At the same time, such groups demonstrated a clear separation between the social classes, an insulation of those in black Atlanta who did not need monthly relief checks—like W. A. Scott and Ben Davis. Hope, for example, was the wife of Morehouse president John Hope. Her Neighborhood Union did necessary work to assist underprivileged black Atlantans, but that aid came with its own version of paternalistic control. The group often met in the Morehouse presidential mansion, a place that the vast majority of black Atlantans would never experience, to coordinate aid. In teaching working-class citizens about home care, sponsoring health classes, and fighting against prostitution, the group was setting the terms by which they would provide aid and thus drew significant distinctions between the classes. Theirs was, as Karen Ferguson has described, a "politics of respectability" that often made them closer to whites of a similar class than to lower-class members of their own race. The black upper class lived in a world far different than that of the common black southerner in the Depression-era 1930s.[37]

All black Atlantans, of course, suffered under the weight of the "racial caste system," but within the black enclave of that system, leaders of the community separated themselves from the rest by capitulating to white interests and scapegoating the poor and uneducated for not conforming to white middle-class standards. "For decades," notes Michelle Alexander, "black elites engaged in private rescue efforts to make black communities tidy, clean, and respectable in a futile effort to gain white approval." That stance affected elite black Atlanta's response to the New Deal, as they favored reform efforts that benefited themselves over and against the sort of aid that would sustain the black working poor. "Some of the most discriminatory federal programs of the New Deal era," Alexander explains, "received strong support from African American bureaucrats and reformers who presented themselves as speaking for the black community as a whole." The black elite were positioned as authorities on black needs, often convincing those below their station that their inability to conform to that accepted ideal "was, after all, their own fault."[38]

Much of this class separation in black Atlanta reached back to Reconstruction, when black political participation and business formation created an elite that sought to distance itself from the vice associated with the poor and unemployed black population in the city. Alcohol in particular was seen by many black elites as a distinct problem among the poor and unemployed. Whites were just as vocal about the black saloons, blaming them for postbellum rising crime rates and using them to scapegoat black men for sexual violence against white women. A political movement among white activists in the early century also led to a push to disenfranchise black men to ensure that black elites would not assume any kind of approximate equality with whites. The racial line had to be maintained at all costs. This all came to a head in the Atlanta Race Riot of 1906, in which dozens of black Atlantans were killed and many more wounded. Despite the restrictions on black voting and other white retrenchments that followed, the fear of further violence led civic leaders of both races to establish a line of communication, aiding racial cooperation to some degree but simultaneously deepening the divide between upper- and lower-class black residents of Atlanta. It was, for the city's black elite, an attempt to find the order of a system to replace the "order" maintained by racial violence.[39]

"There are also certain psychological and social factors that must not be overlooked," wrote Frank Marshall Davis. Black-white contact within class or profession was possible in northern cities. "In Chicago an artist may associate with whites of similar interests," for example. "A Harlem physician may mingle with white doctors; a Bostonian may be the only Negro in his class at Harvard." Such wasn't possible in the South. "In hostile Atlanta, Negroes must turn to other Negroes. 'Race consciousness' develops as a defense mechanism," Davis explained. "If a Negro institution can satisfy the needs of the people, then it is no longer necessary to patronize inimical whites."[40]

In such an environment, the black press thrived. It was both a creator of order and a conduit of information that spread news of racial violence. G. James Fleming credited five factors with contributing to the growth of the black press in the 1920s and 1930s: increased literacy, a realization by black middle-class businesspeople that there was profit in selling solely to a black customer base, residential segregation brought by urbanization, a rise in per capita income, and a realization that Redeemer retrenchment in the Gilded Age had fully extended into the twentieth century and that black communities needed a voice in that particular wilderness.[41]

That voice became louder as Scott's business developed. Maria E. Odum-Hinmon argues that the *World*'s move to become a semiweekly, then a triweekly, then a daily, was pushed in part by racial tension in Atlanta at the beginning of the decade, as the black demand for news grew in proportion to the population's fear of violence. The Ku Klux Klan was prominent in the city. Another white supremacist group, the Order of the Black Shirts, developed specifically to drive black workers from Atlanta, making the case that "city jobs" were "for white folks." Expansion, then, became a way that Scott could figuratively return fire.[42]

Returning fire was important. Stephen Duncombe has argued in his study of zines that the publications are "a shadow map" of the country, and the black press can be described in much the same way. A shadow map, in Duncombe's formulation, "is the property of people who possess very little. What they do possess is the ability to give things they don't own *new meanings*." This was the work of the black press, particularly in Atlanta: translating a racist world through a black lens. The *World* and other papers, like zines, were engaged in a "semantic rearrangement of components of the objective world," and they were designed to give "people who are materially impoverished material with which to fashion their sub-cultures."[43]

Many of the pages of the early *Atlanta World* were devoted to race relations, and lynching in particular; Scott knew what interested readers. The *World* always covered sensational crimes and provided a significant amount of sports coverage. The paper held a virtual monopoly on news of the African American community in Atlanta after the collapse of the

Independent, but its scope was far larger than the city limits. Atlanta's central place in the lives of African Americans gave the paper a national resonance, and it used that resonance to establish its broad-based newspaper syndicate throughout the South.[44]

"A glance backward at 1931 will show the Southern Newspaper Syndicate has accomplished what no other Negro newspaper organization ever dreamed of doing," one advertisement boasted. "A chain of Negro newspapers published three times every week," which included a rotogravure section and comics. "The publishing of news while it is news, [is] made possible by SNS publications on a more than one-issue-a-week basis." The Syndicate also provided "full time employment for 51 well trained young Negro men and women and part time work for 500 more." It was a legitimate achievement in so short a span. "Pardon us if we sound chesty," the paper crowed. Its accomplishments were "a monument to Negro business and publishing life and a credit to those who have made and read the various SNS papers."[45]

The various SNS papers, however, did come with attendant baggage. Beginning in 1930, Scott had a decades-long disagreement with Claude Barnett of the Associated Negro Press. His strategy of allowing locals to include some news copy, which was set and printed in Atlanta, led Scott to believe that he really only needed one membership in the ANP. Barnett, however, argued that each paper that used ANP material should be required to be part of the organization. Scott's claim that others were the publishers and that the Syndicate was essentially just a printer was the kind of argument he would repeat unsuccessfully in a Jackson, Mississippi, libel case in the 1940s (see chapter 5), and it continued to be a sticking point between him and Barnett. Scott's claim helped facilitate the black press in the South by reducing costs for locals who wanted to start newspapers, but Barnett's argument that it did so at the expense of the ANP was surely true.[46]

"Again," Barnett wrote to Scott in March 1931, "without permission from us and against our rules, you have given service to other papers which you publish. This we cannot longer permit. Those papers must take out membership in order to use service." He also made it clear that the ANP would not grant the *Birmingham World* membership, as the service already had a member paper in Birmingham, "which has steadfastly refused to permit the inclusion of another member." Things hadn't improved by June. "Let's get straight on the whole matter," Barnett stated. "You can't expect us to serve five papers for the price of one."

He offered the Syndicate half the normal rate for each paper as an olive branch.[47]

Scott responded that "there was a time that we did print occasionally as many as seven papers," but the Syndicate did so sporadically, as "they were small papers and in the experimental stage." Because of that irregularity, the SNS had discontinued the printing of "all individual papers under outside management" and instead had started branches of the *World* in other cities like Birmingham, Columbus, and, beginning in late June 1931, Memphis. "You can readily see they are merely branches of the *Atlanta World*. At these branches we only have a circulation man and an office clerk," Scott explained. "WE HAVE NO ADVERTISING MAN IN THESE CITIES. WE MERELY NAME THE PAPER AFTER THE TOWN IN WHICH WE START." Columbus had lost money since its founding, he claimed. Birmingham and Memphis looked a little better, but they had yet to secure local advertising. As a counteroffer, Scott proposed the two dollar weekly charge for ANP service be raised to five: two dollars for Atlanta and one for each of the Syndicate's member cities. A frustrated ANP agreed to the terms.[48]

Scott's desire for growth was evident early in the paper's existence. He hired local agents to hawk subscriptions door to door in Atlanta's black neighborhoods. He solicited advertisements from both white and black businesses. Department stores such as the national Sears, Roebuck and the local Rich's advertised heavily in the paper. Like many of its counterparts, the *World* also advertised skin-whitening creams and similar products in every edition, providing at the very least a subtle argument against the paper's more boisterous claims about representing blackness in the South. In one advertisement, for example, the Syndicate asked, "Why publish a Negro newspaper?" Only in such newspapers, it explained, "can a complete coverage of ALL news effecting [sic] or involving Negroes be found." People could read about themselves. Black newspapers helped "the interests and rights of Negroes individually and collectively be preserved." They provided employment for people "who otherwise could not enter the field of their choice (and for which they are prepared) because of the steel bars of racial prejudice." Advertising in black newspapers, the ad argued, provided a road map for readers of stores that actually catered to black customers. That was undoubtedly true, but the paper's emphasis on advertising hair straighteners and skin whiteners served as a reminder of a generic conservatism that didn't always live up to such pronouncements.[49]

As a newspaper concerned with black rights advocacy but otherwise taking broadly conservative positions—running advertisements for such skin products, not advocating direct confrontation against discrimination, and encouraging good behavior and saving money as the bedrock for survival in a white-dominated city—the *World* was particularly interested in businesses that served the black community. The *World* sponsored "Negro Trade Week" in October 1932, supporting and encouraging support for the spectrum of black businesses across Atlanta. Black insurance companies were one example. Though black companies did well, many black customers chose traditionally white insurance companies, trusting their longevity and expertise for securing their futures. But the *World* took the lead in the heart of the Depression to encourage its readers to move to black insurers, which were just as capable as any other. No one, the paper claimed, should complain about black unemployment, even during the Depression, if he or she wasn't going to support black businesses.[50]

Editorially, the *World* responded to the Depression by calling on the federal government to provide jobs programs that treated black applicants fairly. Jobs, the paper argued, were far more important to the black South than were relief packages. Meanwhile, locally, the *World* was diligent about making its readers aware of relief opportunities when such opportunities were available. The paper reported on meetings detailing various New Deal policies and how they related to black Atlantans. The *World* was particularly troubled by the growing trend of minimum wage scales, because the ability of companies to pay black workers less than whites was often the only thing keeping black workers employed. The more minimum wages existed, the more logical it was for companies to fire black workers and replace them with whites. It was a position that would later lead many of the Syndicate's employees into a bitter strike.[51]

The *World* also kept its focus on black higher education. It covered Atlanta's black universities extensively, particularly in 1929, when three of the six formed a loose union. By World War II, the other three joined them in the Atlanta University Center Consortium (the largest organization of its kind in the world). While it lauded events in Atlanta, the *World* also advocated for black colleges in general. When President Rayford Logan was fired from Virginia Union University in 1932 for "radicalism" after asserting that black colleges should be led by black presidents, the *World* defended him. The paper also consistently advocated for continued federal funds for Howard University, always a tenuous prospect with conservative or racist legislators arguing that it was a waste of taxpayer money.[52]

The paper's principal emphasis, however, remained at home. W. A. Scott had graduated from Morehouse, as did other Scott family members. Other Scotts attended other Atlanta schools. The city's black colleges were, if for no other reason than school pride, extensively covered. The same could be said of Booker T. Washington High School, which many of the Scotts and most other black leaders in the city had attended. It was, for example, Martin Luther King Jr.'s high school. And so, when Washington High did not comply with a school board decision to shorten the school day, and one hundred students walked out in protest in January 1934, the *World* marginalized the protesters and supported the school, even though the principal responded by reducing the school day just as the protesters wanted.[53]

The paper was particularly interested in black history, enthusiastically supporting the Association for the Study of Negro Life and History's Negro History Week, lauding its founder, Carter G. Woodson, and in 1934 beginning a book review section to emphasize those values. The *World* devoted space to full-page congratulatory advertisements from both black and white businesses concerning black progress for the 1934 Emancipation Day, advertised as the seventieth anniversary of emancipation. Historian Alton Hornsby sees the *World*'s rotogravure section as part of this emphasis on education and culture. It claimed to be unique to SNS papers and featured pictures of black leaders all over the world. "When you look at the pictures in the *World*'s rotogravure section," the paper advertised, "you see the photographer's art produced on the highest plane and in the most advanced manner yet devised by the most modern newspapers."[54]

The *World*, like almost all black newspapers, included news from the churches, but it extended beyond the common information about services and special programs. The *World* gave full reports of religious conferences and national meetings and consistently reported the annual appointments of Christian Methodist Episcopal and African Methodist Episcopal bishops. The paper also had a substantial social news section. Atlanta's role as an educational hub with a large black middle class created a situation where the city's black social life was less tied to church activities than it was in other cities. The *World* also covered black crime extensively, as would so many of the Syndicate's member papers, using lurid stories to draw in readers. It justified the practice by arguing that it would not play simply to the elite, but would report on matters affecting all black citizens. White papers never reported black-on-black crime, and the *World* understood that its readers wanted to know about it.[55]

The *World*, however, was inherently concerned about the causes and consequences of such crimes. Without equal justice before the law, "a new respect for the rights of others is formed by black and white," the paper argued in January 1932, "and the Negro through education learns to keep his head where a murder might result, Dixie will continue to lead the nation in homicides and the intra-race murder rate of Negroes will far outstrip the annual lynching toll." It tempered such broad esoteric critiques with calls for better treatment by police and more moral actions by the black community. The paper called for better jail facilities, for legalizing the "numbers," and for black policemen to patrol black areas of the city.[56]

Scott was driven by such social issues, but even more by a desire for economic success. "He was one of the most unrelenting persons I ever knew," said columnist Ric Roberts. "He was brilliant, cynical and hard." Editor Frank Marshall Davis recalled that Scott was "capable and determined, and enjoyed himself most when matching wits with an opponent." He "made enemies freely, drove his car with the same recklessness with which he ran for touchdowns as a halfback at Morehouse College, led an active love life and ruled his family with an iron thumb." Roberts described Scott's willingness to be brutally honest as "a strange thing. It was the honesty of complete independence." In November 1933, the ANP briefly discontinued service to the Syndicate for failure to pay its bills. Scott was able to restore service and delay payment, but he continued to let the bill lapse. On February 1, 1934, the ANP gave him until March 1 to take "some decisive action on your part."[57]

Scott would not be able to take decisive action, however, as his penchant for making enemies ultimately doomed him. He was murdered in 1934 soon after the ANP's ultimatum. "My associates here join me in sincere regret at the passing of Mr. Scott," wrote Claude Barnett on behalf of the ANP. "He had done so much in so brief a time and possessed such courage and daring vision, that he was needed in his field. We will miss him." But they didn't forget the bill, writing again soon after about payment. Scott's brother C. A. had taken over the reins of the Syndicate and responded quickly with two weeks' payment.[58]

C. A. Scott was born in Edwards, Mississippi, in 1908. He did his collegiate work at Morris Brown and Morehouse in Atlanta and at the University of Kansas. One friend of the Scotts explained that C. A. "was not the equal of his brother." They were "different types altogether. W. A. Scott would have developed the South into the same thing that *Ebony* has developed the United States into. C. A. would not do that. He would rather protect the family situation. The poppas and the mommas of the family, and so forth and so on. Things like that. Conservative in developing the business, in the interest of his family."[59]

C. A. saw himself differently. "I was basically a New Deal Democrat with Roosevelt all during the thirties and the forties," said Scott. "Because of the issues—voting rights, rural electrification, 1935 University Homes, minimum wages, social security." This was a characterization many would dispute. John Ingham and Lynne Feldman argued in 1994 that during the Great Depression, Scott and the *World* took a conservative Republican position, opposing much of the New Deal, including the National Recovery Act, and arguing that black citizens in need wanted jobs rather than relief. The paper advocated for the support of black businesses, even in times of economic hardship, stressing black insurance companies in particular. Alton Hornsby has argued that the paper opposed discrimination in Washington, D.C., in the 1930s and military racism during World War II. Such positions were not mutually exclusive, and Ingham and Feldman and Hornsby are right. The paper opposed the National Recovery Act and other government spending programs during the New Deal. It also celebrated Franklin D. Roosevelt's Black Cabinet and pointed out the oxymoronic nature of fighting against the Nazi regime with a segregated military. After the war, Scott supported the Republican Party, Dwight D. Eisenhower, and a more equitable two-party system in the South.[60]

The reason for this discrepancy in interpretation is that the *World* engaged in a practical radicalism that sought winnable racial battles and reserved its most caustic criticisms for events away from Atlanta, providing protective cover for the paper. "Black publishers and editors in the South got little except grief from a mixed bag of critics—liberal and conservative, black and white, North and South," John Egerton explains. "If they were at all conciliatory on social issues, they were viewed as timid and Uncle Tomish; if they were combative, they were called recklessly radical; if they tried to entertain or amuse or titillate as well as inform, they were dismissed as sensationalist rags. But in their denunciation of segregation and its crippling effects on all Southerners, the black papers were not only first and right but prophetic; the problem was not with them but with the whites who ignored their warnings."[61] This mixed model would be mimicked throughout the South in this period, leaving interpretations of the black press's activism confused and contradictory. It was a model prompted by the need to survive and fueled by the need for financial solvency.

"W. A. was big minded," said C. A. Scott. "He saw radio stations on top of the Odd Fellows Building. I used to kid him a lot. He was going to build him a big mansion on Ezra Church Drive. He was going to start home building projects in Memphis and Birmingham and promote 'em through the paper." Death, however, put those plans in limbo. C. A. explained, "I took, ah, the view if we preserved the paper we would preserve his memory, you see." W. A. was "a great entrepreneur, a man of vision, and courage, and he liked power."[62]

"He didn't get up to the political interest so much; but he was interested in economic power," said C. A. Scott of his brother. "My goal was to have a free newspaper—to talk and speak. Even if I didn't have any money or a big house. I was for freedom and to influence other people. If I hadn't been in publishing, I'd have been a minister. My father was one. Where I could speak. That's the next freest profession to the press." Of course, events didn't always bear this out. At the end of the summer of 1934, C. A. fired the *World*'s circulation manager, W. C. Kelly, and "Mr. Kelly left disgruntled." He was so unhappy that he planned a rival paper, the *Atlanta News*, to derail the success of his former employer. Though the *News* never made it off the ground, the effort demonstrated the cutthroat rivalries that could exist in the business.[63]

Whether economic power was either brother's ultimate goal, the paper's coverage and advocacy was in aid of making money, and understanding its advertising strategy is important to understanding its overall project. Take, for example, one representative week in July 1934. The ads included a heavy presence of medial and dental suppliers, national products, banks, furniture stores, and funeral homes; theaters were the most consistent daily advertisers because they were placing daily listings of their showings. The Georgia Railroad Company was also a consistent advertiser, as changing schedules and rates required regularly updated advertisements.[64] That month, the paper took in $2,171.20 from its advertising efforts for papers across the country. The Syndicate papers brought in $287.02 in advertising, and the rotogravure sheet brought in $635.13. Local advertising made up an additional $2,042.09. The Ziff company (discussed below) brought in $793.04. The SNS made up $161.02 of that total, the rotogravure weekly $508.73, and local advertising $123.29.[65]

The W. B. Ziff Company, headquartered in Chicago, represented white periodicals, but it did much of its business as a national advertising agent for the black press. Contracting with Ziff had been another major step for

W. A. Scott. When publishing just the *World,* he was only able to do local advertising, but creating the Syndicate allowed him to solicit national advertising and thus create a larger cash pool. The Syndicate was the only Ziff client from the South.[66]

In October 1934, for example, the Scott organization took in $2,372.94 in general advertising, but another $1,281.69 was accrued from the Ziff agency, demonstrating the monetary benefits brought by national advertising, which was made possible by the creation of the Syndicate. Of the $3,654.63 total, $2,497.61 (68 percent) came through the *Atlanta Daily World.* Another $1,014.65 (just under 28 percent) came from the rotogravure weekly. Only $142.37 (less than 4 percent) came from the Syndicate itself.

One year later in October 1935, the Scott company totaled $3,570.70 in advertising revenue. This time, $1,892.54 (53 percent) came through the *Atlanta Daily World.* The rotogravure weekly brought in $1,129.61 (just under 32 percent). That meant a little more than 15 percent ($541.83) came through the Syndicate. Its influence in the Scott monetary hierarchy was growing. And because of that influence, the company was relying less on the Ziff agency. Only $554.88 (15.5 percent of the advertising total) came from Ziff that month. The balance of power in the Scott businesses was changing.[67]

The other source of revenue for the Scotts was printing for the Syndicate. In the early 1930s, the Syndicate charged a member thirteen dollars to print two hundred copies of an eight-page paper. Scott told prospective member papers that the cost simply covered printing and that profit came from the national advertising placed in the editions. "Each week you will have to mail your local news and advertising by special delivery in envelopes furnished by us," the Syndicate explained to its members. "We want to make it absolutely clear that you are the owner and publisher of the paper. We are only the printers."[68]

John H. McCray of the *Lighthouse and Informer* explained how SNS syndication worked. The Scotts arranged this kind of deal for eight pages:

Two columns (40 column inches) of local news at no extra charge, which was inserted on up to four pages. Where local copy exceeded two columns, the extra was charged for at so much per column inch; when local news was inserted on more than the four pages fixed in the contract, an extra per page charge was made for "make-up." Advertisements sold locally were charged for at so much per column inch (originally 8¢ to 10¢ per column inch). The syndicate reserved rights to national advertising it could obtain for local newspapers, a practice which led to disputes between SNS and owners of the local papers.

The SNS contended that its use of news stories out of any of the papers it printed was vital to the total operation, that its staff selected the best stories from all papers and shared these without prejudice with the membership. This meant, in most cases, wider distribution of some story or editorial appearing in a locally owned paper and a broader appeal for public help in cases where civil rights and racial incidents were involved. In addition, McCray explained, "a locally owned paper printed by SNS was far more attractive than one the typical locally owned plant could get out. SNS papers carried one or more pages of sports, mostly from the South, a woman's page, a theatrical page and an editorial page. The editorial page however depended on what the local owners wanted."[69]

Of course, the expansion of the Syndicate into new markets had a greater economic effect on the SNS than did the income generated from printing contracts with the new papers. Advertisers in those new markets had an incentive to do business with the SNS. In March 1940, for example, Bee Dew Products, a Detroit-based cosmetics company founded by Vivian Smith Nash, became a regular Syndicate advertiser, paying $25.20 weekly for six inches of SNS advertising at $4.20 per inch.[70]

The bill for the *Jackson Times* edition for the first week of September 1936 was $36.63. Scott wrote to W. D. Holder, the paper's manager, congratulating him on a fine issue. "You had a very good paper," he told Holder. It was less than a week after the edition's appearance, but Scott was insistent. "I am sure you have collected on your ads by now and will send us your balance due no later than Sept. 17, 1936." Dealing with small, volatile, often short-lived papers created a desire in the Syndicate for prompt payments.[71]

In 1937, the *Birmingham World* ran a special edition for the American Cast Iron Pipe Company, one of the city's largest businesses and one that hired a significant number of black workers. The paper charged twenty dollars for 40 inches of front-page publicity, eighty-seven dollars for 174 additional inches of display advertising, and nineteen dollars for 76 inches of pictures. Then there was thirty dollars for 1,500 copies of the eight-page paper, fifteen dollars for 1,500 copies of a four-page supplement, and sixteen dollars for the composition and makeup of the supplement. The *World* added 16 inches of editorials and 19 inches of news at no additional cost. It was a synergistic effort with a prominent local employer, raising almost two hundred dollars prior to sale and distribution while bettering relations with a white business and alerting readers to a source of potential jobs. This was another benefit of the Syndicate, whose reach allowed Scott to expand his advertising base and create relationships with powerful white southern businesses in the process. It was a practical response to the needs of black workers during the Depression.[72]

The Syndicate's original editor was Frank Marshall Davis, who had, claimed an editorial from the Negro Writers Guild, "carved for himself a very unique place in the annals of Negro editorial accomplishment. He is known far and wide for his unbiased militancy." The editorship was the opening chapter of his life; Davis would later become an activist for black rights, a creative writer of the Chicago Renaissance, and a business owner and labor advocate in Hawaii.[73]

The first edition of W. A. Scott's *Atlanta World* on August 5, 1928, opened with a declaration by its publisher titled "A Dedication to the Public," which positioned the paper as speaking for the disadvantaged.

> That the bulk of the Negroes in the United States live in the South; that the race problem is a problem which concerns primarily the South; that if the race problem is to be solved, the men who do it will be Southern products; these are irrefragable truths alive in the minds of all thinking Negroes; these are truths which are continually manifest in the hearts of all Negroes who have a race consciousness and race pride.
>
> That the Negro has no sectional Newspaper representative in the Southland; that the Negro is viewing his race news, such as it is—chiefly crimes of thieves and murderers—primarily through the optics of a host of prejudiced white papers which take pride in flaunting the black man as a vicious enemy to society; such are the facts brought before us in our daily contacts.
>
> The publishers of *The Atlanta World* have felt the need of a Southern Negro newspaper, published by Southern Negroes, to be read by Southern Negroes. It is in a sincere effort to fill that need that *The Atlanta World* is being presented to the Southern public for its approval or disapproval. The responsibility of a Negro newspaper is to dispense to the public good, wholesome, information to enlighten our people of what his brother is doing; and to serve as a guide and organ of expression for matters of vital concern to the Negro.
>
> To carry out in full faith that responsibility, we dedicate to the public this initial issue of *The Atlanta World*.[74]

It was a unique manifesto, which demonstrated that the Scotts saw their project as a decidedly southern venture. They would bind the black South with a grapevine of information to counteract the misrepresentation and lack of concern by the dominant white southern press. Theirs would be a grapevine strengthened by a practical radicalism that sought to argue for rights without directly attacking those denying them. And it was poised to grow.

Chapter 2

*Race, Representation, and
the Puryear Ax Murders*

As the sun rose in Memphis on May 2, 1932, Stanley Puryear crept into the bedroom where his wife and eight-year-old daughter were sleeping. He raised an ax and began hacking the little girl into pieces. When his horrified wife awoke, he began chopping her too. He then calmly left the house and found Will Jamison walking along the street. He offered Jamison three dollars to help move some whiskey. Jamison was black, Puryear white, and the racial and socioeconomic codes of the Depression-era South virtually assured that Jamison would agree. Puryear led him back to the house, where he shot his potential helper, leaving Jamison stumbling in the street, mortally wounded. When the police arrived, Puryear told them that Jamison had killed his family and that he shot the black intruder in self-defense.[1]

Had Jamison died immediately instead of some hours later, Puryear's plan inevitably would have worked. White southern law enforcement was eager to believe stories of black criminality. But Jamison lived long enough to deny any involvement in the crime. "He shot me down when we got to the house," he said. "I don't know anything about the things that happened inside."[2] That left Puryear as a prime suspect. The investigation, the trial, and the conviction would captivate Memphis, along with the South and much of the nation, but coverage was decidedly different depending on the press. White papers emphasized the victims of the ax murderer and the family saga that led to their deaths. Newspapers of the SNS and other black papers emphasized the heroism of Jamison, another casualty of the crime who also suffered the secondary crime of character assassination after his death. It was, for the black press, another example of whites making assumptions, scapegoating black victims, and trivializing their deaths. The difference in white and black coverage of the crime demonstrates that the outcomes of rights debates between white and black were so different in places like Memphis because the assumptions that created the argumentative starting points were so different. In the Puryear ax murders, white and black commentators saw one seemingly

clear-cut incident in two entirely different ways. That difference was significant, and black newspaper readers supplemented mainstream white
news coverage with their local African American press. Whites did not
read those supplements. The black community had long been built on
the distinct nature of its information systems, from kinship networks to
the black press, which created a more complete body of knowledge than
that of whites. This knowledge highlighted the inequities of Memphis
society while simultaneously ensuring that white and black readers of
newspapers would continually talk past one another, insulating both black
Memphis and white Memphis and making interracial communication that
much more difficult.

Puryear ran the SAP Auto Parts Company, an automobile junkyard. He
claimed in the days after the attack that Jamison stole two pistols, sixty
dollars, and a watch, but police found none of the items on Jamison in his
wounded state. Police captain Frank Glisson was satisfied that Jamison
"had no criminal record in the past." Jamison told police his version of
the events three times, the captain explained, "and never varied."[3] Thus
after the funeral for Puryear's wife and daughter, police took him and his
twelve-year-old son, Porter, into custody and questioned them at length.[4]

Puryear's father and brother owned the Puryear Drug Company in the
Tennessee Hotel building—not an elite Memphis family, but a respectable one—and vigorously defended Stanley's version of events. "There
has never been any domestic trouble in my brother's home," said P. R.
Puryear. "He was a kind, devoted husband and father. I believe he loved
his little girl even more than his son. His wife's relatives will tell you the
same thing." Jamison, meanwhile, could have entered the house through
the back porch or two unlocked windows. "My brother kept two pistols
on the bureau in his room where he slept with little Porter. The negro
picked those up, and had collected Stanley's clothes and his watch before
he murdered Mrs. Puryear and the little girl. He dropped them after he
was shot."[5]

The local *Memphis Commercial Appeal* did pair such accounts in the
early days after the crime with Jamison's deathbed statement. "I spent
the night at a house on Beale Street," said the dying Jamison. "A little
after daybreak I was at Beale and Third when a middle-aged man drove up
and said he would give me $3 to help him move some liquor. I went with
him and he told me to wait in the garage. Then he called me up to the
back porch and he shot me and I run. I didn't have no ax. I didn't go in the
house, and I didn't hurt nobody."[6] At the same time, the *Appeal* claimed

that Puryear was "in a state of collapse" in his home after the ordeal, with a police guard outside the house "to keep traffic moving and to keep the morbidly curious from overrunning the premises." The crowds, however, came anyway, watching the Puryear house from across the street.[7]

The *Memphis Commercial Appeal* had long been a bastion of white supremacy and white southern thinking. The *Weekly Appeal*, one of the two papers later combined to create the *Commercial Appeal*, was founded in 1841 as a Democratic rival to the young city's Whig newspaper, setting its course as a champion of white southern antebellum politics, state sovereignty, and the sanctity of slavery.[8] For example, the *Commercial Appeal* celebrated its centennial anniversary with a booklet in which Robert Talley boasted proudly that at the onset of the Civil War, the *Appeal* "had been such a strong advocate of Southern rights that Southerners had praised it as 'the voice of the Confederacy' and Northerners had assailed it as 'the hornet's nest of the rebellion.' It was certainly the former and very likely the latter for, in the light of those flaming times, the Memphis *Appeal* was unquestionably 'the greatest rebel of them all.'" Talley argued that it was "more than a newspaper, it is a Southern institution."[9] And of course the implication of such a statement was that it was a white southern institution.

In the early twentieth century, the *Commercial Appeal*'s racial stances were mixed. In 1917, the paper published the time and place of an upcoming lynching. In 1923, however, it won a Pulitzer Prize for its editorial opposition to the resurgent Ku Klux Klan. But that opposition was based on a stated devotion to law and order, certain lynchings apparently were accepted, and white southern critics of the *Commercial Appeal*'s stance argued that the paper's editor, C. P. J. Mooney, was a Catholic. Despite its frustration with the Klan, however, the *Commercial Appeal* remained a white southern paper. In the fall of 1936, the paper was purchased by Scripps Howard, a newspaper chain founded in Cleveland that had spread across the country, predominantly outside the South. It became less a part of the Confederate ideal and more a part of a national conglomerate.[10]

The story presented by the city's other white daily, the *Press-Scimitar*, clearly privileged Puryear's version of events. The *Memphis Press* (later the *Press-Scimitar*) was founded in 1909 by Ross B. Young, a journalist originally from Ohio, who used the paper over its first two decades to fight machine politics in the city, a crusading spirit continued by Edward J. Meeman, an Indiana journalist who replaced Young as editor in 1931. The progressive stance that Meeman and his predecessor took against Edward H.

"Boss" Crump and his Memphis political machine, however, did not extend to a corresponding racial progressivism.[11] "Cloud-muted sunlight drifted lazily across the worn steps of the Church of St. Thomas," the paper reported on the Puryear funeral. "The world went lightly about its every-day affairs, but within the church a symphony of grief rose upward and seemed to hang to the ancient rafters as heads were bowed before the bodies of Mrs. Stanley A. Puryear and her daughter, Aurelia, victims of an ax-man who crushed their heads early Monday morning." In the *Press-Scimitar*'s coverage, Puryear was broken but brave. "I'll never see her any more," he repeated between sobs. "But I've got you, Buddy," he told his son. "I've got you."[12]

"I love my family," said Puryear. "I didn't do this thing." Police may have believed Jamison's story, but the *Press-Scimitar* was sure to point out the police captain's statement that "on the other hand, after talking with Puryear I would be convinced that his version of the slaying was the truth." The paper's coverage demonstrated that the case amounted to a choice between the upstanding white man's account and the vagrant black man's, and thus it was only a matter of time until Puryear was officially cleared of wrongdoing.[13]

Still, the ax used in the crime was Puryear's and his "negro maid" told police that she had previously seen it in the house. Both his wife and daughter were insured for $500 each. "The negro started to run and I let him have it," said Puryear, claiming that he rushed into his wife's bedroom after hearing her screams. "But he kept on going out the back door and I went back to look after my wife and baby." He told police that Jamison "started blazing away with both guns, and I opened fire with a shotgun I kept by my bed. The Negro dropped, but got up and ran from the house." Puryear claimed to have left his house at 2:30 a.m. to go to his garage to ensure that the night watchman was guarding the business, but the Fox-Pelletier Detective Agency, which guarded the garage, claimed that the watchman had made his hourly patrols and that "the seals [he] put on the office door and yard gate early in the night were intact when [he] made the last round this morning."[14]

Puryear's explanation was clearly unconvincing, and police and the attorney general announced that they would continue to investigate.[15] Those investigations were separate; the attorney general's office was tak-ing "an unusual interest in the murders," according to the *Commercial Appeal*, "because of their cold-blooded brutality and unusual features."[16] The coroner ruled that the deaths of the two Puryear victims came at the hands of "parties unknown," but Stanley Puryear openly admitted to killing Jamison "and only regrets that he did not do the job more thoroughly." When the grand jury met, then, it was to decide whether or not to charge Puryear with murder in the killing of the supposed black intruder.[17]

Police inspector Will Griffin was confident: "We've shot Puryear's statement full of holes." Police charged Puryear with Jamison's murder while attorney general W. Tyler McLain planned to send the facts of the case to the grand jury the following week. "The grand jury presentation will deal with every known fact in the case," the attorney general promised. "It will cover more than the specific slaying of Jamison." McLain was confident: "We are getting some statements now that will make them sit up and take notice." He explained that there had been no blood on Jamison's hands and none on his clothes, save at the point of gunshot entry. "Would it be possible for a person to hack two bodies as those of Mrs. Puryear and the child were hacked and still get no blood on him?" he asked. "Possible but not probable."[18]

White Tennessee's willingness to accept black witness testimony, whether in the courtroom or in a deathbed statement, had a long and fraught history. An 1815 Tennessee law provided for trials of slaves who were accused of crimes. They would be tried in front of a jury of "freeholders or slave-holders," but those jurors were welcome "to take for evidence the confession of the offender, the oath of one or more credible witnesses, or such testimony of negroes, mulattoes or indians, bond or free, with pregnant circumstances, as to them shall seem convincing." That welcome only held, however, when slaves were the defendants.[19]

Tennessee's legalization of black testimony in criminal cases came between 1868 and 1871, the latter the year that neighboring Kentucky did the same. In 1868, the Reconstruction legislature passed a law to "make the rules of evidence in the Federal and State courts uniform." It was a vague statute, and when the Tennessee legislature amended it in 1871, it did so in yet another vague manner, but after the December passage, witness rules in state civil and criminal trials were in line with the federal code, meaning that testimony would be accepted from any witness deemed credible. Neither statute explicitly mentioned race, color, or previous condition of servitude, but they did not have to. The first law was passed in the wake of the Fourteenth Amendment, which promised due process and "equal protection of the laws." In between the two state evidence efforts, the nation ratified the Fifteenth Amendment, which made "race, color, or previous condition of servitude" a household phrase nationwide. As of

December 1871, Tennessee officially accepted black people's testimony in criminal trials.[20]

By the Depression era, the testimony of black witnesses was an assumed part of the criminal code, even if it was, in practice, a rare occurrence in the prosecution of white defendants accused of crimes against white victims.[21]

Jamison's testimony, however, was not the only evidence against Puryear. There was additional damning, if circumstantial, evidence. Puryear's wife, for example, had to be rescued in 1925 when she was found in the couple's burning house unconscious. Puryear had a close association with a local woman named Mary Sunshine Walker that whispers around Beale Street insinuated was sexual in nature.[22] The next turn in the case came when it was learned that Puryear was a violent opponent of Catholicism and that his wife and daughter had adopted the faith. His daughter, Aurelia, had taken her first communion less than twenty-four hours prior to her murder. The *Atlanta Daily World* reported that Will Jamison's aunt gave police the name and address of "the little white girl" to whom Aurelia had worried that her father "would kill her if she became a catholic."[23] It was a strange admission. Though Puryear was an avowed Protestant, his wife had been a devout member of St. Thomas Catholic Church, was active in the parish, and took both of her children with her to church.[24]

The *Press-Scimitar* chronicled the investigation's progress, but gave equal space above the fold to Puryear's denials. "With tears streaming down his cheeks," the *Press-Scimitar* reported, "Puryear professed his innocence of any crime, told of his great love for his dead wife and child and described the 'perfect bliss' that existed before tragedy settled on their little home." Puryear wept openly as he made his denials. "Insinuations of the police are lies, just lies," he claimed. "I loved my wife and baby girl. I lived for them." The fire rescue story was "just a point blank lie," and his relationship with Walker was "merely just a friendship." The paper described its interview with Puryear being interrupted by Porter, Puryear's surviving son. "The boy rushed forward and was locked in his father's arms. Burying his face on the boy's shoulder Puryear wept, his form shaking."[25]

The coverage clearly favored Puryear, but it also ignored the murder of Jamison, making the focus of the story be the mystery of the family slaying. Jamison was the reason Puryear was in jail and the reason his son was so sad, but Jamison's death was otherwise unimportant in the *Press-Scimitar*'s narrative. The same was true of the *Nashville Tennessean*, the state's largest newspaper, which maintained consistent coverage of the ordeal through Associated Press reports from Memphis. The *Tennessean* did reprint initial coverage of the case that included Jamison's statement and did so again when Puryear was arrested, noting the suspect's denials, Jamison's repeated deathbed testimony, and the sheriff's belief that the black victim's claims seemed believable.[26]

A week after the murders, in contrast, the local black newspaper, the *Memphis World*, published a "Jamison Extra Edition" devoted "To Will Jamison Who Vindicated a Race with a Deathbed Statement." The *World* was a recent addition to black Memphis, created less than a year prior to the Puryear murders in a city that needed new voices. "Living conditions for blacks in the urban South reflected their bleak occupational prospects," writes historian David Goldfield. They were "reminders of inferiority." In Memphis, black residents lived in neighborhoods named Slippery Log Bottoms, Queen Bee Bottoms, and Shinertown, names that, in the words of Goldfield, "indicated their disadvantaged topographical position." The people of Shinertown, those in such a disadvantaged position, needed a newspaper to help guide them through the worst economic catastrophe in U.S. history.[27]

And so in June 1931, the Southern Newspaper Syndicate had created the *Memphis World*, led in its early incarnation by editor and manager J. E. Oakes, giving the Georgia organization a triweekly voice far from home on the Mississippi River. By September, Oakes had hired Lewis Ossie Swingler from nearby Crittenden, Arkansas, to be the paper's city editor, and he would eventually take over the *Memphis World* and steer it through the hard years of the Depression. Most of the Syndicate's papers were the creation of locals, and the Scotts acted as a facilitator of the new publications, a syndicator of content, and a printer for each edition. The *Memphis World*, however, was different. It was founded by the Syndicate, serving along with the *Birmingham World* and the *Atlanta Daily World* as one of the foundational entities of the Scott enterprise. The *Memphis World*, unlike its Tennessee counterparts the *Nashville Globe* and Knoxville's *Flashlight Herald*, offered a full page of comics and littered its front page with lurid and sensational crime coverage, generally following the model that the Scotts had pioneered in Atlanta. The paper "enter[ed] the field with no axe to grind or grudges to air in public print," it claimed in its inaugural edition. "The policy of *The World* will be one of sanity and fairmindedness. These columns will be no media for spite work." The editors wrote that "the primary function of a newspaper is to print news.

The Memphis World will not be content until it prints ALL the clean and constructive news originating here." The murder headlines and scandal coverage seemed to push against that claim, but the paper pushed back: "It is the mission of this newspaper to be a mirror. It strives to reflect the things happening." In one early February 1932 edition, for example, the paper grimly reported with no headline or fanfare that the month that had passed in the new year had already witnessed ten race homicides, putting the city on pace to surpass the seventy-five black victims killed in 1931.[28]

Early in its history, the paper encouraged black ministers to become more active in the fight for racial justice. It encouraged black businesses to stop gouging black customers. It actively sought higher wages for black teachers. Such were necessary fights. Black ministers in the South tended to cultivate a personal sense of salvation over and against the activism that was often a hallmark of black Protestantism. Black businesses often took advantage of the fact that they had a relatively captive customer base and raised prices. Teacher pay disparity in Memphis, as throughout the country, left black teachers receiving demonstrably less pay than white teachers. The *World*'s advocacy included a rebuke of the West Tennessee Teachers Association, which had been ineffective at bringing about any substantial change, and the paper favored a new, more militant organization.[29]

Even at its founding, the paper's lush layout included, along with its comics page, a sports page, a society page, and a page of church news. Those pages not reserved for such fare discussed local funerals, murders, traffic accidents, and robberies. The *Memphis World*'s service as a "mirror" reflected a black population struggling with the same ephemeral pleasures and inherent dangers of many socially marginalized and economically limited groups, but it also showed the desire for upward mobility that was part of such a position. The news of national race stories like Scottsboro and the effort for a federal anti-lynching law demonstrated that Memphis was also aware of broader obstacles to race progress. This was the kind of self-awareness that often belied criticisms of the black press as trading only in vice; mirrors serve not only as a reflection, but as a visit from what is most familiar. Just as the pages of Joseph Pulitzer's *New York World* and William Randolph Hearst's *New York Journal* of the 1890s brought readers to the looking glass with scandal to prod them on civil service reform and government corruption, the *World* used society news, church information, sports, and crime to provide meaningful racial news that local white papers would never provide. That the focus of that racial news tended to veer from local events and reflect efforts at self-preservation didn't make the paper any less relevant or meaningful to those moving toward the mirror.[30]

There were also meaningful local stories. In March 1931, for example, a car wreck between a black Tennessean and a white Mississippian on the Mississippi side of the state border led the white driver and the local sheriff to hunt down the black driver in Memphis and murder him in front of a local black family. In the trial that ensued the following year, one month before Puryear's crime, the sheriff concocted a story about self-defense that every black witness denied, but it was enough for the all-white jury to acquit. "A cold blooded murder," the *World* reported, "a crime typical of Mississippi treatment toward Negroes of the Delta state, had its counterpart in Tennessee." The paper understood the risks it was taking but also was outraged at the trial's outcome. Its coverage was able to denounce the murderer and his obviously false testimony because he came from across the border, committing a crime "typical of Mississippi." Left overtly unreported but obvious was criticism of the principal culprits of the failed trial, the all-white jury that freed the murderer.[31] They were local and therefore could not be the focus of the coverage. The *World*'s reporters understood, however, that they did not need to be blatant. Overt criticism of the murderer would lead to an all-too-familiar understanding of the local jury's failure by the paper's readers. Such were the coded references required of the practical radicalism that sought to advocate for victims without alienating the local white population. While the *World* toed such a line in the Puryear case, emphasizing Jamison's heroism rather than Puryear's treachery, in its frustration it also veered into overt criticism, pushing the boundaries of black southern journalism in the process.

The paper's "Jamison Extra Edition" rehearsed the facts of the case with an undisguised interest in the outcome—"A resumé of a few high points in the case will serve the purpose of showing Jamerson [*sic*] was made the dupe of a merciless fiend"—and speculated on the efforts of the grand jury and the likely outcome of their deliberations. "The city awaits the action of the jury with intense interest." It described a dream about Jamison that his aunt claimed was a premonition of his death. She was "a member of the Holiness church and places much value on dreams and signs." The paper also praised "the relentless and open-minded manner in which Memphis police and special investigators have conducted the celebrated Puryear ax murder mystery," in particular their willingness to believe Jamison over and against the denials of his white attacker.[32]

"Friends, sympathizers and other interested persons have been going about town with a donation slip in their hands trying to raise a sufficient amount of money to send his body back to his native state of Mississippi for burial. The funeral directors say that large numbers of the curious, both white and black have thronged the parlors for days in the attempt to obtain a glimpse of the earthly remains of the colored man who has gained so much attention in the public eye in as much as he died in the dramatic fashion that he did." The visitors stood in a silence "which was rendered still more awesome by a knowledge of the forces which had brought this man to his present state. With hats in their hands the spectators stood about helpless in the face of the eternal mystery, Death, but still more helpless in this instance, because the Grim Reaper had assumed one of his grim[m]est aspects. The visitors filed out but with what thoughts?"[33]

Ultimately, the grand jury indicted Puryear a week and a day after the murders. The *World* reported that though Puryear pleaded not guilty to all three charges, he did so in the face of evidence that corroborated Jamison's story, namely two white milkmen who had encountered Jamison on the street and heard an identical version of his story. "Jamison protested his innocence until the very end," the paper reported. He "was buried last Sunday at New Park cemetery. Burial expenses were made possible through public solicitation of funds." For the *Memphis World*, black readers, and the rest of the black press, the case was always about Jamison, but his vindication meant that Puryear had to be guilty.[34]

The *Atlanta Daily World*, the parent of Memphis's black newspaper, opened its own Puryear coverage by explaining, "One of those 'Negro-did-it' crimes where the alleged culprit is crucified on the cross of race prejudice has been checked and discounted by police who today are holding Stanley Puryear for grand jury action charged with murdering Will Jamison, a Negro."[35] But its most common commentary came through reprinting editorials from its Memphis outlet. "Beale street, like a heathen worshipper, had once again offered up the swarthy body of one of her sons as a sacrifice, a peace offering, a propitiation to the malevolent gods of Hatred, Prejudice, Lust and Greed," a stinging *Memphis World* editorial opened. It was simultaneously published in Atlanta, summarizing the black Memphis response to the case. "What happened to Jamison could have happened to you, to me, to any Negro in the city of Memphis who might have come under the shadow of circumstantial evidence."[36]

If circumstantial evidence points aright and Puryear is guilty of premeditated crime, why didn't he choose a white man for his victim? It is assumed that he could have obtained one of his own race as easily as he procured a Negro. Why did he seek among us for a cloak to hide behind? The answer is that Puryear realized what all of us realize—that the Memphis Negro is practically defenseless, that a black man's life isn't worth a dime hereabouts[,] that Negroes have no rights which white men are bound to respect, and that there is not a single local Negro organization which would dare lift its voice in public protest. He realized that despite the fact that other Negroes may have been intimately connected with Jamison, that no local court would unhesitatingly accept their testimony, no matter what he might do to the man in question in their presence.[37]

"His was a death resulting from a social condition, something inherent in our national system. And if it were not that the unfortunate deaths of his wife and child are involved, it is highly probable that Puryear would not now be besieged by the legal forces, for the s[l]aying of a mere Negro. But sometimes Fate plays curious tricks even on white men guilty of killing black ones." It was not just Puryear, however. The white press was also to blame. "It is common knowledge that the white press—North and South—generally over-emphasize Negro crime news." When the Puryear ax murders hit the papers,

> the papers blazoned forth with streaming headlines the fact that one of the persons involved was a Negro. It may be imagined that the average white man upon reading the article on his way home, looked upon every chance Negro passer-by as a potential ax-murderer. He did this not so much because he actually believes it, but because of the suggestion given by the papers. And it is this very suggestiveness which contributes so much to the condition which caused Puryear to use Jamison as a pawn. The papers go a long way in promoting and disturbing racial emotions.

One way to fix the problem was "organized opposition on the part of Negro subscribers. One day's cessation in the use of white papers by Negroes would do more to stop them from painting all of us [as] fiends than any other agency."[38]

The editorial closed by tying together the murder, the trial, and its coverage in the mainstream press. "They took up a collection in colored Memphis to bury Jamison's body. I wonder how many of us realized that we buried a symbol? Who will be the next sacrifice? It's easy to shake your head and say it's too bad, but what about the next victim, future peace offerings to the gods of racial misconceptions? Who will the *Press-Scimitar* next quote in the language of Amos 'n' Andy as saying, 'White folks Ah didn't hurt nobody?'"[39]

"Willie Jamison has shattered a myth," said another co-published screed from the *Memphis World*. "The unknown, penniless man that met death so cruelly, made history when he died. For he proved that some crimes charged to Negroes are but another link in the chain of false testimony that brand our race with the stigma of lawlessness." His story was something new. "For a group of white men to believe a Negro's word against that of a white man seems a revelation. Surely this man Jamison must have had honesty shining in his eyes." The paper explained that the common response to "the merciless questioning of detectives" would have been a forced confession, but "we are thankful that Willie Jamison had enough steel in his torn body, enough bravery and courage in his heart to reiterate his innocence. So thus did a tragic figure die a hero."[40]

At the same time, the *World* took the local *Press-Scimitar* to task for its handling of Jamison's story. "From the [*Press-Scimitar*'s] accounts of Willie Jamison's deathbed statement concerning the Puryear ax murder, he was unable to speak English," the paper declared with frustration. "If the dead man spoke in the language used by that daily, he must have been unable to see the movies, or to read newspapers." The *Press-Scimitar*'s coverage had Jamison saying, "White folks, ah knowns ah's gwine ter die an' ah's tellin' yuh th truf." The *World* admitted, "It is true that Southerners of both races slur their words and have a drawl. But colored people don't use the strange words above in their conversation. Not in 1932." Reporters from the *World* did not hear the statement, but "we believe he spoke English as was described by the other afternoon paper [the *Commercial Appeal*]. And we are forced to believe also that use of such antique dialect is but another way to remind the Negro that he is but a child, unable even to grasp the language of the country to which he gives allegiance."[41]

The *Chicago Defender*'s coverage was titled "Job Seeker Murdered by Man to Hide Own Crime Is Belief." The primary emphasis was on the murder of Jamison, like that of its black southern counterparts, rather than the murder of Puryear's family. "Another perfect crime went wrong here Monday," the *Defender* began, "when the stranger on whom the deeds were to be blamed lived long enough to tell the true story to the police." The authorities began an investigation "after hearing an accused man accuse his accuser." After explaining the known facts at the onset of the investigation, the *Defender* compared the crime to that of Carl Wanderer, a Chicago man who in 1920 murdered his wife and then killed a white drifter to serve as a beard for the crime before finally confessing.[42]

According to the *Pittsburgh Courier*, Puryear "restlessly paces the narrow confines of his prison cell, while Jamieson's [*sic*] words, trumpeting forth from the shadow of his grave, rises [*sic*] to haunt him like a grim spectre."[43] Unconcerned with the fine points, the *Courier* continued to cover Jamison's story, reporting unequivocally before the trial that "Puryear shot him and tried to foist the murder guilt on him."[44] The *Defender* similarly reported that Puryear, "who tried to have a Race man hanged for a crime he himself committed has been caught in the trap he set for the latter."[45] Neither paper seemed concerned with libel law, confidently asserting Puryear's guilt based on Jamison's testimony.

In July, Puryear was again denied bond as he waited for trial, and the *Courier* titled its coverage "Cracker Who Tried to Say Negro Killed Wife Denied Bail."[46] A *Baltimore Afro-American* story was titled "Dying Story Shows Guilt of Ofay."[47] When the *Afro-American* reported on Puryear's indictment, it noted that he was charged "after Will Jamison, a jobless worker, had died in the hospital proclaiming his innocence of the murder of Puryear's family."[48]

As the case progressed, Puryear's lawyers argued vigorously for a change of venue, claiming that their client could never receive a fair trial in Shelby County.[49] They failed, and when the trial eventually got under way in early October, Puryear stuck to his story. He loved his wife and daughter and hadn't killed them. In the hands of the state, however, Puryear was a chronic drinker and a neglectful husband who often spent nights away from the house and never took his wife to the movies. Prosecutors worked diligently to tie him to Sunshine Walker, though he denied any untoward extramarital activity. When Walker took the stand, she also denied an affair. "Was Stanley Puryear ever undressed and in bed in your apartment while you lived on Walker Street?" lawyers asked. Despite her denials, questions such as those led to more sensational coverage of the trial in the mainstream white press, thereby minimizing the role of race.[50]

While investigators had been at least marginally respectful to Jamison's family and the black Memphis community, the testimony of beat patrolman F. L. Gustafson demonstrated that regular black encounters with police were far more problematic. Gustafson had questioned the gut-shot Jamison and ignored his pleas for water and medical attention. "You ought to die," the officer told him, "for killing a WHITE woman and her child. I ought to take my pistol and blow your brains out." When Jamison denied it, Gustafson continued, "You chopped a WHITE woman to pieces. I'm going to kill you." The *Memphis World* was incensed: "Instead of seeing that Jamison, one of the victims of the tragedy, was taken to the hospital for medical attention, these burly gentlemen of the law, grilled him and let him die." It was, the paper explained, "a significant example of the methods of local white policemen in dealing with Negroes." This aspect had been largely absent from the discussion of the case prior to the trial, as the black press focused on getting an indictment rather than antagonizing the local police.[51] It was "one of those queer inter-racial crimes which are so much a part of the Southern pattern of justice," the *Afro-American* explained, "in which colored men are threatened although they lie dying in the gutter." Indeed, Jamison's important statement was only admitted at trial after a bitter fight between the prosecution and defense.[52]

In its closing statement, the *Chicago Defender* reported, the defense "played upon the race prejudice" of jurors to win acquittal. "If you declare this man guilty, the word would go back to Beale St. denizens and make unsafe the bed of every white woman and child in Shelby county. These criminals would learn that all they have to do to escape the consequences of a crime is to say that they were enticed to the home or some other cock and bull story which gullible policemen would believe."[53]

The trial lasted two weeks. William Gerber, the assistant state's attorney, asked for the death penalty for the crime of killing Jamison, claiming that Puryear's motive for the entire set of crimes was the purported other woman, Sunshine Walker, while Puryear's attorneys continued to maintain Jamison's guilt. The all-white jury was out for more than twenty-two hours, and one time the foreman told the judge that there was an impassable deadlock. The judge, however, sent them back to work. When deliberations began, the jury was at a 6–6 draw; it moved gradually to unanimity for acquittal.[54]

The prosecutor was incensed. "Puryear will yet have to stand trial for the murder of his wife and daughter," he declared. "I am going to try him again. I think this jury was the weakest I ever saw, which can be partly attributed to the condition of the country." He was unequivocal. "When the jury turned him loose, it was a miscarriage of justice. It was an outrage." The outcome of the forthcoming trials, however, seemed bleak, as the one murder that was unquestioned was Jamison's, and the jury had determined in acquitting Puryear that he acted with justification, meaning they thought that Jamison most likely killed the defendant's wife and daughter. "As usual in such trials," the *Pittsburgh Courier* reported, "Negroes were referred to by both prosecution and defense in only the most degrading terms."[55]

The *Atlanta Daily World*'s reaction was mixed. Puryear had been acquitted. A "Fulton county grand jury has refused to indict a supernumerary policeman who recently shot and killed his second Negro. Down in Griffin a convict camp warden was set free after he had been indicted and tried for the murder of a Negro prisoner. In Rome three policemen are being tried for the unwarranted shooting of a fleeing Negro gambler." Things seemed bad. "And yet in spite of the blocking of justice on almost every hand, the Negro should still find much to commend, for it was only a few years ago that it was absurd to think of even arresting a white official for the slaying of Negroes." It was a small victory, to be sure, but a victory nonetheless. "It may take years, but the time will come when convictions will be obtained, and, thus the chance of such acts occurring frequently will be curbed."[56]

Meanwhile, the white *Commercial Appeal* was satisfied with the verdict. "The diligence of the police department and the attorney general's office should not relax," the paper urged, arguing disingenuously that the killer might still be on the loose. "No Memphis home is safe so long as women and children can be hacked and beaten to death and the murderers are permitted to go unapprehended and unpunished." Associated Press coverage of the acquittal, printed in papers like the *Tennessean*, described the trial as "growing out of the axe murders of [Puryear's] wife and daughter," rather than mentioning Jamison—the victim in the trial—by name.[57]

Black skepticism about justice in U.S. courts was conditioned by years of inequality, both in the legal system and in the mainstream press that found satisfaction in its verdicts. "Negroes came to look upon courts as instruments of injustice and oppression," explained W. E. B. Du Bois in the early twentieth century, "and upon those convicted in them as martyrs and victims."[58] Black people's experience as witnesses in U.S. courts was fraught with bigotry. Both enslaved and free black residents of Georgia, for example, were only able to testify in court against other black residents, "free Indians," or "mulattoes," but as Glenn McNair has explained, slaves rarely saw the criminal justice system, and when they did, "the criminal justice system was seldom more than another type of chain designed to keep them ever more securely bound."[59]

Still, the racial line seemed to be negotiable, demonstrating that its development was more utilitarian than ideological. Until 1723, for example, enslaved people were barred from all testimony in Virginia capital cases, but that year the rule was changed so that prosecutors could better punish slave insurrections. Leaders had realized that if only enslaved people knew about a potential revolt, then only they could testify to its reality. Slaves were never allowed to testify against white defendants, but the change did demonstrate that their status was variable based on white whims. In the early national period, for example, various states began amending the rules again to allow enslaved people to provide evidence in cases against free black residents and Native people. Again, white defendants were never included, but the sliding scale that southern states created as they accepted or rejected the word of black witnesses was not set in stone.[60]

Such concessions were never considered a looming threat. One white southern newspaper explained in the wake of the Civil War, "With white judges, intelligent white jurors, a proper estimate will always be placed upon negro testimony." As legal historian Melissa Milewski has said, however, late nineteenth-century "trial transcripts reveal a respect for blacks' words often missing from other areas of Southern life." Lawyers who made choices to put black witnesses on the stand demonstrated their confidence that their testimony would be taken seriously by jurors, and such choices did sometimes result in "verdicts based on black testimony, even when such testimony contradicted that of white witnesses."[61]

In the wake of the Civil War, as legal historian Alfred Avins explains, though "some of the southern States had repealed or were disposed to repeal laws barring colored testimony in order to conform to military orders and eliminate the Freedmen's Bureau, the local politicians advised the people that judges and juries did not have to believe such testimony." Still, the Civil Rights Act of 1866 made the effort. Congressional leaders worried about black competency, they worried about state restrictions and their fundamental denial of equal protection, and thus they included the equal protection clause in the Fourteenth Amendment. Black complaints continued to arrive in Congress that their rights to testify were being abridged, so Congress followed the Fourteenth Amendment with the Enforcement Act of 1870, which gave everyone the right to testify, a provision designed in particular to address California's treatment of Chinese residents. Restricting black people from serving on juries for white defendants remained officially justifiable until the Supreme Court ruled in *Rogers v. Alabama* (1904) that such restrictions violated the Fourteenth Amendment.[62]

While Puryear was going through his series of trials, Clarence Norris, one of the Scottsboro Boys charged with raping two white women, appealed his conviction on the grounds that black men were excluded from jury service, and the Supreme Court agreed, arguing that systematic exclusion violated the Fourteenth Amendment's equal protection clause. Michael Klarman writes, "The Norris Court declared that when no blacks had served on juries for a lengthy period of time in a county where many blacks satisfied the statutory qualifications for service, the state was obliged to provide some explanation beyond a simple denial of race discrimination."[63]

Black testimony against white defendants, although officially sanctioned by the country's legal apparatus, was rarely a viable part of the justice system, particularly in the South. That did start to change, however, in the early twentieth century. Historian Bill Boyd describes a 1905 murder case in Valdosta, Georgia, where a long-standing family feud boiled over into a murder-for-hire that put a father and son on trial for a capital killing. The prosecution in that Deep South, largely rural community hinged on the testimony of Alf Moore, a black farmworker from Tennessee, who was first asked to commit the crime, refused, and then witnessed the machinations that ultimately led to the murder. "They came to me and asked me for the truth," Moore testified, "and I told them." Moore wasn't the only witness, but he was the one with the eyewitness account, and despite being grilled on cross-examination by defense attorneys who tried to play on Moore's race to invalidate his testimony, he was convincing. The white father and son who were tried for the crime were convicted of capital murder and hanged at the prison across the street from the Lowndes County courthouse. "It may have been the first time in Georgia history," Boyd writes, "that the testimony of a black man put a white man on the gallows."[64]

Sociologist Nancy Heitzeg has emphasized "the role of the white racial frame in constructing storylines for white deviance, while simultaneously constructing a narrative that condemns Blackness."[65] Amanda Carlin uses critical race theory to trace "the development of the courtroom as white space and the construction of legal narrative and legal truth as distinctly white." Emphasizing the twenty-first-century manifestations of such white spaces and the legacy of such disparities in their creation, she argues, "The courtroom has created a white space through the historical and consistent exclusion of people and narratives of color."[66]

By December 1932, with the help of such exclusions, Puryear was out of jail on $34,000 bond, the *Pittsburgh Courier* reported. At the same time, the paper noted that Memphis led the nation in rate of homicide, averaging 36.1 per 100,000 people, compared to the national average of 8.5. The homicide rate for black citizens was an "appalling" 81.6 per 100,000, ten times the national average and more than two and a half times the average for Memphis whites. "Included among the homicides," the *Courier* reminded its readers, "is the sensational Puryear ax murder[s]."[67]

Puryear ultimately faced trial for murdering his wife the following year, but on November 29, 1933, his second murder trial ended in a mistrial, the jurors unable to come to a consensus on Puryear's guilt. The judge only allowed their deliberations for twenty-one hours before dismissing the case, to the frustration of many in the courtroom. "That's the workinist jury I ever got hold of," the bailiff said to the press. "I think we could have gotten together," said one juror. "I do too," said another.[68]

Puryear had his third trial a year later in November 1934, and the prosecution again asked for the death penalty. Again Puryear testified, as did his son, Porter. "I saw my daddy with a shotgun," the young Puryear said. "I was scared so I ran and got in bed with my mother and sister. I felt something wet on my sleeve and I got out of the bed and turned on the light. It was blood on my sleeve and I saw my mother was hurt." Despite this gut-wrenching testimony, Porter also told the jury that he saw his father with an ax, making his story largely unhelpful to the defense. Mary Sunshine Walker testified again, and this time she was "more chic and auburn haired than when she testified" in the first trial. While prosecutors were unable to get the death penalty, they were finally able to get a conviction after a four-day trial and two days of jury deliberation. Puryear was sentenced to fifteen years in prison.[69]

In August 1935, however, he was out again on another bond after appealing his sentence. And he was back in the news with another accusation against black people. Puryear claimed that he was attacked in his garage by two black assailants who robbed his safe, taking $2,000 and a diamond ring before striking him over the head with a lead pipe. The *Courier* was doubtful. "Police are looking askance at this story for several reasons," the paper claimed. "One is that neighbors heard no outcry, saw nobody but a white woman, who evidently made the telephone call, enter the place and there was no evidence either inside or outside of the garage of any struggle or any disturbance."[70] This was yet another racially motivated concoction by Puryear, this time presumably for financial compensation after years of litigation.

Despite the new controversy, the Tennessee Supreme Court granted Puryear a new trial in April 1936 for the murder of his family, claiming in its opinion that the district attorney had attacked defense counsel with "improper, prejudicial and inflammatory" comments during his closing statement to the jury. "Unjustified attacks upon the defendant's counsel are unjustifiable" was the court's tautological explanation.[71] The retrial took place in June 1937, and again he was convicted, this time sentenced to serve twenty years for his crime. "The jury reached its verdict on the third ballot giving the maximum penalty for second degree murder," the *Memphis World* reported. "For colored citizens of Memphis interest in the Puryear case goes back to the slaying of Will Jamison."[72]

Still, though he had yet to be tried for murdering his daughter, Puryear was out again on bond after his second conviction, pending yet another appeal. And again he proved unworthy of that bond. In December 1937, Puryear was again in trouble for slashing a nightclub operator in a brawl in a Memphis hotel room.[73]

This time, his luck had run out. The Tennessee Supreme Court in March 1939 finally sustained Puryear's conviction. "The voice of a dead man, having cried out for retributive justice against his slayer since that fatal Monday morning he lay dying at old General hospital seven years ago, has at last been heard and answered by the Tennessee supreme court," the *Memphis World* reported.[74] Two years later, on November 1, 1941, at the age of forty-seven, Puryear died of a diabetes-related heart attack at the state penitentiary.[75]

One of the most important contributions of the black press in a southern town was the reporting of stories that white dailies would otherwise ignore, or providing black emphases in stories that would otherwise go unreported. Such was the case in the Puryear ax murders and the shooting of Willie Jamison. Coverage in the white daily press centered on the grisly murders of the family and the interesting role a black man played in the case. The *World*, however, devoted pages to Jamison, defending his innocence, supporting his statement, telling his life story, highlighting his family, and memorializing him in a way that white papers would never think to do, particularly considering their original assumption of his guilt. These moments of advocacy bonded a paper to its community by serving as its representative and advocate in the public sphere, no matter the racial compromises made of necessity along the way. The Memphis paper's relationship to Atlanta also broadened that sense of community to much of the black South, as syndication in the *Atlanta Daily World* and other SNS papers brought the heroic and tragic story of Jamison, over and against that of the Puryears, to a regional audience.[76]

"The newspaper in your community is the only way in which you can keep informed of local and round-the-world happenings among Negroes," a *World* advertisement argued. That community paper "provides employment for men and women of our race who otherwise would not enter the field of their choice" because of "the steel bars of racial prejudice." The message was clear. Papers like the *World* not only provided what black readers could not get from white counterparts like the *Commercial Appeal* and the *Press-Scimitar*, but also stood as a dam against racial prejudice. In a world where a white husband and father could chop up his family with an ax, then kill a local black man to frame him for the crime, such dams remained vital.[77]

Chapter 3

The Unsolved Murder of William Alexander Scott

W. A. Scott was coming home late again. It was just after 10:15 p.m. on Tuesday, January 30, 1934, when he turned into the garage at his home at 181 Ashby Street. He parked the car and left the garage, planning to enter his house and rest after another in a long line of long days. But he never made it. A gunman wearing a dark overcoat was lying in wait, hiding behind the back porch of Scott's house. He shot his victim three or four times, hitting him in the hip and back, before fleeing through the garden. The South's most influential black newspaper publisher never recovered. One of his writers, I. P. Reynolds, would later call it "the shot that was heard in nearly two million Negro homes."[1]

The murder of Scott was never solved. There were, however, suspects and a series of potential motives that might have driven someone to kill the publisher. The murder, those motives, and the far-reaching aftermath of his death demonstrated the interconnected web of the black upper class in Atlanta and the volatility of those connections, particularly evident in the competition between successful black businesspeople. That competition could literally be cutthroat, and such behavior was abetted by a criminal justice system that only concerned itself with black crime for the purpose of reimposing a version of bondage on the black race. Constructions of black criminality, then, were simply a function of white prerogative, often leaving the black victims of violent crimes without any approximation of justice. Such a system insulated perpetrators of antiblack violence and ensured that they were protected from criminal prosecution in crimes like Scott's murder. While the Depression further devastated an already distraught black southern community, and while racism circumscribed life for almost all black southerners and rural southerners in particular, a small group of urban upper-class black businesspeople in the South lived in a world with much the same roar as the 1920s, and that culture, combined with the lack of consequences for violently competitive behavior, made Scott's assassination possible.

His assassination, the subsequent investigation, and the ultimate trial that acquitted the most obvious suspect provide lenses through which the often-ignored Depression-era black southern upper class takes shape. Theirs was a world of overlapping interests and contentious rivalries, as everyone in that insular world sought to protect their place during volatile economic and racial times. The ascension of Atlanta's black elite, the murder of Scott, the investigation that followed, the list of potential suspects, and the events of the resulting trial demonstrate how those relationships functioned and the racial boundaries that limited their growth.

The history of white policing of black crime reached back to an earlier era. Slaves' status as property often kept them out of the white criminal justice system in the antebellum period, but that status gave way to an increased public vulnerability after the war as white southerners retrenched, using a lack of criminal justice infrastructure to justify the insidious and deadly convict lease system. That system was built on criminalizing trivialities in order to collect free labor. It was less concerned about black criminality against black victims. That went for the black upper class as well as those existing on the economic fringe.[2]

Throughout the period of convict leasing and beyond, black people in Georgia also had to worry about mob violence against them. As Fitzhugh Brundage has noted, Georgia witnessed 458 lynchings between 1880 and 1930, with mob killings happening in 119 of 159 Georgia counties. The broader South witnessed almost 4,000 more. Black economic success was a reason for murder, as was conviction for crime, but by far the most common reason was the supposed threat black men posed to the virtue of white women. Whatever the reason for individual murders, the broader justification came in the form of pseudoscientific race descriptions that depicted the black population as fundamentally childlike and inherently criminal.[3]

Sociologists like Herbert Spencer and William Graham Sumner drew on a misinterpretation of Charles Darwin's evolutionary theory to argue that modern industrial societies mirrored life in the animal kingdom. The principle of survival of the fittest, they wrongly argued, meant that because Europeans were the most prosperous and the most widespread of the earth's human populations, they were the "fittest" for life in civilized society. This was a narrative, notes historian Talitha LeFlouria, that "refused socioeconomic or even psychological duress as a credible factor in eliciting violent and nonviolent criminal behaviors." Instead, black crime "was cast as an irredeemable race trait." From Italian criminologist Cesare Lombroso to Alabama physician Josiah Nott, doctors championed the kind of pseudoscience that propped up such theories, which led to "the belief that blacks were an infantilized and separate species."[4]

Atlanta, of course, was home in much of the early twentieth century to W. E. B. Du Bois, one of the founders of a more scientific sociology. Du Bois could see such problematic perspectives playing out in front of him. "If my own city of Atlanta had offered it to-day the choice between 500 Negro college graduates—forceful, busy, ambitious men of property and self-respect," he argued, "and 500 black cringing vagrants and criminals, the popular vote in favor of the criminals would be simply overwhelming. Why? Because they want Negro crime? No, not that they fear Negro crime less, but that they fear Negro ambition and success more. They can deal with crime by chain gang and lynch law, or at least they think they can, but the South can conceive neither machinery nor place for the educated, self-reliant, self-assertive black man."[5]

Thus, even with money and respectability, all black citizens in Atlanta were marginalized by race and the segregated society that attended white southern bigotry, and that bigotry simultaneously created a policing leniency when it came to murder. W. A. Scott's ability to maneuver through the labyrinthine system of deferences and restrictions that constituted Jim Crow Atlanta, particularly as a new money upstart in an old money town, created conflict and rivalry. So did his personal life. Scott married his first wife, Lucile McAlister, in 1922, and they had two children. In 1929 he married his second wife, Mildred. In 1931, he married his third, Ella, who lived with him for roughly eighteen months before he suggested she go to Reno for a divorce, because he was planning to marry his secretary. W. A. Scott and Agnes Maddox, his fourth wife, were married in October 1933.[6]

It was scandalous to be sure. The Maddox family was understandably shocked and upset by the marriage, their new in-law's fourth in eleven years. The couple, however, stayed several days at the Maddox home after their honeymoon. There Scott apparently reconciled with his wife's family and seemed to have successfully smoothed things over with almost all of the Maddoxes. The one member of the family not present during the visit was Agnes's brother George, who had lived in Chicago for the past two years. He arrived back in Atlanta on the morning of January 30, 1934, the day Scott was attacked. Scott had received several threatening letters from Agnes's family in the weeks before his shooting.[7]

The attack on that cold January night left Scott fearing a second assault as the ambulance came to take him to Harris Memorial Hospital, the first private hospital in Atlanta that served African Americans.[8] While attending Scott, Charles Powell, the hospital's founder, received a mysterious letter with a crudely drawn picture of a pistol in the corner. Powell described the letter as saying in part, "This forty-five will get you. We notified Scott a month ago and he was hard-headed. Hard-headedness is dangerous for you, also. Don't get yourself in trouble for nothing or it will be dangerous for you, also. You took Scott in the hospital too soon."[9] That kind of intimidation affected Scott as well. Throughout the last week of his life, he demonstrated a near constant fear about the possibility that someone would arrive to finish the job. He thus requested a move to MacVicar Hospital at Spelman College. It was there, under the watchful eyes of the Spelman nurses on the afternoon of February 7, that Scott died, leaving a will, a mystery, and a confused and hurting family.[10]

Scott's will was a strange document. Created and signed on the night of February 6, just hours prior to his death, it began by disposing of "the *Atlanta World* and all of its subsidiaries and assets." Twenty percent went to his brother C. A. Scott, who was also named in the will as "the General Manager for all my newspaper businesses." Twenty percent went to Scott's mother. He then listed his other brothers and sisters without providing specific percentages, and also listed his two sons without providing typed percentages. Instead, curiously, "51%" was written in ink. His children also received "the proceeds of all my insurance policies" and "all vacant lots purchased by me from National Benefit Life Insurance Company, Receivers." Scott named his first wife, Lucile, and Austin T. Walden as "guardians" of the children's new estate, as trustees who "are authorized and directed to dispose of the real estate devised hereunder from time to time as may be found necessary."[11] The will would become a source of public controversy, but it also demonstrated a problem fundamentally foreign to the bulk of black southerners in the midst of the Great Depression.

Murder was murder, however, a crime that knew no class, and on February 10 detectives arrested George Maddox, Agnes's brother, for killing Scott. At the inquest that followed, Harry Rogers, the surgeon who had operated on Scott, testified that when the patient first arrived at Harris Memorial, he claimed that the shooting was the result of a deal he had just closed for the purchase of the Odd Fellows building on Auburn Avenue. When his brother C. A. arrived, however, and asked, "W. A., who shot you?" Rogers testified that Scott replied, "I believe George Maddox shot me." Rogers also described Scott's request to be moved to Spelman's hospital, claiming that the patient seemed to be in constant fear. That fear was only exacerbated by threats like the one sent to Dr. Powell, which seemed to indicate something larger than a brother's anger at work, perhaps even the specter of organized crime. Scott kept two policemen outside his room as guards until the day of his transfer. This was a significant point. Though Harris was a private black hospital, white doctors did frequent it, and a white face in the building would not have been strange. Spelman's MacVicar would be an all-black affair, making sure that any potential white assassin could not go unnoticed. Still, Scott's mother claimed to have been in the room when he called for Agnes, kissed her, and said, "Sweetheart, George shot me. You know your daddy and your brother said they were going to get me." Powell testified that Scott discussed the identity of his killer with him three times. The first two times, he described his killer as white. The third time, he described his killer as either white or a "Negro of light complexion," which could have referred to George.[12]

This was, to be sure, a unique method of negotiating the racial line for an upper-class black power broker in the urban South. But if Scott had run afoul of white moneyed interests, he had done so in aid of acquiring the Odd Fellows building. "His decision to purchase the Odd Fellows building, [the] biggest Negro edifice in the South, was for two reasons," Frank Marshall Davis explained. "To adequately house the *Atlanta Daily World* and his increasing business interests, and to give him the enjoyment of ousting his third ex-wife who operated a beauty parlor on the ground floor." The Odd Fellows building had officially opened in 1913 and quickly became the center of black Atlanta. At the building's dedication, the *Atlanta Independent*'s Benjamin Davis, a leader of the Odd Fellows, stood arm in arm with Booker T. Washington. "In every way," Washington reflected, "I found that this building represented the rapid upward march of the colored people of Atlanta and of Georgia at large."[13]

As of the early 1930s, the fortunes of Davis and the Odd Fellows had diminished, giving Scott the opportunity to negotiate for the purchase of the building. Attorney Walter Dillon testified about the potential connection of the shooting to the sale of the Odd Fellows building, explaining that there were three different bidders for the prize. On the Tuesday night that he was shot, Scott had insisted on completing the deal, fearing that one of his competitors was trying to eliminate him from contention. When Dillon arrived at the hospital on the morning following the shooting, Scott told him to "go right ahead with the deal."[14] Real estate—particularly high-profile real estate like the Odd Fellows building in a city that limited black access to meaningful property—provided social legitimacy, which was a commodity in itself. It was (or at least it became) worth dying for.

Meanwhile, the Maddoxes were concerned with demonstrating their own form of legitimacy, arguing that there was no family animosity toward the marriage of Agnes and W. A. that could have caused her brother to kill the publisher. George Maddox Sr. took the stand to claim that after finding out to his satisfaction that Scott had been properly and completely divorced from his previous three wives, he had no problem with his new son-in-law. He even claimed to have called a Dr. Sessions in Washington, Georgia, about making a trip with Scott to negotiate a loan for the Odd Fellows building.[15]

When Agnes entered the funeral home for the inquest, accompanied by her mother, she immediately walked to her brother and embraced him while cameras snapped photos. She corroborated her father's story. She denied any objection by her family to the marriage. She acknowledged that Scott had told her from his hospital bed that George was to blame for the shooting, but claimed that he seemed delirious when he said it. The testimony of Agnes was the bombshell moment of the inquest, the former socialite and secretary turned fourth wife attempting to exonerate her brother for the murder of her husband. When Scott's older brother Aurelius was called, he testified that in a conversation with Agnes, she told him to "keep his nose out of this or he'll get bumped off." The confusion in all of the conflicting testimony won the day. The inquest exonerated George Maddox Jr., returning a verdict of "death at the hands of parties unknown."[16]

The day after the coroner's inquest, the Scott family made its first public announcement that it would pay a $200 reward for information leading to the arrest of the guilty party. "The Scott family is asking the aid of all Atlanta in an effort to apprehend the murderer." They asked the help of all religious and social organizations in the city. Scott, after all, was one of Atlanta's foremost citizens. "If a man of his accomplishments and national renown can be slain and the murderer allowed to go his way and mingle with decent men, what can one expect following the killing of the average citizen?" The paper also asked its readers to send donations to add to the pool of money to actually catch the criminal.[17]

In response, the Atlanta Baptist Ministers Union met at Wheat Street Baptist Church. There, the pastor of Ebenezer Baptist Church, Martin Luther King Sr., made a motion to donate money to the reward fund to find Scott's killer. "We should not be silent on a matter of this sort," said King. "As ministers we should speak out. If a prominent citizen like Mr. Scott can be ruthlessly slain and the murderer remain free, the same fate can befall others." The other ministers agreed, and the organization donated fifty dollars to the reward fund.[18]

Atlanta Negro Chamber of Commerce officials also pledged to the fund, arguing that the murder was just another example of the city's need for black police officers in black neighborhoods. Scott was killed in the First Ward, which was 95 percent black. The Negro Chamber of Commerce had several times petitioned the city for black policemen for such neighborhoods. It was an interesting demand, considering that no one was making a case that the murder represented a broader criminality among the black population of Atlanta and that the murder seemed to have a specific motive within the insular world of upper-class black Atlanta, which black policemen would have been helpless to prevent. But it demonstrated the understanding among African American citizens that such fundraising efforts wouldn't have been necessary had the prominent victim been white and that there was a fundamental lack of consequences for violent crime in the black community, which could have been mitigated by the presence of a black law enforcement presence that saw solving such crimes as paramount.[19]

Meanwhile, the *World* complained that Atlanta's white daily press was implicating the *World*'s and the Syndicate's editorial policy as a motive for the killing. The paper denied that Scott had any role in a November 1933 Scottsboro meeting at Holsey Temple where Ku Klux Klan members distributed flyers and the police had to keep the peace. Scott was accused of speaking at the meeting, but the paper denounced the claim. Furthermore, he wasn't responsible for editorial policy. "Blaming 'what he said in his editorials' for his death is a tale outdoing the fabrications of Ananias and Baron Munchausen." The paper did its best to situate itself in relative proximity to its white counterparts, arguing that it "constantly fought communism as a menace to the Negro in Dixie. The *World* has battled lynching, unjust distribution of public funds, disfranchisement, legal murder, unjust court decisions and murder of both an interracial and an intraracial nature in the belief that it is the sworn duty of every newspaper to fight for the rights of its readers." Still, the *World* never received "any threats from even the most rabid Negrophobists for its editorial stand." The frustrated paper closed its screed with a final plea. "Let those who seek a motive for the untimely passing of our beloved founder and owner, seek a better reason for his fatal shooting and penetrate through the smokescreen of a radical editorial policy. Blaming the contents of the *World* for the tragedy is in the same class with trekking to the North Pole to shoot African elephants."[20]

The Holsey Temple meeting had been a fundraiser for the defense of the Scottsboro Boys. The meeting was organized by the International Labor Defense (ILD), the legal arm of the American Communist Party, and led by the Reverend J. Raymond Henderson of Atlanta's Wheat Street Baptist Church. Twenty-two members of the Klan surrounded the church, passing out leaflets opposing communism and black rights and stopping the ILD leaders from entering the building. The tension ultimately boiled over after a photographer for the *World* tried to take pictures of the Klan members. Police arrived soon after, and it was most likely the instigation by an employee of the paper that drew suspicion of Scott's involvement. The previous year, the *World* had published an editorial by Henderson in which he criticized capitalism and supported the communist cause, but that was certainly not the paper's editorial position. In fact, the *Atlanta Independent*, the precursor to the *World*, had a far more radical reputation than did Scott's paper. The son of Benjamin Davis, the founder and publisher of the *Independent*, was a Harvard-educated lawyer and communist who served as defense counsel for black labor activist Angelo Herndon.[21]

At the time of the Holsey Temple meeting and in the months surrounding Scott's murder, the president of the Atlanta chapter of the NAACP was Austin T. Walden. The ILD criticized him (and the NAACP) for playing into the hands of white Atlanta interests and for not publicly supporting African Americans suspected of being communists. The animus between the radical left and the black leaders seeking to excise communist connotations from black advocacy was palpable. At the same time, when Angelo Herndon's attorney organized a committee to support the legal defense of the communist labor leader, it received support from ostensibly non-communist black leaders like Jesse Blayton, who led the Atlanta Negro Chamber of Commerce and worked with Walden and Lorimer D. Milton (discussed below) at the city's Citizens Trust Bank. It was a situation rife with internecine disputes about the best strategy for achieving equality, and any newspaper that attempted to report on both sides of those disputes was bound to receive a healthy amount of resentment from each. The fault lines were bounded by class tensions and the participants' desire to maintain a level of respectability that would insulate them from their social inferiors. When influential upper-class black Atlantans used the intensity of radicalism and a willingness to associate with communists as measuring sticks for legitimacy, it created a real divide among them as to exactly what the maintenance of respectability should entail. There were thus two politics of respectability, and the different definitions had real victims in the early 1930s. The cases of Herndon and the Scottsboro Boys could remain relatively theoretical to many in black Atlanta's business district, but Scott was a real victim incredibly close to home.[22]

In response to the controversy, C. A. Scott sent an open letter to Atlanta's three white daily newspapers "asking you and all the law-abiding white and colored citizens of Atlanta" to help catch the killer. "We feel that every honest citizen of Atlanta, whether white or black, will desire the apprehension of the murderer for the preservation of law and order on which our social system depends. No slayer should go unpunished—and when an upstanding citizen is shot in the back without giving him an even chance for his life, the time is ripe for public sentiment to crystallize into definite form and ferret out the gunman."[23] This was an obvious attempt to speak to white Atlanta in its own language—Scott talked about "law and order," for example. It was almost lynching talk, with its emphasis on the "social system" ensuring that criminals not "go unpunished." Scott understood his audience and actively sought whatever help he could find for his brother, even if that help came from the relatively antagonistic white population. It was the necessary rhetoric of a black southern elite negotiating a criminal justice system where race provided the ceiling and class provided the floor.

In early March, C. A. Scott traveled to Durham, North Carolina, for a conference with officials of the North Carolina Mutual Life Insurance Company. On his return, he stopped in Johnson City, Tennessee, where he spoke at West Main Street Christian Church. "There have been rumors," said Scott, in what was clearly a speech intended for a broader audience than just the small congregation, "that the editorial policies of W. A.'s papers had something to do with the murder and that northern white capital was being used to spread propaganda throughout the south contrary to southern ideals. The Scotts are southerners and know southern ideals. We were born in the south. We live in the south, do business in the south and intend to stay in the south." He explained that he and his brother never actually wrote editorials for the paper. He then revisited the family's denials about the Holsey Temple meeting and explained that his brother had not been an agitator. "In fact, he only spoke in public upon one or two occasions since he started the *Atlanta World*." C. A. was not the only sibling to travel to North Carolina Mutual. In mid-March, Aurelius, who had already intimated his dissatisfaction with the status of his brother's murder investigation, wired a statement to the Associated Negro Press claiming that after several trips to both Atlanta and Durham, he had concluded that "my brother's death was due to a well-laid plot for control of his newspaper."[24]

Well-laid plots were a dominant feature of the cutthroat business practices of the Auburn Avenue business district. Heman Perry, for example, whose company owned the printing equipment that Scott would use to publish his paper's earliest editions, arrived in Atlanta in 1908, and in 1909 he began implementing a vision of a black business infrastructure in the city that would create economic independence, but his efforts also demonstrated the glass ceiling that existed for black businesses in the city, as prejudice kept his operations limited in their scope, and the resulting financial problems ultimately led to his downfall. "Among black businessmen," Historian Alexa Benson Henderson explains, "Perry's situation served to heighten the belief that, as blacks grew in the economic sphere, they tended to arouse the suspicions and hostility of white groups."[25] Suspicions and hostility, of course, were characteristic of black business rivals as well.

One of those rivals was Alonzo Herndon, who arrived in Atlanta in 1883 and by the early twentieth century owned a number of barber shops that catered to a white clientele. In 1905 he created the Atlanta Mutual Insurance Association, which would later become the Atlanta Life Insurance Company. His growing wealth and the business rivalries that it engendered led Herndon to a remarkable conspicuous consumption, and he invested heavily in domestic and commercial real estate in an effort to control as much territory in the city as possible.[26] The potential for violence in such empire building was obvious, and it was made worse because the black business class was able to operate largely without the fetters of the white criminal justice system, which didn't concern itself with black victims of crime.

Herndon created Atlanta Mutual from a group of faltering benevolent associations that were unable to meet the deposit requirements created by new Georgia regulations. Herndon took over the business after his bid was chosen over several others, including white institutions. One of the administrators later admitted that the group "decided to let this institution remain as it began, a race institution." Such was the business climate in Atlanta: white and black entrepreneurs could be competitors for corporate bids but would never serve on integrated boards of directors. White participation in black business enterprises could come either as customers in service industries, such as the clientele for Herndon's barber shops, or as business owners trying to make a profit from black purchasers, such as the bidders for Herndon's benevolent associations. If white and black businesspeople were meeting at the corporate level, they were always doing so as competitors, and despite Herndon's success, the reality of white supremacy ensured that such competitions were never waged on equal grounds.[27]

A group of those white business leaders had been responsible for the explosion of Atlanta's business sector in the 1920s, growing predominantly white concerns and connecting them and the city to the nation's business infrastructure. A sustained growth campaign by the white Atlanta Chamber of Commerce and a movement known as Forward Atlanta led companies like Chevrolet, Nabisco, and Lay's to locate in the city. Mayor William Hartsfield worked to bring in aviation companies. "Atlanta, the whole South, even in the twenties and thirties was sort of suffering from an inferiority complex," explains attorney Harold Sheats. "And the Forward Atlanta campaign pretty much broke the ice." It only broke it, however, for those white business leaders. As historian Clifford Kuhn notes, the Forward Atlanta campaign "did not include any black citizens in the effort, did not solicit a single black company, and made no effort to gain jobs for black residents." There were more than a hundred black businesses on Auburn Avenue in the early 1930s, and many of them spread their influence beyond the bounds of Auburn, serving black customers across the South. At the same time, the street did serve as a dividing line for commercial equality in the city.[28]

Heman Perry and Alonzo Herndon led two such enterprises, but they were not the only empire builders on Auburn Avenue. In the 1920s, Austin Thomas Walden was retained as counsel by Citizens Trust, the city's most influential black bank, a position that soon expanded to include a role as vice president. It was there that he worked with Lorimer D. Milton and Clayton Yates, bank employees who had left to start a successful pharmacy in the community's Odd Fellows building before returning to the bank in 1924. Walden was, for a period in the late 1920s, the only black lawyer in Atlanta. The virtual monopoly that he held in the black legal profession gave him carte blanche, in the thinking of Aurelius, to manipulate as he saw fit, and he did act as sole guardian for the children's estate in the first months after Scott's death. The principal element of Scott's estate was the newspaper business, which was a thorny issue considering the problematic description of the division in Scott's will, with "51%" written next to the names of the Scott children, which therefore indicated it would be administered by Walden himself. A battle ensued between the Scott siblings, who argued that the 51 percent was meant for them, and Walden, who argued that it was for his charges. Of course, Walden claimed that his certainty came from the fact that he was with Scott on his deathbed drafting his will. The Scott siblings claimed that the fact didn't breed certainty, it bred the legitimate suspicion of corruption. The court, however, agreed with Walden. The children, under the regency of Walden, took majority control of the Syndicate.[29]

Aurelius Scott was outraged. "I spent one week with W. A. before his death. I know the hospital matter first hand," he wrote. "Mr. Walden, attorney, inserted his name as guardian in W. A.'s will unknown to W. A. and my mother and C. A. and all of us. That is the crux of the matter. Mr. Walden gets $25,000 in cash, 600 lots and 51 per cent of the business as it now stands."[30] W. A., he argued, was forced to dictate his will on his deathbed when he wasn't in his right mind, thus creating the 51 percent controversy. He recalled a meeting of the Cooperative Publishers in New York two years prior when members told his brother that "no big business managed by colored people could ever be safe in a southern town like Atlanta." W. A. had resented that kind of talk and responded by praising the South and its people. But current conditions, Aurelius concluded, had proven him wrong. On top of everything else, he claimed that the "action of several persons in connection with the all-day hearing of the coroner's jury was so suspicious that it was evident that they were not only shielding the killer but were spending money to do so."[31]

Aurelius believed that his brother's death was the result of three factors: his editorial policy, the Odd Fellows real estate deal, and a hostile move to gain control of the Syndicate. "The killing is the result of a mastermind plot, involving some of Atlanta's best people," he charged. "The plan has worked so successfully that W. A. Scott's own money is being used to cover up the murder and to release the killer." (It is worth noting that Walden, as guardian of the Scott children's fortune, was the only person not a family member using "Scott's own money.") On the night of his death, claimed Aurelius, W. A. asked to have his "white doctor" call his lawyer and family, but fearing that the "white lawyer" would not arrive in time, he sent for Walden. "Unknowingly, my family is on good terms with business men whom W. A. often said meant him no good whatever. They did not buy his paper and were jealous of his success. Atlanta business men had made several attempts to operate a newspaper and had failed," he argued. "As soon as W. A. died, leading business men, for the first time, got their pictures in W. A.'s paper."[32]

The *World* denied Aurelius's conspiracy theories, but if there was a rift between C. A. and his brother, it was a relatively small one. "I hasten to say that the better element of Atlanta society demands that the murderer of W. A. Scott be brought to justice," wrote the new publisher. "Four months have elapsed and seemingly nothing has been done." C. A. was "most astounded by the lack of enthusiasm and interest on the part of the guardians of W. A.'s two minor boys who now control thousands of cold cash dollars which came direct to them from insurance policies. . . . Others have also received insurance claims on the deceased['s] life. They must contribute cash to bring the slayer to the bar of justice." It was, essentially, a more subtle way of doing what Aurelius was trying to do. C. A. was calling out those who had gained financially from the death, and he implicated them by default for their lack of interest in finding the killer. The interconnected web of the black upper class in Atlanta and the volatility of those connections ultimately killed the publisher, he argued. Having a white police force that didn't concern itself with black-on-black crime ultimately poisoned lower-class black neighborhoods, and it made high-level black capitalism even more cutthroat than it would normally be. This was yet another boundary that cordoned off the world of the black southern urban elite. C. A.'s charge was a more political version of his older brother's claims. The two people who gained the most from Scott's death were Austin Walden and Lorimer Milton, who, as president of Citizens Trust Bank, carried the debt on the Scott estate. But there were other factors at work as well. Later, C. A. would be even more explicit. "I am now definitely convinced that my brother's life was taken as the initial step in a well planned scheme to get possession of the *Atlanta Daily World* and allied papers," he told the Associated Negro Press. "If he had been killed instantly the Scotts would not have been in control of the business today. But W. A. fought death courageously until he could make his will. His death was planned about thirty days before he was assassinated."[33]

In early June, Aurelius Scott returned to Atlanta and spoke with Georgia's solicitor general. He argued that his brother had been a threat to businessmen of Atlanta, who feared that Scott's empire was growing too large too quickly and would ultimately become a threat to everyone (again enforcing those artificially constructed cordons). In one letter to a Memphis correspondent, W. A. had written, "When you have been in the business as long as I have, you will know that playing up to the big dogs makes them play away from you, and my manner of progress for this type of man from now on is—to hell with them. If they want to blow their horns through my papers, pay off first." Aurelius portrayed his brother as a man who refused to play the establishment's game. "He didn't drink, smoke, and couldn't dance, and above all, he didn't hobnob with Atlanta business men. He was too much of a hardheaded, fearless business man." And that businessman, Aurelius explained, was negotiating the purchase of the Odd Fellows business block where he planned to open several businesses, including a new drugstore that would directly challenge an existing store owned by Clayton Yates and Lorimer Milton.[34]

That was significant. In July, the *Atlanta Daily World* first reported that a syndicate of Milton, Yates, J. B. Blayton, and Walden had purchased the Odd Fellows building (even though Walden was still managing the estate of Scott's children) for roughly $54,000, which was paid to local receivers for the National Benefit Life Insurance Company. National Benefit owned the building, but the long-successful insurance company had gone bankrupt in the hard days of the Depression, and Milton, a "well known Atlanta businessman and cashier of the Citizens Trust company" went to Washington, D.C., to negotiate with the receivers. Along with the five-story Odd Fellows building, the group was also said to have purchased the building's two-story annex, which housed Bailey's Royal Theatre, and other businesses extending down to the Butler Street corner of Auburn Avenue. The deal "has been termed the largest on property in a Negro section of Atlanta in years."[35]

With this new—and suspicious—information, Aurelius accused Walden and Milton, along with "a local woman and a Chicago gangster," as the murderers of his brother. (Walden and Milton were described as "a well-known lawyer and a pharmacist in Atlanta.") The attack, Aurelius argued, was because of the Odd Fellows building deal. Scott had negotiated to buy the building for $45,000, with $2,000 down, aided by "a leading North Carolina insurance man." Gilbert V. Bryan, the receiver for National Benefit Life Insurance, refunded the $2,000 in July and resold the property for $54,000 to Milton, Yates, Blayton, and Walden, "all members of the board of directors of the Citizens' Trust Company."[36]

Lorimer D. Milton grew up in Washington, D.C., before attending Brown University for both his bachelor's and master's degrees. John Hope, Brown's first black graduate and the president of Morehouse, chose Milton, Brown's second black graduate, to teach at the Atlanta institution. Milton also began working at Citizens Trust Bank and started moving his way up the corporate ladder, all while also maneuvering for control of a local drugstore housed in the Odd Fellows building. His role with the bank gave him an interest in the *Atlanta World*. "I started that paper," he later boasted. "W. A. went to Morehouse College while I was teaching at Morehouse, and that's how he got to know me. I had a printing company, and when Scott knew that I owned that printing shop, that is, my bank owned that printing shop, then he came to me to let him use it. And so I let him use the damn equipment. I didn't charge him a damn thing for it."[37] As of 1934, however, his relationship with the Scotts had obviously changed.

Whether the deal fell through or the pressure applied by Aurelius Scott became too great, Milton and Walden's investment group did not buy the Odd Fellows building. In August, a white real estate agent named Henry M. Pitts, whose identity went undisclosed at the time, purchased the building for $47,000.[38] So Walden and Milton divested themselves of any financial interest in the Odd Fellows building, allowing others to purchase it and supposedly disproving Aurelius's theory because of the divestment. Next they sought to parlay that momentum by announcing that they were initiating a defamation suit against the *Baltimore Afro-American* in September for publishing Aurelius's claims in a "false and malicious article without so much as making any investigation of its truth or falsity." The case, however, never materialized. Such a suit would have required testifying under oath and a demonstration of the falsity and maliciousness of Aurelius's claims. Whether Walden and Milton didn't pursue the case because of fear they might incriminate themselves or because public announcement of the potential suit served the same purpose as an actual trial, they never actually filed.[39]

But Aurelius would not stop making his case. "Mr. A. T. Walden, local attorney, is using the courts to cover up the murder of the late W. A. Scott, and is now taking illegal possession of my brother's $500,000 estate," Aurelius claimed in 1935. "We have pleaded with Mr. Walden to resign from the will, in which he placed his name, unknown to my dying brother and the family. Mr. Walden admits to the family that he made the will from his own head, and we would have to raise W. A. Scott from the grave to change it. He also remarked that he would 'tear up' the business, if we even tried to move him." And the scheme wasn't an accident. "Mr. Walden and Prof. Milton, were bitter business enemies of my brother, in the effort to get the Oddfellow building, that caused the gangster type murder, at the outset."[40]

There was at least some reason for the suspicion of Aurelius. In December 1937, the legatee distribution from W. A. Scott's estate totaled $10,000. According to Scott's will, C. A. and Emmeline received 20 percent

($2,000) each. Austin Walden and Lucile Scott received 51 percent ($5,100) in guardianship for the children. Scott's other siblings split the remaining 9 percent, receiving $128.57 each. It was clear, however, that the estate was suffering as time passed. The percentages remained the same for each of the legatees in December 1939, but this time C. A. and Emmeline only received $600, Lucile Scott and Austin Walden received $1,530, and the other siblings received $38.57 each.[41]

Walden and Milton had done so much for black Atlanta. They would go on to do much more. But their behavior in the wake of W. A. Scott's death remained suspicious. The claims of Aurelius never centered on either Walden or Milton actually pulling the trigger. Maddox always seemed the most obvious culprit for the murder itself. His motives, however, and the role that Walden or Milton may have played in them remained in question.[42] The two men were provided safe haven by the relative lack of concern from Atlanta's white criminal justice apparatus. These wealthy black men lived their lives and moved in circles far different than most in black Atlanta during the Great Depression, and they maneuvered to control properties and businesses catering to the majority of that population. The black upper class was, in that sense, a benevolent oligarchy. Meanwhile, leaders like the Scotts edged as close to the racial line as possible in order to secure the pride of place that came with inclusion in the business class. Maintaining that place could be a cutthroat affair. And it could get you killed.

But no one was punished for the crime. The official investigation languished (if it hadn't completely stalled), and the Scotts decided that they had no choice but to build momentum on their own. Among the attorneys used by the Scotts during the original coroner's inquest was Reuben A. Garland, a white Atlanta lawyer who stayed on the case through the remainder of 1934, collecting his own evidence to implicate Maddox in aid of getting an indictment. C. A. Scott funded Garland's private investigation into Maddox's story, doing the job of white authorities to develop a scenario for the crime that would be accepted by those same white authorities even if the evidence seemed to point to a "scion of a well known Georgia family."[43]

Though the new evidence came largely from a private investigation, it certainly seemed to be a kind of progress that white investigators had been unable to make, either because of a lack of interest in a black crime or because of the unwillingness of black witnesses to be forthcoming with local white police. "It is stated by some," reported the *Afro-American*, "that much more interest was shown by the solicitor's office in pressing the trial of Angelo Herndon on 'fluke' charges than has ever been shown in any efforts so far to bring Maddox to trial." Prosecutors agreed to take Garland's findings to the grand jury, even though the previous year's coroner's inquest had been inconclusive. Six different witnesses to Scott's deathbed proclamations of Maddox's guilt appeared before the grand jury, along with "several others to whom Maddox had made incriminating statements shortly after the shooting." The state claimed that it would, at the time of trial, prove that the Maddox family was hoping to acquire the *World* and the Syndicate—the murder was, in effect, a family conspiracy. The Fulton County grand jury returned a true bill and formally charged Maddox with murder.[44]

William Schley Howard, the Maddox family's attorney, expressed surprise at the grand jury's decision. Most of the evidence presented, he argued, was rehashed from the previous year. It was a conspiracy theory more than actual evidence, and it left even the pro-indictment *World* in a pleasant state of shock. "The indictment came as a distinct surprise to Atlantans, many of whom had just about come to the conclusion that the case was closed." The *World* noted that the "insistence on the part of both white and colored business friends" of Scott, combined with the work of Reuben Garland, ultimately had secured the indictment. It was a refrain that the paper would repeat at every available instance. Garland had "been retained by both white and colored business friends of the late publisher."[45]

The message was clear. White people were working to get the indictment. White people were the lawyers prosecuting the case. White people were the detectives. The *Atlanta Daily World*, and by extension the Scott family, used whiteness to validate both the importance and the justness of its cause, even as the family itself was doing the work in lieu of an apathetic justice system. It seemed a quixotic situation, at best, considering the broader disingenuousness of the southern white population. After all, "many persons believed," reported the *Chicago Defender*, "that his mysterious slaying was due to the dislike in which he was held by the white business men of the city, who derided his editorial policy and envied his success."[46] The problems inherent in such stances by the *World* became even more apparent as events unfolded.

In the days preceding the trial, there was discussion about potential record witness counts and extended days of testimony, but the prosecution only called eight original witnesses and closed its initial case on the afternoon following jury selection. The defense was more thorough, calling a litany of alibi witnesses. George Maddox Sr., for example, repeated his story about calling a Dr. Sessions in Washington, Georgia, to help finance the Odd Fellows building purchase. Maddox Senior had visited the hospital several times to see his new son-in-law, and he testified that Scott told him that the shooting was a result of the Odd Fellows deal. The defense lawyers were far more systematic than the prosecutors, spending days establishing Maddox Junior's alibi and forcing their counterparts to act more diligently when producing rebuttal witnesses.[47]

One of the witnesses was Austin Walden, who testified to Scott's death-bed proclamation of Maddox's guilt and described being called to Spelman to draft the dying man's will. The defense pressed him on the existence of hostility between Scott and Milton and between Scott and himself. He denied that there was any animosity. He also denied, as reported by the *World*, "that he had heard of any plot or scheme to kill Scott to keep him from buying the Odd Fellows building." The case never really delivered on the new information promised by the prosecution, which emphasized the poor character of Maddox's alibi witnesses rather than new evidence. Still, the *World* was confident. "Driving straight for the death penalty in the case," it reported, Garland and the prosecution "continued an onslaught on the defendant's badly crippled 'alibi.'" Surely there would be a conviction.[48]

There would not. It had been the longest trial involving a black defendant and a black victim in the history of Georgia, but the relatively short three-hour deliberation by the all-white jury returned a verdict of not guilty. An incredulous *World* called the verdict "a surprise" and reminded its readers of the jurors who had let Maddox go. "These are the twelve men who voted 'acquittal' for George Maddox, Jr., after a week length trial in the slaying of W. A. Scott," the paper announced on its front page, before listing the names.[49] It was, however, misplaced surprise. The lackluster prosecution was symptomatic of a society relatively unconcerned with black victims of crime. The reality of a three-hour deliberation in the longest trial involving a black defendant and a black victim in the history of Georgia spoke to nothing else if not white apathy.

Ralph Matthews, the *Afro-American*'s correspondent in Atlanta for the trial, played the role of Alexis de Tocqueville, looking at both the trial and the race relations it represented as an outsider from Baltimore. And he was shocked by what he experienced. Matthews walked down Auburn Avenue in an early version of man-on-the-street reporting. He asked passersby whether they thought Maddox would be convicted. No one thought he would. "He has William Schley Howard for his attorney," said one resident. Matthews thought that the lawyer mattered less than the facts of the case. "Most people," he reported, "seemed to pity me."[50]

While Matthews admitted that the case's outcome had proved the local observers to be correct (the outcome was, he argued, "no surprise, not even, perhaps to the kinsmen of the dead publisher, who sought a conviction on the old Mosaic law, 'an eye for an eye and a tooth for a tooth'"), he was baffled by the respect shown to Howard, who had used "epithets which sent my blood curdling under his violent onslaughts." Howard's harangues at "nigger women" had only been one example in a trial filled with such terms. His closing argument to the jury "was punctuated with some of the vilest epithets for the race it has been my ill-fortune to hear in any courtroom," but among the black population listening, it "was hailed in the corridors as a masterpiece of eloquence. I could not quite understand the workings of the Georgia mind that could swallow such insults without resentment."[51]

Matthews's man on the street tried to explain: "This is the kind of speech it takes to win in a Southern court." It was this attitude that Matthews couldn't understand. After Maddox had been freed by the coroner's jury the previous year, he argued, "the state did absolutely nothing to solve the murder." It was the Scotts themselves who paid investigators, found witnesses and evidence, and hired Garland, who then acted as one of the lead prosecutors in the case. "The mere fact that these steps had to be taken is a reflection on the diligence (?) of the commonwealth where our citizens are concerned," he stated. "Had Scott been white the same prejudiced language which saved Maddox would have sent him to the chair, because evidence in cases involving the latter circumstance does not have to be so conclusive in Georgia."[52]

Matthews had driven in a few short paragraphs to the core reality of the situation of black upper-class urban Atlanta. The murder was tragic, and there was a possibility that it was actually a white man who killed Scott. But white men had played a role in the death whether or not one of them pulled the trigger. The world of relative privilege that existed for the Scotts, Maddoxes, Waldens, Miltons, and Davises was always going to be limited by the white ceiling that stunted its growth. Even more important, and certainly most frustrating to Matthews, black urban southerners seemed to accept such ceilings as a matter of course. Everyone Matthews interviewed assumed that Maddox would walk. No one was surprised at the language used by the white lawyers. No one even seemed to notice that all of the white men were addressed with honorifics and called "Mister" while black witnesses were called simply by their first names. It was the cost of doing business at best, Stockholm syndrome at worst.

William Schley Howard called the prosecution witnesses "gutter snipes" and "a band of infamous perjurers." One witness was "an old, greasy, dirty black buzzard." Another was "a dirty, contemptible nigger, and I don't mean Negro. N-I-G-G-E-R." At one point, Howard told the jury that "if a colored man can get a fair trial anywhere in the world, it is among the God-fearing, law-abiding white people of the South among whom he has been raised." Of course, his opponent, Garland, wasn't appreciably better, calling the Maddox family "the smartest bunch of assassins who ever wore black skins."[53]

The *New York Amsterdam News* agreed with the *Afro-American*'s criticism. It was "a murder trial reeking with disgrace and embarrassment for scores of Atlanta's best families, with defenseless women subjected to insults, scornful and opprobrious epithets at the hands of defense and prosecution." The trial was "a seven-day exhibition of the indignities which colored women must suffer in the courts of the South. There were thinly-veiled assertions that the morals of colored women were not all to be desired, regardless of social strata, while preeminent male witnesses were attacked as perverts."[54]

If Atlanta's upper-class black leaders served as a benevolent oligarchy in the African American community, they remained constantly aware that the bounds of their success were always limited by the far less benevolent apartheid state that surrounded them. Their situation was, to be sure, better than abject poverty, better than Klan victimization, and better than the chain gang, but it was a uniquely liminal space in the southern social hierarchy that obviously had its own set of rules and assumptions. The lack of effective policing in the black community gave business rivals latitude to deal with each other with impunity, which also meant that the victims of that impunity would remain unavenged.

The rivalries were real. The *Afro-American* interpreted the battle as between the old and new money black southern families. "The Maddox family represents the old type of Southern aristocracy," the paper reported. "George Maddox, Sr., has been a resident of Atlanta for thirty-odd years. He has been an employee of the Southern Railroad for twenty of these years, during which he has rubbed elbows with the finest and most influential people of the South as a dining car waiter." That kind of "association with the Dixie noblesse gave him a certain prestige in sepia society. He is Mr. Maddox among his own and George to the whites which is a term of endearment."[55]

Meanwhile, the Scotts were "of the new commercial type who have lifted themselves by their own bootstraps from obscurity to a place of financial independence and prominence." For that effort, "they have incurred the hatred of the whites and the envy of their own race." Additionally, the pitfalls of the publishing business "created for them many enemies in both races. Editorial policy, diametrically opposed to the ideology of the Southland, has alienated the whites and the scandals divulged in the news stories have embittered many of their readers." The *World*'s readers, of course, were working-class blacks. "These are the primary factors, the underlying currents beneath the fight that is being waged, with the crowded spectators about evenly divided for conviction and acquittal."[56]

This division, the *Afro-American* argued, is what drove the marriage between Scott and Agnes Maddox. W. A. was hoping to solidify his reputation, and thus his company's reputation, by marrying into an established family. It was, the paper claimed, a marriage to bolster Scott's power, and the Maddox family was enraged by it.[57]

The Maddox brother scandalized by that hasty marriage had combined with Milton's early contact with the Scott estate, Walden's guardianship of the victim's children, Ben Davis's collapse in the wake of Scott's success, and the mysterious possibility of white interests competing for the Odd Fellows building or angry about Scott's journalistic politics to create one of the most compelling unsolved murder mysteries in Atlanta's history. Milton, Walden, and Davis all had connections to National Benefit Life Insurance, all had connections to the Odd Fellows building, and all had financial interests in the Scott estate; two of the three, Milton and Walden, stayed involved in the estate after Scott's murder. They were also three of the most important luminaries in black Atlanta, and they and Scott all seemed to rotate around an Odd Fellows axis on Auburn Avenue, around which the entire solar system of black Atlanta revolved.

Along with the intrigue, the murder and its aftermath demonstrated the constraints of the system in which Scott, Milton, Walden, and Davis operated. The conspicuous consumption that defined black empire building in Atlanta had led to competitive rivalries that could drift into violent reprisal because of a policing system apathetic about the crimes in which black citizens were victims. Although Scott died, his newspaper and the Syndicate did thrive after 1934. But so did the constraints of that system. The white business and civic leadership that placed a ceiling on black people's ability to rise (and felt completely comfortable using ugly racial slurs in court) reacted angrily when they perceived that upper-class African Americans were using their money or status for racial activism. Meanwhile, white criminal justice leaders hardly reacted at all when black crime resulted in black victims. Instead, they emphasized black criminal prosecution based on the labor needs of the white business and civic leadership. This formula abetted the interests of black empire builders and, at times, allowed them to get away with murder.

Chapter 4

The SNS, Gender, and the Fight for Teacher Salary Equalization

In 1938, Walter Mills, a school principal in Anne Arundel County, Maryland, sued his school system in federal district court with the help of the NAACP, alleging that his salary and the salaries of the teachers in his charge were far less than those of white teachers, violating state laws mandating separate but equal education. He had watched in 1936 and 1937 as similar efforts in Montgomery and Calvert counties had ended in salary equalization without definitive rulings, and he wanted an official mandate.[1]

Later that year, on the other side of the South, B. M. Jackson founded a new newspaper, the *Galveston Examiner*, in the island city just off the coast of Texas, facilitated by SNS syndication. It would only survive for two years, which was typical of small Scott Syndicate start-ups without the resources or readership to maintain long lives.[2] Jackson's paper reported on its front page in December 1939 about Mills's success—a federal court ruling had mandated salary equalization for black teachers in Maryland— and about its hope that the ruling would establish a precedent for the rest of the South. The Anne Arundel County school board had fixed salaries at different levels based solely on race, the *Examiner* explained, and the court decision mandated one salary schedule for public school teachers regardless of race. Of course, as Galveston and other southern regions discovered, the Anne Arundel ruling was a beginning, not an end, in a fight for pay equalization that would continue for years. Still, the *Examiner* was hopeful.[3]

Coverage of the suit was ubiquitous in the nearby *Baltimore Afro-American,* and its pages have provided strong source material for historians of the effort to equalize teacher pay. That effort was one of the core rights fights in the South, although almost all of its post-Maryland outgrowths were below the state's border, making the region's smaller, less-recognized black newspapers vital to interpreting the movement for their readers.[4] The Anne Arundel suit was led by a male principal, but the salary equalization fight was the principal effort at gendered race advocacy during the era of World War II, as the bulk of black teachers were women. This was a generation prior to the slow trickle of school desegregation, so various advocacy groups, including the NAACP, worked for equality within the segregated system, making the case that black teachers did the same work as white teachers and therefore deserved equal salaries. The fight witnessed successes and failures in the late 1930s and 1940s, and it was a fight that the Scott Syndicate's black southern press was uniquely suited to cover. The SNS newspapers were in communities where strikes and lawsuits commenced. They too were struggling for equality in a business that was fundamentally dependent on segregation. The papers were dominated by men but were advocating for salary equalization in a profession dominated by women, problematizing that advocacy and often creating a paternalistic proxy fight that played on common tropes of dependent femininity. Black southern newspapers often get short historical shrift because they were short lived, and so few were saved. But they held significant sway with the black population in their cities and states, and they served as conduits of local information about teacher salary equalization fights across the region. The black press encouraged new outgrowths of those fights through SNS syndicated coverage throughout the South and reversed traditional gender roles by acting as male stewards for female leaders and activists.

To be sure, there were plenty of male teachers, some of whom worked diligently for salary equalization, and there were also a number of female journalists and editors, even in the South and even as part of the Scott Syndicate. And the vast majority of black southern teachers and black southern journalists, regardless of gender, believed that black teachers deserved the same salaries as their white counterparts. But when black male journalists in the South advocated for and reported on teacher salary equalization efforts spearheaded by women, that mediation came with paternalistic assumptions and language that often diminished the pioneering roles female teachers played in those fights.

Public education in the South was slow in coming, but upon its arrival in the nineteenth century, what began as yet another male-dominated endeavor evolved into a female-dominated profession. In North Carolina in 1884, for example, only 731 of the state's 2,231 black teachers were women. By 1900, there were just as many women teaching as men, and in the coming decades, the profession would fall predominantly under the purview of African American women. The same evolution can be seen among white teachers. In 1920 the total teaching force was 85 percent female; in 1930 it was 81 percent. That number fell somewhat in the 1930s, as a male backlash against married women working (a scapegoat for the Depression) diminished the number of female teachers somewhat, but even with that hindrance, the profession remained 78 percent female. The percentage of female teachers rose precipitously again during World War II, as many men were drafted into the military.[5]

Not only were the numbers of black teachers growing, so too were their credentials. The number of black teachers in southern states with bachelor's degrees rose from 12 percent in 1930 to 72 percent in 1950. This was a project aided by the fact that economic necessity and philosophical outlook had kept black education from following the white trend of single-sex education, allowing black women to take advantage of the education that had developed post-Reconstruction to qualify themselves as teachers. As historian Glenda Gilmore has explained, black southerners emerging from the slave period valued "strength, initiative, and practicality among black women," and the "system of higher education they constructed reflected those ideals." Until 1890, North Carolina paid teachers an ostensibly equal wage, though black teachers were asked to do much more, often responsible for classrooms with pupils ranging from five years to nineteen. As the teaching force became more female, however, and white Redeemer politicians found more and more clever ways to punish the descendants of formerly enslaved people simply for not being slaves, public school pay scales separated more and more.[6]

In the seventeen states and District of Columbia that mandated segregated public education, the average salary of black teachers was roughly half that of white teachers in 1930. That average rose to 65 percent by the end of World War II and 85 percent by 1950. "It was black men's exclusion from the political sphere," explains Gilmore, "not black women's willingness to work for low wages, that caused African American teachers to be poorly compensated." Thus it was a fight, despite the early role of Walter Mills, that was led by courageous black women. Activist Septima Clark described her work for salary equalization as her "first effort in a social action challenging the status quo." Likewise, the influential South Carolina NAACP secretary Modjeska Simkins began her most prolific period of activism in the teachers' salary movement. In addition to their activism, women were also the teachers and thus the plaintiffs—Mills and several others excepted—in equalization lawsuits throughout the South. As historian John A. Kirk has noted, the gendered equalization effort was coordinated by the NAACP, and thus "from grassroots African American women's activism in teachers' salary equalization suits to Ella Baker's role in the NAACP's national office, African American women played a vital part in the dramatic rise in NAACP membership and activism in the 1940s."[7]

Exemplary of such a statement is Lulu B. White, the executive secretary of Houston's NAACP chapter, who, while not a plaintiff in the city's teacher salary equalization case, was "intimately involved" in it. After a victory, White "used every possible means of communication—newspapers, pamphlets, lectures, rallies—to inform teachers of the role" of the NAACP.[8] Those newspapers were, in Houston and throughout the South, largely dominated by men, thus emphasizing again the reversal of gender norms as they publicized a rights fight led and dominated by women. Salary equalization lawsuits and activism have been detailed in many studies with many different approaches.[9] This chapter, however, is concerned specifically with journalistic mediation, with how black southern newspapers reported on salary equalization (one of White's "means of communication") and the consequences of the deviation from social norms for black southern rights fights in the postwar era.

African American women began carving a significant place for themselves in their own communities following emancipation, though the pressures of poverty and a male-dominated black culture made significant gains difficult. As Hazel Carby has argued about the nineteenth century, black women, in both self-definition and popular understanding, became intrinsically contradictory upon attempting to enter the public sphere. They were both active adherents to "the dominant discourse of white women's politics" and social outsiders who were on the opposite side of the cultural color line. In this environment, black women activists and writers had to construct a "discourse of black womanhood" because the domestic and literary ideals that shaped the late nineteenth-century cultural definition of womanhood only created a definition of white womanhood.[10]

Paula Giddings argues that racism and sexism, though fundamentally different, stem from the same "economic, social, and psychological" forces, and in the struggle for equality, black women often have compromised their feminist leanings for the sake of African American struggles and sometimes have compromised their African American identities in order to ensure that black womanhood remained viable.[11] Jacqueline Jones sees that a continuously shifting economic climate from antebellum times to the present often has marginalized and subjugated working-class and poor people—urban and rural, black and white, male and female—but African American women, already firmly in the grip of a cultural double bind, have suffered unique (and frequently greater) hardships throughout the nation's various social, political, and economic manifestations. In the public workforce, "black women" often were relegated to "black women's work," a further distinction in gendered employment that is often overlooked by historians. In their private lives, women served and supported their families, but they were also general facilitators of community spirit in black society. The propagation of dual roles within dual roles and double binds within double binds created an economic situation almost impossible to improve, even without the machinations of the U.S. economy and the turbulent transition from slavery to freedom to Jim Crow to general economic oppression.

Following World War I, both black and white women struggled to escape domestic service and develop their viability as a legitimate segment of the workforce with a wage almost equal to that of their male counterparts. But again, unlike white women, African American women had no choice but wage labor, and the development of "white women's jobs," such as secretarial and sales work, only limited black women's choices. The Depression of the 1930s hurt an already hurting black population, forcing black women to shoulder even more of an already heavy burden. Through the work they were able to find, however, African American women unionized, took a growing interest in politics, and developed a sense of black consciousness. With the early development of civil and women's rights issues between World War II and *Brown v. Board of Education* (1954), Jones's black women largely eschewed Giddings's compromises and sided squarely with their black identity and the principal struggles of civil rights. The necessity of their labor to feed their families, their obvious inequality with white women, and their exponential economic and supportive influence on black communities made this choice relatively simple.[12]

Men's domination of the black press remained a relative constant. Robert Abbott and his nephew John Sengstacke founded and controlled the *Chicago Defender*. James H. Anderson founded the *New York Amsterdam News*. Robert L. Vann dominated the *Pittsburgh Courier*, and P. B. Young the *Norfolk Journal and Guide*. In the Deep South, where the bulk of the teacher salary fight developed, the growth of newspapers was facilitated by the Scotts, the *Atlanta Daily World*, and the Scott Newspaper Syndicate.[13]

This is not to say that the history of black southern journalism did not include women and did not have previous intersections with the teaching profession. Lucy J. Cochran, for example, began working at the *Lexington*

Herald before starting her own Kentucky paper, the *Lexington Record*, and aligning it with the Scott Syndicate from 1934 to 1936. Even earlier, women had an important role in black southern journalism in the nineteenth century, feeding particularly from the boom in black newspapers in the 1890s. Of the forty-six female journalists in the last two decades of the nineteenth century studied by historian Gloria Wade-Gayles, more than half were from the South. The journalists in Wade-Gayles's study came from all economic backgrounds. Ida Wells, originally from Mississippi but more famously working in Memphis, and Victoria Earle Matthews of Georgia, who worked at papers across the country, were both from impoverished backgrounds. Mary Church Terrell of Memphis and Josephine Turpin Washington, on the other end of that spectrum, were born into relative wealth. Still, when they joined the journalistic ranks, they made virtually no money. All of Wade-Gayles's subjects, Matthews excepted, were teachers simply to make ends meet. Black journalism in the South was a business just as misogynistic as any other, with the same glass ceiling as other industries, but this did not make women any less crucial.[14]

Women from outside the region also came down to cover civil rights efforts of various kinds. Perhaps the most famous arrived in the years after the teacher salary fight: Chicago's Ethel L. Payne, known as the "First Lady of the Black Press," worked for the *Chicago Defender* in the 1950s and 1960s and spent time in the South covering the civil rights movement from the Montgomery bus boycott to the March on Washington. Still, northern reporters like Payne were tourists in the region, and editors like Cochran were the exception rather than a rule in a gendered business that coded journalism as a functionally male endeavor.[15]

The Scotts and the *Atlanta Daily World* did have women from the family working in leadership roles in the family business, but that business did not own most of the papers it printed. Instead, local southerners and would-be journalists wrote articles and editorials about the news in their area, generated advertisements for local businesses, and then sent that collected material to Atlanta, where SNS staff would organize a layout using the local news, add national news from the *World* and other syndicate papers, print the finished product, and then send it back. It was a system that allowed almost anyone to become a journalist, and the bulk of those who took that opportunity were men.[16] Those men reported on teacher salary fights and became the de facto public advocates for women in the proxy fight for equalization. This could, to be sure, create legitimate problems of interpretation.

In 1935, for example, Nathaniel N. Baker, a bellman for several different hotels in Pensacola, Florida, who had only a high school education, founded the *Pensacola Courier* and edited it until the early 1950s, when his wife, Cora, took over.[17] Pensacola is in the more traditionally conservative southern region of the Florida panhandle. The couple's paper was correspondingly reticent to directly attack white supremacists, but one of its most sustained fights was common to much of the black South in the late 1930s and early 1940s: the struggle for the equalization of teacher salaries. The equalization fight was spearheaded by the NAACP, which, as Tomiko Brown-Nagin has explained, "perceived African-American educators as being at once a core constituency of, and a political threat to, the association's agenda." The fight for equalizing teacher pay was important because of the fundamental injustice to black teachers and the ancillary demeaning of black children's education, but it would also help the NAACP to "shore up its support among educators," who composed "a large segment of the NAACP's middle-class constituency." The fight dominated much of the wartime period. It also continued beyond it.[18]

Albert McKeever's *Jacksonville Progressive News* was founded in 1938, facilitated by the Scott Syndicate, and lasted until the mid-1950s. In April 1941 the paper reported on renewed efforts by Florida teachers to "continue their fight for equal pay." In May, a Jacksonville minister from the African Methodist Episcopal Church began a fund to help the teachers in their fight, noting a case in the U.S. District Court in Pensacola as a "first step in this program." In October, the paper covered a local teacher who had filed a petition with the board of public instruction for equal pay. The move followed a meeting of more than three hundred teachers at a local church to raise money for the Duval County Teachers Association, which had been created to enable the fight for equal pay. "Never before," the paper reported, "have we seen such an interest taken by any group to launch a fight for a cause of the Negroes in this city." An editorial that month praised the teacher, Mary White Blocker, for submitting her petition. "A WOMAN HAS BLAZED THE WAY," the paper proclaimed. "Do we have any men to follow in her footsteps? We need better sewerage, better streets, better schools, better parks for our children, better police protection and many more improvements that we are entitled to." These were achievable goals if people started publicly advocating for them.[19]

Or, more accurately, if men did. It was a contradictory message, boldly proclaiming a woman's success but immediately calling on men to meet the other social needs of the community not specifically gender coded as female. This kind of mediation had ignored the push for abolition, the Progressive-era reform movement, and the swelling ranks of the Women's Army Corps (WAC) and the Women Accepted for Volunteer Emergency Service (WAVES), reflecting and reinforcing the ceiling on women's influence in the public sphere. Septima Clark, Lulu White, and Modjeska Simkins refused to accept that ceiling, but the efforts of the press in gender coding their work while chronicling their success created barriers for the recipients of that mediation, making the maintenance of the ceiling almost assured.[20]

Salary equalization, however, was far from assured. In June 1942, the *Progressive News* reported on a plan offered by the local school board that would base salaries on the results of an examination that all teachers in Duval County would be asked to take. If they chose not to take the exam, their salaries would be frozen at their current level. The NAACP protested the measure because white teachers had no real incentive to take the exam, while black teachers had to take the test in hopes of something approximating equalization.[21]

And so the fight continued. In May 1943, the paper covered a meeting of leading black educators in Jacksonville who supported the National Education Association's backing of the Thomas-Hill bill "for the equalization of educational opportunities throughout the nation." The $300 million appropriation would have provided proportionate funding for black schools in segregated areas, and Florida would have received almost $5 million, "which will increase greatly the facilities and salaries of all teachers throughout the state." Thomas-Hill was an effort to equalize state school systems, which often varied greatly, particularly during wartime when many people abandoned their low-paying teaching jobs for war-based work opportunities. The federal government would have appropriated money in particular to the poorest states with the sparsest educational infrastructure in order to increase teacher pay and keep schools open longer. The South's paltry school infrastructure made it a prime candidate for such funds, and the bill was even cosponsored by Alabama's Lister Hill, but when the U.S. Senate included an amendment regulating how states must spend money for both white and black schools, ensuring equal development of the two, Florida's senators joined their southern colleagues in abandoning the bill they had once supported.[22]

North of Jacksonville in Savannah, Georgia, there was the venerable *Savannah Journal*, founded in 1918 as a vehicle for the city's black Republicans. In 1940, the *Journal* underwent a sea change, taking on a new editor,

Asa H. Gordon, and joining the Scott Syndicate. Gordon was also the director of the Divisions of Social Sciences and of Research Publication at Georgia State College (now Savannah State University), coming from South Carolina State A&M in Orangeburg. "Dr. Gordon is a man of culture and fine character and by study and contact possesses a very excellent education," said M. F. Whittaker, president of the college in Orangeburg. "I think of him as an able educator, a brilliant scholar, and a cultured gentleman." In August 1941, however, Georgia State chancellor S. V. Sanford dismissed Gordon (against the recommendation of school president B. F. Hubert) over editorials Gordon had published in the *Journal* about the salaries of black and white professors. Sanford Beaver, the white chair of the board of regents, sent a letter to alumni stating, "Prof. Gordon was not reelected to his position at Georgia State College for the reason that he had written one or more articles expressing dissatisfaction over the fact that he and others were not receiving the same salaries that were being paid to white professors for similar work." Gordon had accepted the position knowing what the salary was and therefore had no right to argue, Beaver claimed, and the professor certainly had no right to argue in public. Gordon's attitude "seemed calculated to injure the faculty morale of our fine Savannah unit, with the result that the Chancellor thought it would be more appropriate for Prof. Gordon to wage his fight for equal salaries from the outside, rather than from inside of the University System."[23]

Gordon's *Journal* was outspoken. After receiving criticism for an editorial criticizing black teachers in the area for not fighting for pay equalization, in March 1942 the *Journal* ran an editorial from the *Atlanta Daily World* that complimented the courage of local teachers in filing a suit in federal court asking for salary equality. The suit, filed by William Hunter Reeves of David T. Howard Junior High School and the NAACP, was supported by black teachers across Atlanta, who "have agreed upon a systematic plan of raising the necessary funds to prosecute their case if need be." This was the kind of organization that had yet to come to Savannah.[24]

In April 1942, Gordon wrote an open letter to Georgia's white teachers, encouraging them to support equalization and join the chorus of their colleagues across the South. Equalization meant taking teacher pay seriously, and salaries in Georgia for all teachers, white and black, were "far below the requirements for maintaining the American standard of living for any professional group." In addition, "any federal aid to Georgia which will benefit Negro education will also benefit white education." The open letter, published on the occasion of the annual meeting of the state teachers association in Savannah, reminded teachers that equalization was "the first step toward democratic education" in the state, "as paradoxical as this may seem to some blinded with racial bigotry. We hope there are few of these among you."[25]

In December, the paper chided the Atlanta Board of Education for suspending William Reeves, the junior high school instructor who had sued to equalize the wage scales for black and white teachers. The move "clearly reveals [that] the common purpose of the board is to coerce the Negro teachers of the Atlanta system and compel them to keep out of any effort for equalization of salaries in Georgia." The editorial used North Carolina as a counterexample, lauding the state for responding positively to the equalization movement and celebrating the movement's principal proponent, James E. Shepard, president of North Carolina College for Negroes. It quoted an influential white newspaper that had called Shepard "the Booker T. Washington of his race in North Carolina." Reeves was doing much the same work in Georgia, though the state wasn't treating him as such, and so the paper pledged "to stand squarely by" him in his fight.[26]

It was the *Progressive News* strategy in reverse, a different kind of gender coding that found male activists worthy of public celebration in a fight that was dominated by women. The *Journal*'s praise for Reeves was not misplaced, since he was fired for his advocacy, but he was one of many teachers, the majority of them women, who were working for equal pay in Atlanta. When that gender selectivity was combined with Gordon's coverage of North Carolina, which used the male university president as an exemplar of the state's salary equalization activism rather than one of the teachers with far more skin in the game, the paper created a damsel-in-distress vision of advocacy where men championed other men for saving female victims from the bad behavior of a third, more dastardly group of men.[27]

Just up the coast in South Carolina was John Henry McCray's *Lighthouse and Informer*, which became one of the most important and influential Scott Syndicate newspapers. McCray was born in 1910 near Youngstown, Florida. He grew up in Lincolnville, South Carolina, and Charleston before attending Talladega College. There, he got his start in journalism, working for the Talladega College monthly, the *Mule's Ear*, where he tackled everything from world peace to the beauty of sunrises and sunsets. After his education, he took a job as the city editor of the *Charleston Messenger*. Feeling restricted, however, McCray started his own paper, the *Carolina Lighthouse*, in 1939. He moved the paper from Charleston to Columbia the following year and combined it with the local *People's Informer* to create the *Lighthouse and Informer* in the summer of 1940.[28]

Like many others, McCray went into journalism because he was frustrated at the amount and type of representation of black southerners in the mainstream white press. In 1940, he began a column called "The Need for Changing," which highlighted civil rights issues like poor academic facilities, white men preying on black women, lynchings, and equal pay for black teachers. "What has the South ever done for the Negro?" he asked. "Nothing they didn't have to do. Everything that has been done has been done by the Negro, or by the threat of Federal court action." In a September 1941 editorial, the *Lighthouse and Informer* analyzed a new law providing a "slight pay increase" for black teachers. This law "may mean a few dollars more for the colored teachers," the paper explained, but "it has done nothing toward 'equalizing teacher pay.'" It also noted that teachers' salaries were paid mostly by the state but supplemented by the county, and while the state payment was to be increased, nothing was to stop the counties from limiting their contributions in equal measure. With the national movement for equalizing teacher salaries under way, the South Carolina law was a half measure at best. Soon, however, the law turned out to be not even a half measure, as the governor, working in conjunction with the white Palmetto State Teachers Association, told black teachers that they had to go through a process of qualification to prove themselves equal to white teachers. The *Lighthouse and Informer* denounced the "appeasement plan" again in December, calling the notion of qualification "fallacious."[29]

The teacher salary equalization issue was never far from the top of McCray's agenda. One of the dominant strategies for equalization in South Carolina was the use of Ben D. Wood's National Teacher Examination to demonstrate the functional equality of black teachers to their white counterparts. Other assessment standards included the teacher's level of education and time served in the classroom. In May 1944, the Charleston County School Board created a new salary schedule that provided a measure of equalization based on a teacher's number of years of college and number of years of service to the school system. But a measure of equalization was not full equalization, and the county did its best to use creative accounting to keep paying white teachers greater salaries. It was the kind of deliberate speed that the Deep South would use time and again to avoid equality policies of all kinds, but teacher salary equalization delays were frustrating to McCray considering the length of time that the

Lighthouse had been advocating for the change. Early in 1945, the paper published a letter written by a white female student at Winthrop College celebrating the success of the teacher salary equalization case in Richland County. That letter was picked up by the Associated Negro Press and widely distributed, though the student asked after syndication that the name of her school be removed from the letter, obviously feeling blowback from the administration.[30]

In March 1945, the southern and western regions of the National Negro Publishers Association (NNPA), with C. A. Scott serving as vice president for the southern region, called for a special meeting at Mississippi's Jackson College "to work out strategy for fighting for equal education in the Southern States." This was particularly in response to the Supreme Court's 1938 *Missouri ex rel. Gaines* decision mandating that states provide black educational opportunities equal to those for whites, through either integration or the creation of equivalent institutions.[31] McCray was hopeful, writing to the *Atlanta Daily World*'s C. A. Scott that he was convinced that the March meeting "was a turning point in our section and that a new trade and a new south are the inescapable results." At that meeting, the group had created the Southern Negro Conference for the Equalization of Educational Opportunities, with the *Houston Informer*'s Carter Wesley as president, Scott as vice president, and McCray as a member of the committee. It was, however, an all-male group and focused its attention on collegiate education and voting rights. The NNPA had been founded in 1940 to support black publishers throughout the country, working for the success of both the black press and the black race; it held annual meetings to coordinate its efforts. Still, the organization was dominated by men and represented a business dominated by men, and it kept its equalization efforts focused on male-dominated higher education, not out of malice but out of tunnel vision.[32]

Perhaps the epitome of the southern teacher salary equalization fight and its intersection with black male journalism was in Alabama. The shadow of Booker T. Washington loomed large over the state in the first half of the twentieth century. That shadow was evident in the presence of industrial education, to be sure. But it was also there in the "cast down your bucket" approach taken by many black journalists in the state, who walked the same fine line that Tuskegee's leader walked between race advocacy and currying favor with white elites.

The most important Alabama newspaper in the first three decades of the twentieth century was Oscar W. Adams's *Birmingham Reporter*. From

1906 to 1934, Adams hewed close to the thinking of Booker Washington while associate editors T. W. Coffee and William Pickens railed against segregation and disenfranchisement, particularly in light of honorable black service in World War I. But sticking with Washingtonian theory, the editors made the argument that the continued denial of black rights would push Negroes "toward radical parties in their search for a remedy against these awful conditions." The *Reporter* continued to speak out against injustices. The paper made the Ku Klux Klan a particular target and in the early 1930s covered Scottsboro extensively.[33] The *Birmingham Reporter*, however, did not survive past the first few years of the decade. There were more than two dozen black newspapers in 1920s Alabama, but there were only fifteen in the 1930s, owing largely to the Depression. The *Reporter* folded at that time, as did the *Birmingham Eagle*, *Birmingham Weekly Voice*, *Dothan Star*, and *Mobile Weekly Press*. Only a handful of new papers appeared in the 1930s, and most survived only briefly.[34]

In 1931, the Syndicate saw an opportunity in the state's capital and founded the *Montgomery World*, which was edited and published by the Reverend John D. Dowdell and his nephew James Bozeman and lasted until the end of 1935. To replace the *World* after it faltered, the SNS made another, more successful attempt in Montgomery, the *Alabama Tribune*, founded in 1936 and lasting until 1964.[35] This substantial relationship would bind Atlanta and Montgomery for decades.

In March 1941, a staff writer at the *Alabama Tribune* reported on the state's attempts to avoid paying equal salaries to black teachers. White leaders had suggested "lowering the pay of white teachers, cutting the school term," or attempting a version of equalization "by an additional outlay of $2,000,000 by the State Legislature," all plans designed to create resentment among the white population, to make them feel slighted in what they saw as a zero-sum game of rights. "All these 'tactics and schemes' have been detected by Negro educators," the paper reported. Teacher salaries were no longer just an issue for teachers. They were an issue for everyone. "Sentiment seems to be, to use the phrase of a Montgomery newspaper editorial, 'devoted to making the American schools absolutely free and equal.'" This was an important, racially divisive issue, but even in its clear stand on the side of pay equity, the article remained guarded, letting its reporting make its case and couching its complaints in quotation marks and attributions. Schemes by lawmakers to lower the pay of white teachers or cut the school term were not simply "appeals to resentment." They were "interpreted by Negro thinkers" as appeals to resentment.[36] The paper made its case carefully, explaining the issue to its readers and pointing them in the direction of advocacy without expressly engaging in that advocacy itself, for fear of courting retribution for the attempt at what some Alabama whites were sure to see as undermining their children's education.

One of the most significant southern interpreters of teacher salary equalization and other rights efforts was the *Birmingham World*, edited by Emory O. Jackson. The *Birmingham World* had been founded by W. A. Scott in March 1931 as one of the first links in the SNS chain. "The Scott family was a black family from Atlanta that owned the paper," explained Joe Dixon, editor of the *Birmingham World*, at the turn of the twenty-first century. "They subsidized the newspaper when they owned it. They all worked on the newspaper—they had someone in advertising, somebody was in editorials, somebody was in photography, and somebody was in management. It was a real family business." That it was, but the paper's first leader was not part of the family. He was a family friend. Under the initial editorship of Gaines T. Bradford, the *World*'s circulation grew to 7,500 by 1935. Bradford was an Atlanta native who went to Birmingham at the request of his friend W. A. In 1937, however, he and his family were off to Omaha, Nebraska, and H. D. Coke took over the operation, a position he held until 1941.[37]

Both editors allowed local events to dictate their coverage. On the editorial page of the October 4, 1932, edition, for example, the paper explained, "The *Birmingham World* does not make the news; it merely prints it. Whether that news is good or bad, it is the moral duty of any newspaper worthy of the name to publish it in its columns." The paper acknowledged criticism of its constant coverage of crime and murder, but pointed out that as of October, there were already sixty-five homicides in Birmingham in 1932. "What are you and others here who object to seeing this sort of thing in print doing to wipe out the evil?" the editorial asked in challenge. The *World*, it argued, mirrored the community. "If this community is sick of bloodshed and murder, then the various clubs, churches and civic organizations ought to back the *Birmingham World*'s campaign to eradicate the atrocity." Helping the situation meant an effort to "demand full punishment for the killers," not an attack on the newspaper that lifted the veil on the acts.[38]

It was a good argument, and one that kept the paper a staple of the community. Deborah McDowell in her memoir, *Leaving Pipe Shop*, talks about the importance of the newspaper in her home. "The *Birmingham World* was Alabama's oldest black newspaper. Blacks turned to it for reports, announcements of community happenings and for an angle on local and national events missing from the majority paper, the *Birmingham News.*"[39]

In 1941, just as the state's salary equalization fight began, Emory O. Jackson took over editorial duties for the *Birmingham World*, and he remained in that position until 1975, using the paper to fight for civil rights in one of the most notoriously racist cities in the South. "Emory Jackson was a man that really brought this paper to where it is," recalled Joe Dixon. "He did the voting rights, he challenged Bull Connor all the way to the segregated law. [Connor] dealt with no black officers, no black firemen. Emory Jackson and this newspaper led the fight. In addition to what he did in the city of Birmingham, Emory would leave at night and go into the black belt areas and other areas of this state. He would train other blacks in the methods of getting blacks registered to vote."[40]

Emory Overton Jackson was born in Buena Vista, Georgia, in 1908, but he grew up in Birmingham's Enon Ridge area, a black middle-class neighborhood on the city's west side. He then moved to Atlanta to attend Morehouse, where he edited the school's *Maroon Tiger* newspaper. He graduated in 1932 and briefly taught high school English before joining the staff of the *World* in 1934 as a sportswriter and book reviewer. He became the editor of the *World* in 1941, and he also led the Alabama conference of the NAACP. He was, unlike many other male editors who acted as mediators of the salary equalization fight, an activist away from the newspaper.[41]

Jackson's sister Ruby Jackson Gainer was a teacher in the city who helped lead the fight for pay equalization in Birmingham schools, a fight aided by Jackson, the *World*, and the Southern Negro Youth Congress, an organization labeled by the FBI as a "negro Communist front in Birmingham." It was Gainer, the bureau noted thankfully, who encouraged the Youth Congress committee working for equalization to remove two members because of their association with communism. Jackson was a member of the Southern Negro Conference for the Equalization of Educational Opportunities, along with C. A. Scott, Carter Wesley, and John McCray, and he and his sister worked diligently for equal education. Since his relationship to the cause was personal, the scope of his coverage and his activism appeared to be less paternalistic than the approach of many of his male colleagues, serving as an exception that proved the rule.[42]

Gainer had been teaching in the Jefferson County system for fourteen years. She was president of the Congress of Industrial Organizations (CIO)

Teachers Local, the Jefferson County Negro Teachers Association, and the Alabama State High School Teachers Association. And she was fired for fighting for equal pay. Jackson lobbied for NAACP intervention in the case. The firing was "purely intimidation designed to scare the teachers" from fighting for salary equalization. "What steps best to take at this point I am unable to say," he told teachers association leaders, but he did want the plan to be comprehensive. "I feel that we should mobilize public sentiment, organize coalition action, demand a public hearing, test the teachers tenure act, and fight the case clear up to the U.S. Supreme Court."[43]

On April 29, 1945, a federal judge enjoined and restrained the Jefferson County Board of Education from pay discrimination based on race. A report in the *Birmingham Post* in November 1946 revealed that 55.6 percent of black teachers in the county held degrees and that the number continued to improve. That month, Jackson wrote to the local school board asking if the *World* could have a reporter at their meetings to ensure that the equalization of teacher salaries was being complied with as ordered by the courts. The board agreed, "because we hold no secret sessions and we have nothing to conceal," although the reply did claim that the process might take up to three years and that "there is no binding agreement as to non-degree teachers." The board wanted "to be fair and equitable in all of our dealings with all of our teachers and we are trying to make adjustments as rapidly as possible."[44]

In January 1947, the white *Birmingham News* endorsed equal pay. That same month, a delegation from the CIO Teachers Union conferred with the school superintendent about salaries. In April, a contempt of court case charging that the school board was willfully violating the antidiscrimination law was referred to a special master for examination. On May 1, Ruby Jackson Gainer and other activist teachers received termination notices. After Gainer requested a reason for her dismissal, the board cited "insubordination, neglect of duty and other good and just causes." On May 21, she had a public hearing before the board, where local leaders spoke and national leaders sent telegrams in support of her. Jackson called a meeting of the local NAACP's Legal Redress Committee to develop a strategy to remedy both the firings and the unwillingness of Jefferson County to comply with a 1945 court decision mandating equal pay. "The crisis in the equal salary fight is upon us," he claimed. "We must prove equal to it."[45] In retaliation for these actions, eight days later, on May 29, Alex Crawford, the husband of the principal of Praco High School, where Gainer had taught for the previous two years, attacked Emory Jackson in his office, blaming him for the controversy surrounding the school. Despite all of the efforts on Gainer's behalf, however, on June 3, the board unanimously voted to terminate her contract, and two days later the Birmingham branch of the NAACP launched its Educational Defense Fund campaign. Jackson was the chair of the defense fund and was still working to raise money in September 1948 despite legal setbacks and physical attacks.[46]

The Jefferson County Teachers Union, Local 683 of the United Public Workers of America, CIO, sent information to its members explaining the Alabama tenure law of 1940 and encouraging teachers to "know your tenure rights!" The Committee for Alabama of the Southern Conference for Human Welfare issued its own denunciations. One of its circulars declared that the schoolchildren of Jefferson County "received a practical lesson about what democracy is *not* on May 1. On that date their County Board of Education answered contempt of court proceedings against itself by cancelling the contracts of several county teachers." It described the saga and urged readers to contact the school board and demand action. The union did much the same.[47]

Jackson's plan to fight the firing of Gainer and her colleagues in Jefferson County was multifaceted. He wanted "outstanding white and Negro citizens" to write members of the school board. He also hoped to convince organizations to pass resolutions, and he encouraged people to sign petitions against the actions. He wanted the Alabama State Teachers Association (ASTA) and its corresponding principals group to "make a favorable statement on behalf of Mrs. Gainer." He was doubtful it would happen, however, as "several ASTA higher-ups in Birmingham appear to be parties to the frame-up firing of tenure and non-[tenure] teachers."[48]

Jackson's worries about the ASTA seemed justified. A year later, in August 1948, he noted that the group had not produced the money to fight the salary equalization case. "It appears that we are going to have [to] blast those in the ASTA who defeat the will of the teachers. I am about fed up on it and am now ready to carry the case to the jury of public opinion." Again, however, that case was made at a meeting of the NAACP rather than in a scathing editorial in the *World*, but Jackson convinced the group to launch a Teachers Defense Fund drive to raise $1,000 for the equalization suit. His newspaper covered the drive but without editorial comment. Such was the nature of the mediation of the black press. Jackson could be far more radical on behalf of his sister and her colleagues as a leader of the local NAACP than he could ever be in his newspaper, the result of a different kind of coding, which made southern black newspapers responsive both to social mores in the black community and to fear of white reprisal when it came to journalistic activism against local white resistance to equality.[49]

In June, Jackson was involved in "the Gainer Dismissal Case or the Contempt Suit against Dr. J. E. Bryan and the Jefferson County Board of Education." Ruby Jackson Gainer wrote to the local NAACP, asking for a "liberal contribution" to help the Jefferson County Teachers Defense Fund continue the case. "This decision was won in the Supreme Court of Alabama," Gainer's letter explained. "The attorneys are confident of ultimate victory in both cases if we have the courage and the finance[s] to fight to the end." Jackson responded to the request by sending a circular to NAACP members in Birmingham explaining the case. Black teachers wanted $300,000 "in unpaid differential salaries, growing out of an alleged violation of a non-discrimination . . . decree of the Federal Court." Gainer had led the fight and was fired in retribution and to frighten others away from action, he wrote. Jackson also solicited the aid of the Jefferson County Progressive Democratic Council to raise money for the Teachers Defense Fund campaign. He then became chair of the fund, successfully accomplishing the group's goal of raising $1,000.[50]

Letters from around the country flooded the Jefferson County Board of Education urging the restoration of Gainer's job and equalization of pay. The teacher had moved to Pensacola but returned in late August 1948 to explain the case and "to tell the story of how for the lack of funds the case is slowed up in the courts." Meanwhile, Sara Walsh, director of the National Teachers Division of the CIO, wrote to the *Pittsburgh Courier* asking for coverage of the Birmingham fight and to the National Women's Trade Union League of America, the United Council of Church Women, and the Congress of American Women asking for support. There was also a letter-writing campaign to Governor James E. Folsom urging action in the case. The *World* reported on such news when it happened, but Jackson saved his most ardent activism for when he was away from his typewriter. Again, social mores and southern journalistic precedent offered him little choice.[51]

A successful resolution for black teachers was slow in coming, and the salary equalization problem in Birmingham stretched into the next decade. In October 1950, Talladega College's B. A. Jones sent a letter (using a pseudonym) to the editor of the *Birmingham News* explaining the inequities of the Talladega school system in detail and urging compliance with the pay equalization order. It was a controversy remarkably similar to Birmingham's. Talladega's school board members had argued that the black principal of the black school there was behind them, which abrogated their responsibility in acting. Jones argued, however, that "concurrence may be a condition of [the principal's] continued employment." He wrote that "the most effective defense against legal action by Negroes is not the employment of a subservient Negro as principal." It was, instead, compliance with equality mandates. Assuming that the *News* wouldn't publish the letter, he also wrote directly to Jackson, explaining that the problem in Talladega was not a militant school board but "an unreformed 'cracker'" serving as superintendent. He urged the *World* to cover the problem in Talladega and welcomed its publication of his letter. Jackson declined to publish the letter, and he did not cover Talladega either. But he was still working diligently on behalf of teacher and school equality, and he provided a detailed report late that month on the front page of the paper, citing the funding differences for every school in Birmingham. "It is estimated," wrote Jackson, "that $116 more is spent on a white high school student than on a Negro," a figure that "by no means narrow[s] materially the differential gap in education under the 'Separate but Equal doctrine.'" The report, based on numbers released by the city's board of education, focused on building funds at white and black Birmingham schools, but such discrepancies only served to reemphasize the similar funding differentials in teacher pay. This was the kind of nongendered coverage that was not available in other southern newspapers with modest circulations and male editors.[52]

In June 1951, the *World* responded to the federal court decision that black public school facilities in Clarendon County, South Carolina, were unequal to those for white students; the court had ordered officials to move immediately toward equalization and to report their progress. It was "the first such verdict that has been rendered regarding public school facilities in a deep-south state," and the *World* classed it as a "significant victory." The plaintiffs had asked for an end to segregation. That didn't happen, and the paper acknowledged the disappointment, but it chose to emphasize the victory of equalization over and against the defeat of desegregation.[53]

In June 1953, Bill Nunn, the *World*'s managing editor, urged Jackson to take over a project documenting educational inequality in the South. He wanted numbers on spending and school enrollment. There had to be an economic corollary to the moral case. "In trying to prove to our reading public that the south's theory of 'separate but equal' will never work educationally," he argued, "we must get the facts and figures." Jackson responded by writing to C. G. Gomillion at Tuskegee, who sent him data from 1936 to 1951. The numbers were stark, demonstrating massive disparities in enrollment, building values, and capital outlay per student. Spending for black pupils was only 30 percent of spending for white pupils in the 1936–1937 school year. That disparity had shrunk through the remainder of the 1930s and 1940s, reaching just below 72 percent by the 1950–1951 school year, but even that progress left a vast spending gap that disadvantaged Alabama's black students in immeasurable ways, particularly when broader capital outlays, building values, and other figures became part of the calculations.[54]

The lack of paternalism in the *World*'s coverage of teacher pay was most likely due to Jackson's relationship with his sister, the plaintiff in the equalization case. In other gendered controversies during World War II, such as the rape of Recy Taylor, the problematic mediation was evident. On September 3, 1944, Taylor was kidnapped while leaving church and was then raped by six white men, who admitted the crime to police. Still, they were never indicted, igniting protests from the black community in Alabama and across the country. Among those outraged was E. G. Jackson, editor of the *Alabama Tribune* and Emory Jackson's brother, who teamed with Eugene Gordon from the communist *Daily Worker* to confront Alabama governor Chauncey Sparks and demand an investigation into the case. He helped organize meetings and generated petitions, along with allies such as E. D. Nixon, Rosa and Raymond Parks, Rufus Lewis, and Johnnie Carr. This was the leadership group that would, argues Danielle McGuire, "lift Martin Luther King, Jr., to international prominence a decade later, after their leading organizer was arrested on a Montgomery bus."[55]

Taylor's case was a symbol of the age. An all-white, all-male jury dismissed the case in October 1944. After months and months of activism led by the black press and, in particular, by Rosa Parks, the attorney general finally sought a grand jury indictment. But that jury too was all-white and all-male, and in February 1945 it failed to indict any of the men who had confessed. The verdict stunned and frustrated black Montgomery, but McGuire has described the case as bringing "the building blocks of the Montgomery bus boycott together a decade earlier." Those building blocks, however, could only be gathered by the coverage of the black press. "Decency calls for the protection of womanhood," wrote Emory Jackson in the *World*. "Permit womanhood anywhere to be abused, you leave it without sufficient protection everywhere. Erring men who escape punishment in one instance will feel no restraint against any woman anywhere, if in the interest of selfish idealism, the Grand Jury should feel impelled to indict the guilty." The *World* made the case that allowing crimes against black women was a gateway to crimes against white women, about whom the grand jury might be more concerned.[56]

This was a calculated paternalism, to be sure, as Jackson used familiar tropes in an effort to urge prosecutions for Taylor's attackers. Those tropes, so familiar to the white men who might be convinced to indict, were the same tropes that black male journalists were using in aid of promoting teacher salary equalization. Through Taylor's recovery and the teachers' wage fight, the tropes themselves remained constant. They arose, for example, in the *Arkansas World*'s coverage of salary equalization events centering around Little Rock's Dunbar High School. Called by Mark Tushnet the "most important salary suit of the 1940s" and described in detail by historian John Kirk, the Little Rock case sought to remedy vast racial disparities in public school teachers' pay. For the 1941–1942 school term, black primary school teachers made an average of $331, while their white counterparts made an average of $526. The secondary school rate was $567 and $856. The local Classroom Teachers Association created a Salary Adjustment Committee, both dominated by African American women, to plan a case with the aid of the NAACP. Ultimately, Dunbar's English Department chair, Susie Morris, headed the lawsuit.[57]

Thurgood Marshall, who handled the Little Rock case, wrote to Roy Wilkins impressed with the women leading the charge. "These Southern Teachers have acquired new backbones," he wrote. The black press coverage, however, was less enthusiastic about the female leaders. Both the *World* and the *Arkansas State Press*, the city's two leading black papers, covered the equalization fight. The *State Press*, led by L. C. Bates, praised the NAACP and the steps the case was taking "in the direction of liberalism and Americanism." It was wholly supportive, but what coverage remains stripped the effort of its gendered relevance. The *World*, too, supported the effort, but focused its sympathy not on Susie Morris but on Dunbar's principal, John H. Lewis. In May 1943, after fourteen years at the school, Lewis submitted his resignation under pressure from the school board, largely because of his participation in the equalization suit, which had finally been tried in October 1942. The principal expressed no regret, arguing that to cooperate with the board against his black faculty would have been "contrary to his principles of justice and right." The

World covered the resignation with undisguised gratitude. "World history records that every great movement of any worth required the martyrdom of a strong and courageous character of the times before success was accomplished," the paper wrote. "The Negro teachers and citizens of Little Rock and Arkansas possess such a martyr to the cause of equal citizenship and rights." By all reasonable standards, the paper's martyr should have been Morris, but instead it was the man who resigned in sympathy with her cause.[58]

In Grambling, Louisiana, a Lincoln Parish town just south of the Arkansas border, the Syndicate's *Bayou State Register* was published by Collie J. Nicholson, sports information director for Grambling College. In 1951, a *Register* editorial castigated S. L. Jones, editor of the *Southern Advocate*, another northern Louisiana black weekly, and an appointee to Governor Earl Long's Civil Defense Advisory Board. Jones, who had earlier been part of the SNS with a different Depression-era newspaper, claimed, "Our teachers are being paid better salaries than any other state in the Union," which was decidedly wrong and which the *Register* saw as a way to excuse the administration. Louisiana's black teacher pay still had not arrived at equalization more than a decade after that particular movement had materialized. Jones's position was "a typical example of the type of stuff some Negroes spout out in an attempt to keep white people thinking they are 'all right.'" Jones was standing "on very thin ice, trying to represent all Negroes when in fact he represents very few." He and those of his ilk stood "in a despicable and unsavory light" and did far more harm than good. This was a direct shot at another black editor in a state without very many black editors. At the same time, the attack was not about the sustained fight for teacher pay; it aimed not at advocating for a predominantly female teaching corps but instead at disparaging a male rival.[59]

In Kentucky, the *Louisville Independent News,* another male-owned paper associated with the Scott Syndicate, had covered the December 1939 report of a special committee appointed by Kentucky governor Happy Chandler to study equal education in the state. That committee recognized the legal right of black students to attend the University of Kentucky and other institutions of higher learning, including the University of Louisville, "harmonizing our state laws with the United States Constitution." Plans for the transition, however, remained in process. In October 1941, almost two years after Chandler's committee report, student Charles Eubanks filed his second complaint against the University of Kentucky, suing for undergraduate admission to the school. To stop him from attending and to conform to the Supreme Court's opinion in *Missouri ex rel. Gaines*, the Kentucky legislature established Kentucky State College as his case was pending, hoping to provide a black alternative to his admission to the all-white institution. Though Charles Hamilton Houston and Thurgood Marshall worked diligently on his behalf, the case dragged on for years, and Eubanks eventually dropped it in 1945. The *News* covered it until the end, rightly interpreting Eubanks as a symbol of the racial divisions in Kentucky higher education and the failure of the government to live up to its promises.[60]

Covering the men involved in higher education equalization fights was a fundamentally different endeavor than covering the women's effort to equalize teacher salaries in public schools, but the *Independent News* was diligent about responding to both. In November 1940, a Louisville teacher, with the aid of the NAACP, joined the chorus of her southern counterparts and petitioned the board of education to make her salary equal to those of white teachers, beginning the process of equalizing all black teachers' salaries. The *Independent News* covered the effort in depth, prompting the school board to act quickly and agree in January 1941 to equalize salaries beginning with the new school year in September. Thurgood Marshall, representing the NAACP, refused to drop the lawsuit, however, arguing that "it is desirable to have some sort of decree in this matter so that the question will not come up again." It was a good strategy. White school boards had not proven particularly trustworthy. The trial was set for October, but again he was disappointed by Kentucky, as the teachers agreed with the court's dismissal that month after signing new contracts that gave them equal pay. The black female teachers were uninterested in being dictated to by men who assumed they knew best, whether they were white politicians or NAACP lawyers. The women just wanted equal pay.[61]

The gendered divisions in education went even further. The month prior to Chandler's equal education report, the *Independent News* asked an incumbent state legislator running for reelection about the status of the "Married Teachers' Law," a statute that prevented schoolteachers from marrying until they had accrued five years of teaching experience.[62] It was a bizarre sexist holdover that only three states still maintained, but the most telling part of the *News*'s story was the interview itself (a black newspaper interviewing a white politician), which was treated as an afterthought by the paper. Most black papers south of Louisville didn't have that kind of access, and those that did usually were not interviewing legislators about race-neutral issues. This article was something of a watershed precisely because it was not a watershed.

Glenna Matthews argues that the historical gender gap in the United States developed through a constant battle over access to the public sphere. Certainly this battle was more than territorial, and for the bulk of U.S. history it was relatively one-sided. But through the conscious, often incremental ventures of women, public space in all its forms—cultural, political, legal, semantic—began opening to include both genders. This was how women were able to enter the education profession to begin with.[63] The pushback against such gains was multifaceted. Sara Evans emphasizes the cycle of contradictory presentations of women's roles and the psychological frustration it engendered in the decades after World War II. When women criticized those roles, they experienced backlash from both men and a significant number of women. Following the war's end, for example, the Equal Rights Amendment went down to defeat in the Senate in July 1946.[64]

Black women, and black teachers in particular, were especially at risk, gripped by the dual oppressions of race and gender and fighting the tropes of both in activist struggles like salary equalization. Unlike the general trend of civil rights, black and white women moved steadily from unified advocacy to separate striving, seeing less and less in common with each other as years and issues passed.[65] In instances like teacher salary equalization and increased higher-echelon job opportunities, however, black teachers were already striving separately. While the salary equalization movement did not achieve a seminal legal victory that provided blanket equalization for black teachers, it did, in most instances, improve their salaries. It also convinced the NAACP that creating equality within "separate but equal" schools was a nonstarter and that attacking segregation itself would be the most effective strategy, and it grew the NAACP in the South and put black women at the forefront of the civil rights fight.[66]

But when those women's efforts were mediated through the black southern press, and SNS papers in particular, their role was minimized through paternalistic assumptions and reporting that played to the mores of the day even as, for the first time, a substantial southern black press corps covered a race rights fight led by women in a vocation dominated by women. The gendered mediation not only diminished the roles of the women, but ultimately diminished the significance of the teachers' salary equalization fights in the well-worn narrative of twentieth-century equal education fights. The equal education struggles became the core of the pre- and post–World War II civil rights movement as—surely to the relief of the *Jacksonville Progressive News*—men began to follow in the women's footsteps.

Chapter 5

Expansion beyond the South in the Wake of World War II

Phoenix was a destination, not a starting point. That was particularly true at the onset of the last major wave of the Great Migration. Alberta Gibson moved in 1912 to Phoenix from Texas by way of California, and there she became a laundress, working to support her mother and young son. By 1937, she had taken over the local newspaper, the *Phoenix Index*, founded in 1936 by the Reverend W. Gray. There was no long history of black newspapers in Arizona because the black population there was small. The state's first African American paper, the *Phoenix Tribune*, began in 1918, a child of the first wartime wave of the Great Migration. It was followed by the short-lived *Western Dispatch* and then the *Index*.[1] Gibson wasn't a native Arizonan, and she knew that most of her readers weren't either. So after taking over the paper from Gray, Gibson took a measured but unusual step for a western newspaper and aligned the *Index* with the Scott Newspaper Syndicate. In a town where most of the black people were migrants, she assumed, the news of Phoenix needed to be leavened with news of the South. The Arizona capital would be the westernmost point in the SNS orbit.

Gibson's *Index* was called "A Paper with a Purpose" and urged its readers with another slogan, "Don't Spend Your Money Where Your People Are Not Welcome."[2] The paper claimed to be politically independent and vowed that it "shall at all times, regardless of any set rulings or regulations, present the news completely, impartially and free from hatred." Columns encouraged readers to boycott companies that used racist depictions of black characters in their advertisements. They railed against law enforcement officers who "allow mobs to take their prisoners and proceed to do with them as they wish." These were problems that would seem all too familiar to southern readers, who found *Index* columns reprinted in the *World* or one of its regional counterparts.[3]

After the onset of World War II, however, there was obviously a shift in coverage toward the war effort. Full-page ads from the U.S. Office of Civilian Defense described the steps readers should take in the event of an air raid. Stories throughout the paper described and lauded black people's participation in the war effort and evinced a marked frustration that the massive increase in the number of black soldiers had not come with a commensurate expansion of the number of black officers. After all, the *Index* argued in a 1942 editorial, "The Negro mess boy who set a standard of bravery at Pearl Harbor was but carrying on a tradition that started with Crispus Attucks, the first to fall in the Revolution." Not only was black bravery in World War II vital to the effort, it was also part of a historical investment in the cause that dated to the birth of the nation.[4]

This was the kind of dualism that defined the national black press during the war. Black newspapers had been accused of sedition during World War I and were accused of not aiding the war effort in the lead-up to and during World War II. In both instances, the editorial positions of the black press, which argued for the fair treatment of black Americans, was the cause. "The press was admittedly biased and made no pretensions of objectivity when it came to the need for equitable treatment of blacks," argues historian Roland Wolseley. This is an important observation. Black press advocacy was happening on the front pages. It was inherent in the news itself, making black newspapers something fundamentally different from other papers in the United States. White journalist Westbrook Pegler argued that black weeklies, "in their obvious, inflammatory bias in the treatment of news resemble such one-sided publications as the Communist *Daily Worker* and [Charles] Coughlin's *Social Justice*." *Ebony* later did a study of this supposed disloyalty. "Far from being parlor pinks, most Negro publishers are arch-conservatives in their thinking on every public issue with one exception—the race problem. The owners of the biggest newspapers have but two main missions—to promote racial unity and to make money." The SNS seemed to bear out *Ebony*'s conclusion, but whatever the mission of any black paper, it was undoubtedly true that none was engaged solely in a project of strictly objective journalism.[5]

The era surrounding World War II was a period of transition for the Syndicate, as the company followed black southerners who were spreading west as far as Phoenix and north into Michigan, where the SNS found a stable, profitable home, as did so many other southern migrants. At the same time, labor disputes, traditionally associated with northern industrial centers, made their way south, calling attention to wage disparities in the Scotts' business. Expansion outside the South and labor problems at home mirrored national issues during the war era, but the papers of the Syndicate also grappled with the war itself, attempting when possible to point out the similarities in the racial exclusion policies of Nazi Germany and the American South. It was a time of transition for the SNS in expansion, in labor relations, and in the way Syndicate papers discussed race and foreign policy.

Black coverage of World War II was an advance on the press's previous take on World War I, when editors had taken phrases like "patriotism" and "Americanism" and adapted them to arguments for equal rights. A "war to make the world safe for Democracy," as Woodrow Wilson had the country believe, should have augured nothing less. That being the case, as William G. Jordan has explained, the black press during World War I became "a frontier between black and white in which the terms of racial coexistence were negotiated and renegotiated through written and verbal exchanges that were conditioned by the ever-present threat of force." That force was even more menacing during World War II, and so that pattern of negotiation and renegotiation remained.[6]

Doubts were rampant among black communities about the onset of World War II, with black workers barred from defense jobs, a segregated military, and all of the other racial problems throughout the country. "The claims of the Negro minority to democratic recognition were vastly heightened by the war. Resentment against exclusion from many branches of the armed forces and from defense industries, coupled with segregation, flared in the Negro press and was vigorously voiced by Negro agencies," explained a 1942 report from the American Civil Liberties Union. "Cast upon the larger world stage of exploitation of the darker races in the colonies of the democracies, their cause in the United States is taking on a new significance in the conduct and aims of the war." Shortly after the bombing of Pearl Harbor, a *Pittsburgh Courier* reader named James Thompson wrote a letter to the editor reminding the paper of such problems, and he emphasized that while victory abroad was important, the pursuit of equality and democracy on the home front was the only thing that would make such a foreign conquest worthwhile. The *Courier* developed the Double V campaign in 1942 in response to that letter: "Democracy: Victory at Home, Victory Abroad." The paper sent posters to its distributors throughout the country and published endorsements of the idea on its front page. It never criticized the war effort, but it did tie the fight for racial justice in the United States to the fight overseas against an opponent who was segregating certain groups deemed inferior, denying rights to those groups, and ultimately murdering many of them. It wasn't a difficult case to make.[7]

And it was a case that bore fruit, at least to a limited degree, for the journalists who made it. In 1944 alone, the first black correspondent, an *Atlanta Daily World* reporter, was admitted to the White House press corps; Franklin Roosevelt met with a group of National Negro Publishers Association members who discussed the concerns of black Americans and the black press in relation to the war and eventual peace; and reports of black combat troops appeared in U.S. newspapers, sent from black correspondents embedded with the soldiers. "The Negro is not taking advantage of the present global conflict to further his own advance, for his militancy was evident long before the outbreak of World War II," explained commentator Samuel Perry in 1942, adding that "criticism is not by any means sedition." He assured his readers that "the American Negro has been, and always will be, loyal, but . . . he seeks a larger share in the democratic way of life. In brief, the Negro press is fully behind our national effort to win this war."[8]

Syndicate papers did not participate in Double V, because it was a competitor's promotion, but many validated its spirit, particularly when it came to racial justice claims back home and even more when those claims arose along the more common routes of the Great Migration. "One newspaper chain, the Scott Newspaper Syndicate, has invaded the Negro press field," reported a study of the black press in 1938. Its papers had spread throughout the country following that migration trajectory. "All of these papers are printed in whole or in part in the offices of the *Atlanta World*, thus effecting an economy in production costs and permitting the use of up-to-date shop equipment, but at the same time compelling excessive uniformity and the minimization of local news in the various papers of the syndicate." That was certainly true, but what the study omitted was that it was uniformity that had created campaigns like Double V, and local news content varied with the amount of such material submitted by the local publisher.[9]

When W. A. Scott died in February 1934, accolades arrived from all over the country from civic leaders, ministers, rival presses, and the newspapers of the Syndicate, which he had spent so much time building. As Scott made clear early in the process, he wanted his business to be national, and so when a tribute arrived from the Syndicate's most far-flung representative in 1934, the *Detroit World*, the statement stood as both a note of appreciation and a symbol of what Scott had accomplished. "We, the members of the Staff of *Detroit World*, hereby honor and pay our respect to the most outstanding Negro publisher, the late W. A. Scott," it said. "His monument is one which stands as an inspiration to Negro youth throughout the world, as proof that even those things which seem impossible, can be done. We, therefore, pledge ourselves united to support the principles for which he fought in journalism, and express our confidence in his successor, C. A. Scott." The tribute was signed by the paper's staff, including the Hamtramck editor, Leroy G. White.[10]

This act of kindness was repeated by scores of similar outlets, but it was significant because it served as a public statement of the budding relationship between Atlanta and Detroit, which would remain through the era of the Great Depression and the war years. The Syndicate supported newspapers in Arizona, Connecticut, Illinois, Indiana, Iowa, Kansas, Michigan, Minnesota, Nebraska, New Jersey, New York, Pennsylvania, and Wisconsin, in addition to all of the southern states. This was a significant nonsouthern presence, fostered particularly during the war years, for a newspaper group that began by reminding its readers that "Negroes are different in Dixie." Leroy White would become a more and more important connection between Georgia and Michigan as the years progressed, but in the early 1930s, in the wake of Scott's sensational death, White was still an employee, answering to the *Detroit World*'s managing editor, Golee B. Bryant.

Bryant was a crusader and a founder, along with Morris Lewis, secretary to Congressman Oscar DePriest, of the Congress of Youth, which served as an organizational body for a "national Negro youth movement" in Detroit and the region, an effort to mentor kids and make them more successful. His paper reflected his activist bent. When, for example, the white students of Hamtramck High School and St. Florian Roman Catholic Church combined to plan a moonlight dance and decided to bar the black students from attending, White (the *World*'s Hamtramck editor) and Leonard Troutman (president of the *World*'s Jovial Juniors Club of Hamtramck) immediately protested to the principal, who responded by announcing that "every student in the High School should be welcome to attend any affair bearing the school's name."[11] It was a victory against the creeping incursion of Jim Crow and a demonstration of the kind of activism black reporters undertook. Instead of keeping a measured, objective distance and reporting on the crisis, White and Troutman acted to stop the discriminatory practice, then reported on what they did.

White had a vision of a journalistic empire much like his southern counterpart W. A. Scott—the creation of a newspaper chain across his home state of Michigan. He began in March 1938 with his first publication, the

Michigan State Echo, headquartered in Lansing, and then expanded with more papers in cities around the state; SNS material provided non-Michigan content. White's principal battle had always been housing. In February 1942, Detroit's defense housing coordinator publicly decided to "uphold Negro occupancy" of defense housing but continued to delay the action in response to pressure from angry local whites.[12] The controversy led to rioting later that month, leaving fourteen people injured and twenty in jail. In April 1942, the *Detroit World Echo* reported the federal government's plan to "place Negroes in the Sojourner Truth Defense Housing Project." Leroy White was on the interracial Sojourner Truth Citizens Committee, which called on the mayor to put those plans in place. Upon the announcement of the federal order, Detroit police commissioner Frank Eamans resigned. "It was under Eamans['s] direction that police prevented Negroes from occupying the project on February 28th which precipitated the resulting riot." The government order followed a mass demonstration of roughly ten thousand people at the statue of Sojourner Truth in Detroit's Cadillac Square. In addition, a federal grand jury indicted three of the white leaders who had incited the earlier riot in an attempt to block black entry into the project. Meanwhile, black people in Detroit waited for the project to open to them. Protesters marched in front of city hall with signs reading "Negroes have landed in Australia, when do we land in Sojourner Truth?" Finally, they landed at the end of April: new black tenants entered under armed guard amid the taunts and protests of angry whites.[13]

In March 1943, a new controversy developed when the federal Public Housing Authority refused to "rescind the ban against Negroes at Willow Lodge Housing project," which led to a protest letter "from 20 leading citizens" directly to Roosevelt, asking him to correct the decision. While he was in Detroit for the June NAACP conference, Emory O. Jackson "had a highway view" of the battle over the Willow Lodge housing project. "Housing is a fighting word here," he wrote. "People are living as thick as the sands of Florida."[14]

Tensions over housing boiled over in June, and the *World Echo* was perfectly placed to cover the violence (and the Syndicate was perfectly placed to spread the coverage through its member papers). The setting was Belle Isle, home to segregated city beaches on the Detroit River. When black swimmers moved into the "white" part of the area, the whites attacked. Soon more than 200 sailors from a nearby naval base joined them. Word of the battle spread through the city, particularly the fact that whites were attacking individual black swimmers. (One account had a baby being thrown from a bridge.) That, of course, spread the riot all over town, with black neighborhoods fuming and white mobs roaming the business districts looking for new victims. Ultimately more than 6,000 federal troops calmed the violence, and at its end there were 34 dead and more than 700 injured. Property damage ran into the millions. Twenty-five of the dead were black, and 17 of those were killed by white policemen tasked with stopping the violence. Along with the dead and wounded, the property destroyed, and the federal troops in the city, 1,300 people sat in jail, arrested for their role in the protests.[15]

The *World Echo* was positioned to both cover the tragedy and call for calm. It described the more immediate cause—"a widespread rumor that a colored woman and a child had been killed by whites at a beach"—and the broader stated cause by civic leaders: "an organized national fifth-column conspiracy to break our national unity and disrupt the home production front." The paper's coverage was comprehensive, from the incident at Belle Isle to eulogies for the dead to a statement on the rioting from President Roosevelt. White men had beaten black men near city hall. Tear gas canisters flew all over the city. The police killed two people "at an apartment hotel where, police said, Negro snipers were firing from upper windows. Gunfire and gas grenades from the police drove out all occupants." The paper was also sure to mention that editor White was among the leaders who "issued appeals calling upon the rioters to stop fighting." Days after the riot, the city named a committee of twenty-five people tasked with bettering racial issues and working to "prevent a recurrence of riots."[16]

A large portion of the black press focused on the issues of hiring discrimination, segregation, and the rampant racial violence in the country at the onset of World War II, rather than emphasizing the national unity that Franklin Roosevelt was urging. The strategy became a controversy on April 28, 1942, when a series of articles by Westbrook Pegler criticized the black press, and the northern black press in particular, for putting their own interests above those of the nation. Papers like White's engaged in what Pegler termed "'gent's room' journalism" and created a massively unhelpful paradox by placing advertisements for specious products in the same editions as lofty, high-minded editorials. Black editors responded in kind, which led more white journalists to make similar criticisms to those of Pegler. And those criticisms were usually condescending. "The smoke from big black cigars supercharged the sticky heat of the basement cafeteria in Chicago's Wabash Avenue YMCA," described *Time* magazine. "A well-dressed, pipe-smoking Negro rose to address the third annual conference of the National Negro Publishers Association. His 75 listeners, full of fried chicken and Pepsi-Cola, were still wrought up about the issue of their press and their race." *Time*'s racist account was reason enough for the meeting, but the principal topic of conversation was Pegler's criticism of the black press's sensationalism and use of World War II as a cudgel in the fight for race rights. The black publishers railed against Pegler as a "traitor" but did not denounce him with a formal resolution.[17]

In the fifth of Pegler's articles in mid-July, he made attempts at amends, but the damage had already been done. The publicity prompted the Roosevelt government to call many black editors to Washington, D.C., in 1942 to encourage them to deemphasize race agitation for the duration of the war. There was, however, no formal agreement that promised them any race progress in return, as Roosevelt had tried with A. Philip Randolph in January 1941, so the government's effort failed. The papers of Michigan and throughout the North maintained an unapologetically activist stance that looked decidedly different from that of their counterparts in the South. When the editors continued their inflammatory attacks, the government responded by launching an FBI investigation into both the *Pittsburgh Courier* and the *California Eagle*. The *Courier*, unsurprisingly, fired back. "This sort of thing is an obvious effort to . . . frighten Negro editors into silence. . . . We suggest the FBI investigate those forces . . . within America that are fostering and spreading Fascism and disunity by treating Negroes as second-class citizens."[18]

The reactions of white southern newspapers were mixed. Many presses in the region supported white supremacy without question, but others were more liberal. The *Louisville Courier-Journal*, for example, reported favorably about black leaders and civil rights efforts and "sometimes launch[ed] campaigns against some evil in the system of racial segregation as it exists in the South." Or, closer to Syndicate headquarters, "We can't do much pointing of the accusing finger at Adolph [*sic*] Hitler or ell Doochey for trying to give their people an exaggerated idea of the supremacy of their blood," admitted Ralph McGill, the moderate editor of the mainstream *Atlanta Constitution*. "We have the Klan."[19]

The expansion of the Scott Newspaper Syndicate outside the South to places like Phoenix, Detroit, and Minneapolis during the war years belied the reality that during World War II, there was a reduction in the number of newspapers, although there was an increase in the circulation of

Table 1. Legal Form of Ownership for Black Newspapers, 1945

Ownership Form	Number of Papers	Combined Average Circulation
Individual proprietorship	59	431,675
Partnership	21	237,611
Corporation	40	1,037,274
Other	16	102,500

Source: Blackwell, "Black-Controlled Media," 21.

those surviving. Control of black information and the wealth that resulted from it was moving into fewer and fewer hands. Individual proprietorship, for example, remained the most common form of newspaper company in 1945, but more than 57 percent of the total circulation of black papers came from papers owned by corporations (see table 1). The rise in circulation during World War II led black newspapers to woo advertisers selling national products. As dependence on advertising increased, papers were more vulnerable to forces beyond the walls of their offices.[20]

In the late 1930s and 1940s, the FBI devoted significant attention to the black press, whose reporting on race and discrimination was seen as detrimental to national unity. Along with visiting the *Afro-American* and *Pittsburgh Courier*, the FBI visited the *Norfolk Journal and Guide*, ostensibly because of antidiscrimination editorials being printed by publisher P. B. Young. Soon the FBI made its way to the *Atlanta Daily World*, interviewing columnist Cliff MacKay about external influences on editorial policy. Both the *Courier* and the *World* published editorials decrying the practice of pressuring the black press. The *Courier*, with a circulation of approximately two hundred thousand, came under the government's watchful eye but did not experience the same level of scrutiny as some of its counterparts. "The investigation was a farce. They never harassed anybody or threatened anybody. They just expressed their dissatisfaction at what we were doing," said *Courier* columnist Frank Bolden. "They suggested that we protest in another way or wait until after the war. But to my knowledge, they never threatened to arrest anyone or told anyone they had to do something." The FBI also sent letters of complaint to Syndicate paper the *Birmingham World*, which had criticized J. Edgar Hoover for not hiring black agents.[21]

This was not an isolated incident. Patrick Washburn has argued that "the investigation of the black press during World War II was far more massive than previously indicated by historians" since all critics of the government were interpreted as legitimate threats. Harry McAlpin, the

World's White House correspondent, reported in 1945 that government officials had planned "to completely demoralize the press by accusing it of sedition," but the program collapsed when the Justice Department "refused to cooperate with the interested military authorities and the 'keep-the-Negro-in-his-place' planners."[22] It was that kind of intimidation that helped convince the *Courier* to launch its Double V campaign and to make the case that race loyalty did not mean disloyalty to the country and the war effort.

There were several black journalism syndicates in this era: Carl Murphy's *Afro-American* papers, headquartered in Baltimore; a series of newspapers associated with the *Pittsburgh Courier*; the SNS; and Sengstacke Newspapers, with the *Chicago Defender* at the company's head. John H. Sengstacke, who took over from his uncle Robert Sengstacke Abbott, was born in Savannah and grew up in Woodville, Georgia. Still, after attending the Hampton Institute and Ohio State, then moving on to various journalism posts before joining the *Defender* in 1934, he crafted a journalistic ideal far from that emanating from his home state.[23]

Despite the differences in the various black press syndicates, there were commonalities in the production of World War II–era black news. In a contemporary analysis of the press in the 1940s, sociologist John Burma argued that though black newspapers continually moved to defend a middle- and upper-class economic position, their emphasis on race rights for all classes was strong. The black press both shaped public opinion and united African Americans under the banner of the information it generated. In 1945, *Fortune* magazine analyzed the front pages of black newspapers, coming to the unsurprising conclusion that "the Negro press is an interest-group press; its chief concern: Negro progress."[24] Rightly so. But the level of that interest, or at least the level of a newspaper's willingness to demonstrate that interest in the face of white resistance, differed based on both region and syndicate.

All of the black press used the war to expand their international scope, using the wartime treatment of black soldiers and comparisons to Hitler's Germany to press for further rights. In the *Pittsburgh Courier*, that expansion led famously to the Double V campaign. In SNS papers beyond the bounds of the South, the same message was clear without the syndicate-specific branding. At the same time, the press was careful in its treatment of discrimination in the military. As historian Lee Finkle has explained, black newspapers argued against the poor treatment of black servicemen, "but the press at the same time took a strong stand against any disobedience on the part of black troops," believing that "the postwar status of blacks would largely depend upon an unblemished military record." Balancing both immediate and long-term goals, then, was the priority. The newspapers did that by giving "total support to any action that did not result in a violation of military orders."[25]

The most important black southern newspaper outside the Scott Syndicate was P. B. Young's *Norfolk Journal and Guide*. The *Guide* early opposed migration. It opposed Garvey and the Universal Negro Improvement Association. It supported the New Deal relief programs and wanted rights for black citizens but remained moderate and gradualist, frustrating many in Virginia and the Chesapeake upper South by not engaging in more radical behavior. Young helped found Virginia's first NAACP chapter and served as an early president, but he did not aid its growth after World War II. As Henry Lewis Suggs has explained, Young and his paper "did not spearhead the drive to desegregate schools, interstate transportation, and housing." Many in "the New South's emerging black middle class" saw him as "a conciliator, a race man, a person the mayor called upon if a black presence was needed."[26] That mattered. Young's was the largest paper in the South. Even though the *Guide* only served the region's far northeastern corner, Young's behavior has become representative of the whole, characterizing the black press in an area where editions of smaller southern newspapers were never saved. Despite certain affinities at certain points, the *Guide* and the papers of the Scott Syndicate were not the same and at times were not even similar. The characterization doesn't hold when expanded beyond the bounds of Virginia.

His conciliatory thinking led Young to chair a meeting in Durham, North Carolina, in October 1942 that created the Southern Conference on Race Relations. Two years later, the group merged with a white counterpart to create the Southern Regional Council. The arguments of the Durham group were incredibly moderate. Young made clear that the original meeting was not "to press for racial equality," as that might engender a white backlash. After the 1944 merger, Young and other moderates successfully steered the group to a similarly cautious position, avoiding attacks on segregation and refusing to rock any racial boats.[27]

The Southern Regional Council was headquartered in Atlanta, and its attitude was symbolic of the city's public racial position. The *Atlanta Daily World* did its best to take advantage of the city's pseudo-progressivism during the war. The paper pushed to repeal the poll tax in 1941, and Georgia ultimately repealed it in 1945. After the U.S. Supreme Court's

Smith v. Allwright (1944) decision struck down the white primary,[28] the *World* began a massive voter registration drive through its member papers, which helped expand the number of black registered voters in the years following World War II. Such efforts were also beneficial in that they increased the paper's exposure, thus driving circulation, which in turn drove advertising rates, whose income kept efforts like voter registration drives afloat.[29]

Sociologist Lincoln Blakeney studied the *World*'s editorials from 1932 to 1947 and argues that they were principally concerned with interpretation, simply explaining relevant news items to the paper's readers. After these explanatory editorials came the work of persuasion or crusading for various causes and concerns. The vast majority of the editorials in the period dealt with local issues, they were written in-house, and they emphasized education, politics, and law enforcement above all else. Those would probably be the main topics in most black newspapers of the period, but the *World*'s emphasis was where it distinguished itself as a distinctly southern entity, demonstrating the practical radicalism it deemed necessary for peace and profit. Its educational editorials, for example, called for better schools, for more money to improve the education of black students in Georgia, arguments that specifically avoided calls for integrated schools. The paper's push for more effective law enforcement stressed the unsafe conditions in black neighborhoods. Punishments for crimes needed to be more severe. Black criminals who harmed black victims needed to be prosecuted more sternly. The police brutality claims and the jeremiads about the dangers of white policing that filled the editorial pages of newspapers in Detroit were largely absent.[30]

Many editorial choices were driven by financial concerns. Ruth Scott, W. A. and C. A.'s youngest sibling, produced a master's thesis in Atlanta University's Economics Department in 1939 demonstrating that the correlation between circulation and advertising rates for black weeklies was strong in metropolitan areas, but less so when the total black population was much smaller. This was true for the one daily in her study as well, demonstrating that the problems northern black newspapers wrestled with were not necessarily foreign to those in the South; for all the talk about regional differences, commonalities did exist beyond the issue of racial discrimination. The *World*'s revenue stream came from circulation, advertising, and the Syndicate. For smaller papers, like the one in Hamtramck, advertising rates were determined less by total circulation and more by economic need based on total production costs to the Syndicate.

For papers like the *World*, higher circulation created higher advertising rates. Voting rights drives, then, served the Scotts' financial interest while also creating a stronger black citizenry, which could only redound to even stronger circulation down the road.[31]

The *Atlanta Daily World* also secured its flank by running an open shop, rejecting unionism for its employees. In 1940, reporter Davis Lee gloated about "the Federal Government nabbing the *Atlanta World* for violation of the Wages and Hours Act." The frustration employees felt about their low wages lingered through the next year. On December 1, 1941, the *World* ran a story titled "Why Workers Want Organization," which described the need for labor unions to protect vulnerable black workers. Just below the story's dateline, however, was a disclaimer: "This article doesn't express the views of this paper." The next morning, the *World* announced on its front page that "several members of the *World* mechanical department, who are affiliated with the Local 470, AFL Typographical Union," had called a strike "in an effort to force the execution of a contract which provided for a 'closed shop.'" The paper claimed to have made concessions to the workers and blamed Austin Walden, "administrator of the W. A. Scott estate," for the breakdown in negotiations. Management, the paper wrote, claimed that the closed-shop contract "would void some of the rights of the legatees, who actually own the Scott estate."[32]

The strike continued through the week. On its sixth day, Cliff MacKay wrote a glowing front-page column about the valiant nonunion workers putting out the *World* every day, using his praise of those still at work to subtly denigrate the striking employees. When the strikers refused to return to work during negotiations, as suggested by a federal mediator, the *World* again used its bully pulpit to make itself appear the victim. It was a strong tactic. One full week after the strike began, the striking workers signed an agreement in the office of Judge John L. Cone, commissioner of conciliation for the Labor Department, headquartered in Atlanta. The employees agreed to return to work while continuing negotiations through December. Management had a solid upper hand, and the efforts of the workers for a closed-shop, unionized paper were thwarted. They stayed at work. C. A. Scott had outmaneuvered them.[33]

While the *World* had a clearly patriotic approach to U.S. foreign policy, particularly when it came to fights like World War II, it also covered the independence movements in Africa extensively, addressing the absence of such coverage in the white press. From 1943 to 1946, the founder's son W. A. Scott III served in the intelligence bureau of the army, principally as a photographer. It wasn't a position common to black enlistees, but his experience in media had created a special circumstance. His photographs enhanced the *World*'s and the Syndicate's coverage of the war. The younger Scott was also among those who liberated the concentration camps from Nazi control.[34]

The willingness of the paper to wrap its more racialized coverage in a veneer of patriotic duty and its pragmatic reporting on the country's relationship to injustice would ultimately pay dividends. In September 1942, Claude Barnett, director of the Associated Negro Press, wrote to C. A. Scott about the possibility of "admission to the Washington correspondent's staff" for a member of the black press. He noted that the reason black reporters weren't allowed in the White House press corps was "a social one. You see at Government expense they have those swell lounges set up where they lay around, smoke and drink and they don't want any Negroes fraternizing there. There is no other reason." Knowing that the only formal restriction keeping black reporters out of the press corps was the requirement that the journalist represent a daily newspaper, Barnett proposed that the *World* make an application to the White House Correspondents' Association. "Name our Washington representative, Alvin E. White, as your representative there." He told Scott to use White's Washington address. White would file brief daily stories to the *World* to demonstrate that he "worked" for the paper. "You can prove you are a bona-fide daily and that is the only dodge they have, really." After securing the credential, Barnett explained, "we could then abandon the cost of wires or work out some direct representation costs," functionally dropping the official pretense that White was principally a *World* employee and allowing him to continue his work for the ANP. "I think we can force our way into the White House press conferences." Scott liked the idea, if not the immediate plan, and worked within the confines of the NNPA to help create a Washington news bureau and secure a White House correspondent, keeping Barnett in the loop as negotiations developed. Finally, in February 1944, Harry S. McAlpin became the first black reporter to be part of the White House press pool.[35]

It was a signal victory, but the slow pace of change mirrored much of the *World*'s strategy. In a 1945 analysis of the paper's editorial policy, one commentator explained that the *World* "has been a strong advocate of political rights programs," but the paper expressed that advocacy by taking "a steady stand upon and strong approach to securing full citizenship rights for Negroes in Georgia." While the paper ardently supported

Table 2. Papers and Periodicals Read by People in
Oliver's Study, Exclusive of *Atlanta Daily World*

Paper or Periodical	Number of People
Atlanta Constitution	66
Pittsburgh Courier	34
Atlanta Journal	31
Chicago Defender	6
Afro-American	4
Life	3
Norfolk Journal and Guide	3
New York Herald Tribune	2
New York Times	2
Reader's Digest	2
Time	2
California Eagle	1
Christian Science Monitor	1

Source: Oliver, "History and Development," 29.

steps taken to secure those rights, it "takes mild issue with local and state-wide political officeholders who do not recognize this differential in Georgia democracy."[36]

"It cannot be said that the *Atlanta Daily World* has a strong editorial policy," wrote Sadie Mae Oliver in 1942. "At times it does carry a series of editorials mildly supporting or denouncing some issue." As an example, Oliver described the 1942 Atlanta mayoral election, in which Scott supported Dan Bridges. When Bridges lost to William Hartsfield, Scott changed his allegiance. "One may conclude that a bit of pressure was brought to bear on *The World* press by such an occurrence." That kind of pressure consistently played on the militancy, or lack thereof, of the paper. "Editorial staffs must be strong and willing to face issues intelligently and with courage," noted Oliver. "This appears to be the greatest weakness of the world's only Negro daily paper."[37]

Because of this, many readers turned to the *World*'s northern counterparts. In her study of its readership, Oliver surveyed seventy-five people, a cross-section of the black Atlanta population, all of whom were regular readers of the *Atlanta Daily World*. Among the questions she asked was about other papers they read. Their answers were telling (see table 2).[38] Though the bulk of the people in Oliver's study claimed that the principal reason they read the *World* was for local news, the column inches the paper devoted to local news were dwarfed by sports and comics (see

Table 3. Reading Interests of People in Oliver's Study

Feature	1st Choice	2nd Choice	3rd Choice
Local news	48	8	12
Educational features	27	14	8
National news	26	16	10
Programs (radio and theater)	22	23	28
Editorials	21	15	11
Industrial-political	21	10	16
Sports	20	20	17
Religious or church items	17	17	13
Business items	16	8	17
Women's features	16	7	15
Puzzles (crossword and games)	15	13	24
Society column	15	22	13
International news	11	17	13
Personal items	11	9	18
Crime	9	9	24
Funeral notices	8	9	23
Comics	8	6	16
Advertisements	8	11	14
Juvenile news	7	7	16
Fiction	2	7	13

Source: Oliver, "History and Development," 31.

tables 3 and 4). It was the kind of formula that would lead Scott and the *World* to later come under fire for conservative civil rights stances, but the paper always advocated for equality in its practically radical way, in the spaces between the sports and the comics and the crosswords. In 1944, for example, C. A. Scott joined thirty-two fellow southern editors and writers, most of them white, some of them archconservatives, to create the Committee of Editors and Writers of the South. They produced a report, "Voting Restrictions in the Thirteen Southern States," which argued that the vast majority of southerners didn't vote, far more than in any other region, and that the lack of political participation allowed a small group of officials to run the region to its own ends. There weren't any policy prescriptions in the report, and they didn't demand that voting restrictions for minorities be lifted, but there was what historian John Egerton has called "a public declaration of opposition to the status quo." The following year, Scott helped to form the Citizens Democratic Club of Fulton County, the principal goal of which was to fight against Georgia's white primary.[39]

Table 4. Number of Inches Devoted to Items in a Typical *World* Issue

Feature	Inches	Feature	Inches
Sports	160	Society column	25
Comics	120	Editorials	24
Religious or church items	60	Puzzles (crossword and games)	22
Advertisements	46.5	Juvenile news	20
Local news	45	Crime	20
Programs (radio and theater)	45	International news	18
Fiction	39	Funeral notices	15
Women's features	30	Industrial-political	15
Educational features	30	Personal items	9
National news	30	Business items	6

Source: Oliver, "History and Development," 12.

To be sure, this was not the kind of activism that filled the pages of Detroit's black newspapers, but the *World*'s advocacy moved to the limits of what was possible in the cloistered world of the Jim Crow South. This was a fraught time in the history of African America, as the demographics of the South changed with the last major wave of the Great Migration and as the seismic eruption of World War II upended long-held assumptions about rights and democracy. The Syndicate's ability to adapt regionally, economically, and philosophically put it on a path to success in the postwar era. There would be new opportunities to challenge Jim Crow and lay the groundwork for the coming civil rights movement.

Chapter 6

Percy Greene and the Limits of Syndication

On Saturday night, February 27, 1943, Percy Greene, editor and publisher of the *Jackson Advocate*, went to his office on Farish Street, the hub of black Jackson, Mississippi. Throughout the day he had been hearing rumors that involved Edward Tademy, the black principal of the Smith Robertson School. Smith Robertson was the first and most prominent public school for Jackson's black residents. It was the alma mater of Richard Wright and the symbol of progressive education in the city, making Tademy a prominent public figure because of his leadership role in the school. The principal, according to the talk that wafted through Jackson, had made unwanted advances to several women from Jackson College who were working at the school, which also served as a World War II ration station. Tademy had promised them jobs and that he would fire the existing faculty, everyone said. Then he became "violently amorous," advancing on one of the women "until her dress was almost torn off and she screamed for help." It was juicy Saturday night gossip, and it was everywhere. So Greene decided to publish it.[1]

Greene had founded the *Advocate* in 1938, and in October 1940 he joined the Scott Newspaper Syndicate. The SNS provided syndicated material for the *Advocate*, and it printed the newspaper on Auburn Avenue, Atlanta's version of Farish Street. So when Tademy sued for libel, he sued the Scotts. The resulting case spent the next three years in the courts, and in the process it helped define both the scope of responsibility for newspaper syndicates and the limits of their influence. The black press in the South served a black population that was largely impoverished and rural, and it relied on syndicates such as the SNS to provide the information to tie them to the networks that constituted the grapevine throughout the region. Thus the case proved to be vitally important not just for Jackson and Atlanta, but for all the rural areas that relied on black southern syndication. It also demonstrated the inherent risk that syndicates took when reprinting local content. In this case, the *Advocate* ultimately severed its relationship with the Syndicate. The paper and the SNS moved down separate (yet ideologically parallel) tracks in the following decades.

Mississippi's black press began after the Civil War, developing in fits and starts through Reconstruction and the Gilded Age and finally becoming a legitimate and strong presence in the early decades of the 1900s. But in the first half of the twentieth century, the visibility of the black press in Mississippi began to recede. The eighty-seven papers that had existed between 1900 and 1920 became eighteen by 1940. By 1953, there were only eleven. Without urban centers and with a virtual apartheid system in place in Mississippi, the ability of the black press to survive, let alone succeed, was dramatically hindered. Since there was no real black middle class in the state outside the small urban core, there was no real way to make black journalism profitable. Most editors and publishers had other jobs as doctors, teachers, or, even more often, Baptist or Methodist ministers.[2]

Only seven Mississippi towns prior to the Supreme Court's *Brown v. Board of Education* decision had more than 4 black newspapers in their histories. Of the 116 black newspapers published in the first eight decades of the twentieth century, 69 came from those same seven towns: Vicksburg, Natchez, Meridian, Jackson, Hattiesburg, Greenville, and Mound Bayou. The average newspaper circulation was between five hundred and a thousand, a far cry from the circulation numbers of larger papers in cities outside Mississippi. But historian Julius Eric Thompson argues that information sharing in rural areas, which included passing newspapers from one to another, increased the number of readers.[3]

The black press focused on segregation, voting rights, and lynching. But the stifling racism of Mississippi did not allow editors to really inveigh against injustices. The papers instead typically reprinted wire stories about such issues. Social news, church updates, and entertainment information usually dominated the pages. Thompson notes that what advocacy existed "shows them subscribing to the school of thought of Booker T. Washington."[4]

Greene's *Jackson Advocate*, for example, highlighted black success stories and often criticized black Mississippians for contributing to some of their own problems, such as the tenuous health of black people in the state capital. In late 1941 Greene's editorials called on his readers to better their health so they would not have to rely on a white medical establishment that was not always interested in helping to cure them. He also used his editorial page to inveigh against black-on-black crime. White police were not inclined to deal with such disputes vigorously, so black behavior needed to improve on its own. When the paper talked about equality, it did not clamor for integration, but argued instead for equal standards within the segregated system. Editorials stated that black teachers, for example, deserved equitable pay in relation to their white counterparts. The *Advocate* often railed against Germany and Japan and supported the war effort. Like many of its contemporaries, the paper was not shy about reminding readers that fighting for equality at home was a logical outgrowth of fighting for equality overseas. Also like most papers in Mississippi, it endorsed Protestant Christianity as the ultimate saving grace of all sufferers at home and abroad. Such was the *Advocate*'s method—urging readers to solve their own problems of health and crime, rather than arguing for better treatment from doctors and police, or arguing for equal pay in a segregated educational system rather than advocating for segregation's end. This was a familiar practical radicalism that insulated the paper from potential white anger or reprisal for stances that whites might find too extreme. White Mississippians, of course, had a low bar for what they deemed radical. Thompson argues that "Greene was caught between the old Booker T. Washington position of economic emphasis versus a strong demand that discrimination should end at once."[5]

The *Advocate* quoted Washington's Atlanta Compromise regularly, but under Greene's leadership it became the most radical paper in the state, calling for black voting rights and political participation. Editorials calling for voting rights were understandable to whites (though not popular), and their enactment would not require increased contact between the races. Thus such editorial positions were considered relatively safe ground. They allowed Greene with plausibility to convince his readers that he had their best interests in mind and to mollify white politicians that he could steer black public opinion away from integrationist demands. Greene often lobbied in his newspaper for the Mississippi state legislature to fix problems of race relations in the city and state. At the same time, he assured whites that his motives included the best interests of both races of Mississippians. As Thompson points out, Greene was a paradoxical figure who argued for black rights without really arguing for the renunciation of Mississippi's conservative political system. It bears repeating that in Mississippi, the *Advocate* was the radical newspaper.[6]

Greene was born in 1898 in Jackson, and he developed in an age of Jim Crow, when Booker T. Washington was the model of black southern activism. He graduated from high school and took some classes at Jackson College before migrating north to various points in the Midwest and then serving in the First World War. After his honorable discharge, Greene returned to Jackson and fell into journalism not because of training or long-standing desire, but because he was barred by racism from other options, such as the law.[7]

Greene's paper had "a wide circulation and . . . several thousand subscribers in Jackson, Mississippi and in its immediate vicinity," said the court filings. It was "circulated by mail, by delivery to its subscribers, by newsboys on the streets, by sales at news stand[s], and otherwise, and is and was read by thousands of persons over a wide territory." Without any formal circulation numbers for the *Advocate*, it is impossible to know exactly how many people read the paper or were influenced by its news coverage. Still, the number of potential readers was large. Jackson's black population was just under twenty-five thousand, and Hinds County's was just over fifty-five thousand. There were more than a million black residents in the state. The potential influence of the *Jackson Advocate* was extensive. In his testimony during the original libel trial, Edward Tademy said that the paper was circulated widely in Laurel and Hattiesburg, roughly ninety miles away.[8]

The black population was generally impoverished, particularly during the Great Depression; however, a small middle class developed, particularly in Greene's Jackson, which had its share of Washingtonian economic groups, such as branches of the National Negro Business League and Negro Chamber of Commerce. Though Jackson's black middle class was large enough that the majority of Greene's advertisers were black businesses, white advertisers still made up a critical part of the *Advocate*'s income.[9]

That dependence made toeing the racial line all the more important for the publisher. Greene and his newspaper were already lightning rods for controversy and remained so in the decades to come, but the controversy usually was generated in his own community. While Greene supported the integration of the military during World War II, for example, he opposed A. Philip Randolph's proposed March on Washington for Jobs and Freedom in 1941 to gain integration. Militancy only hardened white attitudes, he believed, and the state of black progress rested on cultivating benevolence from whites. Though he was a tireless champion of black voting rights, Greene remained a Washingtonian accommodationist on most other civil rights issues, frustrating activists and his readers throughout the state.[10]

After he founded his paper, Greene's status in the community grew. He was a Mason, an Elk, and a Knight of Pythias. He volunteered with the Selective Service System in the early years of World War II. He even maintained a correspondence with James W. Silver, head of the Ole Miss History Department, who wanted copies of the *Advocate* for his students to read at the state's venerated lily-white institution. Of course, even Greene's success did not come without controversy. In the months following his Tademy editorials the FBI began investigating whether or not Greene was receiving kickbacks for his Selective Service work. The allegations centered around Greene charging fees for helping registrants fill out their paperwork. They were never proven, and the case was ultimately dropped, but it was an issue nonetheless.[11]

And then there were the Tademy editorials themselves. On March 6, 1943, Greene became mired in yet another controversy for simply commenting on the local talk of the town in his editorial column, "Up and Down Farish Street."

> FARISH STREET SATURDAY NIGHT: The Ole Ave. was agog with gossip Saturday night as everywhere folks were asking one another and me "have you heard about Fessor" Tademy, the principal of Smith Roberson School and then for fear that I had not herd and to be sure that I would hear they'ed began telling one of the most revolting stories of moral degenercy and depovity regarding the Principal of Smith Robinson School.[12]

Greene explained that a group of young women were assisting at the school while people were registering for the ration books issued by the federal government during World War II. "After making amourous advances to the many of them to whom he gave his telephone number for future contacts," wrote Greene, "supported by his promise that he was going to get rid of most of the teachers next year and give them all a job with the last one to enter his room he became so violently amourous, until she resisted his advances he cought her with such persistence until her dress was almost torn off and she screamed for help."

It was, he admitted, just a rumor being bandied about on Farish Street, but it was being discussed by everyone. "In Professor Tademy's case I am inclined to the old adage of 'Where there is so much smoke there is bound to be some fire,' and to every parent in the city of Jackson who looks to the school as an aid in installing into their children the finer virtues of manhood and womanhood the usefulness of Professor Tademy as Principal of Smith Robinson School and as a teacher in the Jackson public school system is over." The onus for action was now on the school superintendent. "Professor [O. B.] Cobbins, despite of the reluctance that he might have to act against

Professor Tademy on a 'Morals' charge, as Supervisor of Negro schools must now come face to face with the delemma continued in the injunction, 'Judge ye not less ye also be judged,'" Greene argued. "Upon the failure of Prof. Cobbins to act immediately in the case of Prof. Tademy the Negro citizens of Jackson should carry the case to Prof. [Kirby] Walker less these periodic outburst of stories of moral laxety regarding school teachers be reflected in the lack of high moral and spiritual influence of the schools."[13]

It was a damning exposé, but it was also an unsourced editorial that was devastating to Edward Tademy. Greene, however, was not done. The following week, he published another screed on the subject, this time with far more venom. "Everybody was still talking about 'Fessor' Tademy who, as more and more is heard about his approaches upon those young girls over at Smith Robinson school the other day, justifies the 'Hep Cats,' up and down the Ole Ave. in comically referring to him now as 'Fessor Tademy The Great Lover.'" While there was still some amusement in his writing, Greene's frustration was real.

> What most folks wanted to know was what was going to be done in "Fessor" Tademy's case and the best I could do was tell them what I heard that "Fessor" Cobbins, The Supervisor of Negro Schools said about the case when the Principal of the schools asked him about what he was gonna do. "Fessor" Cobbins when the question was put up and said that he couldn't act cause "Fessor" Tademy's case hadn't been "OFFICIALLY BROUGHT TO MY ATTENTION."
>
> When I said that [to] a couple of folks with children going to school one of them up and said, MY LORD ABOVE what kind of official notice does "Fessor" Cobbins want other than a public and disgraceful scandal that grown folks, children, and everybody else is talking about up and down the streets of the city. One fellow says to me if that kinda story was to start about a teacher on the other side of the fence he would have had to leave town on the first train, and said further that now Tademy ought to be put out, and a lot of cleaning up ought to be done around Lanier High School. I hated to hear him mention Lanier High School on the account of my friend Prof. [Isaiah Sumner] Sanders being the Principal out there [since 1935] and whose personal character I see as above reproach. Which led me to wish that he was in a position of greater authority so as to exert a greater influence on the whole Negro Public School System.[14]

This was not personal, wrote Greene, "but sometime when you get to close to a thing you can't see as somebody standing way off looking, and the reason folks try to show people things sometimes is to help and not hurt and ain't nothing never beat criticism and especially the kind that make folks mad." There were other problems at Smith Robertson. "There are a number of houses of shady reputation in the vicinity of the school where the students hang out when they ought to be in class or study; that there are too many girl students permitted to leave and return to the school after unlimited experiences of marriage and otherwise. And too much 'Society and Fraternalizing' of students and teachers." There was, to Greene's mind, only one viable solution: "Sometime you can't help an old house with paint, you just have to tear off some old and put on some new boards."[15]

Edward Tademy was the principal of Smith Robertson and the president of the Eighth Educational District of the Mississippi Association of Teachers in Colored Schools. He began his teaching career in St. Joseph, Louisiana, but spent the bulk of his time in Hattiesburg, where he taught for ten years before moving to Jackson. There he joined Central Methodist Episcopal. He taught Sunday school. He had been married to his wife, Rhoda, for sixteen years.[16] He was, by all prior accounts, an upstanding citizen.

On February 27, the Eighth Educational District had hosted a meeting, the theme of which was "educating for victory and freedom." It was an important event with representatives from across the five counties that comprised the district. Greene, too, was at the meeting. Sitting on the dais, he noticed the teachers laughing to themselves and pointing as Tademy, who presided over the meeting, rose to speak. This was not completely surprising. Tademy was short, fat, and incredibly nearsighted, and his appearance was often the butt of jokes. Unfortunately for the principal, however, the laughter was not about his looks. Even without Greene's questions, the teachers at that meeting were talking about the incident at Smith Robertson. It was, according to the editor, the predominant subject.[17]

Greene went to the college to verify the stories and then "to several other people who by that time—everybody was talking about it, in the pool rooms[,] in the neighborhoods, my wife, and everybody else was talking about it." Jackson College's dean, Henry T. Sampson, told Greene that "everyone of those girls had made report that Professor Tademy had made some advance to them, and that it was unfortunate that they had told it and they had been unable to squash it, but it got out to be common rumor all over town."[18]

Tademy felt that he had to do something. In September 1943, he filed suit in federal district court over Greene's claims that Tademy "made love to several high school students when they were signing up for Ration Book No. 2," asking for $25,000 in actual and punitive damages. How the damages were described was significant, because the hit to Tademy's reputation was not all encompassing. At the time of the suit, he was still the principal of Smith Robertson, still president of the Eighth Educational District of the Mississippi Association of Teachers in Colored Schools, and still assistant secretary of the Jackson Negro Christmas Cheer Club. Tademy's complaint argued that the articles "expos[ed] him to public hatred, contempt and ridicule." Such was the case for punitive damages. He also claimed that the articles "reflected upon the professional integrity of plaintiff and tended to inure and damage plaintiff in his profession," though that would be much harder to prove.[19]

Tademy's lawyer was Ross Robert Barnett, who would later become Mississippi's infamous fire-eating segregationist governor and cause so many problems for the black press.[20] His lawsuit, however, was not directed at Percy Greene, who wrote the articles and edited the *Jackson Advocate*. Instead, the defendant was the *Atlanta Daily World* or, technically, "the estate of W. A. Scott, deceased," and thus each surviving member of his family, led by his brother C. A. Scott, who headed both the *World* and the Scott Newspaper Syndicate and served, by the 1940s, as administrator of the founder's will.[21]

W. A. Scott was born in 1902 in Edwards, Mississippi, the son of a minister who moved to Jackson in 1914 to start a new church. The elder Scott was also a printer, and he constructed the William Alexander Scott building on Farish Street to house his Progressive Printing Company. Greene was boyhood friends with the brothers W. A. and C. A. Scott, and their father's printing business was Greene's first exposure to black publishing. The Scotts would complete their secondary education at the high school department of Jackson College, just a few short years behind their friend Percy. In 1943, the Scott Newspaper Syndicate totaled roughly sixteen newspapers and was still influential, particularly in Jackson, where the brothers' boyhood friend edited a paper that was part of the group.[22]

At stake in the case against the Scotts was the nature of black press syndication in the 1940s. The Scotts and the *Atlanta Daily World* did not "own, publish, manage or control the *Jackson Advocate*." Instead, Percy Greene and his staff wrote articles and editorials about the local news in central Mississippi, generated advertisements from local businesses, and then sent that collected material to Atlanta, where SNS staff would organize a layout using the material, add national news from the *World* and other syndicate papers, print the finished product, and send it back to Jackson. The Syndicate's contact with the local content was limited to proofreading and the occasional addition of a headline.[23]

This situation created the fundamental importance of the Tademy libel case. Without the relationship with Atlanta, Greene's paper could have survived (and did survive after the relationship ended). Greene had his own Jackson constituency and an outsized reputation in the state. Still, he would not have attained his initial success without a benefactor agency like the SNS, which allowed individuals with few resources to create newspapers. For the vast majority of southern black newspapers, both within Mississippi and without, would-be journalists and entrepreneurs required those syndication and printing connections with larger firms to create a viable news network throughout the region. The Tademy case tested the limits of culpability in the relationship between syndicate printers and their member newspapers—and thus the growth limits for black newspapers in the South. While the alleged libel occurred over a distinctly Mississippian incident in a distinctly Mississippian newspaper, Percy Greene's friends in Atlanta were heavily invested in its outcome.

W. A. Scott's four brothers, three sisters, mother, and two sons all had the responsibility to deny Tademy's charge, and while they all did deny it, their denials were by no means uniform. Most family members alleged that the defendants did not "own, publish, manage, control, sell or circulate the newspaper described in the complaint as the *Jackson Advocate*." Scott brothers Lewis (also known as L. A.) and Daniel claimed that "the defendants have had nothing to do with the operation or control of the newspapers in spite of continued efforts to get possession of their property since the death of the late W. A. Scott, manager and co-founder of the newspapers." Their brother Aurelius, who had been at odds with the family since W. A.'s murder, had a similar caustic response, not only denying Tademy's charges, but using the opportunity to charge his family members with incompetence and corruption.[24] It was clear that the Scott family's fight was not only an effort to define the limits of their culpability in defamation suits resulting from the actions of their member papers, but also an internecine battle between members of the family, whose stake in the business founded by W. A. Scott was far from equal.

Under cross-examination, C. A. Scott claimed that the Syndicate averaged about sixteen newspapers at any one time. "We have certain standard non-controversial non-partisan matter that we give these various papers we print," he said. "Then, they supply the local stuff for the editorial page, social page and sports, and we supply four pages of standard material that is non-controversial, non-partisan that is circulated, to these various cities." Scott explained that the Syndicate was different than the Associated Negro Press, which provided content for any paper that paid for the service, but the SNS did provide syndicated material written or rewritten in Atlanta for use in member papers.[25]

The Scotts printed and sent between one and two thousand copies of the paper to Jackson. "We charge them so much for each column of newspaper composition we set up," said Scott, "so much per inch for the advertising, so much for making up the page, and so much per hundred copies for the paper, and we print those papers, in most cases, if they haven't paid us in advance, c.o.d." That generally totaled roughly fifty dollars per week. The Syndicate set a paper's local material, then inserted material from the *Atlanta Daily World,* the ANP, or other member newspapers. The paper's editor could choose which material he wanted included, or he could allow those choices to be made in Atlanta. Most important for Scott was the fact that the Syndicate did not edit the local material. It did occasionally generate headlines for articles that didn't include them, but it did not change the submitted copy. "I did not know about the article," said Scott, referring to Greene's description of Tademy's behavior, "until I got a copy of the suit." Scott had never met Tademy, had never received any correspondence from him, and had never been asked to retract anything printed for the *Jackson Advocate.*[26]

In her turn on the witness stand, C. A. Scott's mother, Emeline, explained that among the additions that the Syndicate included in its layouts for member papers was national advertising that profited the Atlanta group. She admitted that it did benefit the Syndicate if member papers had the largest circulation possible, but reminded the court that neither the Scotts, the *World,* nor the Syndicate read any of the submitted material for content.[27]

The *Advocate* had a circulation between 2,500 and 3,000. It was a small operation with only two employees. Syndication allowed for such arrangements because Atlanta did the yeoman's work of production. The *Advocate* charged roughly forty cents per advertising inch and then charged for the paper itself. The Syndicate charged the *Advocate* for various services. "The payment is based on $1.00 a galley in excess of two galleys submitted per issue, or ten cents per inch, make-up for new advertising, and five cents charge, make-up charges for new advertising, with additional charge of $1.50 for inside make-ups, and $3.50 for extra front page make-up,"

Greene explained in his testimony. "What we pay them is determined by what we have for them to make up."

> Naturally we don't have the same amount of advertising each week. We may have four or five hundred inches one week and the next week we would only have twenty-five.
>
> Q. You pay according to the amount of advertising?
>
> A. And copy. We pay them $1.25 per galley for copy.
>
> Q. What do you mean by galley?
>
> A. A galley is a certain number of inches of printed matter. A galley measures about 6½ inches.[28]

Greene and the Scotts had an agreement for printing that had been originally confirmed in a simple letter from Atlanta to Jackson. After Tademy issued the suit, however, the two formalized the relationship with a signed document for the purpose of cataloging the various responsibilities of both parties in the relationship. Scott further explained when recalled for additional testimony that articles without a dateline definitely came from Greene. Articles from the ANP or SNS might have been chosen in Atlanta or might have been clipped from the *Atlanta Daily World* by Greene and sent with his local materials to be included in his *Jackson Advocate*.[29]

For most observers, however, the minutiae of syndication relationships in the southern black press were the angels dancing on the heads of so many pins. Black Mississippi wanted to know what happened at the school. During the last week of February 1943, the Office of Price Administration had asked public schools to help issue Ration Book No. 2, and the white superintendent of the Jackson city schools, Kirby Walker, had charged Tademy with heading the effort at Smith Robertson. Tademy had twenty-one teachers from his school and thirty-six students from Jackson College to assist with the process.[30]

The group from Jackson College was mostly women. Their stint at the school lasted for a week, and it was quickly apparent to many of them that Smith Robertson's principal was overly familiar. Among the Jackson students was Irma Anderson, who claimed that she was alone in a room when Tademy entered and tried to put his arms around her. He tried to kiss her, but she refused. He offered her his telephone number, but she refused. "Mr. Tademy," she told him, "I once had respect for you, but I don't have it now." The following day, Tademy again went to Anderson, this time promising her a job at the school after her graduation if she agreed to keep quiet about his advances.[31] She did not keep quiet, however, and told the leader of the group from Jackson College. That student reported the incident to the school's dean of students, who then reported it to the college's president. Still, when Tademy filed suit and Anderson originally had to supply a sworn statement to court officials, she denied that the incident took place. "I didn't want to go to Court," she admitted during the trial. "I figured this would be what it was, and I said no; in fact to everything he asked me I said 'no.'"[32]

Tademy denied the charges. He had never tried to put his arms around Anderson, he said. He had taught her at nearby Lanier High School prior to his move to Smith Robertson and hers to Jackson College. "If I wanted to do anything mean," he said, "I could have done something mean maybe five or six years ago with them, because they were . . . high school students over at Lanier." Tademy's theory was that the accusations came from a cabal of Jackson College members. Greene had attended Jackson College, as had Tademy's original competitor for the position of principal of Smith Robertson. Anderson was obviously still attending. The administrators of the school believed her story. "I understand the Scotts [also] attended Jackson College," Tademy told the court.[33]

At Smith Robertson the week following the ration book distribution, Henry Bell, the school's janitor, showed Tademy a copy of the *Advocate*. Shocked and angry, Tademy went to confront Greene. Tademy "showed him the places where he mentioned different things that I did, accused me of, told him not a word of it was true, and that he should have talked to me before putting anything in a paper like that, and I asked him to retract, and of course, he was very discourteous and refused to do so, told me to go sue him."[34]

Greene denied being discourteous, but admitted that he had refused to retract his articles. "I had verified all of this stuff by conversation with teachers in the school," said Greene, "with the officials of Jackson College and other persons," including Dean Henry T. Sampson. Greene's two daughters attended Lanier High at the time, and he claimed that his only interest in printing the material was because he wanted the best, most reliable people in charge of Jackson's schools.[35]

Greene's motives bore little on the judge's finding of fact in the case. Tademy claimed that more than four hundred people had asked him about the charges. A former colleague, a teacher then residing in Arizona, wrote him to say she had heard about the scandal. "It is," Tademy said, "practically interfering with my work in the community seemingly." People read gossip and discussed gossip, "and perhaps sooner or later it might affect my work in the community if it keeps on." Tademy claimed that while he still held his job at Smith Robertson, "my supervisor said that in case that we fail in this case, that the public would force them to ask my resignation, not that they wanted to do it, on the truthfulness of this, but the public seem to be heated up over it."[36] It was clear that Tademy's reputation had taken a hit. Arguing, however, that "perhaps sooner or later" tangible consequences would come from the publication was not substantive proof of actual damage. Thus Tademy lost his initial suit in federal district court in January 1945, and he appealed to the U.S. Circuit Court of Appeals.

In the original decision, Robert L. Russell, a federal judge for the Northern District of Georgia, ruled that a Georgia statute argued that anyone seeking punitive damages for libel had to first alert the would-be defendants to give them an opportunity to retract the problematic material. Mississippi had no such statute, but when suing in Georgia, Russell ruled, the plaintiff had to follow the Georgia rules. It was a victory for the Scotts, the *World*, and the Syndicate, but it was not a decision that completely abrogated their culpability. Russell was ruling on a fine point of the law, not claiming that Tademy's accusations were unreasonable.[37]

In the Fifth Circuit Court of Appeals the following year, a three-judge panel doubled down on Russell's original ruling, arguing that "the judgment should have been one of dismissal without prejudice because of the plaintiff's failure to comply with the Georgia notice statute governing newspaper libel actions." The court argued that it was unconcerned with "the evidence or the findings made on the merits" because such was beside the point if the Georgia law was applicable to the case. They found that it was, and Tademy lost again. And again the Scotts won without a clear definition of their role in the libel.[38]

So Tademy set out to prove that the damages he sought were not merely punitive. He was actually suffering. In 1947, he filed another suit. Included in this complaint was a more elaborate explanation of his "great humiliation, embarrassment and mortification as a direct and proximate result of said libels, slanders and the publications thereof," and he also made some more tangible claims of actual damage. He said that he "actually lost his job as superintendent of a school in the City of Jackson for two years, which paid him the sum of approximately $2400.00 per year, making a total in the sum of $4800.00." With this amount and his continued pain and suffering, Tademy kept his asking price at $25,000.[39] He also continued to maintain that he had complied with the Georgia law that required him to notify the defendants and allow them the opportunity to print a retraction. That remained a problematic claim, which had been quashed in the appellate court, and the Scotts' response emphasized the error. Federal judge Robert L. Russell heard the case again and agreed with the Scotts. That claim was invalid. But the rest of the family's attempts to have the case dismissed failed. There would be another trial.[40]

The most pressing issue of this proceeding was Tademy's sight and its effect on his job. He had almost no vision in his left eye and only marginal vision in his right. He had received a cornea replacement and could only see out of his right eye with a contact lens, an incredibly rare device in the 1940s. Though there was plenty of confusion about just what a contact lens was, Tademy's essential argument was that he had used one the year prior to his firing, so the troubles with his eyesight could not have been the reason for his unemployment. Kirby Walker, the superintendent of Jackson public schools, however, claimed that Tademy's dismissal was directly and only related to his eyesight. O. B. Cobbins, Jackson's director of colored schools, validated Walker's testimony. Tademy's vision problems, he claimed, were the sole reason for his dismissal. Still, Cobbins, unlike Walker, admitted to being aware of the sexual harassment controversy and said it was a well-discussed topic among teachers in the city.[41]

The new testimony helped demonstrate to Judge Russell that, if nothing else, "the publication of the two articles in question likewise, in some measure at least, contributed to his failure to secure employment as a teacher for at least one year, 1945–46. Furthermore, the libelous articles will affect him to some extent in the future." Tademy's eyesight, however, was surely another determining factor in his failure to find employment, and the suffering described by the plaintiff had been dismissed in the first trial. Russell awarded Tademy $1,000, which the *Atlanta Daily World* quickly paid.[42] The case had come to an end.

It was not without its consequences. The boyhood friends who had cemented their adult relationship through a syndication agreement had severed that bond in July 1946, when Tademy's original appeal was before the Fifth Circuit Court of Appeals. The relationship had been strained by the case, as the Scotts essentially took the blame for Greene's assertions. They also paid the bill, and the court costs for two federal civil trials surely outstripped the small fees that Greene had paid to the *World* for syndication. Black southern printing and syndication services, however, were few and far between, so Greene signed a printing agreement with Patton Publishing, a white Jackson firm, to keep his newspaper afloat.[43]

Greene was able to make such a deal because of the Washingtonian credentials he had established throughout the decade. Arguing for political rights while willingly sloughing off social rights had paid off, just as it had for Booker T. Washington, who had been able to parlay his own voting rights activism and social accommodationism into white philanthropy for black education throughout the South. Whether solidifying his paper's relationship with local whites strengthened Greene's position in Jackson or the end of the Depression modified the purchasing power of subscribers and advertisers, the *Jackson Advocate*'s circulation grew through the rest of the 1940s. Meanwhile, the Syndicate also experienced continuing success. The SNS had thirteen member newspapers at the time of the *Advocate*'s move to Patton Publishing. It kept between nine and thirteen throughout the rest of the decade.[44]

Syndication among the black press in the first half of the twentieth century is often misunderstood. The *Chicago Defender*, for example, created several member papers to expand its reach. So too did the *Pittsburgh Courier* and the *Baltimore Afro-American*. At the same time, there were news services like the Associated Negro Press, which provided national news copy to black newspapers.[45] But the Scott Newspaper Syndicate combined printing services and news copy to create a vehicle for small operations throughout the South and the Midwest that provided African Americans with news that concerned them. For small publishers in Mississippi and elsewhere, that relationship could be absolutely vital, but as the Tademy case demonstrated, the connection between the syndication service and its members could also be problematic. The work of the Syndicate helped formalize knowledge among the black population, particularly in the South, providing information that readers could get from no other source. At the same time, its influence stopped at the water's edge of the opinion page. In most cases, those opinions aligned. Both Greene and the Scotts remained Washingtonian conservatives, and both the *Atlanta Daily World* and *Jackson Advocate* were known for their moderate positions on civil rights activism as the 1940s gave way to the 1950s and 1960s. Still, there was no fundamental requirement that the Syndicate and its member papers be aligned. And in the era before World War II and the civil rights movement, when the SNS was serving many newspapers beyond its own *Atlanta Daily World*, fact-checking a story about locals behaving badly in a Jackson, Mississippi, high school was practically impossible.

There was obviously a significant difference between meaningful rights activism and local gossip about a community leader becoming "violently amourous," but that did not diminish the importance of the latter story. The Tademy case enthralled many in black Jackson and frustrated the Scotts in Atlanta, but more substantively, it allowed the courts to draw the lines of culpability for syndicates that published the work of others. Even though the SNS eventually lost the case, it was a small judgment and decided on technicalities, thereby providing, even in defeat, a form of insulation for the *Atlanta Daily World* and its Syndicate as it created a viable black southern news network. Formalizing news coverage across a region dominated by Jim Crow was fundamentally important to the development of a unity of thought among black southerners in the generation before the civil rights movement. That unity, that grapevine, could have developed regardless of the outcome of Edward Tademy's libel suit, but the consequences of his case provided for the first time a horizon line for the Syndicate's responsibility in printing the black South's news.

Chapter 7

Davis Lee and the Transitory Nature of Syndicate Editors

On the evening of May 30, 1927, twenty-three-year-old Davis Lee brought a woman named Audrey Dixon to a party at Willow Grove Park in his hometown of Bel Air, Maryland. There he got into an argument with Wesley Buchanan and several of his friends, presumably over Dixon. In her telling, Buchanan and his friends trapped Lee and pulled a gun. So Dixon hit Buchanan's arm while Lee stabbed his assailant in the chest. Lee and Dixon then left the party, driving thirty miles south to her house in Baltimore. The police were waiting for them. "I stabbed him in the chest with my pocket knife," said Lee after his arrest. "He died immediately." Lee was tried for second-degree murder, convicted in November, and sentenced to eighteen years in prison.[1] It was, perhaps, the most inauspicious start ever to a career in journalism.

That career would span the next half century and would be as outsized as Lee's entry into the business. He began writing in prison. After being paroled, he founded several newspapers over several decades, evolving from a crusader for civil rights to the rare black defender of southern segregation. He was almost unimaginably litigious, evolving from libel lawsuits in his early career to later million-dollar suits against the NAACP, which stemmed from imagined conspiracies by black activists against the honesty and virtuousness of his stances against forced integration. Lee's journalistic endeavors existed on the margins, hubristic and controversial by necessity in order to keep his several fledgling business enterprises afloat.

Despite his radical stances and controversial life, the case of Davis Lee demonstrates the difficulties that existed for black journalists and small-time publishers between the 1930s and 1960s. Most created weekly papers with circulations in the hundreds, staffed by fewer than five employees and relying on syndication services like the SNS to fill the spaces between local news, editorial commentary, and the advertising that kept them solvent. The economics of the business understandably left them shifting with the winds of those elements, and though Lee shifted more than most, his case is demonstrative of the plight of black journalists in small markets in the middle of the twentieth century, a plight that is vital to seeing a full picture of the Scott Newspaper Syndicate. Survival dictated that journalists and would-be publishers create a customer and advertising base for themselves by either crusading for black rights or moderating their stances to play to local white interests, and the strange career of Davis Lee is exemplary of both of those efforts. He began with the *Baltimore Afro-American*, a rival organization, but his career took him through various individual efforts with the Scott Syndicate, then back to the *Afro*, then back again to independence. Loyalty to any given syndication service, of course, was not a prerequisite for potential newspapermen, and his movement, if not his politics, were common among Syndicate customers.

Lee was born and raised in Bel Air, where he attended the Harford School of Journalism and Law, one of the region's public secondary schools. It was a promising start, but the murder of Wesley Buchanan and the eighteen-year sentence that followed was a significant hindrance to his progress. In prison, Lee was a machine operator in a textile factory. While there, he helped his fellow inmates learn to read and write, but he also wrote himself, submitting stories and editorials to various papers and making a journalistic name while behind bars. "I work in the pants factory during the day, and do all of my writing (two syndicated weekly columns, short stories and essays) at night, from six until ten," he explained. "Every spare moment between times is utilized in reading. I read 12 daily papers, 50 or 60 colored weeklies when they come in, two new novels each week, besides a number of magazines." That work helped Lee achieve parole after serving six years; he had convinced Carl Murphy, president of the *Baltimore Afro-American*, to supply him with a job, which apparently convinced the parole board of his stability. The *Afro*, founded in 1892, was one of the largest and most significant black weekly newspapers in the country. "I am positive, Mr. Murphy, that my future mode of living and achievement will fully justify you in coming to my assistance. I am determined to make good, all that I ask is a chance."[2] It was a request that would bind Lee to Murphy for the next decade.

That decade was the core of the Depression era, and the economic crisis created the distinct social and journalistic landscape that Lee entered, even as he was serving his sentence. As early as 1931, Lee was writing reports on conditions at his prison and submitting fiction stories to the *Afro-American*. "He seems to be able to smuggle mail past the guards and undoubtedly is a clever chap," Carl Murphy commented. In December 1932 Lee reported on the *Blackman,* a new monthly publication from Marcus Garvey and, after the closing of the *Negro World,* the official organ of the Universal Negro Improvement Association. His devotion to the association's politics ultimately garnered Lee his first national exposure.[3]

In May 1933, he wrote to columnist and provocateur George S. Schuyler, who responded in his *Pittsburgh Courier.* Lee was upset with Schuyler's criticism of Marcus Garvey and the "infantile paralysis of Garveyism." Garvey's, according to Lee, was one of the greatest "movements that was ever conceived in a black brain" and was founded with honorable intentions. Lee saw virtue in the back-to-Africa movement and thought that the black population could work to convince the government to help. "There may be bloodshed, but the end is worth the sacrifice." Schuyler, however, was adamant. Garvey was "unquestionably a great rabble rouser," but he "was and is without executive ability." More important, he was "a man who robs and deceives his followers," and the notion that the U.S. and African governments would help subsidize the back-to-Africa movement was unlikely at best. "Garvey and his disciples are all wrong." Lee fired back in the *Courier,* blasting Schuyler's "ridiculously puerile" attack on Garvey. "Every reasonable man knows" that Garvey's honesty and integrity "are beyond reproach."[4]

In April 1933, Lee wrote an editorial for the *Afro* in response to the conviction of Scottsboro Boy Haywood Patterson, turning his frustration at the verdict into a screed against white Christianity. "Young people have listened with extreme fortitude to their absurd and asinine ravings about their white God," he wrote, "but from the treatment accorded us, the way that innocent members are lynched and crucified on the cross of prejudice and white supremacy, we are forced to the conclusion that Christianity is a huge joke, and only serves to further the unjust oppression and exploitation of us, and that this god is a myth."[5]

Lee soon produced "The Future of the Negro," a controversial pamphlet that examined the black experience in the wake of economic collapse, which hit the black community twice as hard, first because of financial hardships and second because of the "fear and hate" propagated by angry, disaffected whites. Thus, he concluded, the "only hope of economic salvation lies in the redemption of Africa." W. E. B. Du Bois, Schuyler, and others were opposed to the back-to-Africa movement, argued Lee, but their leadership had proven to be a failed proposition in the face of the Great Depression. Lee defended Marcus Garvey's ideas, acknowledging his faults and that he "erred in the execution of some of his plans," but concluding that his ideology was sound, and the vast majority of his critics acted out of jealousy more than anything else.[6]

Lee was released from prison in early March 1934. Finally free, he married Lucile Davis in Baltimore in October and announced that the couple would head south after the wedding so that he could meet some lecturing obligations. It was a discouraging trip. South Carolina tenant farmers were "on the verge of starvation." Charleston was even worse than the rural areas. Residents were "wholly at the mercy of the whites." Housing conditions were virtually unlivable. The high school curriculum was incomplete. The streets in "the colored ghetto of this historic city of the South" had no paved streets or sewer system. Even more problematic for Lee was the state of the black business community compared to the one in Baltimore. "There are 40,000 people here, and they do not have one decent restaurant, store, or barber shop." There were plenty of churches, however, and the ministers seemed to be the wealthiest black residents of the city. "They have fairly decent homes and ride in sumptuous automobiles, while those who support them live in houses not fit for dogs to live in." Even worse, the city had surrounded a large oak tree on Ashley Avenue with a fence. It had been the sight of twenty lynchings, "and the good white folks are preserving it as a warning to other dark-skinned brethren."[7]

The residents of Charleston did not take kindly to his interpretation. Writing to the *Afro*, E. B. Burroughs, the president of Charleston's branch of the NAACP, countered that even in the poorest section of Charleston, all of the streets were paved; the tree on Ashley Avenue was never the site of a lynching, much less twenty; and there was a relatively thriving black business infrastructure in the city. But Lee wasn't just inaccurate, he was a con artist, Burroughs charged, adding that Lee had colluded with a "local newspaper man" to create a business guide for the black community. This "Negro Business Guide," however, was less to help Charleston and more to help Lee and his associate, who "charged anything they could get, some 75 or 50 cents, for the same size space. There was no proofreading done and it was printed on paper that was about the cheapest obtainable." Lee's visit was nothing more than "a grand racket." Burroughs's response was one of several angry reactions the paper printed in its pages, all from residents of Charleston who saw no truth in Lee's report.[8]

Lee acted as a correspondent for the *Afro* as he made his way down the coast. After Charleston, Lee ventured to Savannah, Georgia, where he found conditions no better. He reported on the Coffee Bluff community, a group of fishers on the Coffee Bluff River. He spoke of the "tribesmen" there as if he were on an exotic safari. The people lived in "old and dilapidated" log cabins, near "three or four white families who live close enough to exploit them." Their food, their lifestyle, and their sanitation were substandard. There was no public school. The people were "filthy and unsanitary." And they were always under the thumb of local whites.[9]

Lee had not given up his militancy. While in Savannah, he took a trip to the still-active Hermitage plantation "where I saw one hundred or more male members of my race working for one dollar per week." A white caretaker took him on a tour of the grounds, showing him the meager slave huts that were still on the premises, the auction block, and the overseer's house. The sights "made me feel like crying, fighting, doing anything to avenge the wholesale atrocities perpetrated upon my people." As he was leaving, he was stopped by "two little ragged colored boys" who offered to show him "de big oak whar dey usedta hung de slaves." Devastated again, he "drove back to Savannah, packed and left."[10]

In December, Lee reached Jacksonville, which, whether part of the initial plan or not, turned out to be his final destination. There he submitted a tortured report to the *Afro* about Granville G. Bennett, a black man beaten to death by white police officers after he refused to confess to stealing some clothes. "Citizens of this prejudice-ridden city are in an uproar," he reported. The local NAACP was "making a thorough investigation" and sponsoring a private autopsy.[11]

Lee's goal was a paper of his own, and with only fifty-four dollars in December 1934 he founded the *Jacksonville Mirror*, the first of many such creations over the course of his career.[12] While a prison sentence was a unique entrance into the business, Lee's path to publishing—experience in journalism without a formal education—was common. For example, Henry Houston, publisher of the *Charlotte Post*, a contemporary paper of Lee's *Mirror*, began his work in the business as an office boy at a young age. "I have never had but one job outside of the newspaper business. That was when I worked as an insurance agent for several years," said Houston. "I attended the city schools and have never been to nobody's college."[13]

To fill the gaps between his reporting and editorials, Lee—like Henry Houston before him—became a member of the Scott Newspaper Syndicate, but his time in Jacksonville was short. The *Mirror* billed itself as "Jacksonville's only colored standard newspaper," but it wasn't, and that bravado combined with Lee's penchant for sensationalism precipitated a "double-barreled newspaper war" between the *Mirror* and the rival *Florida Tattler*, published by Porcher Taylor, throughout the first months of 1935. The "war" crescendoed with Lee swearing out a warrant against Taylor for criminal libel, claiming that a *Tattler* article "hurt his paper's circulation and damaged his reputation" when it described his criminal past. The *Afro-American* wanted no part of the conflict. In a letter to Taylor, *Afro* president Carl Murphy explained that Lee did not work at that time for his paper. "He was an unpaid member of our staff at one time. You have our permission to give him the devil." Lee ultimately solved his problems in Jacksonville by leaving. After six months, he sold his paper for $2,000 to Walker Commercial College.[14]

After his exit from Jacksonville, Lee maintained his association with both the *Afro* and syndication services like the Associated Negro Press. His exposé detailing the lives and "actual slavery" of Tennessee sharecroppers appeared under an ANP heading in June. He produced a similar report on the horrors suffered by Texas sharecroppers the following month for the *Afro*. In July 1935, he wrote to Murphy about his trip through Texas and his plan to travel west through the remainder of the year. "If you would like for me to write some exclusive stuff for the *Afro* while on the Coast at space rate I would be glad to." And he did just that, sending several pieces to the *Afro-American* and the ANP during his travels.[15]

In February 1936, Lee reported for the ANP on the NAACP's successful push to get Western University graduate Benjamin Price admitted to the University of Maryland Law School. It was an early example of Lee's positive contact with and reporting on the NAACP, a position that changed drastically in the decades to come.[16]

That summer, Lee again hit the road, even traveling to Birmingham for an ANP interview with the Scottsboro Boys. In that interview, Haywood Patterson told Lee that he and his fellow defendants would be willing to be represented by local Alabama lawyers instead of their current team, headed by New York attorney Samuel Liebowitz. It was something of a coup, raising Lee's profile and helping establish his credentials. The problem for Lee, however, was that even with successful scoops, he couldn't seem to avoid controversy. Libel charges and financial problems dogged him throughout 1936. He eventually left the road in Topeka, Kansas, and settled down (as much as Lee ever settled down) and began publishing another newspaper, the *Capitol Plaindealer*, again contracting with the Scott Syndicate in September 1936.[17] This newspaper was a modification of an older paper, the *Topeka Plaindealer*, which he took over after marrying Thelma Chiles Taylor, the daughter of its founder, in July. Lucile Davis had died of pneumonia in February.[18]

Lee continued his tendency toward investigative journalism in Topeka. One advertisement for the *Plaindealer* announced, "It is chuck full of real live news—you must read this paper—it is the eyes and nose of Topeka—sees all and prints all worth printing." His activism also spread beyond the bounds of writing. In January 1937, for example, he headed an interracial Kansas delegation of the National Unemployment League on a trip to Washington, D.C.[19]

But the *Plaindealer* folded, and soon Lee was on the road again, this time moving to North Carolina to start other papers. As of September 1937, Lee listed himself as the general manager and managing editor of the Outlook Publishing Company, headquartered in Winston-Salem and publishing the *Winston-Salem Outlook*, the *Greensboro Tribune*, and the *Forsyth Liberal*.[20]

In late 1938, he left North Carolina to take over the *Savannah Journal*. Savannah was in the heart of the region he had found so offensive earlier in the decade. From there he reported on mob violence, acts of racial terrorism, regional elections, and the failures of Jim Crow. Both for the *Savannah Journal* and in his freelance reporting for the *Afro*, he did his best to publicize local lynchings. He also worked with attorney Austin Walden of the Georgia NAACP to help stay the execution of Marion Hunter, a black Savannah man accused of killing five people, because black people had been excluded from the grand jury.[21]

Lee's advocacy always tended toward the dramatic. In May 1940, he told the story of Leroy Linzy, a black man from Marlow, Georgia, who had "been held in peonage on a turpentine plantation owned by D. B. Warnell, a State Senator, for eleven years and threatened with a stretch on the chain gang if he left." Linzy escaped, and accomplices took him to Savannah, where Lee contacted the FBI. Fearing for the lives of his family, however, Linzy made his way back to Marlow, where he planned to murder the foreman of the plantation. Lee rushed to the scene, saving Linzy and ultimately helping to steer the case into federal court. It was a clear acknowledgment of debt peonage and the fight against racism, which overwhelmed many of the black citizens of Georgia. Lee also reported on Ku Klux Klan activity in nearby South Carolina.[22]

His activism could be a frustrating endeavor. At one point, Lee wrote to Murphy about the possibility of writing an exposé about black journalism in the South called "Editing a Paper in Hell," which had been prompted by watching a judge sentence a black woman to thirty days in jail "because a poor white man said she cursed him." He described a litany of racial injustices that he witnessed every day. "You don't have the slightest idea about the pressure that is brought to bear on a colored editor in Georgia, if he has manhood." A similar letter referred to the region as Hades. "When I leave here," he told Murphy, "I don't even want to see the south on the map."[23]

Later in 1940, he made his escape, this time heading north to Newark, New Jersey, and leaving the Scott Syndicate to work for his original benefactor full time. In October 1940, the *Afro* board authorized the creation of a Newark office, with Lee at its helm. "It is necessary to be extra careful, temperate and discreet in handling affairs because your main job is to keep business running smoothly without breaks and to keep everybody working harmoniously yet productively at highest efficiency," Murphy told him. "You are in charge of the office from now on."[24] By all accounts, Lee's relationship with the home office seemed to be strong. In December 1941, he joined a local Newark committee to promote the sale of war bonds. The following month, he accepted an award for his *New Jersey Afro-American* "for most progress during the year." In September 1942, the *Afro-American* included Lee in a feature about those who "make the wheels go round in 6 *Afro* offices."[25]

In March 1942, he appealed to the Fair Employment Practices Committee (FEPC) to hold hearings in Paterson, New Jersey, because of the number of defense contractors refusing to hire black workers. He ran a photo, reprinted in the *Baltimore Afro*, of his donation on behalf of the paper to the Bridgeton chapter of the NAACP to help the organization prosecute a white police officer accused of killing a black man in Atlantic City. He reported favorably on an NAACP investigation into a May 1942 race riot on Long Island. He reported on the plight of black southern migrants trying to escape the horrors of tenant farming, who then found themselves in Farm Security Administration camps that were desolate and poorly maintained.[26]

In late October 1943, just months before his break with the paper, Lee penned an editorial castigating southern senators for killing an education bill that would have provided millions of dollars of funding to public schools. It was a stand he wouldn't continue to take for long. In late September, the *Afro*'s personnel director had filed a critical report on Lee's management of the Newark office. "Mr. Lee must be told that it is up to him to get along with his staff as a means of developing a closely-knit and productive unit," the report said. "If he cannot curb his temper and use of profanity, he should be removed as manager and given a roving assignment." The Newark operation had been "loose" and had "carried on without due regard to company rules, regulations and directives." The personnel director had traveled to Newark to investigate in response to accounts that Lee had brandished a gun during one office row. In December 1943, Lee's circulation manager was arrested in the office for marijuana possession. At that point, Carl Murphy designated Lee for assignment and deposed him from the Newark office.[27]

Even that minimal version of employment was short lived. By April 1945, Lee had severed all ties with the *Afro* and formed the *Newark Telegram*, originally a typical black weekly featuring local news and crime stories. A March 1946 editorial, for example, pilloried Senator Albert Hawkes for not supporting the FEPC, and a bold announcement told the paper's readers to "Join the NAACP."[28] But it did not remain typical for long. Freed from the constraints of established journalistic operations in Baltimore, Pittsburgh, and Atlanta, Lee and his paper underwent a significant change.

In 1948, the *Roanoke Times* reprinted an editorial from Lee's *Telegram*. He had returned to the South, as he had done in 1934, traveling to meet with newspaper distributors, but he came away with a vastly different impression of the region he once condemned. "The racial lines in the South are so clearly drawn and defined there can be no confusion," he wrote. White and black were separated, and that separation served as a functional road map of stores and restaurants that were amenable to black customers. Segregation allowed everyone to "know the score," unlike the situation in New Jersey, where racism was diffused but omnipresent. In addition, segregation also helped foster the development of a black middle class of business owners who, specifically because of segregation, had a captive audience for their services or products. "There are some sore spots down there," he argued, "but it is not as bad as it is painted." It was not hatred that whites felt toward black people, but instead a feeling of superiority that could be mitigated by an expansion of black capacity. "White people of this country are not only our friends, but they want to see us get ahead as a race." Black activists did not need to spend money trying to convince white people that they were equal. They should simply "fight for recognition, justice, civil rights and equality" within the race and "demonstrate to the world by our living standards, our conduct, our ability and intelligence that we are the equal of any man." The white South would then accept the black South on its own terms.[29]

This was a Washingtonian message that was a full turn from his earlier impressions of the South. It was also a more extreme version of what many of his fellow Syndicate and southern editors chose to emphasize. Percy Greene's *Jackson Advocate*, for example, highlighted black success stories in Mississippi's capital and often criticized its black citizens for contributing to some of their own problems. The reasons for Lee's about-face remain a mystery, but whether the change was based on opportunism to create publicity, bitterness over his break with the *Afro* and other established black news outlets, a sincere (if bizarre) philosophical change, or some combination of the three, it was clearly one that white southerners liked. Virginia senators Harry Byrd and A. Willis Robertson both read Lee's editorial into the *Congressional Record*, Byrd describing it as "one of the most accurate and clearest presentations I have ever seen of the racial controversy," an article that "should be read by every patriotic American."[30]

Patriotic black Americans were not as impressed. John McCray of the *Lighthouse and Informer* formerly had a cordial relationship with Lee. "I am the man who established the *Lighthouse* originally," Lee said. "I had McCray running it for me, but it made no money, so I turned it over to Mc-Cray." That was true, and though he didn't stay with it long, the *Lighthouse* became by far the most successful endeavor founded by Lee. But Lee's editorial supporting segregation turned the two into foes. "To Governor [Strom] Thurmond and the several daily newspapers" that quoted and reprinted Lee's editorial, McCray suggested that they "check on the gentleman." Lee had come to the South "to do some of the bountiful business he now says exists" in the region, founding the *Savannah Journal* in 1938. But he failed miserably and fled north to Newark. "In fact, the gentleman ran out on a bondsman who had bailed him out of jail on a criminal libel charge." If Lee's white acolytes wanted to champion a black message, they should choose "one for whom there is respect and esteem among Negroes. Lee has neither." In reference to Lee's work prior to December 1943, McCray assured readers that "his worshippers' eyes would pop out if they could but read some of the views he wrote eight years ago." He closed by arguing that "white people sometimes commit monstrous blunders by clinging to words of a Negro they know nothing about."[31]

McCray's criticism continued in the following issue of his weekly, and he reported on the letters he had received from "irate South Carolinians" who said that Lee was "a traitor and nincompoop" who ran a "trashy journal." McCray added, "The Negro newspaper people would be very happy were the Dixiecrats to adopt him permanently." The *Afro-American* also excoriated its former employee: "It should be the responsibility of reputable individuals and organizations to bring these impositions to their attention promptly. Nothing spreads faster than a lie." By October 1948, Thomas W. Young, president of the National Negro Publishers Association, had publicly denounced Lee, explaining that he was not respected among the community of black journalists and should not be assumed to be representative of that fraternity. The final word on Lee's editorial came from Lester Granger, executive director of the National Urban League, who considered Lee's "cringing editorials on the South and the colored citizen as the most harmful action taken against our case by any colored American."[32] And that kind of harm made Lee a celebrity among white supremacists.

In the late 1940s, Lee published an article titled "Black Supremacy" in the right-wing anticommunist magazine *Plain Talk*. He used the space to ridicule black congressman Oscar DePriest for attempting to integrate a Washington, D.C., restaurant owned by white North Carolina congressman Lindsay Warren. In the summer of 1948, Lee went after "outside agitators," claiming that they were destroying the racial balance in the South. Thurmond, as noted by Sid Bedingfield, "hailed Lee as the true voice of black southerners."[33]

Lee's work continued to be a favorite of white southern congressmen and newspapers. In 1949, Louisiana senator Allen Ellender read another Lee editorial into the *Congressional Record*, this one in response to the Truman administration's proposal for federal civil rights legislation. "Does Mr. Truman and the advocates of civil rights know that millions of Negroes in the South are not affected by segregation and discrimination?" Lee asked, in a complete reversal of the reporting in his early journalistic career. He argued that the region provided the best potential base for future economic growth, despite its general poverty. "The South is still the poorest section of our Nation," he concluded, "and it is only human that southern whites will provide better schools, hospitals, etc., for their own than for Negroes. After all, they carry the bulk of the tax load."[34] This was a message that Ellender and his colleagues wanted heard and a message that gave Lee the publicity to keep his fledgling business afloat.

It was also a message that veered sharply from that of Booker Washington, who never argued that "it is only human" that white schools and hospitals would receive more economic resources than those for black students and patients. That isn't to say that black southern journalism was not generally more conservative than its northern counterpart. "When it comes to Negro newspapers you can't measure Birmingham or Atlanta or Memphis Negroes by a New York or Chicago Negro yardstick," claimed an SNS editorial. The *Atlanta Daily World* maintained a staunch position against Jim Crow and its effects in the post–World War I world, but after World War II, when the movement became more intense and organized, the *World* turned to protect the status quo. "Undoubtedly," notes Henry Lewis Suggs, "the *World*'s 'conservative' approach was a turning point in the history of black journalism in Atlanta." At no point, however, did anything published in the *World* advocate discrimination or superior facilities for whites because "they carry the bulk of the tax load."[35]

In a 1950 editorial, Lee returned to a still problematic but far more Washingtonian position. "It appears to me that the first things should come first, and that our economic well-being is of greater significance than the privilege or right to attend a white school or to associate with white people on an equal basis provided by Supreme Court decisions and pressure legislation." He argued that he wanted to see black people "enjoy every right, privilege, and opportunity enjoyed by any other American," but he opposed "agitation designed to deprive the other fellow of a right to be associated with his own kind exclusively, if he so desires." He cited the NAACP's graduate school desegregation cases in Oklahoma and Texas and argued that a handful of graduate school entries "is of no benefit to the millions of our people who are in need of the bare necessities of life." Black educational success, he argued, had always been funded by white people, through legislative decree and, most important, tax dollars. Thus "instead of spending thousands of dollars to finance unnecessary court fights for privileges which will cost the race millions in lost valuable friendships and racial good will, our leaders should go into the Negro ghettoes and force the local grocer to carry prime meats and sell to our people grade A products which will make us healthy."[36]

It was not a good argument, depicting as it did black economics as a zero-sum game, but it was a familiar one, and it had the benefit of not being completely wrong. Still, Cliff MacKay, managing editor of the *Afro* and former editor of the *World* and the Syndicate, awarded him "this week's crocheted bandana" in November 1950. "A word of caution to 'Uncle' Lee's good white Southern friends. You better look up this brother's record (prison, that is) before you build him up so high!"[37]

Also in 1950, Lee appeared on the FBI's radar while giving FEPC speeches in Birmingham. The bureau had received information from an executive at the Southern Natural Gas Company that Lee had communist ties back in New Jersey. Lee was known "among the colored people as being a small-town racketeer and a petty extortioner." In 1943, the agency had recorded him as railing against Jim Crow in a speech and vowing to fight against it "with the backing by the National Association for the Advancement of Colored People," but something had clearly changed.[38]

"Davis Lee expresses the antithesis of the American creed when he declares that fighting for and winning justly due citizenship rights loses good will and friendships," argued the NAACP's Roy Wilkins in 1951. "On the contrary, such activity increases respect, which is vastly more important than mere good will." He made the point that Lee's demands for economic redress were not exclusive of rights activism. "Among the colored, there is a decreasing number of honest Uncle Toms who really believe that colored people must accommodate themselves to the whims of white people just because whites are white and colored are not," Wilkins said. "Then there are dishonest Uncle Toms, full of a kind of guile, industriously working their own accommodation racket for their own benefit." Wilkins didn't name Lee as one kind of Tom or another. But he was a Tom, and thus he was a problem.[39]

E. D. Nixon, founder of the Montgomery Voters League and a leading member of Alabama's Progressive Democratic Association, was among those who signed a public letter printed in the *Montgomery Advertiser* protesting a 1953 planned appearance by Davis Lee at the city's municipal auditorium. It worked. Only seventy-five people showed up for the speech, and only twenty-five of those were black.[40] "All kinds of wild stories are being told about the poor down-trodden Negro; how he lives in terror 24 hours a day," Lee had written in his *Telegram* in 1952. "It so happens that I just returned to Newark from these States under attack, and I found none of these conditions." Lee acknowledged that "there have been two or three isolated instances" of violence and injustice, but they were rare occurrences. Herman Talmadge, the white supremacist governor of Georgia, was scolded as "a bigot and a Negro hater," but "he is neither." It was a strange ledge from which to dive and was, of course, completely wrong. "What Governor Talmadge is doing for Negroes speaks much louder than anything he could say against them." But as shocking as such statements were, his pronouncement about Charleston, South Carolina, was perhaps even more problematic: "I was in Charleston recently; I found more democracy being practiced there than in any northern or eastern city where I have visited. There is no Negro section there. Negroes live everywhere, and on most streets the next door neighbor is white."[41] Not only were these statements completely false, but they were a direct contradiction of his earlier outraged writing about his experience in Charleston. There are methods of circuitous reasoning that could perhaps place this version of Lee's thinking in a theoretical line with his former Garveyist bent. But proclaiming the virtues of white Charleston was a renunciation of the most basic principles that Lee originally had espoused.

It should come as no surprise that Lee opposed the Supreme Court's *Brown* decision. Southern states had spent millions of dollars to "give Negroes equal school facilities," Lee wrote in 1954. "Now after these States have spent millions as they were requested to do, a group goes back into courts declaring that the Negro is not now satisfied with equal facilities, that the separate but equal law is unconstitutional, that nothing less than integration will do. That doesn't seem fair to me."[42]

He continued to make that case. Lee's *Newark Telegram* editorial on *Brown* and integration as a bad idea was republished in full on the front page of J. Oliver Emmerich's *McComb Enterprise-Journal*, a white Mississippi paper that had been searching for black voices opposed to *Brown*. "Southern Negroes may lose a lot more than they gain. Integration in the North and East is not a howling success. This movement to integrate the schools of the South is loaded with more racial dynamite than appears on the surface and the Negro will be the one who is blown away." Again, Lee's argument was defensible (if ultimately wrong) and not as accommodationist as much of his later material seemed. Still, the *Savannah Tribune*, a Scott Syndicate paper, slammed Lee's views: "We have our doubts about any literate Negro who says he willingly accepts the practice of segregation and discrimination."[43]

In 1955, Lee's willingness to do just that convinced the FBI to try to develop him as an informant. His newspaper, the *Telegram*, took "a position concerning the Negro Question indicating that the Southern Negro has not been treated too badly by the White." That sounded good to the bureau, but Lee was "a controversial figure" and had "been charged with several minor violations concerning obscene literature." In addition, the FBI's Savannah office had approached Lee about the possibility, and he had declined. The bureau decided not to press the issue.[44]

In the spring of 1956, Lee began giving speeches in Alabama school districts, invited by county superintendents of education to discuss integration, with the obvious intent of demonstrating that even black experts disagreed with the idea. In 1957, he argued that the Supreme Court "has given the Negro civil rights in exchange for jobs, bread, and shelter." The minimum wage had led to the firing of thousands of black workers. Farm policy "threw thousands of Negroes out of jobs and homes." Northern companies that were building factories in the South to avoid the reach of unions only hired white workers. Job opportunities would supply economic opportunity, and economic opportunity would take care of education and politics. "Don't promise [black people] civil rights and full access to the ballot, and flood the Nation with Hungarian refugees to take his jobs." Of course, the problem with such claims is that civil rights and economic opportunity were not mutually exclusive propositions. Still, those arguments, however wrong, were not incendiary. Similar misinterpretations of cause and effect befuddle many political thinkers today. Business owners did take advantage of the minimum wage to fire black workers. Northern factories did run from unions and discriminate in hiring. Lee's mistake was in tying the opportunism of racist business practices to governmental civil rights policy or, even worse, to black southerners themselves. What began as a wrongheaded but understandable argument devolved into absurdity, but it did get him the publicity he craved. In another editorial, he claimed that North Carolina's "Negro schools, in most instances, are better than the white."[45]

During this period Lee relocated to the region he had once seen as hell, settling in Anderson, South Carolina, and forming the *Anderson Herald* (while still sporadically publishing editions of his *Newark Telegram*). In 1958, Lee sent letters to white businesses in South Carolina to solicit funds for a special school edition of his *Herald*. "I know that you do not operate a business to accommodate Negroes, but I am sure that you are interested in the current efforts afoot to force integration upon the races in the south," he told them, before explaining that "Negro schools are better, newer and more modern than the white schools" and that black South Carolinians would understand if they just had a black voice explaining it to them. Of course, he needed advertisers to make such a project happen.[46] These letters provide a glimpse into Lee's potential motives. With established black papers no longer supporting him, his stories became calculated to curry favor with a new and wealthier set of benefactors.

"The liberals, who are frothing at the mouth and shedding crocodile tears over the plight of the poor Negro in the South, will gladly give him integration, but won't give him a job or provide his family with clothing or bread," Lee wrote. "Negroes can't eat integration. They need jobs. They need the opportunity to develop their talents. The South is the only section of the Nation that offers such opportunities."[47] Claims such as these echoed those of Tuskegee and had the ability to convince white moderates of their veracity in a way that his more phantasmagorical claims never could. And that made them matter more. It made them more dangerous.

Lee's later journalism was concerned about white reaction in the extreme, in large measure because, as Maxwell Brooks noted in 1953, the principal interest of the black press and its publishers was profit.[48] That interest drove an emphasis on circulation, and the desire for higher circulation led the papers to publish the kind of content their readers wanted. And readers wanted militancy. The direction of that militancy, it turned out, could be variable.

Of course, the profit motive and militancy also fed Lee's paranoia and self-aggrandizement. When his battles with the South Carolina NAACP began, his persecution complex metastasized in earnest. "Roy Wilkins has set the NAACP up as the national clearinghouse for Negro thought and opinion," he said. "If a Negro leader expresses himself, and his expressions do not coincide with the policy of that organization, he will be discredited and destroyed. This has happened dozens of times." While this was untrue, it was understandable how a dissenter would come to such a conclusion. But Lee was not satisfied without a liberal dose of hyperbole. "The NAACP is a vicious, undemocratic, un-American organization that is dedicated to the destruction of our way of life," he claimed. "Racial strife, dissension and prejudice [are] sweeping this Nation like a prairie fire as the result of pressure and agitation by this irresponsible organization."[49]

Lee proclaimed in a 1959 edition of his *Anderson Herald*, "Let me state here that I am not an Uncle Tom and I feel that I am a full-fledged, true-blooded American." He just did not believe in forced integration. But in the same article, Lee made the case that "the southern white man taught us to believe in the real God, and in Christ, the Saviour of all men, black and white. This one revelation changed us from a savage into the likeness of God with a soul to save." This was an odd subject for someone claiming not to be an Uncle Tom: "The slaveowners had so much faith in us, that when they went off to the War Between the States over us, that they left black men behind to care for their wives and children. They could not have paid us a finer tribute than this."[50]

In December 1958 the NAACP's Roy Wilkins had penned a letter to the organization's Anderson, South Carolina, branch. He admitted, "We do not know what motivates Mr. Lee. We do not know whether it is the revenue he receives from white advertisers and contributors or whether it is some other factor. We do know that he faithfully follows the line laid down by the White Citizens Councils and other race hate organizations." Wilkins said that Lee "publishes what he calls a list of the members of the NAACP in Anderson, S.C. This is a White Citizens Council trick. It is doing the white man's dirty work for him." Lee was "a Negro editor toadying to the enemies of the Negro."[51]

In February 1959, Lee responded with a lawsuit against the national and Anderson chapters of the NAACP, claiming libel and asking for half a million dollars. The criticism, he argued, was retribution for his publication of the membership list of the local NAACP. He also filed suit against the *Baltimore Afro-American* for running the story and including excerpts of his letter to white businesses. He then sued its satellite offices in Newark, Philadelphia, and Richmond.[52]

In June 1962, Lee sued the Anderson District Five school board for not allowing him to use one of the black high schools for "a banquet to honor worthy Negro employees who have worked on a job for 15 or more years." Of course, from his perspective, the board's refusal was the result of NAACP manipulation. "There is no other Negro in this nation who has had the courage, intelligence and the know-how who has publicly opposed the NAACP." The schools allowed the NAACP to hold meetings, but Lee was unable to hold his banquet. He interpreted this as a conspiracy and predictably sued. "The Negro leaders in Anderson could provide the forum for NAACP agitators to peddle their fraudulent stock in trade, and help raise money to create strife and bitterness in our state, while thousands of little Negroes in our midst lack food, shelter, heat, medicine," Lee wrote.[53] It was yet another quixotic effort.

When a group brought a class action suit against South Carolina to integrate the state parks, Lee filed an answer to the original complaint, arguing that as a member of the racial group filing the class action, he was opposed to their claims. He also filed a countersuit, citing the South Carolina NAACP as his principal target and asking for $10 million. He argued that the attempt to integrate the parks would lead to their closure. "Now if the state did close all of the parks, who would be hurt?" he asked in an editorial. "The answer is simple, it would be little Negroes and little white people." The suit was, in his mind, an obvious ploy by the NAACP to raise funds for its coffers on the backs of those most vulnerable. It was an argument that had long since run its course and no longer convinced anyone.

He lost on both counts: the Fourth Circuit Court of Appeals ruled in April 1964 that the parks had to be integrated and that Lee had no standing to include additional parties in his counterclaim.[54]

Despite the drama, or perhaps because of it, Lee was still attempting to expand his business during this time. He had formerly published the *Savannah Journal*, which came under heavy criticism from many outlets, including the *Los Angeles Sentinel*, which referred to the paper as a "scandal sheet." In December 1960, Lee essentially took over the venerable *Savannah Tribune*, eighty-five years old and one of the papers that originally had criticized his pandering. But it was an uneasy marriage. Lee had negotiated a price of $20,000 with Willa Ayers Johnson, to be paid over the course of what he described as a six-month "lease with an option to buy." Lee's lawsuits against the NAACP in South Carolina, however, made Johnson incredibly uneasy. The problem became more acute after students boycotted a local high school when its principal was fired by the white school board. Lee's *Tribune* supported the firing and denounced the "NAACP students strike." It was the last straw, and in May 1961 Johnson and her husband shut down the plant and changed the locks. Lee interpreted the move as the result of collusion with the NAACP and sued for $250,000 in damages, charging that there was a conspiracy between Johnson and the Savannah branch of the rights group.[55]

In 1962, Lee went even further, visiting Jackson to meet with the Mississippi Sovereignty Commission in an effort to raise money for the lawsuit against the South Carolina NAACP. He met with Governor Ross Barnett himself ("the most cordial and gracious chief executive that it has been my pleasure to meet"). A federal judge had issued a ruling that South Carolina schools had to integrate by September 1962 or lose federal funding. Lee claimed the law was unconstitutional and wanted to fight it. He argued that white southerners "would not get to first base" pursuing the case, but "if Negroes would institute such proceedings, the whole world would sit up and take notice." Lee was game for the job, but he hoped for a stake from the commission. "If I could get $15,000, I could stop these pressure groups and the federal government in their tracks." The Sovereignty Commission's director, Albert Jones, responded to Lee, encouraging his "very good idea and effective efforts in process." Fifteen thousand dollars, however, was unrealistic. The commission politely declined.[56]

By 1963, Lee was publishing his *Herald* only sporadically, but it remained caustic. In an opinion piece that year, for example, Lee blamed civil rights "pressure groups and the Kennedy Administration" for the state of "the race issue." South Carolina in no way restricted black voting, he argued. The fact that so few black voters were registered was the result of apathy bred by the civil rights movement itself. "Dr. Martin Luther King, Jr., and his organization," he wrote, "has done the Negro more harm than good." King and his contemporaries were opening themselves to the possibility of becoming the tools of communism, and "one of the greatest tragedies that could befall any race is to have its youth contaminated by communistic controlled and directed pressure groups."[57]

North Carolina journalist Reed Sarratt classes editors like Lee as the exception, but notes that "a few Negro editors" called for the maintenance of segregation, arguing that "the help of the white man was necessary to Negro progress and that the greatest gain was to be made within the framework of a segregated society." The second part of that proposition is unquestionably true, though the first part might not accurately depict Lee's thoughts. White Charleston editor Charles Waring considered promoting Lee as a bulwark against integration, but after learning about both his reputation and his criminal past ultimately decided against it. Waring knew that Lee was critical of the NAACP, as did the NAACP, which attempted to discredit Lee in the black press. Journalist Charles H. Behling describes Lee's *Herald* as "a study of paradoxes."[58]

An internal NAACP memo tried to explain the publisher. "Generally, a person is identified in terms of his personality, character, outlook, and accomplishments. In this regard, Lee is a complex person to describe. But at first glance one notices that he is well informed and highly intelligent." His newspaper reputation was one of "being a master exposé artist," and thus he was "always feared and hated by 'upper class' Negroes." It was that fear of journalistic retaliation that bought him a level of cover for his more outlandish pronouncements. The NAACP report claimed that he was a personal friend of Roy V. Harris, president of the Citizens Councils of America: "Lee is a friend of the Ku Klux Klan and regularly addresses their assemblages." The hatred he had earned from members of his own race led to a fear for his life, and he carried a revolver. Lee kept letters of introduction from segregationist southern senators and drove around the region "in his high powered, mobile-telephone equipped convertible," meeting with white business owners and leaders, drumming up support and advertising for his newspaper. "Lee's 'program' in its pure state consist[ed] of selling segregation." He was "a dangerous man." His cultivation of southern segregationists meant that any black opposition he faced would be threatened with potential layoffs or other reprisals.[59]

This was a dramatic turn for someone who had started his career by describing his plight as "editing a paper in hell." Davis Lee continued creating controversy for the rest of the 1960s and throughout the 1970s and 1980s before passing away in South Carolina in 1987. He was, to be sure, an extreme case. But his evolution over the years and his willingness to create small-time paper after small-time paper, adjusting his position on issues and getting himself noticed so as to keep his enterprises afloat, is an example of what many black journalists, particularly those working in the South, had to do to compete for readers. Surely a case as operatic and hubristic as Lee's was not the common experience, but neither was, for example, Madam C. J. Walker's experience common to the budding black middle class of the late Gilded Age. Still, historians use her as an example because even though her experiences were bigger and broader than most, there were commonalities—selling to a black customer base and sustaining internal economic growth—with her counterpart business owners in black neighborhoods across the urban North. So too Davis Lee demonstrates what his counterpart newspaper publishers were doing in small towns across the country and the South in particular in the middle of the twentieth century. Few of them made the transition from murderer to publisher, from rights crusader to segregationist, but each had to stop and start, each relied on self-aggrandizement and syndication, and most publications ultimately had short life spans, just like Lee's myriad publications.

Despite his extremism, Lee is an exemplary model of an SNS customer. For small-time black newspaper publishers trying to exist during the racial tumult of the mid-twentieth century and in competition with larger black weeklies, editing a newspaper in hell was hard.

Chapter 8

The Life and Death of the Scott Newspaper Syndicate

Atlanta was a racist city, limiting the rights and political power of black people and at times surging violently against them. In other ways, however, Atlanta was not typical of the broader southern experience. A significant black elite, fed by the city's black colleges and the black business class centered on Auburn Avenue, was able to use its influence to gain concessions from whites, all the while, as Alton Hornsby has described, "exercising great care not to offend the southern caste system." This created a unique dynamic. "In the cities, for a long time, the South had, or seemed to have, a *stable* population," James Baldwin explained. "That is, the South was certain that the nigger 'knew' his place, the boundaries of which were, presumably, fixed forever by the existence of the Black 'middle class.' This 'class' had an exceedingly complex usefulness in the Southern city, whereas it had virtually no resonance in the North: the Northern city demolished, simply, any meaningful relationship at all between the Black and the White communities."[1]

Of course, the scope of the black elite's effect was originally limited by the white primary. But after 1946 and the fall of Georgia's primary rules, the city's black leadership was able to use its power to influence the votes of working-class African Americans and gain significant leverage in local elections. In the 1949 mayoral election, for example, a combination of upper-class whites and the vast majority of black voters reelected incumbent William Hartsfield. It wasn't a coalition as such, since nothing about the group was structured, but the overlapping interests of the two demographics became the key to Atlanta's political kingdom throughout the following decades.[2]

Though the Supreme Court in Texas's *Smith v. Allwright* (1944) had ruled the white primary unconstitutional, Georgia unsurprisingly assumed its validity in the immediate aftermath of the decision. Still, the year prior to *Smith*, firebrand governor Eugene Talmadge had been defeated in the Democratic primary by Ellis Arnall, who in 1945 was able to lower the voting age from twenty-one to eighteen and, on February 5, repealed the poll tax. This progress spurred the *Atlanta Daily World*, working in conjunction with the National Association for the Advancement of Colored People and the Atlanta Civic and Political League, to lead a drive to register black voters. But though around 3,000 voters registered, there was still the white primary, which kept many from bothering with what seemed like a symbolic (and potentially dangerous) gesture at best. The campaign was given new life, however, when Atlanta congressman Robert Ramspeck resigned, forcing a special election on February 12, 1946—a special election where the white primary did not apply. The *World*, the NAACP, and the ACPL immediately redoubled their efforts, and by election day, 6,876 black voters were registered. And Georgia's white primary was soon to fall. Just two months later, on April 1, 1946, the Supreme Court ruled in *Chapman v. King* (1946) that white primaries were unconstitutional in Georgia, just like they were in Texas. The *World* took credit for "registration of about an additional 75,000 Negroes to vote in the Democratic primaries in 1946 after removal thru the courts of the 'White Primary' bar."[3]

The special congressional election vote had been much smaller, but the black registration total wasn't marginal. Of the two leaders among the nineteen candidates, Helen Douglas Mankin campaigned for the black vote. Her principal challenger, like most of the other candidates, did not. With all but the Third Ward—which included Precinct B, the black precinct—reporting, Tom Camp had a lead of 156 votes. But 956 of the 1,040 votes cast in the Third Ward went to Mankin, giving her the victory. Columnist Thomas Stokes commented on the magnitude of the event, noting that "this election experience followed a thorough course of preparation by the intelligent Negro leadership which is taking its obligation seriously."[4]

The success in the special election increased the momentum for further registration, deemed by every black leadership group in the state as an absolute necessity after former governor Eugene Talmadge's entry into the 1946 gubernatorial race. His opponent, James Carmichael, became black Georgia's choice by default, but the effort to elect him had to be far greater than what was needed in a local congressional election. This wouldn't be an urban vote. It would be statewide. The massive new voter registration drive in 1946 was pushed heavily by the *World* at the direction of C. A. Scott. The paper encouraged registration at every turn, tracked the progress of black registrations in the state, and included registration pleas from its advertisers. All of the paper's employees were required to register. The *World* wasn't alone, as every black church, every black organization, and every black business worked for the cause. But the *World* was the binding glue for all of them, and it was unequivocal. The campaign closed on May 4 with 24,137 black voters registered, more than 21,000 of whom lived in Atlanta. Though there were 56,854 registered white voters in Atlanta, and though Talmadge still won the election, the ratio had dramatically changed.[5]

The *World* was a consistent champion of voting rights in Georgia. "That was one of the things that we emphasized greatly—voting," said Ruth Scott Simmons, youngest of the Scott siblings, "and even the struggle to get the vote." When black voters in Atlanta began to flex their political muscle in local elections, the *World* reported diligently on both the role of the black electorate and the response of city government to the clout of the new voting bloc. Mayor William Hartsfield, for example, began denouncing the vigilantism of groups like the Black Shirts and the KKK.[6]

The paper's editorial masthead beginning in 1945 quoted President Franklin Roosevelt: "The right to vote must be open to all our citizens irrespective of race, color, or creed—without tax or artificial restrictions of any kind. The sooner we get to that basis of political equality, the better it will be for the country as a whole." When, for example, two petitions were filed in federal court in July 1946 charging a massive voter purge of black registrants, one in Atlanta dealing with Fulton County, the other in Brunswick dealing with Coffee, Pierce, and Atkinson counties, the *World* trumpeted the actions on the front page, describing the intricacies of the legal maneuvers in detail. By comparison, the white *Atlanta Constitution* mentioned the filings on page fourteen.[7] The discrepancy demonstrates how vital the black southern press was in its role as a grapevine for the black population and as an alternative news source that supplemented stories underreported (or not reported at all) by the local white press.

During the 1949 election season a group of black elites in the city created the Atlanta Negro Voters League, chaired by Austin T. Walden, who had been so intimately involved with W. A. Scott's murder in 1934 and its aftermath. C. A. Scott was a member of the league, and his paper publicized its endorsements for various city and state races. The group was able to broker deals with white leaders, trading votes in exchange for favorable conditions for black residents of the city, which led historian Alton Hornsby to call Walden "the New South's first black political boss."[8]

The paper had consistently championed the hiring of black police officers for the city, and eight black men became officers in April 1948, appointed by Mayor Hartsfield in response to black political leverage. The *World* also argued loudly against two initial policies: the black officers were stationed in a basement away from white officers and were disallowed from arresting white suspects. "It was as if eight new superheroes swooped down onto Atlanta's historic Auburn Avenue area," explains the *World*'s twenty-first-century managing editor, Maria Odum-Hinmon, describing a situation similar to that in nearby Chattanooga, which also witnessed the hiring of black officers in 1948. "Hundreds of people, young and old, lined the sidewalks to catch a glimpse of them or possibly even shake their hands." Scott's paper heralded the officers, and he had also worked with officials to help choose them. "This afternoon at the Butler St. YMCA," the *World* reported in early April, "a long-awaited precedent will be set when eight Atlanta Negro police officers will assemble at their precinct headquarters and be dispatched for active duty in the city."[9]

It was a victory, but there were also brutal losses. In 1946, for example, Scott had worked with a local minister on a project to raise more than $10,000 to defend a group of black sharecroppers in Walton County after one of them allegedly stabbed a white man who was flirting with his wife. Ultimately, however, the mob had its way, and two black couples were lynched on the side of a country road outside Monroe, Georgia, in what historian Laura Wexler has called "the last mass lynching in America." The *World* covered the story in detail and with the most vigorous advocacy against lynching, sometimes using comparisons to the Holocaust perpetrated by the Nazis to drive its point home. In response to a complete lack of action by white authorities both locally and at the state level, President Harry Truman authorized a federal investigation in July, and the newly created Citizens Defense Committee met in Atlanta to raise funds to prosecute violations of black rights in Georgia. Scott spoke at that meeting and, frustrated with the lack of action in the case by August, wrote an open letter to Governor Ellis Arnall calling for "the immediate establishment of Negro units of the National Guard in this state," arguing that it would "alleviate this feeling of insecurity among the great masses of Negroes in this state, and at the same time, cause the masses of white people to realize that we have certain elementary rights secured by the constitution that must be respected." He published the letter on the front page of the *World*. The killings had renewed discussions of a federal anti-lynching law, and the paper also reported on that, but the new bill stalled and the FBI claimed to have found no conclusive evidence in the Monroe lynchings and therefore couldn't indict anyone.[10]

The paper did much the same in January 1948 when Rosa Lee Ingram and two of her sons were convicted by an all-white jury and given the death penalty for the murder of a white sharecropper the previous November. The Ingrams claimed self-defense, to no avail. Again the *World* covered the case in depth, and again the paper combined its coverage with advocacy. It raised money for the defense, and it raised money to support Ingram's remaining children. When the NAACP and the communist-affiliated Civil Rights Congress jockeyed for leadership roles during her appeal, the paper unhesitatingly sided against the communists. The Ingrams' sentences were eventually reduced to life in prison, and they were eventually freed in 1959. The case was another testimony to the paper's support of black people's rights. When the *World*'s leadership "thought that a mockery of justice had been done," writes Odum-Hinmon, "it stepped in and became an active participant in the news it covered—not just a chronicler of events."[11]

The Monroe lynchings and the Ingram conviction were signposts of the racial problems in Georgia. The lynchings in particular were a precursor to the race-baiting gubernatorial campaign of Eugene Talmadge. The *World* saw these incidents not just as a reversion to an older generation of white behavior, but as something insidious and new. "Nothing more dastardly has happened in the memory of Georgians to disgrace the name of the state," the paper editorialized. While the furor around the Monroe lynchings was fresh and while Talmadge was parading his racism around the state, a group of working-class white bigots in the city formed a new group, the Columbians, whose goal was to prevent integration in the city through force and intimidation.[12]

In May 1947, the *World* and the Syndicate worked to ensure that the state's attorney general, Eugene Cook, would follow through on the efforts of former governor Ellis Arnall to prosecute groups like the Columbians and the Ku Klux Klan. Because of public pressure, Cook promised that the "Klan case will be tried." It was a case that would be prosecuted "purely on a legal basis devoid of any political color or fanfare. Our sole purpose in bringing the suit was to revoke the charter of the Klan and we will use our best efforts to see that this purpose is accomplished." The suit commenced the following month, and the Klan responded by voluntarily surrendering its charter to the state. It was a temporary victory and a shrewd Klan move to avoid a legal ban by the courts. Cook was ecstatic at the surrender, as was the *World*, but the paper clearly understood the ramifications of the move. It "means that the order has only ended its corporate status of the national organization. The Knights of the Ku Klux Klan may apply for a new charter here or in any state. The charter has been dissolved but the Klan may still function as an organization."[13]

The tension in Atlanta, however, went beyond villains in white hoods. Postwar housing shortages in the city led to battles over affordable housing, with whites trying to carve out territory for other white residents out of already existing black neighborhoods. One agreement in particular convinced black residents on Sells Avenue to give up their homes with the understanding that black residents on nearby Ashby Street would be protected. But they were not. In early June 1947, "under cover of darkness," two white men planted a bomb between two houses in the Sells-Ashby area "in an attempt to strike fear into Negro inhabitants of the neighborhood." The bombing seemed to be prompted by the arrival in the neighborhood of "a white vegetable peddler," who had purchased the home of a black resident. In preparation for more potential violence, the residents were "instructed by police to shoot if they catch anyone about their houses attempting to bomb them." This did not stop the bombers, however, as more incidents continued through June and July. Either the local Columbians or the Klan were supposed to be behind the actions, but whoever was doing the bombing, they were continuing without being caught, leading many to assume the police were supportive of the acts. "What's the difference whether it is a Columbians' hate group, the Ku Klux Klan members or just plain white supremacists whose greatest joy consist[s] in making life hard for Negroes?" a *World* editorial asked. "It all adds up to the same thing so far as Negroes are concerned."[14]

Against that backdrop, in March 1949, Scott sent an internal memorandum to Syndicate publishers notifying them of a $50,000 libel action against the *Atlanta Daily World* by two white policemen, which had been filed under a new restrictive libel law in Georgia. The suit was in response to a report by the paper of police brutality against a black woman in her home. Scott assured the publishers he would stand by the story, which was "based entirely upon sworn affidavits by the woman concerned." He described the suit as "part of the pattern of intimidation that is taking place in the South, generally, and Georgia, particularly, as a result of action for the Civil Rights program." While Scott told the publishers that "we do not intend to be intimidated into suppressing vital news in connection with the defense of the rights of our people," he did admit that "we are exercising extra care in publishing matter that might unnecessarily cause litigation. Because, as you perhaps know, libel suits can be expensive and perhaps, completely destructive." That expense could come in many forms. The *Chicago Defender*, for example, called Georgia's statute a "new notorious libel law, believed to have been conceived for the purpose of instilling fear in the Georgia press." The suit against the *World* was the first under the stricter statute. The *World*, however, had no intention of rolling over for such tactics. The paper answered the charge by claiming that the reports were based on sworn affidavits by the victim and that there was nothing malicious about such coverage. Though the cops ultimately dropped the suit, the message had been sent.[15] This was an important moment in the evolution of black southern news coverage: the first time Scott acknowledged an intent to back off race stories that might cause legal action by white people. It was a pivot point, and the Syndicate's practical radicalism became a more conservative stance in the following decades.

According to Ruth Scott Simmons, the paper "provided an opportunity to write and disseminate news as we saw it, and as the facts presented it, because there was a problem of the general press of direct accounts by Negroes, about Negroes, and other circumstances." And that led to smaller but still significant activism. The *Atlanta Daily World*'s style sheet, for example, insisted that the names of people of all races and nationalities be capitalized, that all names receive at least the titles of "Mr., Mrs., or Mlle.," and that the first names of unmarried women be included, rather than only providing initials.[16] These were policies designed to correct the inequities of the white papers.

Then there were larger activist actions. In 1954, Frederick Mosley, a black man, was arrested in Atlanta for allegedly raping a local white woman. While he was in custody, police included him in a lineup for a different crime, and another woman accused him of rape in a 1953 incident. Mosley was a gospel singer and the father of a seven-month-old child at the time of his arrest, and he made the case to an all-white jury that no one "in his right mind" would commit such a crime with a baby at home who needed him. "I have never committed no crime like that in my life," he said, "and I never will." *World* reporter George Coleman covered the trial, highlighting the inconsistencies in the victims' testimonies and the problems with the women's memories of events and their role in police lineups. Such were minor details to the white jury, which convicted Mosley of the second rape and sentenced him to death.[17]

Coleman's coverage of the case demonstrated not only flaws in the prosecution, but outright lies by witnesses and police. Mosley had been arrested in June, just weeks after the Supreme Court's *Brown v. Board* decision. "All I know is they broke every rule they had," Coleman recalled in a later interview. "I went to the NAACP and asked them to help this

Table 5. Mean Number of Column Inches per Issue and Percentage of Coverage of Black Americans in *Atlanta Constitution*, 1950s

Category of Coverage	Column Inches (Percentage of Coverage)
Civil rights–related	8.83 (40%)
Everyday life	7.92 (35%)
Stereotypical	4.83 (22%)
Minority life	1.00 (4%)
Total	22.58 (1.25% of each issue)

Because of rounding, the percentage column adds up to more than 100%.

Source: Martindale, *White Press and Black America*, 81.

man. They wouldn't touch it." The organization wouldn't touch it because despite the lineup issue and its legal ramifications, there was also incriminating evidence that Mosley was guilty. Coleman went to other groups as well, again with no luck. Finally, he worked with Mosley's fellow gospel singers to hold programs and raise money for a series of appeals, which resulted in a series of stays of execution after clear demonstrations that evidence had been withheld from the jury. Coleman reported on all of them, emphasizing the minutiae of the case that provided striking evidence of Mosley's innocence, but also emphasizing the work done by activists and fundraisers to help the cause of freeing him. The case carried on through 1954 and 1955. Austin Walden and the NAACP did get involved to a limited degree on the legal front, particularly as the case moved into 1956, but it was ultimately a fool's errand. Mosley was executed on June 29, 1956, and in keeping with his star-crossed life, he was granted another thirty-day stay of execution just ten seconds after his death. Coleman turned to print to take the NAACP and everyone else who failed Mosley to task. "It was the greatest failure of my life," Coleman later said. His coverage never overtly declared Mosley's innocence. It remained fundamentally objective. At the same time, it was activist reporting that emphasized a case that was clearly corrupt and that did not receive comprehensive treatment in white newspapers.[18]

Coverage of black citizens accounted for only about 1 percent of the *Atlanta Constitution*'s total page space in the early 1950s (see table 5). The *Constitution* eliminated black citizens entirely from the society and financial pages and segregated a distinct "Colored" obituary section. And it was not alone. The mainstream media, David Welky has argued, played a prominent role in a "reassertion of traditional values." At the same time, "conservatives dominated the inner circle of the Associated Press." And even if they didn't, the Associated Press's dependency on its member papers inclined it to cater to perspectives those papers would support. The Kerner Commission report charged that the white press in the early 1950s demonstrated a massive indifference of white society toward black America.[19]

The black press, for C. K. Doreski, helped erase "a destabilizing, institutionally forced signification" that was part of the dominant American narrative. William G. Jordan describes the black press during this time as a "parallel public sphere" that allowed its readers to examine alternatives to mainstream coverage and arguments against dominant racial mores. Importantly, though, there was "no impermeable barrier" that "separated black discourse from the rest of the public sphere." And so there was interaction, the black press's "diminished voice" often making its way into mainstream coverage.[20]

In November 1944, the *Atlanta Daily World* had eliminated its Monday edition, the result of a "newsprint shortage and a reduction in personnel in the mechanical department." But there were still victories. In March 1947, the Senate Rules Committee unanimously voted to issue credentials to a *World* reporter for the congressional press galleries "over the protests of the credentials committee of newspaper men." Louis Lautier's credentials were hard earned. He was the *World*'s Washington, D.C., correspondent and head of the news service for the NNPA. He, the NAACP's Charles Hamilton Houston, Howard Law School's George Johnson, and others testified in front of the Senate Rules Committee before the press credentials were awarded.[21]

This success was not necessarily expected, since the paper's growth through the years was often more tenuous than it appeared. Lucile Scott (W. A. Scott's wife and the family's matriarch) explained that though her husband left all of his property and insurance policies to his sons following his murder, "he didn't put money in the bank in his name. When he died there wasn't a penny in the *Atlanta Daily World*." And so "I had to return the money back to them," to "the business."[22] By 1945, the *World* listed its circulation as 23,000 and the Syndicate's circulation at 79,950. The paper was charging nine cents per advertising line, and the Syndicate was charging thirty cents per line. The organization was staffed with roughly ten reporters that year. The office of the *World* at 210 Auburn Avenue at that time was a shotgun setup, with an editorial area just behind clerical desks in an open office, which was hugged by a corridor that led up three steps to a similar space for reporters. Even farther back was a space filled with a flatbed press, linotype machines, and hand presses, each station along the way, from the front door to the back alley, filled with ink-stained employees. "I knew it would work because it was needed," C. A. Scott later said of steering a black newspaper through the Depression and World War II. "Don't give a man something he doesn't need. That's worse than wasting their time."[23]

Scott, of course, was steering more than just a newspaper. Jesse B. Blayton, so close to Lorimer Milton and Austin Walden at the time of the murder of Scott's brother in 1934, founded WERD in October 1949, the first black radio station in Atlanta, and after it began broadcasting, the *World* provided on-air news throughout the day. Even that kind of expansion, however, was secondary to the company's syndication program. Ruth Scott Simmons explained:

> Once a week, they would send us their copy and we would print their paper. And I think what made Atlanta so well-known among blacks all over the country is that these individual papers would have predominantly Atlanta news and news of general interest to blacks everywhere. We would only give them so many pages within that paper of their local news. The front page would be mostly theirs and maybe the second or third, but for the biggest part of it, it would be the same news that was in the *Atlanta Daily World*. And by printing our paper every day at the time, we had a lot of news.[24]

And a lot of advertising. In 1948, the company dealt with 472 advertisers just for the *Atlanta Daily World*. Some were small firms, some were large. Some advertised once that year, some in every edition.[25] That was before Syndicate advertising and the revenue streams from member papers, printing jobs, and the weekly rotogravure sheet. It was a massive undertaking, one that was unique to African American publishers in the Deep South.

The population that read the papers clearly understood their reliance on advertising. Describing the Chicago black press in the early 1960s, newspapers deemed far more radical than those in the South, St. Clair Drake and Horace R. Cayton explained that readers "do not expect the Negro press to be Simon-pure; they merely expect it to be interesting and to put up a fight while it tries to make money." Still, the need to remain solvent and the increasing hold on the black newspaper trade by fewer and fewer corporate entities concerned many in the late 1940s. Walter White predicted in 1948 that the black press would ultimately cease its more radical activism because the increase in production costs and corresponding catering to advertisers would force it to subsume the desires of its readers to such overwhelming forces. Columnist Ted Poston worried in 1949 that black newspapers were "sometimes more concerned with profits than principles." Writing in 1953, however, Maxwell Brooks noted that profit as the principal interest of the black press actually drove an emphasis on circulation, and the desire for higher circulation led the papers to publish the kind of content that their readers wanted. And readers wanted militancy.[26]

Of course, the papers and their militancy were not uniform, even within individual operations. "Newspaper publishers are apt to be primarily business men whose interest in race welfare is secondary to their interest in selling newspapers," the *New Republic* explained. "It is not they, but the men they hire, who make their papers worth-while; the editors, the columnists, the reporters. These are the men who are qualified to speak of the sufferings and aspirations of Negroes, for they are still part of the race."[27]

The notion that the *World* and its subsidiaries maintained a largely conservative profile because of dependence on a white advertising base is simply false. The paper's largest advertisers were black-owned businesses, principally insurance companies, with hundreds of other Atlanta businesses throwing in. There were also thousands of classifieds and other smaller advertisements. One of the *World's* largest advertisers was the NAACP. If people were going to be offended, they were going to be offended by the ubiquitous presence of NAACP advertising over and against any specific editorial. As Roi Ottley explains, with large national, corporate advertisers providing supplemental revenues unrequired for the daily operation of black newspapers, those papers were largely free "to speak out boldly on social and racial questions" and to be "almost radical in their economic outlook." The black press remained in 1955 and 1956 much as Gunnar Myrdal had found it a decade earlier: "able to operate relatively freely and unmolested."[28] There were plenty of predatory loan and finance companies among the paper's advertisers, but they weren't going anywhere because of an editorial position either. As of the early 1950s, the *World* was not in danger of faltering financially because of a dependence on white advertising.

Its smaller subsidiary papers may very well have been in that position, particularly in the South, but those papers seemed to be the ones that raged loudest against the machine. Thus the common economic argument for what some have called southern journalistic conservatism, but was actually a more practical journalistic radicalism, a proxy advocacy, holds little weight, though that has remained the most prevalent historical understanding. Rather, a fear of some white business losses combined with a liminal position between the white and black worlds, a role as connective tissue between the two, seems to have driven much of the *World*'s policy. It was a role much like those of administrators at southern historically black colleges and universities (HBCUs), going back to the days and arguments of Booker T. Washington.

Washington and other black college leaders were responsible for sustaining viable black institutions, but they also had to take the attitudes of powerful whites into account. They were making solid middle-class citizens of their pupils and interpreting respectable blackness to white southern benefactors, and the balancing act they performed between those two worlds often made them seem like accommodationists to black critics who wanted to use their newfound collegiate educations in aid of reform. The press was another important black southern institution whose leaders walked that line between powerful whites and the black critics who wanted to use the education gained from the paper's news for more radical reform. Meanwhile, evidence abounded throughout the region that violence and bankruptcy were usually the rewards for more extreme forms of activism, which would have killed the black press, broken the grapevine, and eliminated a viable buffer in that liminal space between white and black.

In 1949, for example, there were ten different insurance companies catering to black customers that were going to keep advertising regardless of editorial policy. In total, they spent $5,024.66 on advertising in the *World* that year; the two largest contributors were the Life Insurance Company of Georgia and Atlanta Life Insurance Company. The city of Atlanta advertised often in the paper, but the total cost of those ads was only $407.12. The Atlanta Board of Education spent another $46. But five different insurance companies brought in more revenue than the city. It is possible that Atlanta would have diminished its advertising in the paper had the *World*'s editorial policy been more aggressive, but the city needed the paper to get information to its black citizens. Such relationships were mutually beneficial and more than likely would not have diminished (and certainly would not have disappeared) based on the paper's editorial bent. The Atlanta Black Crackers baseball team paid $667.16 in advertising, even in the post–Jackie Robinson era. The NAACP contributed $254.44. The National Negro Publishers Association spent $3,480.72. These businesses and organizations were among the 426 separate advertisers that paid for space in the *Atlanta Daily World* in 1949.[29] Economic fear of a strained relationship affecting white advertising dollars simply did not exist. The white advertising in the *World* was there because those companies were seeking black business; they were not acting in a charitable or subsidy role. And their dollars were exponentially outpaced by advertising from black firms with an even greater vested interest in the community.

The numbers for 1953 were remarkably similar. The Atlanta Black Crackers had folded after baseball's integration, but more radical groups like the Atlanta Negro Voters League had taken the team's place as significant advertising presences in the *World*. The National Negro Publishers Association was no longer listed in the advertising records, but its place had been taken by groups like the Westside Voters League. Atlanta advertisers had become more rights conscious in response to events of the early 1950s, making a turn away from rights consciousness by the paper, including the ads, a quixotic move at best and certainly not a necessity. The Life Insurance Company of Georgia and the Atlanta Life Insurance Company remained the largest insurance advertisers. The NAACP's advertising share increased to $387.84 in 1953. And the city of Atlanta was still advertising at roughly the same rate as it had in 1949.[30]

In 1954, despite the tumult of *Brown* and the angry white response to the Supreme Court's decision, advertising remained relatively constant. The city of Atlanta did not stop advertising in the *World*. The totals for insurance companies catering to black customers were down from their previous massive influence, but the NAACP's number was higher than ever before. Groups like the Westside Voters League and the Atlanta Business League remained a strong presence, and the white businesses that catered to black customers, both stores that were local and those that were part of national chains, kept advertising in the paper because they still wanted those customers despite the political turmoil. The NNPA returned to the paper as an advertiser in 1954, and the total number of entities advertising in the *World* rose to 451, up from the total in 1949.[31]

While the *Atlanta Daily World* was functionally synonymous with the Syndicate, the proverbial head of the snake, its letterhead and other materials described the paper as a "Member [of the] Scott Newspaper Syndicate," emphasizing the broad coalition of papers over the individual leader. Throughout the late 1940s and early 1950s, the paper employed five advertising salesmen each year. There were several commission rates, ranging from twenty-five cents to five cents on the dollar. By far the most important of those solicitors was James Russell Simmons, who outpaced his peers comfortably each month. The evolution of his success demonstrates the evolution of the paper's success. In March 1947, for example, Simmons sold just over $2,000 in advertising. In March 1948, his sales were just over $2,500. In March 1951, Simmons sold more than $3,100 in advertising. In March 1952, he sold more than $5,000 and even more than that in the following March. In the tumultuous year of 1954, Simmons's sales were down, and he collected just under $3,600 a month in ad revenue. But 1955 witnessed another spike to more than $4,700 in monthly sales. Simmons's counterparts experienced similar waxing and waning in their fortunes. The rise of sales and then the stumble in 1954 mirrored the fortunes of the southern black press in general, with postwar economic success leading to increasing stability before the civil rights movement made the market more volatile. The *World*'s size and longevity provided a hedge against much of that volatility, however. Rights fights certainly sold papers, and the paper saw a rise in circulation after *Brown*, just as Simmons and the other salesmen saw an increase in advertising revenue in 1955.[32]

In 1952, the *World* accrued $312,832.42 in gross sales, averaging $26,069.37 per month. Sales fluctuated between a low of $21,000 in August to a high of $33,000 in December. In 1953, the paper did even better, earning $330,261.33 in gross sales, an average of $27,521.78 per month, and that success was spread relatively evenly, with January, April, August, and December totals all hovering above $27,000. Significantly, 1954's gross sales remained consistent with previous years, totaling $321,892.95 and averaging $26,824.41 per month. July was the most successful month with more than $30,000 in sales, and March was the least successful with just under $24,000. These numbers demonstrate that the paper was insulated from much of the civil rights commotion around it; white retrenchment following *Brown* hurt smaller black news organizations in the South that didn't have the *World*'s pedigree. The paper had the longevity to find a baseline acceptance among white leaders. Events surrounding race rights shaped the paper's coverage and editorial position, but they did not in any significant measure affect its bottom line.[33]

Though the Syndicate presses in Atlanta printed the Birmingham paper, the organization paid printers and binders in Memphis to handle its other semiweekly. The *Memphis World* employed one principal advertising salesman and two less regular solicitors. Each week it reported its credits and debits to the home office of the Syndicate. In January 1954, for example, the paper took in $1,428.56 in revenue, the vast majority of that total ($1,043.78) coming from advertising sales. In addition, $364.11 came from newsboys, $18 from new subscriptions, and $2.67 from cash sales. Meanwhile, the paper accrued $248.22 in debits that month, its expenses including gasoline, phone calls, office supplies, stamps, truck repair and rentals, and photographs for the newspaper. It left a profit of $1,180.27, demonstrating the value of the semiweekly to the financial viability of the Syndicate.[34]

That relationship, however, still caused tension. In the fall of 1951, Claude Barnett and the Associated Negro Press had to deal with the same problems the Syndicate had given them back in the days of William Alexander Scott. Barnett desperately sought copies of member papers in order to discover whether they were using ANP material without individual subscriptions to the service, but C. A. Scott was recalcitrant. "We publish only three papers," he told Barnett, referring to the *World* editions in Atlanta, Memphis, and Birmingham. "For the other publications we serve only as printers." That was, of course, untrue, just as it had been in the late 1920s and early 1930s. "If they only serve as printers," a frustrated Barnett wrote, "why use ANP news in these other papers? Shouldn't they have individual memberships????"[35]

Scott used the same tactic in the early 1950s that his brother had used two decades prior—he ignored Barnett. "I hate to keep bothering you about the group of SNS papers," Barnett wrote to Scott in February 1952, "but it is important to us to have a chance to see the papers which ANP service is going to." The quarrel had not stopped even as the Syndicate's existence was coming to a close. In February 1955, the ANP increased its monthly cost by twenty dollars, and when Scott protested, Claude Barnett explained, "When you consider the fact that in serving the *World* we are also servicing a score of your subsidiary papers, which in one or two instances prevents our being able to sell the local paper, it seems only fair." Scott replied that there were only ten papers, not a score, and that they rarely used national news anyway. That was not true, and it had never been true, and Scott agreed to the rate hike.[36] Much of the Syndicate's success had been facilitated by its ability to take advantage of the Associated Negro Press for its member papers without paying its fair share. It seems likely that without that advantage, the Syndicate's financial solvency would have been compromised early in its life.

One way to gauge the development of the Syndicate through the 1940s and 1950s is by using the company's taxable wages and number of employees as functional indicators. As a general rule, employees in Atlanta took

Table 6. Growth of Syndicate Employees' Taxable Wages, 1940–1954

Year	Taxable Wages ($)	Number of Syndicate Employees	Number of Memphis Employees	Number of Birmingham Employees
1940	69,602.73	74	5	10*
1941	65,753.65	76	7	NA
1942	61,504.72	56	5	NA
1943	70,412.48	64	7	2
1944	84,239.27	71	8	4
1945	95,654.13	72	8	3
1946	113,300.79	66	8	4
1947	124,831.56	61	8	5
1948	145,458.40	74	7	6
1949	141,297.42	65	7	5
1950	148,675.62	76	6	5
1951	147,069.47	80	8	4
1952	154,478.82	77	6	5
1953	155,069.46	78	8	5
1954	169,855.42	78	7	5

*The high number of Birmingham employees in 1940 is the result of particularly frequent turnover that year.
Calculated from Annual Return of Excise Tax on Employers of Eight or More Individuals for Calendar Years 1940–1954, box 27, Tax Records, 1940s–1950s, Atlanta Daily World Records.

home the most pay, employees in Memphis the second most, and the few at the small *Birmingham World* the least. That trend held for menial employees as well as those at the head of the various enterprises. Lewis O. Swingler, leader of the *Memphis World*, tended in every year to make a higher salary than Emory O. Jackson, for example.[37] Birmingham's proximity to Atlanta made it more dependent on the home office. Memphis had more latitude, the need as time went on for more employees, and a workload that redounded to higher pay.

The systematic growth in taxable wages over time demonstrates that though the number of newspapers associated with the Syndicate clearly decreased, their stability made the enterprise a profitable venture. "Is the Negro press dying or growing?" asked sociologist John Burma. "Actually it is doing both—decreasing in numbers [of papers] and growing in circulation."[38] The same was true of the Syndicate (see table 6).

The company also gave significant salaries to women during this period. The second highest paid employee in Birmingham in 1944 was female. One of the salary leaders in Memphis was a woman. There were no fewer than fifteen women in the Syndicate hierarchy in Atlanta in the top third of the salary list, and only two of them had Scott as a last name.

Table 7. Yearly Payroll Totals (Gross Pay in Dollars)

	1950	1951	1952	1953	1954
Memphis	11,786.89	14,070.58	12,856.53	10,959.52	11,288.00
Birmingham	7,720.21	7,599.61	7,989.17	8,856.04	10,074.61
Operators	21,084.30	23,435.55	23,988.76	23,608.11	24,667.83
Administrative, editorial/clerical	48,247.21	52,509.13	58,108.13	58,299.55	70,465.87
Mechanical	48,405.08	52,388.24	54,882.27	59,164.18	64,925.97
Advertising	11,431.93	13,850.39	16,041.42	16,575.51	15,537.56

Payroll 1950, Payroll 1951, Payroll 1952, Payroll 1953, OBV139, 1951–1953; and Payroll 1954, OBV140, 1954–1957, all in Atlanta Daily World Records.

Demonstrating that the hiring of women in well-paid positions was no wartime necessity, there were in 1948 fifteen women in the organization with top-tier salaries, one in Memphis, one in Birmingham, and the rest in Atlanta. It is also worth mentioning that James Russell Simmons, the *Atlanta Daily World*'s principal advertising salesman, often led the company in pay, since he worked on commission. His fortunes fluctuated with those of the paper, but more often than not the situation left him in a beneficial position. That said, none of the Syndicate employees made a lot of money. As Ted Poston pointed out in 1949, "Negro newspapermen were among the lowest paid in the industry," while many publishers maintained "lavish summer homes, extensive real-estate investments, and five- and six-figure incomes."[39] The breakdown of salaries among the various employment categories is telling (see table 7).

Another method of gauging the evolution of the Syndicate in the postwar economy is to examine the company's yearly cash receipts. Of course, cash receipts are not the totality of a business's income, but they do provide a way to measure the part of the company's business coming from the Syndicate, from Memphis, and from Birmingham (see table 8). The cash receipt totals demonstrate the stability of the Syndicate's contribution to the Scott enterprise over time despite its diminishing importance to the company's overall profit. In 1936, the Syndicate's total contribution of more than $25,000 made up almost 30 percent of the Scotts' business. By 1954, that contribution was more than $28,000 but now constituted less than 9 percent of the total. The SNS maintained consistency despite the loss of newspapers over time, but because of that loss the Syndicate was unable to keep pace with the rest of the company's growth.

When the Supreme Court ruled in *Brown v. Board of Education* on May 17, 1954, coverage in the *World* was suitably celebratory, hailing the deci-

Table 8. Yearly Cash Receipts (Dollars), 1936–1954

	Total	Syndicate	Memphis	Birmingham
1936	86,765.35	25,544.90	5,847.00	133.75
1937	87,996.49	25,593.30	4,211.20	3,459.11
1938	88,480.13	26,041.06	7,014.51	3,508.80
1939	98,080.36	31,477.02	6,570.00	5,304.05
1940	–	–	–	–
1941	106,632.83	37,766.80	4,244.42	3,715.98
1942	107,517.91	36,654.61	4,021.47	2,146.65
1943	124,727.82	35,537.12	4,556.71	2,287.49
1944	154,595.11	37,008.63	1,400.00	1,100.00
1945	199,069.62	35,758.26	–	–
1946	213,689.97	33,170.85	5,600.00	3,100.00
1947	232,719.47	34,748.65	1,150.00	100.00
1948	247,241.24	33,840.42	5,100.00	4,400.00
1949	234,343.20	24,783.76	5,775.00	5,017.00
1950	246,946.60	26,645.53	9,000.00	4,300.00
1951	274,446.80	34,251.37	7,211.37	4,500.00
1952	312,856.61	28,497.82	2,350.00	3,800.00
1953	313,829.39	25,311.06	–	3,500.00
1954	324,194.89	28,112.16	–	7,200.00

Source: Cash Receipts, Yearly Totals, OBV7, February–October 1936; OBV8, October 1936–May 1937; OBV9, June–December 1937; OBV11, August 1938–March 1939; OBV13, October 1939–May 1940; OBV15, May–December 1941; OBV16, December 1941–July 1942; OBV18, October 1942–April 1943; OBV20, October 1943–April 1944; OBV22, September 1944–February 1945; OBV25, November 1945–May 1946; OBV27, August 1946–February 1947; OBV30, December 1947–June 1949; OBV32, October 1948–April 1949; OBV33, April–September 1949; OBV34, September 1949–March 1950; OBV36, September 1950–August 1951; OBV38, August 1951–January 1952; OBV41, December 1952–June 1953; OBV43, November 1953–May 1954; OBV45, October 1954–March 1955, all in Atlanta Daily World Records.

sion as representative of a country that was finally living up to its ideals. Preferring pragmatic, cautious responses, many black civic and religious leaders in Atlanta responded to *Brown* by calling for patience as courts and local leadership examined ways to move forward. Notably, and despite precedent to the contrary, the *World* was not among them. *Brown* was the "decision of the century"; it was a "giant step forward for democracy at home and abroad." The paper featured statements from local leaders and the presidents of the schools connected to the Atlanta University Center. Another article, however, cautioned black citizens against "gloating and bragging," explaining that "as in the past, [Negroes] will exhibit the same loyalty and sanity, and they will work quietly along with their fellow Americans in abiding by what the highest tribunal has handed us." It also reported on NAACP meetings to plot the implementation of desegregation. In the days that followed, the paper reported on all of the news developing in response to the decision, the debate that raged as a result, and the white southern denunciations of the Supreme Court. It reported on the responses of white southern dailies, even the most moderate of which, like the *Atlanta Constitution*, claimed to "deplore" the ruling and assured its readers that implementation would take years rather than months. Meanwhile, the *World* had daily coverage of calls by groups like the NAACP for immediate implementation. The paper's editorial page remained adamant that while respectfulness should be the watchword of the day, there could be no compromise on full active engagement of the new decree. When the Georgia governor was defiant, the paper attacked his statements. When the *Constitution* ran editorials that the *World* found problematic, it ran reasoned responses to them. This was the obvious culmination of the practical radicalism that had developed throughout the 1930s and 1940s. Or, as Odum-Hinmon has argued, the paper's coverage of the *Brown* decision "showed that when it came to matters of civil rights during this era, the newspaper spoke up fervently."[40]

As historian James Bradford Murphy has explained, the *World* attempted "to develop racial awareness among its readers to insure the psychic stability of the Negro in the face of racist theories of inferiority." It "worked for the realization of a state of security for Negroes by informing readers of their rights and of the procedures by which they were deprived of those rights."[41] That had been the established role of practical radicalism throughout the preceding two decades, and the *World* sought to play that educational role without running afoul of those who might seek to diminish those hard-won rights. While that formula functionally held past 1954, it fit less appropriately with the events that developed in the years following *Brown*.

The paper was in a controversial position during the civil rights movement. "We had the civil rights movement, on the one hand, demanding seating space at the lunch counter," explained Stanley Scott, a member of the family. "You had the *Atlanta World*, on the other hand, seeking advertisement from the department stores where the sit-inners were demonstrating. So it was a touchy problem there." In the age of civil rights, the *Atlanta Daily World*'s advocacy was spotty at best. In response to the burgeoning sit-in movement, for example, *World* editorials called for restraint. "There is no need for any group to take matters into their own hands in misguided attempts to gain civil rights, when these rights have already been guaranteed by the Constitution of the United States and interpreted and confirmed by the courts. Such attempts merely create general ill-will and set up situations that endanger the lives and property of everyone," the paper claimed. "The answer is to be found at the conference table, ballot box, and in the courts of law; to do otherwise is unsound, dangerous, and impractical."[42]

In response to the Freedom Rides, the *World*'s opinion had not changed: "Calm, quiet, intelligent approaches are the best way to solve complex problems of this sort. Fanatical emotionalism on the one part, only begets fanatical extremism as a reaction." Historian Charles Simmons describes the *Atlanta Daily World*'s editorial policy as an attempt at objectivity. There is, however, no such thing in editorials. He seems to mean a pragmatism that judges each situation independently, after gauging the possible outcomes for both the situation and the paper's best interest. "I think sometimes that when the scholars in the profession talk about objectivity they mean something else altogether," said Percival Prattis. "I think they mean dignity. I think they mean that we should fight like gentlemen and not brawl." The *Atlanta Daily World* needed to keep its circulation high for advertising purposes, which meant it could not be against the rights for which the black South was striving. At the same time, its status in mainstream white society and its desire to protect itself from reprisal meant that overt, unconsidered radicalism was also probably a bad idea.[43]

It was during the civil rights movement that the *World* ultimately faltered in the eyes of activists, earning a reputation as a conservative newspaper quite different from the period of practical radicalism prior to the onset of the first wave of civil rights. Chief among its dilemmas was a series of sit-ins in downtown Atlanta beginning in 1960. The sit-ins, like those in Greensboro, Nashville, and elsewhere, targeted large chain department stores, many of which were significant advertisers in the *World*. So the paper could either maintain its reputation by siding with rights activists or maintain its bottom line by siding with its advertisers. Desegregation, explains Alexis Scott, the third-generation twenty-first-century publisher of the *World*, was "one of those double-edged swords. The *World* fought vigorously for desegregation in its news pages, and then once it attained that goal, it hurt it financially, because they had a brain drain as well as many advertisers saying, 'Well, we don't need to advertise in a black paper anymore. We're all in one big happy family.'" It was an incredibly difficult position, considering that the paper's reputation could come at the expense of survival. Again, the Scotts faced a similar dilemma to that of HBCU administrators. Ultimately, the *World* chose against suicide.[44]

"They were really walking a tightrope," explained Stanley Scott, referring to *World* editors in the 1960s. "Because on the one hand they had to depend on the department stores for their life blood—advertising. And they had to stand up and be counted in respect to the civil rights movement." The paper argued that rights activists should keep their focus on segregated education and voting rights instead of sitting in at lunch counters. The problem with Stanley Scott's analysis, however, is that the paper's revenue stream did not make those department stores necessities for the paper's survival. The Syndicate was gone by that point, making such advertising more important than it was in the 1940s and 1950s, but the base of the *World*'s advertising base was still black.[45]

In addition, the choice to not damage its bottom line ultimately damaged its bottom line. Rival papers that criticized the *World*'s stance grew in stature and circulation. By 1969, the *Atlanta Daily World* was publishing only four editions per week. Still, it is significant that even through the controversy, the *World*'s place in Atlanta—a place it established over the course of the generation prior to World War II—allowed it to survive such a debacle. Roland Wolseley cites Louis Lomax as referring to the *World* as "the one exception" to the general rule that the black press supported the civil rights movement, and he notes the paper's infamous stand against sit-ins to make his case.[46]

The journalism career of Louis Lomax began after an education at Paine College, American University, and Yale, and his commentary on the black press and its relationship to race activism was significant. Discussing black journalism of the 1950s and early 1960s, he argued that the concentration of black businesses in the North was not significant enough to maintain journalistic independence from the need for white advertisers. The northern black press, then, was wholly willing to rail emphatically against southern segregation and race violence—in the process giving itself a reputation for militancy—while simultaneously ignoring a northern urban business climate that put a ceiling on black economic expansion, ignoring high-interest unsecured loans to black customers, and ignoring all the subtler de facto racisms that kept the northern black population struggling. "I know of one Negro editor," he wrote, "who has a fat folder full of evidence—pictures, affidavits, etc.—showing just how Negroes are swindled by some of his best advertisers. These articles will never be run. The businessmen know about the folder, however, and their ads will forever remain in the paper."[47] There was in such a relationship a kind of legitimate power displayed by the black press, an upper hand reached by blackmail, if nothing else, but it was a power that was ultimately limited in scope. As in all cases of blackmail, this power was generated by powerlessness and by need—in this case, a need to keep white advertisers—and because the advertisers still received the business that came through advertisement, it was not they who were the victims of that blackmail. It was instead the readers, those "swindled Negroes," who were the victims.

Lomax pointed out that, for the most part, the black press had been inherently supportive of the rights movement. "The lone exception is the highly respected, rock-ribbed Republican *Atlanta Daily World*." In May 1960, the paper criticized an Atlanta-area economic boycott of white businesses in black neighborhoods that refused to hire black employees in nonmenial positions. The boycott was led by students, most of whom had always seen the *World* as an Uncle Tom rag, and they also formed their own paper, the *Atlanta Inquirer*, a crusading answer to its staid counterpart. The *Inquirer*'s advocacy helped ensure that black doctors could practice in formerly lily-white hospitals, and it supported any and all efforts for black equality in Georgia. Of course, the *World* was not blind to the *Inquirer*'s popularity. Two days after its criticism of the boycott, the paper reversed course and praised student sit-ins as an effective method of change, lending its support to arrested protesters in Savannah and Atlanta. "The case of the *Atlanta World* provided a moral," Lomax concluded. "By failing to support the Negro revolt the Negro press may keep some white advertisers but it will lose its readers."[48]

But by 1960, the *World* and other black newspapers had an advantage that those in the interwar period didn't have. The mainstream press—the white press—had either endorsed the fights for equality or had, at the very least, come to accept the rule of law (whether for moral or economic reasons). In that situation, any argument from potential advertisers that they did not want to be associated with a publication that supported rights activism would have been disingenuous at best. By that time, mainstream newspapers were doing it too. Additionally, the militancy of the black press by 1960 was pushed by the desire of the white press to capture the black reading market. After decades of rights advocacy, the spending power of the black population was greater, its situation far from perfect but clearly improved from that of, say, the 1930s. With better resources and more reporters, the mainstream press was able to cover race stories with a similar advocacy and superior depth, forcing black weeklies to set themselves apart by moving further to the radical left.[49]

Such was not a factor in the interwar period. And that being the case, the *World* was not a civil rights exception in that period. It engaged in a practical radicalism that balanced its position in Atlanta society while still remaining uncompromising on issues of fundamental equality. The paper's management knew in the period prior to *Brown* that advertising wasn't going anywhere if it used its platform for rights in the formula that southern readers had come to expect. It was a desire for change combined with a desire to survive that found the scales tipped, improperly at times, after the post-*Brown* movement began.

Writing in 1951, Howard University professor Lewis Fenderson framed the role of the black press as a "four-purposed social instrument." It informed the black population about news of its members and news that affected its members. It presented a black position on issues to white society ("thus encouraging interracial understanding"). It advocated for black social acceptance. Finally, it provoked responses from the white press.[50] While it is certainly true that the black press did all these things, this book attempts to make a very different case—that the black press, in serving as a reconstituted grapevine in a repressive Jim Crow era, was concerned first and foremost with the initial item in Fenderson's list, compensating for the segregation that existed in journalistic coverage as it did in every other aspect of southern life. The positions presented to white society and the attendant responses by the white press were ultimately ancillary in the pre-*Brown* period to the creation of a social instrument specifically serving the black community.

Fenderson acknowledged a significant divide between northern and southern newspapers but also drew a sharp distinction between small and large publications. Papers from smaller cities devoted more space to articles promoting interracial harmony, whereas the larger papers sought more grandiose, lurid coverage. The tragedy of the situation, for Fenderson, was that white readers generally only had access to one or two of the larger national editions and never saw the smaller journals, which presented a far less sensationalistic picture of black and interracial life. He portrayed southern newspapers as being far more soft-spoken about the breaking of racial mores. When such stories did run, they were brief accounts, rather than longer features as they were in northern black weeklies, a necessity caused by a concern about whites' reaction. As an example, he cited a brief 1947 article in the *Atlanta Daily World* about black delegates being seated at a Republican meeting, a story that "would undoubtedly have rated feature treatment in a Northern paper."[51]

This is the well-intentioned but flawed historical understanding of the southern black press and the small-town southern press that has dominated the historiography. The life of the Scott Newspaper Syndicate demonstrates a different story. When the paper's position is seen holistically rather than caricatured through one brief example, and when the positions of its syndicated subsidiaries are also taken into account, the *Atlanta Daily World* and its contemporaries in small and large towns of the South and along the path of the Great Migration demonstrate a decidedly different picture than that of a soft-spoken surrogate unwilling to challenge racial mores.

Still, while the news articles often reappeared through syndication—even during the civil rights movement—the editorial policies were not altogether uniform. The *Birmingham World* chose not to denounce the Freedom Riders. It remained silent instead. That caution was understandable considering the violent reaction of white Alabamians to the Freedom Riders, but when the activists were jailed, the silence lifted. "In Birmingham a few days ago, some freedom travelers were placed in jail for protective custody. If this were truly protective custody, why not take them to a hotel, why treat them as law breakers? Mob leaders were not arrested. Why were they not arrested for the protection of the good community?" This wasn't advocacy for radicalism. It was a reasonable question about the nature of police claims of protective custody. On May 23, 1961, the synergy of the Syndicate still firmly in place, the *Atlanta Daily World* reprinted the editorial. It was, in a sense, the epitome of halfway advocacy, but it also was a crucial and valid protest against the behavior of the Alabama state police.[52]

C. A. Scott helped organize the Citizens Democratic Club of Fulton County and was the group's president throughout the 1940s, but he became a Republican in 1952. Scott admitted in a 1972 interview, "My mother sorta made me" a "natural born conservative." Though his paper's conservative turn on civil rights didn't happen until the early 1960s, its broader critique of national affairs was consistently Republican throughout its early history. Locally, the *World* was reluctant to specifically criticize or attack politicians. C. A.'s daughter Portia saw his Republicanism as a result of wanting to break the one-party system in Georgia. "And he liked Eisenhower," she said. "He thought he was an American hero." Still, Portia Scott argued that the *World* "was never a Republican paper."[53]

Not everyone agreed, and the Republican turn had consequences for Scott and the paper. The *World* was "bitterly denounced" for its political coverage and its editorial position. The publisher was asked to resign as the leader of the Citizens Democratic Club after announcing his support for the presidential campaign of Dwight Eisenhower and his running mate, Richard Nixon, in 1952. "The club," announced Scott's successor, "would be better off without lukewarm Democrats." Still, Scott stuck to his position. He believed that Eisenhower's victory would "bring greater economic stability domestically, eliminate waste and corruption in government and pass the phases of the civil rights program it is committed to." Even more important, it "will be a boon to the development that takes place, the Negro will receive in this area greater opportunities and more freedom in general."[54]

The conservative turn on rights issues in 1960 ultimately created competition for the *World*, breaking its virtual monopoly on black news in Atlanta. In July 1960, the *Atlanta Inquirer* debuted with overt editorials claiming that it would be the political alternative to the city's other black paper, emphasizing black rights and refusing to compromise on issues of discrimination and segregation. In 1970, a printers strike led by the Atlanta Typographical Union engulfed the *World* after a printer had been, in the minds of some, unjustly fired. The strike stirred the echoes of the 1941 work stoppage and reinforced to many that the *World* had become a bastion of reactionary politics, out of touch with a radical wave that had passed the paper by. Ultimately, C. A. Scott responded by giving up the printing press that had been the backbone of the Syndicate, choosing to abandon in-house printing rather than make concessions to the union.[55]

With the exception of Barry Goldwater in 1964, the *World* endorsed every Republican candidate from 1952 to 1988. When students from the city's HBCUs engaged white businesses such as Rich's department store and other *World* advertisers in the 1960s, Scott was placed in the position of choosing between the citizens who purchased his newspaper and the advertisers who subsidized it. Scott chose the advertisers. Black citizens should focus more "on removing segregation in education, more voting and political influence, equal consideration in the administration of justice at the state level and improved economic opportunities than on places to eat." Of course, black businesses like the *World* and its fellows on Auburn Avenue depended on business segregation for their lifeblood, and most local black businesses opposed the sit-ins (though in a quieter way than the *World*). This stance, however, turned many against the paper. It lost a third of its readership in the 1960s, suffering at the hands of the more radical *Inquirer* and another competitor, the *Atlanta Voice*.[56]

The *World* and its Syndicate counterparts were not, however, the sum of some problematic stands in the early 1960s. From its creation in 1928 to the birth of the Syndicate in 1931 and then to the 1955 birth of the first wave of civil rights, it was a voice far louder and more pragmatically vigorous than normally acknowledged. Describing the *World* in the early 1950s, one reader explained, "It was the only expression black people had. It was just something you were supposed to read. Because if you didn't read it, you might miss something that you ought to know." Annie McPheeters credits the *World* with being among the "organizations that helped in the dramatic and hard-earned hegemony of Negro political awareness and participation" in the early 1950s.[57]

In 1957, E. Franklin Frazier argued that the assumed necessity of black businesses for the broader American economy, or even the economy of black America, was fundamentally wrong. This "myth of Negro business" was a direct result of black middle-class desires and, even more specifically, Atlanta, Georgia, where Atlanta University's business school churned out new acolytes. There was, without question, a budding and unique emphasis on the power of business in Atlanta, stretching back to the 1898 Atlanta University conference, "The Negro in Business," and the creation of Booker Washington's National Negro Business League. "Faith in this social myth," Frazier wrote, was also perpetuated by the black press. And with good reason. Black newspapers were the "most successful enterprises established by Negroes." Evaluating Frazier's description of Atlanta two decades later, historian Robert C. Vowels admitted that the *Atlanta Daily World*'s "impact on the black business community over the decades is difficult to assess," but the *World* and the Syndicate were clearly not in Frazier's "lowest category of small business." The paper unquestionably served as connective tissue for businesses in the city. The Scotts had close, if fraught, relationships with Lorimer Milton, who became the first acting dean of the Atlanta University School of Business Administration, and Jesse Blayton, who became Georgia's first black certified public accountant. To be sure, the *World* was a business first, stretching back to W. A. Scott's original vision for his Southern Newspaper Syndicate. In its role as a business, business advocate, and connective tissue for businesses in Atlanta and in the South, the *World* and its Syndicate certainly played a role in Frazier's paradigm, but that role, critics like Vowels have argued, only redounded to the good.[58]

The Syndicate ceased to exist in 1955 after train service to and from Atlanta was substantially reduced, making timely shipping incredibly difficult. By then, the Syndicate's roster had dwindled to ten papers in four southern states. Many of the papers still with the Syndicate had amassed a significant debt load that also made continuing operations a losing proposition. The first wave of civil rights activism was beginning. The SNS had long since witnessed its peak. And so the generation turned and passed the Syndicate by, but that does not mean that it was a relic. The civil rights movement in the South in the 1950s and 1960s was intensely conscious of media, and activists were consistently willing to appear conciliatory in the face of white anger in order to gain a moral upper hand. The movement was, in this sense, practically radical, a lesson learned from Syndicate journalism in the generation before *Brown*. The SNS had stretched from Atlanta throughout the South, then outside those bounds, following the trajectory of the Great Migration, before returning to its roots in the South and in Atlanta—always Atlanta—as its life came to a close in 1955. Months later the Montgomery bus boycott commenced, ushering in a new form of practical radicalism for a generation that had grown and developed on the succor of the Scott Newspaper Syndicate.[59]

Conclusion

In January 1954, the National Negro Publishers Association held its midwinter workshop at Tuskegee Institute, the first time the NNPA offered one of its major events in Alabama. Representatives from the Syndicate's *Alabama Tribune* and *Birmingham World* were there. The Scotts attended, along with every editor and manager of the *Atlanta Daily World*. Thurgood Marshall, representing the NAACP's Legal Defense and Education Fund, gave the plenary speech. His talk, "The Next Step—Win or Lose," was about the pending school desegregation case that would be decided in May. *Brown v. Board of Education*, of course, would be a win, but there were plenty of next steps to come. The distinctive nature of the civil rights movement that developed after the *Brown* decision had its grounding in the distinctive black southern mind-set that developed as a response to the racism African Americans encountered, but also to the information they received. And to how it was received. Marshall stood on the dais with Jessie Matthews Vann, publisher of the *Pittsburgh Courier* (she took over the paper after her husband, Robert L. Vann, died), and Carl Murphy, editor of the *Baltimore Afro-American* and president of the NNPA.[1] As they had for decades, northern presses had made their way South, but also as they had for decades, they would return home, leaving the publishers of the *Alabama Tribune*, the *Birmingham World*, and the *Atlanta Daily World* to generate a distinctive southern interpretation of events and of the distinctive southern movement that followed.

Brown v. Board of Education was to the twentieth century what Abraham Lincoln's Emancipation Proclamation was to the nineteenth. *Brown* did not end segregation, just as Lincoln's speech did not end slavery. Ten years after *Brown*, for example, there were still no integrated schools in South Carolina, Alabama, or Mississippi. Only 1 percent of black southern children were attending school with whites. But just as the Civil War was a catalyst to make emancipation a reality, the civil rights movement worked to give teeth to the mandates of *Brown*.[2]

Integration and the fight for it was a divisive issue for the black press. While the idea of equality was paramount to the papers, the idea of integration was an inherent threat to their survival. Wolseley cites "remnants of the Garvey days or others concerned about the purity of the black race" when referring to the contested space held by black newspapers, which advocated for equality while realizing that their own economic viability rested on segregation. The position of the black press looked remarkably similar to that of historically black colleges or Negro baseball leagues. Equality could mean the marginalization of the fundamentally black entities that provided such valuable services for their people. Providing choice to consumers when one of the choices had every financial and historical advantage over the other meant that those with fewer advantages usually lost. Integration led to choice, and choice helped kill autonomous black institutions. In 1947, for example, the black press was doing inarguably well, with some papers maintaining record circulation numbers. By the end of the 1960s, however, black press circulations had dipped to between 50 and 75 percent of those numbers.[3]

Beginning in 1954 and fitting that new era, an interracial group of journalists and educators founded the Southern Education Reporting Service (SERS) to report "factually and objectively on developments in Southern education stemming from the Supreme Court decision outlawing segregation in the public schools." Correspondents throughout the region collected clippings and investigated local stories of compliance and noncompliance, publishing the results in the monthly *Southern School News*, a journal of interest to everyone with a stake in the integration fight. That the SERS developed as the Scott Newspaper Syndicate faltered was merely fortuitous timing. The former was not a continuation of the latter. The Southern Education Reporting Service was simply creating a nonbiased compendium of information, and while that did in a sense create a version of those bonds based on the uniformity of information provided earlier by the Syndicate, there was no opinion page, no banner headlines, no action beyond reporting stories related specifically to southern school desegregation. Members of both the Ku Klux Klan and the NAACP were subscribers to *Southern School News*, for example, each seeking updates on the progress of southern responses to *Brown*. There were even staunch segregationists on the SERS board of directors, and the effort ironically demonstrated the pitfalls of such interracial arrangements—even in reporting on desegregation—as white board members were able to appropriate much of the control of the SERS from their black colleagues. Still, in its effort to bind the South through uniform news coverage of integration, there were traces of the Syndicate in its endeavor.[4]

The Syndicate dissolved in 1955, a victim of technological change more than anything else, when a reduction in train service to and from Atlanta made inexpensive, timely shipping virtually impossible. More symbolically, the Syndicate's replacement in the region by the SERS represented the end of an era, made all the more evident by the *Atlanta Daily World*'s often troubled later civil rights advocacy. Carl Senna's *The Black Press and the Struggle for Civil Rights*, for example, doesn't even mention the *World*. The works that do, such as those by Charles A. Simmons and Roland Wolseley, paint the paper with a broad conservative brush, mostly emphasizing its coverage of student sit-ins and economic boycotts in the early 1960s.[5]

Gloria Blackwell argues that black publishers in Atlanta never received "sufficient support" from readers or from businesses and social institutions to "create and sustain a communications network disseminating a potent, pertinent message." She explains that "the two primary, and often opposing pressures upon black-controlled media are the obligation to address the particular needs of African-Americans and the struggle to stay alive." This was an inescapable reality that the life of the Scott Newspaper Syndicate demonstrated time and again. "The most common experience in the history of black media enterprises," Blackwell argues, "has been prolific and promiscuous births balanced by brief emissions, impotence, and death."[6]

Charles H. Loeb, a former employee of the *World* and cofounder of the Syndicate's *Louisiana Weekly* who eventually moved to the *Cleveland Call and Post*, referred to those willing to create black newspapers as people with "high altruism and low pay."[7] The life of the SNS demonstrated that view.

Even in the Victorian era, well before the Scott Syndicate saw the light of day, historian Emma Lou Thornbrough notes, one of the most conspicuous characteristics of black newspapers was "the large number which were started and their low rate of survival. Many were so ephemeral that only their names survive; others were so obscure that not even this evidence of their existence remains."[8] This was a reality that did not change in the years following World War I, particularly in the South, where racism, financial hindrances, and educational deficiencies conspired to keep so many publications small and short lived.

There was a long tradition of the white southern press defending white southern attitudes on race against any available opponent, be it abolitionists or northerners in the antebellum period or anti–Jim Crow advocates as the century turned. The white southern press was largely responsible for building the momentum for post-Reconstruction disenfranchisement laws and for promoting a solid white South. This consistent defense of white supremacy, in harsher or softer tones depending on the location and paper, continued through the entirety of Jim Crow, validating the messages white southerners received in their history lessons, their family discussions, and their public lives: there was a significant cabal of outside agitators "bent on destroying the southern way of life." The list was long and multiracial, including white liberal politicians, judges, unions, communists, and the NAACP, which were all placed under the harsh light of such scrutiny.[9]

That made the black press, particularly in the South, all the more important. "The mass communications media have, over the past forty years, changed America into a mass society," Harold Cruse explained in 1967. "And on the bottom where this mass society emerges stands the Negro, not quite passive as of now, but still subject to manipulation and still politically fragmented, if not more so than ever." Cruse interprets this reality as a "default of the Negro intelligentsia,"[10] but the black press, serving as a constituent part of that intelligentsia, was a vital binding agent in the creation of that mass society, just as the grapevine bound disparate groups of enslaved and freed people through the power of information.

"The Negro press is by far the most effective communication channel leading directly to the Negro people," wrote communist educator Doxey Wilkerson in 1947. "Whoever would influence the economic, political or civic beliefs and behavior of Negro citizens must necessarily approach his audience through the increasingly effective newspapers and magazines." The black press was a "special-interest" press, a "fighting people's press" engaged in "championing the freedom and full democratic rights of the Negro people, stimulating and organizing their struggles, and helping to build an increasingly unified Negro people's liberation movement." Sociologist Benjamin Singer points out in reference to the proliferation of television in a later generation that mass media often serve power and are used to mollify a citizenry. Still, "although mass media may have a conformative potential for majority groups, [they] possess . . . a transformative function for minority group identities." What was true for television and Black Power was also true for the black press and the push against Jim Crow.[11]

"From Harlem to Tougaloo, the Negro press is the most loudly impatient agency for immediate, fundamental change in the status of the race," writes Roi Ottley. "At times, in its honest fury against injustice to black men, it is a kibitzer on the sidelines of American life; and at other times, especially in periods of moral inertia, it is a noisy wailing-wall." Vanderbilt University English professor Edwin Mims, writing in 1926 a call to action for progressives in the South, identifies the black press as "the single greatest power in the Negro race." Asa Gordon, writing about Georgia in the following decade, describes black newspapers as "moulders of opinion, mediums of expression, and developers of racial solidarity."[12]

The *Atlanta Daily World* and the Scott Newspaper Syndicate certainly fit that bill. From the paper's founding in 1928, to the creation of the Southern Newspaper Syndicate in 1931, to the paper's transition to a daily in 1932, and then to the rebranding of the Scott Syndicate after its member newspapers began following the Great Migration out of the region, the company served as a catalyst of "honest fury" and a "developer of racial solidarity." In so doing, it reified the kinship networks developed during slavery and served as a bridge to the post-*Brown* civil rights movement.

It did so pragmatically. That practicality manifested in coverage that sought to attack broader racial disparities without including direct attacks on local citizens and institutions, which might cause physical or economic retribution toward the newspaper. That practicality could also be financial. Newspapers in the North like the *Defender* and *Courier*, for example, or on the East Coast like the *Norfolk Journal and Guide* and *Baltimore Afro-American* had the resources to send reporters to various events important to the race. In the Deep South that simply wasn't the case. Limited financial resources made syndication like that of the SNS even more vital. Having a paper in or near the area of a newsworthy event became the cost-effective equivalent of sending a reporter to the scene.[13] Combined with the Scotts' willingness to effectively bilk the Associated Negro Press for reprinting rights by sharing one subscription for all the Syndicate's member papers, that strategy helped solidify the grapevine and make it cost-effective for small southern communities to have, at least temporarily, viable black media outlets.

Albert Lee Kreiling has argued that the northern black press's denunciation of racial abuse was a ritual, a metaphysical act of atonement by northern papers and for northern readers who had left for greener pastures.[14] The black press in the South had a more immediate job, a more visceral response to the segregation, violence, and disenfranchisement that surrounded it. If the survival of a newspaper was a test of victory in those struggles, then most southern papers clearly lost, but the process of syndication allowed them to exist, even for a short time, to document the collection of large tragedies and small triumphs that constituted southern race relations. Though the life span of most of the newspapers was limited to only months, the continuity generated by the Syndicate provided uniformity and stability to black southern newspaper readers and to northern readers as its members followed the trajectory of the Great Migration. In the process, the Syndicate helped unify communities and provide information unavailable in other venues. The Scott Newspaper Syndicate survived the Depression and bigotry with a practical radicalism that kept it viable in the liminal space between white authority and black needs in the quarter century prior to *Brown*, the Montgomery bus boycott, and the civil rights movement.

Appendix

The Papers of the
Scott Newspaper Syndicate

Proof of the existence of most of these papers and their time as part of the Scott Syndicate comes from a methodical evaluation of the *Atlanta Daily World*'s cash receipt books from 1931 to 1955, which have notations for every month a given paper sent payment to Atlanta (OBV1 through OBV45, Atlanta Daily World Records, 1931–1996, Manuscript Collection no. 1092, Manuscript, Archives, and Rare Book Library, Emory University, Atlanta, Georgia). These notations are not always a reflection of the complete runs with the Syndicate. The *West Virginia Weekly*, for example, was listed in the cash receipt books as beginning with the SNS in the summer of 1934, but research in the West Virginia State Archives revealed that its run with the Syndicate actually began in October 1933. The *Spokesman* (Xenia, Ohio) was never listed in the cash receipt books at all, but it did make an appearance in a separate SNS ledger and thus was added to the list below.

The newspapers are listed in the order they were created, though they may not have joined the Syndicate in the same order. When newspapers share the same date span, they are listed in the order in which they appear in the *World*'s log books. There are four papers (*Globe Dispatch*, *Selma World*, *East Arkansas World*, and *Chattanooga World*) whose existence was demonstrated either by a separate Scott Syndicate ledger or a mention in the *World* itself, but the period in which they existed (between October 1932 and January 1934) is missing from the archival record (OBV136 through OBV138, Atlanta Daily World Records). This is one of three gaps in archival coverage; the others are November 1931–March 1932 and December 1940–May 1941. When a recorded existence of a newspaper was found in the last month prior to a gap or the first month after it, thereby indicating that its existence most likely included time within that undocumented period, the final date of the maximum possible span of the paper's life is included parenthetically.

Additionally, some papers changed their name (for example, the *Bartlesville Voice* became the *Tulsa Voice*, before re-forming again several months later with its original name), and in those instances each incarnation of the paper has its own entry. Continuity additions were made when spans of one or two months separated constituent months in a series. Empty spans of more than two months were considered to be a stoppage in the paper's activity. Lone payments made by papers more than three months after the continuous set have been viewed as late payments for former services rendered. When there were only two mentions of a paper spaced more than two months apart, the record has been left untouched and is included here.

Newspapers marked with an asterisk (*) were part of the White Newspaper Syndicate in Michigan, which was recorded separately in the SNS cash receipt books. The White Syndicate's payment tenure is the final entry.

NEWSPAPER (LOCATION)	TIME WITH THE SYNDICATE
Columbus World (Columbus, Ga.)	March 1931–October 1931 (March 1932) (December 1940) June 1941– March 1955
Birmingham World (Birmingham, Ala.)	March 1931–March 1955
Nashville Independent (Nashville, Tenn.)	March–April 1931
Chattanooga Tribune (Chattanooga, Tenn.)	March 1931
Carolina Enterprise (Greenville, S.C.)	March–October 1931
Memphis World (Memphis, Tenn.)	July 1931–March 1955
Montgomery World (Montgomery, Ala.)	September 1931 (October 1932) February 1934– December 1935
Jacksonville World (Jacksonville, Fla.)	June 1932–February 1934
Nashville World (Nashville, Tenn.)	July 1932–November 1937
Jackson World (Jackson, Miss.)	July–September 1932 (January 1934)
Louisville Leader (Louisville, Ky.)	July–September 1932 (January 1934)
St. Louis Argus (St. Louis, Mo.)	July–September 1932 (January 1934)
Louisiana Weekly (New Orleans, La.)	July–September 1932 (January 1934)
Indianapolis Recorder (Indianapolis, Ind.)	August–September 1932 (January 1934)
Hampton Tribune (Hampton, Va.)	August 1932
Dallas Express (Dallas, Tex.)	August–September 1932 (January 1934)
Charlotte Post (Charlotte, N.C.)	August–September 1932 (January 1934) October 1934–June 1939

Greenville Leader (Greenville, Miss.)	August–September 1932 (January 1934)
	September–October 1934
Cape Fear Journal (Wilmington, N.C.)	August 1932–July 1936
	July–September 1941
Gary American (Gary, Ind.)	August 1932 (possibly through January 1934)
Richmond Planet (Richmond, Va.)	August–September 1932 (January 1934)
Columbus Voice (Columbus, Ohio)	August–September 1932 (January 1934)
Charleston Messenger (Charleston, S.C.)	August–September 1932 (January 1934)
Waco Messenger (Waco, Tex.)	August–September 1932 (January 1934)
Newark Herald (Newark, N.J.)	August–September 1932 (January 1934)
	September–October 1934
Carolina Times (Durham, N.C.)	August–September 1932 (January 1934)
Flashlight Herald (Knoxville, Tenn.)	August 1932 (possibly through January 1934)
Public Informer (St. Petersburg, Fla.)	August 1932–July 1935
Miami Times (Miami, Fla.)	August–September 1932 (January 1934)
Weekly Echo (Meridian, Miss.)	August 1932
Detroit Independent (Detroit, Mich.)	August 1932
Globe Dispatch (Shreveport, La.)	(October 1932–January 1934)
Selma World (Selma, Ala.)	(October 1932–January 1934)
East Arkansas World (Marianna, Ark.)	(October 1932–January 1934)
Chattanooga World (Chattanooga, Tenn.)	(October 1932–January 1934)
Pee Dee Weekly (Florence, S.C.)	(October 1932) February 1934–April 1936
Durham Dispatch (Durham, N.C.)	(October 1932) February 1934–August 1934
Tampa World (Tampa, Fla.)	(October 1932) February 1934–January 1936
Columbus Advocate (Columbus, Ohio)	(October 1932) February 1934–October 1934
Carolina Eagle (Kinston, N.C.)	(October 1932) February 1934–May 1934
Richmond Broadcast (Richmond, Va.)	(October 1932) February 1934–June 1934

Tropical Dispatch (Miami, Fla.)	(October 1932) February 1934–June 1950
Detroit World (Detroit, Mich.)	(October 1932) February 1934–July 1934
New Bern World (New Bern, N.C.)	(October 1932) February 1934–July 1939
Jacksonville Tribune (Jacksonville, Fla.)	(October 1932) February 1934–August 1934
Iowa Bystander (Des Moines, Iowa)	(October 1932) February 1934–October 1935
Hannibal Register (Hannibal, Mo.)	(October 1932) February 1934–April 1937
Fort Worth Mind (Fort Worth, Tex.)	(October 1932) February 1934–May 1938
Cleveland Eagle (Cleveland, Ohio)	(October 1932) February 1934–November 1935
Asheville World (Asheville, N.C.)	(October 1932)–February 1934
Knoxville Recorder (Knoxville, Tenn.)	(October 1932) February 1934–August 1934
Youngstown Challenger (Youngstown, Ohio)	(October 1932) February 1934–November 1940 (May 1941)
Mississippi World (Natchez, Miss.)	(October 1932) February 1934–March 1935
Mobile Sun (Mobile, Ala.)	(October 1932) February 1934–April 1936
Roanoke Enquirer (Roanoke, Va.)	(October 1932) February 1934–January 1936
Brunswick Herald (Brunswick, Ga.)	(October 1932) February 1934–September 1934
Austin Messenger (Austin, Tex.)	(October 1932) February 1934–March 1934
Galveston Voice (Galveston, Tex.)	(October 1932) February 1934–June 1935
Crusader (New York, N.Y.)	(October 1932) February 1934–May 1934
West Virginia Weekly (Charleston, W.Va.)	October 1933–December 1934
Jackson World (Jackson, Tenn.)	March–April 1934
Mississippi Weekly (Vicksburg, Miss.)	March–August 1934
Okmulgee World (Okmulgee, Okla.)	March–May 1934
Clarksville World (Clarksville, Tenn.)	March 1934–July 1934
Chattanooga Dispatch (Chattanooga, Tenn.)	March–April 1934
Cincinnati News (Cincinnati, Ohio)	March–August 1934

National Negro World (New York, N.Y.)	March–April 1934
Pittsburgh Criterion (Pittsburgh, Pa.)	April–November 1934
Mobile World (Mobile, Ala.)	April 1934
Houston Guide (Houston, Tex.)	April 1934–July 1934
Chattanooga World (Chattanooga, Tenn.)	April 1934–October 1934
Marshall Tribune (Marshall, Tex.)	April 1934–January 1935
Selma Post (Selma, Ala.)	April–May 1934
New Orleans Broadcast (New Orleans, La.)	May–September 1934 May–June 1935
Carolina World (Greenville, S.C.)	May–September 1934 January–February 1935
Asheville Record (Asheville, N.C.)	July 1934–November 1935
Michigan World (Detroit, Mich.)	August 1934–August 1937
Palm Beach Tribune (West Palm Beach, Fla.)	August–October 1934
Charleston Telegram (Charleston, S.C.)	August 1934–October 1935
Public Guide (Knoxville, Tenn.)	September 1934–April 1938
Lexington Record (Lexington, Ky.)	September 1934–April 1936
Mississippi Tribune (Vicksburg, Miss.)	September 1934–January 1935
East Texas Messenger (Huntsville, Tex.)	September–December 1934
Greenville World (Greenville, S.C.)	October 1934–June 1935
Chattanooga Observer (Chattanooga, Tenn.)	November 1934–March 1955
Peoria Informer (Peoria, Ill.)	November 1934–April 1939
Jacksonville Mirror (Jacksonville, Fla.)	December 1934–April 1935
Jackson Times (Jackson, Tenn.)	March 1935–September 1936
Spokesman (Wilberforce/Xenia, Ohio)	February–March 1935
Louisville Independent News (Louisville, Ky.)	February–November 1935
Oklahoma Defender (Oklahoma City, Okla.)	March 1935–December 1939
Muskogee Lantern (Muskogee, Okla.)	March 1935
Bartlesville Voice (Bartlesville, Okla.)	March–May 1935 October–November 1935 October 1936–January 1937
Rome Sentinel (Rome, Ga.)	March–September 1935
Atlantic City Eagle (Atlantic City, N.J.)	March 1935 November 1940 (May 1941)
Dayton Progress (Dayton, Ohio)	March 1935–January 1940

Buckeye Tribune (Wilberforce/Xenia, Ohio)	April–June 1935
Corinthian Gazette (Corinth, Miss.)	April–June 1935
Anderson Messenger (Anderson, S.C.)	May 1935–June 1936
Natchez Journal (Natchez, Miss.)	April–May 1935
Toledo Enquirer (Toledo, Ohio)	May–June 1935
Broadcast (Bradenton, Fla.)	May–August 1935
Augusta Journal (Augusta, Ga.)	May 1935–June 1936
Tulsa Voice (Tulsa, Okla.)	June–July 1935
Hot Springs Mirror (Hot Springs, Ark.)	June–July 1935
Temple Times (Temple, Tex.)	July–November 1935
Hub City News (Spartanburg, S.C.)	July–September 1935
Vox Populi (Daytona Beach, Fla.)	July–September 1935
St. Louis News (St. Louis, Mo.)	August–November 1935
Orlando Sun (Orlando, Fla.)	August 1935–December 1936 January–June 1938
St. Petersburg World (St. Petersburg, Fla.)	September 1935–November 1936
Forum (Dayton, Ohio)	November 1935–January 1936
Owensboro Eagle (Owensboro, Ky.)	November 1935–February 1936
Ft. Myers World (Ft. Myers, Fla.)	December 1935
Southern Liberator (Forrest City, Ark.)	December 1935
Waco Post-Dispatch (Waco, Tex.)	December 1935–June 1936
Toledo Press (Toledo, Ohio)	December 1935–July 1936 December 1938–July 1939
Ideal Review (Bridgeton, N.J.)	January–April 1936 August–October 1936
Blytheville World (Blytheville, Ark.)	January 1936
Panama City World (Panama City, Fla.)	February 1936–January 1938
Hartford Advocate (Hartford, Conn.)	February 1936–April 1937
Vidalia Banner (Vidalia, Ga.)	April 1936
San Angelo Enterprise (San Angelo, Tex.)	April–December 1936
Mobile Press Forum Sun (Mobile, Ala.)	May 1936–September 1938
Florida Crusade (Tallahassee, Fla.)	May–September 1936
Alabama Tribune (Montgomery, Ala.)	June 1936–March 1955
Florida Guardian (Ft. Lauderdale, Fla.)	June–August 1936
Omaha Chronicle (Omaha, Nebr.)	July 1936–September 1937
Cuttings (Greensboro, N.C.)	July 1936–December 1937
Cleveland Guide (Cleveland, Ohio)	July 1936–January 1944

Jackson Sentinel (Jackson, Miss.)	September 1936
Capitol Plaindealer (Topeka, Kans.)	September 1936–March 1937
	July–September 1937
Washington Gazette (Washington, N.C.)	December 1936
Rocky Mount Gazette (Rocky Mount, N.C.)	January 1937
Greensboro Tribune (Greensboro, N.C.)	January–November 1937
East St. Louis World (East St. Louis, Ill.)	February–April 1937
Phoenix Index (Phoenix, Ariz.)	March–August 1937
	April 1938–October 1942
Amarillo Herald (Amarillo, Tex.)	March–August 1937
Toledo Tribune (Toledo, Ohio)	March–April 1937
	April–November 1938
Galveston Guide (Galveston, Tex.)	April–June 1937
East Texas Times (Big Sandy, Tex.)	May 1937
Tampa Journal (Tampa, Fla.)	May 1937–October 1937
Tyler Tribune (Tyler, Tex.)	May–September 1937
Birmingham World, Bessemer edition (Bessemer, Ala.)	May–June 1937
Louisville Herald Tribune (Louisville, Ky.)	June 1937–January 1938
Columbus Advocate (Columbus, Ga.)	June 1937–November 1940 (May 1941)
Southern Broadcast (Monroe, La.)	July–October 1937
Connecticut Labor News (Hartford, Conn.)	July–September 1937
Weekly Commander (Clarksdale, Miss.)	August–October 1937
Texas Examiner (Houston, Tex.)	August 1937
News World (Detroit, Mich.)	August 1937–November 1938
Baton Rouge Post (Baton Rouge, La.)	August 1937–May 1938
Florida American (Gainesville, Fla.)	December 1937–August 1938
St. Augustine Enquirer (St. Augustine, Fla.)	March–April 1938
Louisville News (Louisville, Ky.)	March 1938–October 1939
	December 1942–February 1943
	July 1943–February 1945
Pensacola Courier (Pensacola, Fla.)	March 1938–December 1941
	July 1943–February 1947
	October 1947–March 1955
*Michigan State Echo** (Lansing, Mich.)	March 1938–May 1939
Camden Express (Camden, Ark.)	April 1938–October 1939
People's News (Tampa, Fla.)	April–October 1938

Tri-State News (Huntington, W.Va.)　　May 1938–August 1942

Delaware Dispatch (Rehoboth Beach, Del.)　　May–September 1938

Knoxville Progress Post (Knoxville, Tenn.)　　May–August 1938

Florida Tribune (Jacksonville, Fla.)　　June–August 1938

Jackson Echo* (Jackson, Mich.)　　June 1938
November 1938–February 1939

Brunswick Sentinel (Brunswick, Ga.)　　July 1938–September 1940

Grand Rapids Echo* (Grand Rapids, Mich.)　　July–October 1938

Hamtramck Echo* (Hamtramck, Mich.)　　July–October 1938
March–June 1939, December 1939
May 1940
August–September 1941
March 1942

McComb County Echo* (Mt. Clemens, Mich.)　　August 1938–October 1939

Pontiac Echo* (Pontiac, Mich.)　　September 1938–September 1939
February–April 1940

Flint-Brownsville News (Flint, Mich.)　　September 1938–March 1939
(December 1940) June 1941–April 1942

Struggle (Evansville, Ind.)　　September–December 1938
December 1939–June 1940

Helena Informer (Helena, Ark.)　　September–December 1938

Southwest Georgian (Albany, Ga.)　　November 1938–January 1944
August 1946–March 1955

East Carolina News (Kinston, N.C.)　　December 1938–July 1940

East Tennessee News (Knoxville, Tenn.)　　December 1938–February 1947

LaGrange Advertiser (LaGrange, Ga.)　　December 1938–October 1939

New Orleans Observer (New Orleans, La.)　　December 1938–December 1939

Iowa Observer (Des Moines, Iowa)　　January 1939–August 1941
April 1942–December 1945

Charleston Ledger Dispatch (Charleston, W.Va.)　　January–April 1939

Kalamazoo Guide (Kalamazoo, Mich.)　　February–March 1939

Tri-City News (Moline, Ill.)　　April–May 1939

Detroit World Echo* (Detroit, Mich.)　　April 1939–October 1940
October 1941
March 1942–March 1943
November–December 1943

World Telegram (Indianapolis, Ind.)	May 1939–August 1940
Universal Brotherhood (Texarkana, Ark.)	May 1939–May 1940
	October 1940
	November 1941–December 1942
Macon Broadcast (Macon, Ga.)	May 1939–November 1940 (May 1941)
Toledo Voice (Toledo, Ohio)	June 1939–August 1943
Bay County Bulletin (Panama City, Fla.)	June–August 1939
Colored Citizen (Pensacola, Fla.)	July 1939
Southern Sun (Greenwood, Miss.)	June–September 1939
Palm Beach Record (Palm Beach, Fla.)	August 1939–May 1940
Battle Creek Tribune (Battle Creek, Mich.)	August 1939
Twin City Journal (Monroe, La.)	August 1939–July 1940
Illinois Times (Danville/Champaign, Ill.)	September 1939–April 1945
Winston-Salem Post (Winston-Salem, N.C.)	April 1939–March 1940
	September–November 1940 (May 1941)
Port Arthur Flash (Port Arthur, Tex.)	October 1939–April 1940
Blue Grass Tribune (Frankfort, Ky.)	October 1939
Cincinnati Independent (Cincinnati, Ohio)	November 1939–March 1949
	September 1949–March 1950
Falls City News (Louisville, Ky.)	November 1939–June 1943
Indianapolis World (Indianapolis, Ind.)	November 1939–January 1940
Twin City Herald (Minneapolis, Minn.)	December 1939–February 1940
Trenton Record (Trenton, N.J.)	December 1939–January 1940
Buffalo Star (Buffalo, N.Y.)	December 1939–January 1940
Sunlight (Pine Bluff, Ark.)	December 1939–February 1942
*Lansing Echo** (Lansing, Mich.)	January–July 1940
Austin Item (Austin, Tex.)	January–March 1940
South Bend Citizen (South Bend, Ind.)	January–April 1940
Southwestern Torch (El Paso, Tex.)	February 1940–July 1941
Twin City Tribune (Monroe, La.)	February 1940–November 1941
Carolina Lighthouse (Charleston, S.C.)	February–April 1940
Trenton World (Trenton, N.J.)	February 1940–June 1941
Arkansas World (Little Rock, Ark.)	March 1940–May 1953
Galveston Examiner (Galveston, Tex.)	March–June 1940

Milwaukee Observer (Milwaukee, Wis.)	April 1940
Vicksburg American (Vicksburg, Miss.)	July 1940–August 1941
Lighthouse and Informer (Columbia, S.C.)	July 1940–January 1949
Shreveport World (Shreveport, La.)	July 1940–October 1941
What's News (Danville, Ill.)	July–August 1940
Saginaw Echo* (Saginaw, Mich.)	August 1940
Jackson Advocate (Jackson, Miss.)	October 1940–July 1946
District Baptist (Bastrop, La.)	October–November 1940 (May 1941)
North Carolina Citizen (unavailable)	October 1940–June 1941
Savannah Journal (Savannah, Ga.)	(December 1940) June 1941–December 1942
Capital City Post (Tallahassee, Fla.)	(December 1940) June 1941 October 1941
Tampa Reformer (Tampa, Fla.)	(December 1940) June–July 1941
Jacksonville Progressive News (Jacksonville, Fla.)	(December 1940) June 1941–May 1946
Alexandria Observer (Alexandria, La.)	July 1941–December 1943
Meridian Progress (Meridian, Miss.)	August–October 1941
Industrial Era (Beaumont, Tex.)	August 1941–June 1945
Vicksburg Tribune (Vicksburg, Miss.)	November 1941–October 1944
Atlantic City Tribune (Atlantic City, N.J.)	January–October 1942
Danville Star (Danville, Va.)	April 1942–March 1943
Miami Progressive News (Miami, Fla.)	June–September 1946
Florida Record Dispatch (West Palm Beach, Fla., then Tallahassee, Fla.)	February 1947–March 1948 February–March 1949 August 1951–June 1952
Jackson Banner (Jackson, Miss.)	October 1949–June 1951
Nashville Sun (Clarksville, Tenn.)	August 1950–May 1952
Bayou State Register (Grambling, La.)	May–July 1951
Northside Home News (Atlantic City, N.J.)	March–June 1952
Marion County Citizen (Ocala, Fla.)	December 1952–March 1953
Independent Call (Knoxville, Tenn.)	February 1953–March 1955
Florida Spur (Ft. Lauderdale, Fla.)	January 1954–March 1955
*White Syndicate (Detroit, Mich.)	March 1939–December 1943

Notes

Introduction

1. Myrdal, *American Dilemma*, 911.
2. Blakeney, "Sociological Analysis," 7.
3. Hahn, *Nation under Our Feet*, 69, 85. Meanwhile, as Benjamin Fagan has demonstrated, the antebellum black press centered in the North helped to organize liberation programs centered around a concept of "chosenness." See Fagan, *Black Newspaper*.
4. Egerton, *Speak Now against the Day*, 285.
5. Brown-Nagin, *Courage to Dissent*, 1–13, quotes 2, 8.
6. Painter, "Black Journalism," 30–32; O'Kelly, "Black Newspapers," 2, 5; and Dann, *Black Press*, 14.
7. Detweiler, *Negro Press*, 19; O'Kelly, "Black Newspapers," 8, 9; and Guy Johnson, "Some Factors in the Development," 334. See also Kerlin, *Voice of the Negro*. For an example of the racial pragmatism of northern black newspapers, see Glick, "Mixed Messages."
8. Standing, "Study of Negro Nationalism," 69–70; and O'Kelly, "Black Newspapers," 9. Depression figures culled from Thomas, *Human Exploitation*, xiv–xv; Lanctot, *Negro League Baseball*, 6; Hogan, *Shades of Glory*, 224–225; Frederickson, *Dixiecrat Revolt*, 13; and Warren, *Herbert Hoover*, 241–242.
9. O'Kelly, "Black Newspapers," 9; Standing, "Study of Negro Nationalism," 69–70; Alfred McClung Lee, *Daily Newspaper in America*, 178; Odum-Hinmon, "Cautious Crusader," 14; U.S. Department of Commerce, *Negro Newspapers and Periodicals in the United States, 1937*, 1; Blackwell, "Black-Controlled Media," 20; and LeCour, " Negro Press as a Business," 108.
10. Washburn, *African American Newspaper*, 120–121; and Detweiler, *Negro Press*, 152–156.
11. Bedingfield, *Newspaper Wars*, 1–6, 39–63, quotes 1, 6.
12. *Atlanta World*, 28 February 1932, 6. There were at least 241 newspapers associated with the Syndicate. The existence of those papers and the statistics associated with them come from tabulations generated from the daily cash receipt books of the *Atlanta Daily World* and the Scott Syndicate. Statistics and figures about the makeup of the Scott Newspaper Syndicate come from my own data mining of the *Atlanta Daily World*'s cash receipt books, housed in the archives of Emory University. See Cash Receipts, OBV1 through OBV45,

Atlanta Daily World Records, 1931–1996, Manuscript Collection no. 1092, Manuscript, Archives, and Rare Book Library, Emory University, Atlanta, Ga.

13. *Atlanta World*, 28 February 1932, 6.

14. Black et al., "Impact of the Great Migration."

15. Fultz, "Morning Cometh," 98.

16. Myrdal, *American Dilemma*, 917, 920–921.

17. Dolan, "Extra!"

18. Grossman, *Land of Hope*, 78–89; and Henri, *Black Migration*, 79.

19. Doreski, *Writing America Black*, xv, xviii, xxiii.

Chapter 1. Atlanta, the Scott Family, and the Creation of a Media Empire

1. *Atlanta Daily World*, 11 February 1934, 6.

2. Hornsby, "Georgia," 119, 120–121; and Gordon, *Georgia Negro*, 266–267.

3. Hornsby, "Georgia," 120–121. Washington's 1895 speech accepted segregation as a temporary accommodation between the races. In return, he wanted white support for black efforts for education, social uplift, and economic progress. "In all things that are purely social we can be as separate as the fingers," he famously argued, "yet one as the hand in all things essential to mutual progress." His Atlanta Compromise wasn't trumpeting permanent second-class citizenship for African Americans. Instead he wanted black self-improvement that would ultimately earn white respect and thus a seat at the negotiating table as equals somewhere down the road. Many black critics, however, saw Washington's compromise as a slippery slope that would cause more problems than it could ever hope to solve. For more on Washington, see Harlan, *Booker T. Washington: The Making*; Strickland, "Booker T. Washington"; Friedman, "Life in the Lion's Mouth"; Harlan, *Booker T. Washington: The Wizard*; Norrell, *Up from History*; Smock, *Booker T. Washington*; Boston, *Business Strategy*; and Zimmerman, *Alabama in Africa*.

4. Hornsby, "Georgia," 121.

5. *Savannah Tribune*, 7 January 1893, 1; and Hornsby, "Georgia," 122–123.

6. Hornsby, "Georgia," 122, 123, 125.

7. Ibid., 123–126.

8. Ibid., 126–127.

9. Blackwell, "Black-Controlled Media," 67; and Feldman, "Checklist of Atlanta Newspapers," 8.

10. Gerald Horne, *Black Liberation/Red Scare*, 18, 328; Gordon, *Georgia Negro*, 222; and Bacote, "Negro in Georgia Politics," 325. See also Rozier, "History of the Negro Press."

11. Walter White, "Portrait of a Communist"; Gerald Horne, *Black Liberation/Red Scare*, 18, 20; Bacote, "Negro in Georgia Politics," 325; and Dittmer, *Black Georgia*, 61.

12. Davis become one of the most prominent Odd Fellows leaders, and the Georgia chapter had the largest membership in the country, at one time having roughly sixty-eight thousand members. Gerald Horne, *Black Liberation/Red*

Scare, 19 (quotes from Cofer and Davis's son); and Brisbane, "Davis, Benjamin J[efferson], Sr.," 159. See also Phillips, "Sociological Study of Editorials," 12–14; Chambliss, "What Negro Newspapers of Georgia Say," 12; Rozier, "History of the Negro Press," 39; Detweiler, *Negro Press*, 57–58; and Dittmer, *Black Georgia*, 57, 164.

13. Dittmer, *Black Georgia*, 57–58; and Phillips, "Sociological Study of Editorials," 16–17. "The collapse of the Odd Fellows, on which the *Atlanta Independent* was founded," wrote Davis's son, "made the bankruptcy of the paper inevitable." Benjamin Davis Jr., *Communist Councilman from Harlem*, 51. It was during Davis's leadership of the Grand United Order of Odd Fellows that the group contracted for a new building at 250 Auburn Avenue. It opened in 1913, and the *Atlanta Independent*'s offices moved to the building's fifth floor. The building also contained black-owned retail and office spaces. Eventually those businesses included the Yates and Milton Drug Store. In 1914 an annex, including an auditorium, opened, making the Odd Fellows buildings the center of black Atlanta. The total cost of the buildings was $100,000. Velma Maia Thomas, "Centennial Celebration: The Odd Fellows Buildings," *Atlanta Daily World*, 29 April 2013, http://www.atlantadailyworld.com/201304295615/Original/centennial-celebration-the-odd-fellows-buildings, accessed 14 October 2013; Mason, *Black Atlanta*, 18, 24; and Gerald Horne, *Black Liberation/Red Scare*, 21.

14. This even bled into his personal life: Davis had originally named his son Morton, after an Athens postmaster. But after an argument with the postmaster, rooted in Odd Fellows business, Davis changed his son's name to Benjamin Junior. Gerald Horne, *Black Liberation/Red Scare*, 21–22, 27. Horne quotes Davis's son, from an unpublished memoir, on 22.

15. Lisio, *Hoover, Blacks, and Lily-Whites*, 42, 53, 67; and Gerald Horne, *Black Liberation/Red Scare*, 23–24.

16. Gerald Horne, *Black Liberation/Red Scare*, 19–20, 24–25. The Adamson quote comes from Horne, 25, who took it from a letter in the Herbert Hoover Papers.

17. Bullock, "Profile of a Periodical," 95–99.

18. *Atlanta Independent*, 5 January 1928, 1.

19. Dittmer, *Black Georgia*, 163–164.

20. When Aurelius was at Morehouse, he published an annual for the college's 1925–1926 school year, which may have influenced W. A. to later enter the publishing field. Such is the influence of older brothers. *Atlanta Daily World*, 11 February 1934, 8; and Edward A. Jones, "Morehouse College." Their father, a PhD, an educator, and a fraternal leader along with being a minister, would later move to eastern Tennessee, where he preached at Jonesboro, at Washington, and ultimately at West Main Street Christian Church in Johnson City. W. A.'s membership moved there with his father, as there was no church of that denomination in Atlanta. *Atlanta Daily World*, 8 February 1934, 1.

21. Another account has W. A. always scheming to make money. He sold six hundred umbrellas during one school year, quit Morehouse, married his

first wife, and then moved to Florida. *Atlanta Daily World*, 8 February 1934, 1, 11 February 1934, 6, 12 February 1934, 6; and Teel, "W. A. Scott," 159–165.

22. Oliver, "History and Development," 3. While at Morehouse, Scott took an economics course from Lorimer D. Milton, who worked for Citizens Trust, which was the receiver of Service Printing Company following the financial demise of Heman Perry, its owner, in the mid-1920s. Though Milton claimed he never charged W. A., the Scott family disputed that claim, arguing that he wrangled a favorable deal from Milton and Citizens Trust. Ingham and Feldman, *African American Business Leaders*, 582.

23. *Atlanta Daily World*, 8 February 1934, 1, 11 February 1934, 6; W. A. Scott to C. A. Barnett, 6 August 1928; and Agreement, 6 August 1928, both in box 148, folder 7, Claude A. Barnett Papers: The Associated Negro Press, 1918–1967, pt. 2, Associated Negro Press Organizational Files, 1920–1966, Chicago Historical Society, Chicago, Ill. (hereinafter Barnett Papers); and Davis, "Negro America's First Daily," 86. For more on Davis, see Davis, *Livin' the Blues*; and Davis, *Writings of Frank Marshall Davis*.

24. Hogan, *Black National News Service*, 28, 56–74.

25. Davis quoted in Ingham and Feldman, *African American Business Leaders*, 583; and Alexis Scott interview.

26. W. A. Scott to Associated Negro Press, 18 February 1930, box 148, folder 7, Barnett Papers; Oliver, "History and Development," 6–7; and Ingham and Feldman, *African American Business Leaders*, 584.

27. *Atlanta Daily World*, 14 March 1932, 1, 8 February 1934, 1, 11 February 1934, 6, 12 February 1934, 6, 13 March 1934, 1; W. A. Scott to C. A. Barnett, 12 December 1929, box 148, folder 7, Barnett Papers; and Hornsby, "Georgia," 127–130. Along with news from the Syndicate and the ANP, the Scotts got photos for the rotogravure section from both of those sources, International News Photos, Acme Wide World, and other mainstream services. Barnett, "Why Can't We Have Negro Dailies?," reprinted in *Indianapolis Recorder*, 15 January 1938, 13.

Davis was up against a more powerful force than himself in the *Atlanta Daily World*. He lost, and by 1931, the *Atlanta Independent* was running at an economic loss and Davis's influence had diminished precipitously. Still, the paper reported a circulation of 27,000 in 1932, a circulation of 11,250 in 1933, and a similar circulation in 1934, even after it ostensibly folded. *N. W. Ayer & Son's Directory of Newspapers and Periodicals* listed the *Independent* as having a circulation of 10,125 in 1935. The directory, in fact, continued to list the *Independent* into the 1940s, which meant that Davis voluntarily submitted his newspaper to the directory, even though it had gone defunct. Gerald Horne, *Black Liberation/Red Scare*, 23–24; Chambliss, "What Negro Newspapers of Georgia Say," 12; *N. W. Ayer & Son's Directory of Newspapers and Periodicals* (1932), 170; *N. W. Ayer & Son's Directory of Newspapers and Periodicals* (1933), 168; *N. W. Ayer & Son's Directory of Newspapers and Periodicals* (1934), 163;

N. W. Ayer & Son's Directory of Newspapers and Periodicals (1935), 164; and *N. W. Ayer & Son's Directory of Newspapers and Periodicals* (1936), 162.

28. *Memphis World*, 15 April 1932, 2.

29. Jesse O. Thomas to C. A. Barnett, 25 February 1931, box 148, folder 7, Barnett Papers.

30. W. A. Scott to C. A. Barnett, 23 June 1931, box 148, folder 7, Barnett Papers.

31. Blackwell, "Black-Controlled Media," 12; Alfred McClung Lee, *Daily Newspaper in America*, 177; Odum-Hinmon, "Cautious Crusader," 15–16; Gore, *Negro Journalism*, 19–20; and Pride, "Register and History," 18–25.

32. Gordon, *Georgia Negro*, 267–268; W. A. Scott to Associated Negro Press, 4 October 1928; W. A. Scott to Associated Negro Press, 21 October 1929; W. A. Scott to Associated Negro Press, 12 November 1929; W. A. Scott to Associated Negro Press, 30 December 1929, all in box 148, folder 7, Barnett Papers; *Atlanta Daily World*, 8 February 1934, 1, 11 February 1934, 6, 12 February 1934, 6, 13 March 1934, 1; *New York Amsterdam News*, 14 February 1934, 1; Hornsby, "Georgia," 127–130; Allen Woodrow Jones, "Alabama," 43; and Wolseley, *Black Press, USA*, 73–74. As the *World* grew in stature and resources, it became able to send correspondents to major sporting events like Joe Louis fights or black college football rivalries. For the most part, however, it still relied on press agents for coverage of baseball games. It also always held a membership with the Associated Negro Press. The paper's physical plant covered roughly four thousand square feet, a cramped operation to be sure. The office was in the Citizens Trust building at 210 Auburn Avenue. Oliver, "History and Development," 10–11, 13, 22–23.

33. *Atlanta Daily World*, 31 March 1932, 6; and Barnett, "Why Can't We Have Negro Dailies?," 13. The expansion did take a toll on the family. "It seems as if there is about to be a rift in the ranks of the Scott family in the very near future," reported Frank Marshall Davis. "As a matter of fact, it has already occurred to a certain extent." Davis was never specific about "this family fuss," but he did confide that he was frustrated enough that he was open to finding new employment in the field. Claude Barnett of the Associated Negro Press was unsurprised, "because the whole country has been wondering how they were managing to do the startling things which you are doing down that way." The family strain would continue. On 5 June 1935, L. A. Scott, one of the brothers, arrived at the Syndicate offices drunk and in a rage, arguing with their mother, Lucile, and attacking employee Lucien Dupre. When Cliff MacKay and John Calhoun tried to detain him, L. A. punched MacKay as well. He stormed off to the press itself, ripping belts from the machinery and scattering tools before again attacking Dupre. He then left, heading all the way to Bolivar, Tennessee. When he returned later that month, he was arrested. Dupre was confined to his home for four weeks as a result of the wounds he sustained at the hands of L. A. Scott. C. A. Scott to C. A. Barnett, postal telegraph,

8 July 1935; Associated Negro Press to C. A. Scott, 10 July 1935; and C. A. Scott to Percival L. Prattis, 12 July 1935, all in box 148, folder 8, Barnett Papers; F. M. Davis to Claude Barnett, 9 August 1931; and C. A. Barnett to F. M. Davis, 1 September 1931, both in box 148, folder 7, Barnett Papers.

34. Associated Negro Press to W. A. Scott, 22 October 1931; W. A. Scott to C. A. Barnett, 6 November 1931; and Associated Negro Press to W. A. Scott, 6 November 1931, all in box 148, folder 7, Barnett Papers.

35. *Houston Informer*, 23 April 1932, 3; *Boston Chronicle*, 31 December 1932, 1; *Indianapolis Recorder*, 9 July 1932, 2; *Lynchings by States and Race*, 2; Terkel, *Hard Times*, 68; Thomas, *Human Exploitation*, xiv–xv; Wolters, *Negroes and the Great Depression*, 98–113, 196–203; Frederickson, *Dixiecrat Revolt*, 13; and Warren, *Herbert Hoover*, 241–242.

36. Tobin, "Early New Deal in Baton Rouge," 307–308; and *Baton Rouge Morning Advocate*, 13 January 1933, 4. The editorial was provocative, and it was syndicated, also appearing in other Louisiana papers like the *Ruston Daily Leader*, 9 January 1933, 2.

37. That isn't to say that groups like the Neighborhood Union kowtowed to white whims. During the Depression, the group clashed with the white Fulton County Relief Center when indigent whites were given Christmas gifts and indigent blacks were not. Still, by acting as the representative of lower-class blacks to white relief agencies, the Neighborhood Union emphasized class distinctions further while still doing fundamentally good work. The divisions were seen as a fait accompli. Sitkoff, *New Deal for Blacks*, 1:49; Kirby, *Black Americans*, 97; Lerner and Kerber, *Majority Finds Its Past*, 68–69; Godshalk, *Veiled Visions*, 233; and Ferguson, *Black Politics*, 19–24, 29–43, 49–51.

38. Alexander, *New Jim Crow*, 213–214; and Ferguson, *Black Politics*, 5–17. See also Sklaroff, *Black Culture*.

39. For more on the postbellum divisions of black Atlanta by social and economic status, see Dorsey, *To Build Our Lives Together*; and Drago, *Black Politicians and Reconstruction*. For more on the role of the Atlanta Race Riot of 1906 in exacerbating those divisions, see Godshalk, *Veiled Visions*; and Mixon, *Atlanta Riot*.

40. Davis, "Negro America's First Daily," 87.

41. Fleming, "Emancipation and the Negro," 216; and Blackwell, "Black-Controlled Media," 20.

42. Odum-Hinmon, "Cautious Crusader," 38.

43. Duncombe, *Notes from Underground*, 58–60.

44. Hornsby, "Georgia," 127–128; and Ingham and Feldman, *African American Business Leaders*, 585–586.

45. *Atlanta Daily World*, 27 December 1931, 3.

46. Associated Negro Press to W. A. Scott, 25 February 1930; W. A. Scott to C. A. Barnett, 28 February 1930; Associated Negro Press to W. A. Scott, 5 April 1930; Associated Negro Press to W. A. Scott, 30 July 1930, all in box 148, folder 7, Barnett Papers.

47. Associated Negro Press to W. A. Scott, 2 March 1931; Associated Negro Press to W. A. Scott, 7 March 1931; and Associated Negro Press to W. A. Scott, 30 June 1931, all in box 148, folder 7, Barnett Papers.

48. W. A. Scott to C. A. Barnett, 4 July 1931; and Associated Negro Press to W. A. Scott, 7 July 1931, both in box 148, folder 7, Barnett Papers.

49. Hornsby, "Georgia," 128; and *Atlanta World*, 15 January 1932, 2. For examples of advertisements for skin whiteners, hair straighteners, and white businesses, see *Atlanta World*, 27 December 1931, 5, 6, 30 December 1931, 5, 1 January 1932, 5, 15 January 1932, 6, 27 January 1932, 2, 3 February 1932, 4, 17 February 1932, 6, 26 February 1932, 1, 4, 28 February 1932, 6, 2 March 1932, 1, 9 March 1932, 1, 2, 11 March 1932, 1, 13 March 1932, 1, 14 March 1932, 1, 8, 16 March 1932, 1, 17 March 1932, 6, 20 March 1932, 1.

50. Hornsby, "Georgia," 131.

51. Ibid.

52. Ibid., 132–133.

53. Ibid.

54. *Atlanta Daily World*, 2 December 1931, 4, 4 February 1934, 1, 10 February 1934, 1; and Hornsby, "Georgia," 134, 136. The rotogravure section lasted from 1931 to 1937, a victim at the end of expensive printing costs. Oliver, "History and Development," 10.

55. Hornsby, "Georgia," 134–135, 136–137; *Atlanta Daily World*, 2 December 1931, 4; and Ingham and Feldman, *African American Business Leaders*, 586–587.

56. *Atlanta Daily World*, 15 January 1932, 4. In 1948, that final goal came to fruition when Atlanta hired its first black officers. Hornsby, "Georgia," 137.

57. Davis quoted in Ingham and Feldman, *African American Business Leaders*, 581; C. A. Barnett to F. M. Davis, 27 November 1933; and Associated Negro Press to W. A. Scott, 1 February 1934, both in box 148, folder 8, Barnett Papers.

58. C. A. Barnett to F. M. Davis, 12 February 1934; Associated Negro Press to C. A. Scott, 22 February 1934; and Frank Marshall Davis to C. A. Barnett, 22 February 1934, all in box 148, folder 8, Barnett Papers.

59. Oliver, "History and Development," 14–15; and Blackwell, "Black-Controlled Media," 99.

60. C. A. quoted in Ingham and Feldman, *African American Business Leaders*, 586; Hornsby, "Georgia," 129; and Blackwell, "Black-Controlled Media," 102–103.

61. Egerton, *Speak Now against the Day*, 464.

62. Quoted in Blackwell, "Black-Controlled Media," 104–106.

63. Ibid., 104–106; C. A. Barnett to C. A. Scott, 8 September 1934; and C. A. Scott to C. A. Barnett, 18 September 1934, both in box 148, folder 8, Barnett Papers.

64. Records from 8–14 July 1934, in Advertising Sales, June 1934–October 1935, box 1, Atlanta Daily World Records, 1931–1996, Manuscript Collection

no. 1092, Manuscript, Archives, and Rare Book Library, Emory University, Atlanta, Ga. (hereinafter Atlanta Daily World Records).

65. Advertising Journal, July 1934, OBV1, Advertising Sales, February–August 1934, Atlanta Daily World Records.

66. Ziff began working with black publications like the *Chicago Defender* in the 1920s and then moved across the country. Ziff contracted with a large selection of black newspapers and then solicited national advertising from mainstream corporations, arguing that the vast majority of black customers rarely read the white press. In a 1932 publication, Ziff made the case that "no merchandising picture is complete" without an understanding of the African American market. "Dark Market," *Time*, 5 December 1932, 26; "Appoint W. B. Ziff Company, Representative," *Printer's Ink*, 9 March 1922, 36; "Ziff's List of Negro Papers," 392–393; and Ziff, *Negro Market*, 3.

67. Summary Advertising Sold during October 1934, and Summary Advertising Sold during October 1935, both in Advertising Sales, June 1934–October 1935, box 1, Atlanta Daily World Records.

68. Odum-Hinmon, "Cautious Crusader," 39.

69. Quoted in Blackwell, "Black-Controlled Media," 79–80.

70. Account no. 15: Bee Dew Prods., Inc., Advertising Record, 1939–1940, box 1, Atlanta Daily World Records; and *Afro-American*, 4 April 1942, 19.

71. C. A. Scott to W. D. Holder, 12 September 1936, OBV137, Atlanta Daily World Records.

72. "A. S. Scott—Promoter, Special ACIPCO Edition, 14 July 1937," OBV138, Atlanta Daily World Records.

73. In September 1934, Davis resigned his post for "the quieter and more introspective life of authorship." *Atlanta Daily World*, 24 September 1934, 6; and Alexander, *New Jim Crow*, 213.

74. Oliver, "History and Development," 5–6.

Chapter 2. Race, Representation, and the Puryear Ax Murders

1. Police Department, City of Memphis, Report of Homicide, Will Jamison, Negro, Age 27; and Police Department, City of Memphis, Report of Homicide, Aurelia Zina Puryear, white, age 8; Police Department, City of Memphis, Report of Homicide, Aurelia Puryear, white, age 38, all in box 1, folder 55, Criminal Court Files, 1932–1937, Donald F. Paine Collection of Hiram Hall, Eugene D. Blanchard, and Stanley Puryear, MS.3204, Special Collections, University of Tennessee Libraries, Knoxville (hereafter Paine Collection).

2. *Washington Post*, 3 May 1932, 10; and *New York Herald Tribune*, 3 May 1932, 5.

3. *Atlanta Daily World*, 4 May 1932, 1; and *Memphis Commercial Appeal*, 3 May 1932, 1.

4. *Atlanta Daily World*, 4 May 1932, 1.

5. *Memphis Commercial Appeal*, 3 May 1932, 1.

6. *Memphis Commercial Appeal*, 3 May 1932, 1.

7. *Memphis Commercial Appeal*, 3 May 1932, 1. For a full run of the paper's coverage of the murder, see *Commercial Appeal* articles, May 1932, box 1, folder 51, Paine Collection.

8. Thomas Harrison Baker, *"Memphis Commercial Appeal,"* 3–5.

9. Talley, *One Hundred Years*, 16, 67.

10. Thomas Harrison Baker, *"Memphis Commercial Appeal,"* 218–221, 252–256; Talley, *One Hundred Years*, 68–69; and Goings and Smith, "'Unhidden' Transcripts," 372–373.

11. Porteous, "Two Eds of Memphis"; and Meeman, *Editorial We*.

12. *Memphis Press-Scimitar*, 3 May 1932, 1. For a full run of the paper's coverage of both the murder and Puryear's first trial, see Stanley Puryear Articles, 1932, box 1, folder 50, Paine Collection.

13. *Memphis Press-Scimitar*, 3 May 1932, 1, 2.

14. *Memphis Commercial Appeal*, 3 May 1932, 1, 4; and *Chicago Defender*, 14 May 1932, 1.

15. Investigating, however, was difficult. Police announced that too many people had handled the weapon at the crime scene, making the recovery of fingerprints a virtual impossibility. *Memphis Commercial Appeal*, 3 May 1932, 4.

16. *Memphis Commercial Appeal*, 3 May 1932, 4. Mainstream white coverage eventually went beyond the immediate reports and opinions of the local press. In December 1940, for example, *Intimate Detective Stories* featured a sensationalistic account of the crime. Much later, in 1997, local historian William F. Currotto compiled and published what amounted to a scrapbook that rehearsed the most lurid details of the case. Jack DeWitt, "Problem of the Curving Shot," *Intimate Detective Stories* 1 (December 1940): 19–21, 36–38, in box 1, folder 47, Paine Collection; and William F. Currotto, *Stanley Puryear Took an Ax* (Memphis, Tenn.: Patchwork Books, 1997), in box 1, folder 49, Paine Collection.

17. *Atlanta Daily World*, 10 May 1932, 2.

18. *Memphis Press-Scimitar*, 3 May 1932, 2.

19. "An Act to Repeal So Much of the Forty-Eighth Section [of] an Act Now in Force in this State as Provides for the Trial of Slaves for Capital Offences and Directing the Mode [of] Trial in Future," *Acts of the State of Tennessee, 1815* (Nashville, Tenn.: Printer to the State, 1815), 175–176.

20. "An Act to Make the Rules of Evidence in the Federal and State Courts, Uniform," *Acts of the State of Tennessee, 1867–68* (Nashville, Tenn.: Printer to the State, 1868), 94; House Bill no. 152, in *House Journal of the Thirty-Seventh General Assembly of the State of Tennessee* (Nashville, Tenn.: Printer to the State, 1871), 91–92, 133, 347; and "An Act to Amend an Act Passed the 13th Day of March, 1868, Entitled 'An Act to Make the Rules of Evidence in the Federal and State Courts, Uniform,' and the Acts Amendatory Thereof," *Acts of the State of Tennessee, 1871* (Nashville, Tenn.: Printer to the State, 1871), 119–120.

21. §9774–§9805, chapter 4, *Annotated Code of Tennessee, 1934*, 8:684–703. This is not to say that black witnesses were not the object of bigotry. One of

the cases that remained in the minds of Memphis residents in 1932 was a case in St. Louis eight years prior. While the murder trial was held in Missouri, its defendant was Lemuel Motlow of Lynchburg, Tennessee, a nephew of Jack Newton Daniel and an influential part of the Jack Daniel's whiskey business. Motlow claimed that he accidentally killed a train conductor on a railroad taking him back to Tennessee because Motlow was trying to kill a black porter who had been insolent to him. The porter, Ed Wallace, was grazed by a second shot, but testified that he had no quarrel with Motlow. The defendant's lawyers responded by demonizing Wallace. "There are two classes of Negroes in this country. One is the kind that knows its place. These are Negroes we love, care for, and protect," explained one of Motlow's Nashville-based lawyers, Frank Bond. "The other class demands racial and social equality. They want to inter-marry with your daughters and mine. They shall not do it. This Negro Wallis [*sic*] is one of these Negro uplifters." Motlow was acquitted. John M. McGuire, "Case History: Poking Around in Old Court Files from the '20s, Retired Judge Arthur Litz Has Unearthed One of the City's Most Scandalous Murder Trials," *St. Louis Post-Dispatch, Everyday Magazine*, 31 July 1997, 1G.

22. *Memphis Press-Scimitar*, 5 May 1932, 1.

23. *Atlanta Daily World*, 10 May 1932, 2; and *Memphis World*, 10 May 1932, 1.

24. *Memphis Commercial Appeal*, 3 May 1932, 4.

25. *Memphis Press-Scimitar*, 5 May 1932, 1.

26. *Nashville Tennessean*, 3 May 1932, 1, 4 May 1932, 1, 2, 6 May 1932, 11, 11 May 1932, 1, 3. All of the *Tennessean*'s coverage came from the Associated Press; the paper clearly saw the case's broader interest to its readers but did not find it important enough for editorializing or sending one of its own re-porters to Memphis. See *Nashville Tennessean*, 12 May 1932, 3, 19 June 1932, 12, 28 June 1932, 12, 19 July 1932, 10, 20 July 1932, 2, 22 September 1932, 14, 27 September 1932, 6, 28 September 1932, 1, 2, 29 September 1932, 4, 5 October 1932, 1, 7 October 1932, 1, 6, 8 October 1932, 4, 12 October 1932, 14, 19 October 1932, 1.

27. Goldfield, *Black, White, and Southern*, 27. The *World*'s Nashville equiv-alent was the *Nashville Globe*, and that black weekly probably covered the case similarly. Unfortunately, any coverage from the paper no longer survives. The two extant editions from 1932 cover state murders, and the few remain-ing editions from subsequent years do the same, along with coverage of the Scottsboro Boys and other racially charged causes célèbre. But no *Nashville Globe* or *Nashville Globe and Independent* coverage remains from the period of May to October 1932, nor from any of Puryear's subsequent retrials. See *Nashville Globe*, 4 March 1932, 15 April 1932, 6 October 1933, 30 March 1934, 22 November 1935.

28. *Memphis World*, 28 June 1931, 1, 3, 16 September 1931, 8, 9 February 1932, 1. During the Depression, financial problems forced the paper to move from three editions per week to two. Shannon, "Tennessee," 339–340.

29. Shannon, "Tennessee," 340–341.

30. *Memphis World*, 26 July 1931, 1, 8, 16 September 1931, 1, 22 March 1932, 8.

31. *Memphis World*, 15 April 1932, 1.

32. *Memphis World*, 10 May 1932, 1.

33. The paper's coverage of the indictments also noted that "several neighbors have testified since the grand jury session that the Puryears had had a violent quarrel a few days before the ax slaying." *Memphis World*, 10 May 1932, 1.

34. The *World* reported two weeks after the killing that Jamison's uncle Dan had been murdered with a shotgun fifteen years prior in Macon. "He and another man had been joking," Jamison's aunt explained. "Dan, I suppose, cracked the biggest joke. The man got mad and shot half his head off with a shotgun." The first murder was not racially motivated, but it still resonated. The *World* titled its coverage, "Jamison Is 2nd Shotgun Victim in Family." *Memphis World*, 17 May 1932, 1; and *Atlanta Daily World*, 16 May 1932, 1, 2.

35. Jamison had been taken to Memphis's General Hospital, where he died later the same day. he was able to speak to authorities, and the black press's compensatory celebration of his life began soon after. Jamison died on his twenty-sixth birthday; he was born in 1906 in Macon, Mississippi. A reporter from the *Memphis World* interviewed Jamison's first cousin for the Southern Newspaper Syndicate. She explained that Jamison had left Macon in 1920 to work on a government barge crew, which took him north, but he moved to Memphis in 1928. He was planning to go back to work for the barge crew on the day he was killed. Jamison had no criminal record, and investigators had decided that he was most likely innocent of any crime by the time the *World* reporter managed to interview his cousin, but when he was originally shot, the police were not so sure. They had stopped his cousin from bringing him a glass of water, despite his desperate plea for a drink. "His eyes were closed, set for the eternal sleep," the *World* said, but he "was never able to have his last moments lightened with the comforting sight of his closest relative. Instead the man was hammered with a barrage of questions from officers and reporters, and died clinging to his original story." *Atlanta Daily World*, 4 May 1932, 1, 10 May 1932, 2; and *Memphis Commercial Appeal*, 3 May 1932, 1.

36. *Atlanta Daily World*, 10 May 1932, 2; and *Memphis World*, 10 May 1932, 1.

37. *Atlanta Daily World*, 10 May 1932, 2; and *Memphis World*, 10 May 1932, 1.

38. *Atlanta Daily World*, 10 May 1932, 2; and *Memphis World*, 10 May 1932, 1, 5.

39. *Atlanta Daily World*, 10 May 1932, 2; and *Memphis World*, 10 May 1932, 5.

40. *Atlanta Daily World*, 10 May 1932, 6.

41. *Atlanta Daily World*, 10 May 1932, 6. At the same time, the paper was willing to give credit where it was due. When homicide investigator William Lemmer died of a heart attack several weeks following the Puryear murder,

the paper eulogized him as a "friend of Negroes." He had been part of the Puryear investigation and had been an early believer of Jamison's account. "He has tried to make this community as safe for Negro citizens to li[v]e in as he did for white constituents," the *World* reported. *Atlanta Daily World*, 16 May 1932, 6.

42. *Chicago Defender*, 7 May 1932, 3. The Wanderer case became known as the Case of the Ragged Stranger.

43. *Pittsburgh Courier*, 14 May 1932, 6.

44. *Pittsburgh Courier*, 21 May 1932, A1.

45. *Chicago Defender*, 4 June 1932, 1.

46. *Pittsburgh Courier*, 30 July 1932, 4.

47. *Baltimore Afro-American*, 8 October 1932, 22.

48. *Baltimore Afro-American*, 4 June 1932, 10.

49. While the change was being considered in June, they were able to win Puryear a delay until September (he was temporarily released), following the court's summer recess. *Memphis World*, 17 June 1932, 1; and *Atlanta Daily World*, 17 June 1932, 5. In July, Puryear's defense attorneys had Jamison's body exhumed to take fingerprints, an effort to demonstrate that he had a past criminal record for stealing cars, despite the fact that police argued that those crimes were committed by a different Will Jamison. *Atlanta Daily World*, 7 July 1943, 5A.

50. Stanley A. Puryear v. State of Tennessee, vol. 1, 1–3, box 1, folder 57, in Stanley Puryear vs. State of Tennessee—Volume I, December 1934–January 1935 (1 of 4); Testimony of Stanley Puryear, in Stanley A. Puryear v. State of Tennessee, vol. 2, 321–451, box 2, folder 1, in Stanley Puryear vs. State of Tennessee—Volume II, December 1934–January 1935 (2 of 4); and Testimony of Mary Sunshine Walker, in Stanley A. Puryear v. State of Tennessee, vol. 4, 751–781, box 2, folder 3, in Stanley Puryear vs. State of Tennessee—Volume I, December 1934–January 1935 (1 of 4), all in Paine Collection.

51. *Atlanta Daily World*, 7 October 1932, 1A.

52. *Afro-American*, 8 October 1932, 22, 15 October 1932, 9, 22; and *Pittsburgh Courier*, 15 October 1932, 4. Puryear's defense called more than forty witnesses to vouch for him, but the state's evidence contradicted many of their statements.

53. *Chicago Defender*, 29 October 1932, 2.

54. Verdict, in Stanley A. Puryear v. State of Tennessee, vol. 4, 958–960, box 2, folder 3, in Stanley Puryear vs. State of Tennessee—Volume IV, December 1934–January 1935 (4 of 4), Paine Collection; *Atlanta Daily World*, 17 October 1932, 1, 20 October 1932, 7; *Washington Post*, 20 October 1932, 4; *New York Amsterdam News*, 26 October 1932, 16; and *Afro-American*, 29 October 1932, 8.

55. *Afro-American*, 29 October 1932, 8; and *Pittsburgh Courier*, 29 October 1932, 4.

56. *Atlanta Daily World*, 21 October 1932, 6.

57. *Nashville Tennessean*, 20 October 1932, 2; and *Chicago Defender*, 29 October 1932, 2.

58. Bailey and Green, *"Law Never Here,"* xi–xvii; and Du Bois, *Souls of Black Folk*, 179.

59. Cobb, *Digest of the Statute Laws*, 973; McNair, *Criminal Injustice*, 168–169; Jones-Brown, "Race as a Legal Construct," 145; *Chaney v. Saunders*, 3 Munf. 51 (Va. 1811); *Dean v. Commonwealth*, 45 Va. (4 Gratt.) 210 (1847); Rothman, *Notorious in the Neighborhood*, 215–216; and Higginbotham, *Shades of Freedom*, 40. See also Sweet, *Legal History*, 265–464.

60. Thomas D. Morris, "Slaves and the Rules," 1209–1210, 1215; Tischauser, *Changing Nature*, 90; *People v. Hall*, 4 Cal. 399 (1854); McDaniel, "Elizabeth 'Lizzie' Fouse," 275; and Howard, *Black Liberation in Kentucky*, 106–7, 144, 155.

61. *Macon Daily Telegraph*, 25 October 1865, 2; and Milewski, "From Slave to Litigant" (*Law and History Review*), 747. See also Milewski, "From Slave to Litigant" (PhD diss.); and Pincus, *Virginia Supreme Court*, 31–33. For more on black witnesses in criminal and civil cases, see Mangum, *Legal Status of the Negro*, 350–355.

62. Oliver Wendell Holmes's opinion in *Rogers* validated a motion to quash a murder indictment because "jury commissioners appointed to select the grand jury excluded from the list of persons to serve as grand jurors all colored persons, although largely in the majority of the population of the county, and although otherwise qualified to serve as grand jurors, solely on the ground of their race and color and of their having been disfranchised and deprived of all rights as electors in the State of Alabama." *Rogers v. Alabama*, 192 U.S. 226 (1904); Avins, "Right to Be a Witness," 471, 480–481, 484, 488, 497–499, 500–501; and Tischauser, *Changing Nature*, 90. See also Howard, "Black Testimony Controversy"; Delombard, "Representing the Slave"; and Campbell, *Crime and Punishment*, 62–65, 78–81, 129–137.

63. *Norris v. Alabama*, 294 U.S. 587 (1935); and Klarman, "Racial Origins," 65. Part of the reason that black citizens entered the legal system at such peril, whether for jury service, as witnesses, as defendants, or as plaintiffs, was because of the widespread criminalizing of the black population by white leaders and the courts themselves. For more on the early twentieth-century criminalization of blackness, particularly in the development of modern cities, see Muhammad, *Condemnation of Blackness*.

64. Boyd, *Blind Obedience*, 97–108, quote 105.

65. Heitzeg, "'Whiteness,' Criminality, and the Double-Standards," 199. For more on modern aspects of racial discrimination in criminal justice, see Rosich, *Race, Ethnicity*.

66. Carlin, "Courtroom as White Space," 450, 484. See also Gray-Ray et al., "African Americans." Former U.S. attorney Paul Butler noticed when trying Mayor Marion Barry in 1990 that black jurors would sometimes refuse to convict black defendants despite accepting their guilt, or hope that black defendants

would be freed because their behavior was the result of a flawed system or because the prosecution of the crime was racist in intent. This notion of black retribution for racist behavior within white supremacist structures surely played a role in early decisions to keep enslaved people from the witness stand. This conundrum leaves Butler arguing that black jurors should harness the power of jury nullification to keep some nonviolent black offenders out of prison, since "the decision as to what kind of conduct by African Americans ought to be punished is better made by African Americans themselves, based on the costs and benefits to their community, than by the traditional criminal justice process, which is controlled by white lawmakers and white law enforcers." Butler, "Racially Based Jury Nullification," 678.

67. *Pittsburgh Courier*, 3 December 1932, 1, 10 December 1932, 5.

68. *Washington Post*, 30 November 1933, 7; and *Memphis Commercial Appeal*, 30 November 1933, 1.

69. *Memphis Commercial Appeal*, 20 November 1934, 13, 22 November 1934, 13, 23 November 1934, 1, 12, 24 November 1934, 1, 12, 25 November 1934, 1, 5, 26 November 1934, 1, 27 November 1934, 1; *Pittsburgh Courier*, 8 September 1934, A7; and *Washington Post*, 20 November 1934, 1.

70. *Pittsburgh Courier*, 31 August 1935, A3; and State of Tennessee v. Stanley Puryear, Motion for a New Trial, 13 December 1934, box 1, folder 53, in Stanley Puryear vs. State of Tennessee, December 1938, Paine Collection.

71. Stanley A. Puryear v. State of Tennessee, in the Supreme Court at Nashville, December Term, 1935, brief, n.d., box 1, folder 56, Paine Collection; *Memphis Commercial Appeal*, 5 April 1936, 1; and *New York Herald Tribune*, 5 April 1936, 30.

72. *Atlanta Daily World*, 12 January 1937, 2, 2 July 1937, 1; *Memphis Commercial Appeal*, 29 June 1937, 1, 5, 13; *Pittsburgh Courier*, 13 March 1937, 3; and State of Tennessee v. Stanley A. Puryear, box 1, folder 53, in Stanley Puryear vs. State of Tennessee, December 1938, Paine Collection.

73. *Atlanta Daily World*, 30 December 1937, 3; and *Pittsburgh Courier*, 8 January 1938, 3.

74. *Puryear v. State*, Supreme Court of Tennessee, 4 March 1939, *South Western Reporter*, in folder 46, South Western Reporter–State of Tennessee vs. Stanley Puryear, March 1939, Paine Collection. The one victory Puryear had at the Tennessee Supreme Court came following his failed appeal. His lawyer secured him fifteen additional days in the Shelby County jail before being transferred to the state penitentiary. *Memphis Commercial Appeal*, 5 March 1939, 1, 12, 10 March 1939, 11; and *Atlanta Daily World*, 10 March 1939, 2.

75. *Afro-American*, 15 November 1941, 8; *Pittsburgh Courier*, 15 November 1941, 23; *Chicago Defender*, 15 November 1941, 2; and Stanley A. Puryear v. State of Tennessee, in the Supreme Court of Tennessee, box 1, folder 54, Tennessee Supreme Court case, n.d., Paine Collection.

76. *Memphis World*, 10 May 1932, 1, 5, 6; *Memphis Commercial Appeal*, 3 May 1932, 1; and *Memphis Press-Scimitar*, 3 May 1932, 1, 2. (All of the coverage

throughout early May from these two white dailies is similar to the coverage from 3 May.)

77. Shannon, "Tennessee," 340.

Chapter 3. The Unsolved Murder of William Alexander Scott

1. *Atlanta Daily World*, 1 February 1934, 1, 8 February 1934, 1, 10 February 1934, 1, 4, 11 February 1934, 1; and *Atlanta Constitution*, 31 January 1934, 6.

2. The three most comprehensive works on this transition are Alexander, *New Jim Crow*; Muhammad, *Condemnation of Blackness*; and Blackmon, *Slavery by Another Name*. See also McNair, *Criminal Injustice*; Mancini, *One Dies, Get Another*; Fassin and Rechtman, *Empire of Trauma*; Oshinsky, *Worse than Slavery*; and Fassin, *Enforcing Order*.

3. Brundage, *Lynching in the New South*, 105–108. See also Dray, *At the Hands of Persons Unknown*, 245–247, 262, 304–305, 440–442; and Bailey and Tolnay, *Lynched*, 14, 185–188, 230.

4. LeFlouria, *Chained in Silence*, 45–47.

5. Washington and Du Bois, *Negro in the South*, 180.

6. *Atlanta Daily World*, 11 February 1934, 1, 6, 12 February 1934, 6; *Baltimore Afro-American*, 17 February 1934, 1; *Chicago Defender*, 17 February 1934, 1; *New York Amsterdam News*, 14 February 1934, 1; and Davis, "Negro America's First Daily," 86.

7. Agnes Maddox, along with being Scott's secretary, had been a schoolteacher. The *Pittsburgh Courier* called her a "local society celebrity" and noted that she "was mentioned in connection with Scott's third divorce last summer." Maddox originally worked in the Atlanta office of the *Courier* before moving to the *World*. She worked from four o'clock in the afternoon until midnight, "as Scott's business expansion had made it necessary for him to run his plant in three shifts." The *Amsterdam News* was more discreet in its description, calling her a former teacher who was prominent in Atlanta society. *Pittsburgh Courier*, 10 February 1934, 1; *New York Amsterdam News*, 14 February 1934, 1; *Baltimore Afro-American*, 3 February 1934, 1; and *Atlanta Daily World*, 10 February 1934, 1, 11 February 1934, 1, 6.

8. The creation of Harris Memorial was part of a larger trend in the late nineteenth and early twentieth century to create black hospitals in urban areas throughout the country. Mitchell F. Rice and Woodrow Jones Jr. have argued that the reason for this profusion was threefold. First, black physicians needed places to practice. Second, there was a national belief—among both whites and blacks—that a lack of adequate black medical facilities contributed to disproportionately poor health among the black population. Finally, black doctors saw the creation of hospitals as part of a larger effort to lift the social standing of the black community. Rice and Jones, *Public Policy*, 15–18; Articles of Incorporation, William A. Harris Memorial Hospital, box 1, Manuscript Collection no. 1041, Sadye Harris Powell Family Papers, Manuscript, Archives and Rare Book Library, Emory University, Atlanta, Ga.; *Atlanta Daily World*, 3 February

1934, 1, 6 February 1934, 1, 7 February 1934, 6, 8 February 1934, 1, 11 February 1934, 1; *New York Amsterdam News*, 7 February 1934, 2; and *Atlanta Constitution*, 2 February 1934, 7, 8 February 1934, 13.

9. At the coroner's inquest, Powell told the jury that he destroyed the letter after three days because it frightened his wife. He had received the letter around 6:30 p.m. on 4 February 1934 by special delivery. He wasn't home, so the messenger slid it underneath his door. *Atlanta Daily World*, 10 February 1934, 1, 11 February 1934, 1.

10. MacVicar Hospital at Spelman was a thirty-bed facility that usually served Atlanta University Center students. Scott was the exception. The building still stands on Spelman's campus as MacVicar Hall. Audrey Arthur, "MacVicar Serves as Atlanta's Hospital for Blacks in the Late 1920s," *Inside Spelman*, http://www.insidespelman.com/?p=2299, accessed 14 October 2013; and Chang, *Citizens of a Christian Nation*, 6.

11. C. A. Scott was the Syndicate's assistant general manager and had been working for the paper since its inception. "In him," reported the *World*, "W. A. Scott placed sincere trust and confidence." Though it is not included in Fulton County's will records, a copy of the document exists in its collection of records related to the Scott estate. Last Will and Testament of W. A. Scott, Untitled, 1934, Estate 25021, Probate Court of Fulton County, Atlanta, Ga. (hereinafter Last Will of W. A. Scott). Quote from *Atlanta Daily World*, 8 February 1934, 1.

12. There were several reasons for Maddox's arrest. There was an apparent deathbed accusation by Scott that specifically implicated Maddox, and there were also witnesses who placed someone matching Maddox's description at the scene. *Atlanta Daily World*, 10 February 1934, 1, 11 February 1934, 1; *Baltimore Afro-American*, 17 February 1934, 1; *Atlanta Constitution*, 1 December 1927, 7, 22 September 1929, 6, 10 February 1934, 1, 10 April 1934, 10, and 22 March 1937, 7; and *Chicago Defender*, 17 February 1934, 1.

13. Velma Maia Thomas, "Centennial Celebration: The Odd Fellows Buildings," *Atlanta Daily World*, 29 April 2013, http://www.atlantadailyworld.com/201304295615/Original/centennial-celebration-the-odd-fellows-buildings, accessed 14 October 2013; Mason, *Black Atlanta*, 18, 24; Frank Marshall Davis, "Negro America's First Daily," 88; and Gerald Horne, *Black Liberation/Red Scare*, 21.

14. Scott had paid $2,000 to complete the transaction just a few hours before the shooting. Meanwhile, one of his competitors for the Odd Fellows building had purchased $30,000 in bonds held by Emory University as a mortgage on the building. *Atlanta Daily World*, 11 February 1934, 1; *New York Amsterdam News*, 14 February 1934, 1; and *New York Times*, 17 January 1911, 1.

15. *Atlanta Daily World*, 11 February 1934, 1.

16. Agnes told the inquest that she was not allowed in the room while her husband was making his will and that when she tried to read the finished product over the shoulder of one of the Scott brothers, they put it away so she couldn't see it. Scott's will bequeathed Agnes $2,000—the $2,000 that he had

put up as earnest money for his purchase of the Odd Fellows building—and one of two houses that he had purchased from receivers of the National Benefit Life Insurance Company. That relatively small segment of his fortune would "be taken by my said wife in lieu of dower and year support." The will was certainly not a document favorable to Agnes. Last Will of W. A. Scott; *Atlanta Daily World*, 11 February 1934, 1; *New York Amsterdam News*, 14 February 1934, 1; *Baltimore Afro-American*, 17 February 1934, 1; *Chicago Defender*, 17 February 1934, 1; and *Atlanta City Directory* (Atlanta, Ga.: Atlanta City Directory Co., 1934), 670.

17. *Atlanta Daily World*, 11 February 1934, 1, 12 February 1934, 1, 13 February 1934, 1, 14 February 1934, 1, 17 February 1934, 1, 18 February 1934, 1, 19 February 1934, 1, 20 February 1934, 1, 21 February 1934, 1, 24 February 1934, 1, 26 February 1934, 1; and *Atlanta Constitution*, 15 February 1934, 7.

18. *Atlanta Daily World*, 15 February 1934, 1, 27 February 1934, 1, 6, 28 February 1934, 1, 1 March 1934, 1, 2 March 1934, 1, 3 March 1934, 1, 5 March 1934, 1.

19. *Atlanta Daily World*, 15 February 1934, 1, 16 February 1934, 1. Citizens Trust and Lorimer D. Milton were instrumental in forming the Atlanta Negro Chamber of Commerce in August 1932. The bank's J. B. Blayton suggested the need for such a group and then called together a group of black businessmen, including Milton but not any of the Scotts or other representatives from the *World*. The local white chamber aided the organization's development. It had a vested interest in ensuring the success of a black version of the chamber in order to avoid any attempted integration of its own. "History of the Negro Chamber of Commerce," in *Atlanta—You Ought to Know Your Own!*, 13, 44; Franklin M. Garrett, *Atlanta and Environs*, 900–901; and Elizabeth Sandidge Evans, "Atlanta Negro Chamber of Commerce," 1:152–153.

20. *Atlanta Daily World*, 14 February 1934, 1. The *World* was critiqued by the *Pittsburgh Courier* on 10 February; the paper argued that Scott's methods were predatory and that his creation of the *Birmingham World* put the existing *Birmingham Reporter* out of business. But Oscar W. Adams, publisher of the *Reporter*, flatly denied that claim: his paper had "not lost a single line of advertising because of the appearance of Editor Scott's paper shipped here from Atlanta, and if we have lost a single subscriber or sale because of any of Mr. Scott's operations, we have not learned of it." *Pittsburgh Courier*, 3 March 1934, 5.

21. Holsey Temple was an African Methodist Episcopal church on the corner of Boulevard and Chamberlain streets in Atlanta. The only arrest that resulted from the event was of a white Emory student, Nathan Yagol, who was attending the rally. The charge was "inciting to riot" for sitting on the back pew of the church, but it was dismissed the following day. *Atlanta Constitution*, 12 December 1933, 2; *Atlanta Daily World*, 7 November 1932, 2; and Ferguson, *Black Politics*, 61–64. (The *World*'s coverage of the meeting is not cited because the 1933 editions of the *Atlanta Daily World* have not survived.)

22. Scott does not seem to have been associated with the Davis-Herndon group, though noncommunists like Blayton lent their support. Ferguson, *Black Politics*, 62, 64–65; and Brown-Nagin, *Courage to Dissent*, 32. As another example of the fracturing of black Atlanta, in an editorial on 15 February, G. R. Higginbotham paid an interesting sort of tribute, demanding that Scott's killer be captured because of the danger posed to the black community. "There are twelve million Negroes in America," he wrote, "and we have about come to the fork in the road of our civilization where we must take a stand, and not proceed further until we get our bearings." He worried that "human life has become so cheap" and encouraged his readers to vigilance. "We must demand that the assassin of W. A. Scott be brought to justice for our own safety. It is not a question of whether he was, in our opinion, a just or an unjust man. Those are relative terms and if we as judges and gunmen were permitted to bump off everybody who failed to come up to our requirements, there wouldn't perhaps be enough of us left to tell the tale. No man deserves to be bumped off." This kind of language seems to argue that many in black Atlanta were little sorry to see Scott go and were perhaps even unconcerned about catching the killer. *Atlanta Daily World*, 15 February 1934, 6.

23. *Atlanta Daily World*, 9 February 1934, 1.

24. A. S. Scott to C. A. Barnett, Western Union, 12 March 1934; Associated Negro Press to C. A. Scott, February 1934, both in box 148, folder 8, Claude A. Barnett Papers: The Associated Negro Press, 1918–1967, pt. 2, Associated Negro Press Organizational Files, 1920–1966, Chicago Historical Society, Chicago, Ill. (hereinafter Barnett Papers); *Atlanta Daily World*, 13 March 1934, 1; *New York Amsterdam News*, 17 March 1934, 1, 3; and *Pittsburgh Courier*, 17 March 1934, 5. Aurelius had master's degrees from Ohio State and the University of Kansas. He had taught at Bethune-Cookman and West Virginia State. He seemed reliable and legitimate, though as an untenured instructor in West Virginia State's Education Department, Scott's services were terminated in 1935. This information comes from Scott's personnel file, housed in the archives of what is now West Virginia State University, via email correspondence with Ellen Hassig Ressmeyer, the university's archivist. More detailed information from that file is restricted.

25. Henderson, "Heman E. Perry," 220, 231–234, 237.

26. See Merritt, *Herndons*; and Henderson, *Atlanta Life Insurance Company*.

27. Dorsey, *To Build Our Lives Together*, 112, 115–117.

28. Kuhn, Joye, and West, *Living Atlanta*, 89–95, quotes 93–95. See also Franklin M. Garrett, *Atlanta and Environs*, 2:777–997.

29. Milton and Yates would both be honorary pallbearers at Walden's funeral in July 1965. "Funeral Services for Judge Austin Thomas Walden," Austin T. Walden Papers, 1915–1965, MSS 614, ser. II, box 2, folder 1, Atlanta History Center, Atlanta, Ga. (hereinafter Walden Papers); A. T. Walden to Citizens Trust Company, ser. III, box 2, folder 9, Walden Papers; Brown-Nagin,

Courage to Dissent, 17–18; Willard "Chuck" Lewis, *Citizens Trust Bank History*, 4, 11–15; Petition of A. T. Walden to Honorable Thomas H. Jeffries, Ordinary, 17 February 1934, Estate 25024, Probate Court of Fulton County, Atlanta, Ga.; Petition of Lucile Scott and A. T. Walden to Honorable Thomas H. Jeffries, Ordinary, 25 June 1934, ibid.; Special Return of A. T. Walden as Guardian of W. A. Scott II & Robert Scott, Minors, 22 June 1934, ibid.; Annual Return of A. T. Walden & Lucile Scott as Guardians for Robert & W. A. Scott, Jr., Minors, 22 November 1934, ibid.; Petition of A. T. Walden and Lucile Scott to the Honorable Thomas H. Jeffries, Ordinary, 24 June 1935, ibid.; and Petition of A. T. Walden and Lucile Scott, Court of Ordinary, Fulton County, Ga., ibid.

30. *Baltimore Afro-American*, 24 March 1934, 21.

31. *Baltimore Afro-American*, 5 May 1934, 15.

32. The *Afro-American* printed Aurelius's article after sending a telegram to C. A. Scott for comment. His reply was brief but decisive: "Understand you wired Spelman relative to my brother's death. I know the facts. It is unfair to involve Spelman in this matter." The entirety of Aurelius's charge was published in one screed in the *Baltimore Afro-American*, 24 March 1934, 5.

33. *Atlanta Daily World*, 27 May 1934, 1, 3 June 1934, 1; and C. A. Scott to C. A. Barnett, Western Union, 11 February 1935, box 148, folder 8, Barnett Papers.

34. Both Scotts quoted in *Baltimore Afro-American*, 16 June 1934, 14.

35. *Best's Life Insurance Reports*, 471–472; Teske, *Unvarnished Arkansas*, 137; Christian, *Black Saga*, 284; and *Atlanta Daily World*, 12 July 1934, 1. Bond Almand of the law firm Branch and Howard announced the deal. Because of the receivership, the Odd Fellows building was also known as the National Benefit building.

36. Aurelius told the *Afro-American* that W. A. had instructed him from his deathbed to remove the building contracts from his coat pocket, blaming them for the attack. "W. A. backed out of his garage for ten straight nights with a cocked gun in his hand, and had relatives not packed the gun away that night he would have gotten the gunman who killed him," Aurelius claimed. "That same night, keys to his safe deposit box mysteriously disappeared. Just a short time before his death, his operating cash was tied up." *Baltimore Afro-American*, 21 July 1934, 1, 2.

37. Milton began in the bank's accounting department and worked at both Morehouse and the bank from 1921 to 1923. In 1923, he left the bank to purchase an interest in the Gate City Drug Store, which was owned by Heman Perry, a founder of Citizens Trust. The new Yates and Milton Drug Store did very well, even as the Perry empire crumbled. Milton returned to the struggling Citizens Trust in 1927, leaving the day-to-day operations of the drugstore to his partner, Clayton Yates. Milton and Yates were also high-ranking functionaries in Atlanta's First Congregational Church. "Blayton, Jesse B. (December 6, 1897–)," "Lorimer D. Milton (September 8, 1898–February 8,

1986),'' and "Clayton R. Yates (?)," all in Ingham and Feldman, *African American Business Leaders*, 81–82, 86; Willard "Chuck" Lewis, *Citizens Trust Bank History*, 11; Kuhn, Joye, and West, *Living Atlanta*, 105–106; Pomerantz, *Where Peachtree Meets Sweet Auburn*, 176; and "Lattimore [*sic*] D. Milton: Commerce," interview by Bernard West, Living Atlanta Tapes and Papers, 1914–1985, MSS 637, box 38, folder 15, p. 15, Kenan Research Center, Atlanta History Center, Atlanta, Ga.

38. Deed no. 730746, in *Deeds 1508, Pgs. 351–End, Fulton Co.*, 410–411; Deed no. 731565, in *Deeds 1528, Pgs. 1–350, Fulton Co.*, 232–234; Deed no. 765233, in *Deeds 1604, Pgs. 1–350, Fulton Co.*, 89; Deed no. 742086, in *Deeds 1297, Pgs. 1–350, Fulton Co.*, 183–184; Deed no. 610690, in *Deeds 1693, Pgs. 351–End, Fulton Co.*, 355–359; Deed no. 745975, in *Deeds 1554, Pgs. 181–End, Fulton Co.*, 186–187; Deed no. 747852, in *Deeds 1389, Pgs. 351–End, Fulton Co.*, 575–576; Deed no. 777493, in *Deeds 1637, Pgs. 181–End, Fulton Co.*, 251–252; Deed no. 811946, in *Deeds 1691, Pgs. 351–End, Fulton Co.*, 567–568, all in Clerk of Superior Court, Fulton County Courthouse, Atlanta, Ga.; Sixteenth Census of the United States, 1940, NARA microfilm publication T627, roll 732, 61A; Fourteenth Census of the United States, 1920, NARA microfilm publication T625, roll 253, 27A; and Fifteenth Census of the United States, 1930, NARA microfilm publication T626, roll 363, 2B, and roll 365, 44A.

39. Walden cited himself as one of the lawyers (as well as being a plaintiff), along with Baltimore attorney W. Ashbie Hawkins. Hawkins, despite the defamation suit, had a long association with the *Afro-American*. He was even, in a surprising potential conflict of interest, an *Afro-American* stockholder. Regardless, they never filed in Baltimore City Court of Common Pleas, the Baltimore City Court, or the Baltimore City Superior Court. *Chicago Defender*, 15 September 1934, 3; "W. Ashbie Hawkins (1861–1941)," MSA SC 3520-12415, Archives of Maryland (Biographical Series), http://msa.maryland.gov/megafile/msa/speccol/sc3500/sc3520/012400/012415/html/12415bio.html, accessed 15 October 2013; Frederick N. Rasmussen, "1908 Illinois Race Riot Was Impetus behind Founding of the NAACP," *Baltimore Sun*, 11 February 2012, A5; Farrar, *"Baltimore Afro-American,"* 1, 5, 33, 41, 62, 103; and Baltimore City Equity Indexes, in Maryland State Archives, Annapolis, cited in correspondence with the author, 12 December 2013.

40. A. S. Walden, circular letter, 1935, box 148, folder 9, Barnett Papers.

41. Blackwell, "Black-Controlled Media," 112; Ledger, 1937, 74, and Ledger, 1939, 144, both in box 21, Misc. Ledgers, Atlanta Daily World Records, 1931–1996, Manuscript Collection no. 1092, Manuscript, Archives, and Rare Book Library, Emory University, Atlanta, Ga. The percentages remained the same at the end of 1940. Ledger, 1940, 175, ibid.

42. In September, for example, Walden and Milton were both on the dais at Spelman College during a visit by Secretary of the Interior Harold L. Ickes for the demolition of a house on the site of what was to become a massive housing

project for Atlanta University. Walden opened the program with a welcome on behalf of the people of Atlanta. Milton was on the advisory committee on university housing that was appointed by Ickes. *Atlanta Daily World*, 27 September 1934, 1; *Charleston News and Courier*, 20 October 1946, 4; *Kentucky New Era*, 21 October 1946, 7; and *Tuscaloosa News*, 20 October 1946, 2. Forrester B. Washington, Walden's replacement as head of the Atlanta NAACP, believed that C. A. Scott had formed the Atlanta Civic and Political League with J. Wesley Dobbs "with the deliberate purpose of killing the NAACP because Walden was the head of it," largely because of disputes over Walden's administration of W. A.'s will. Pomerantz, *Where Peachtree Meets Sweet Auburn*, 125–127.

43. *Baltimore Afro-American*, 12 January 1935, 1, 16 February 1935, 2; *Pittsburgh Courier*, 12 January 1935, A7; *New York Amsterdam News*, 12 January 1935, 1; *Atlanta Daily World*, 7 January 1935, 1, 2; and Greene, *Temple Bombing*, 305.

44. *Baltimore Afro-American*, 12 January 1935, 1, 19 January 1935, 1, 2; *New York Amsterdam News*, 12 January 1935, 1; and *Atlanta Daily World*, 7 January 1935, 1, 9 January 1935, 1. The indictment led to a manhunt in Chicago for Maddox, leading C. A. Scott to telegraph Claude Barnett of the Associated Negro Press about aiding the investigation to find the murder suspect. C. A. Scott to C. A. Barnett, Western Union, 9 January 1935, box 148, folder 8, Barnett Papers.

45. Howard was legitimately famous, a veteran of the Spanish-American War, a former member of the House of Representatives from Georgia's Fifth District, and a legendary criminal defense attorney. The *Afro-American* proclaimed that he was "known as the South's greatest cross-examiner." He was "reputed to be Georgia's greatest courtroom technician." Howard was "a typical Georgian," the paper reported. He had "spindlelegs and a reddish-brown pompadour, is worshiped by the gentry of color and bears a reputation which strikes awe into any opponent." Garland, in turn, was Howard's "stocky little rival." Howard was assisted in the case by attorney E. L. Tiller. Though the evidence against Maddox was circumstantial, the decision to charge him was "generally considered" by most of Atlanta society, according to J. C. Chunn, "a triumph of justice." See "Howard, William Schley"; *Baltimore Afro-American*, 12 January 1935, 1, 9 February 1935, 1, 2, 16 February 1935, 2; *New York Amsterdam News*, 12 January 1935, 1; *Atlanta Daily World*, 7 January 1935, 1, 9 January 1935, 1, 18 January 1935, 1, 20 January 1935, 1, 6 February 1935, 1, 5; *Chicago Defender*, 19 January 1935, 1, 2; and *Pittsburgh Courier*, 12 January 1935, A7.

46. *Chicago Defender*, 12 January 1935, 1.

47. C. F. Payne, for example, a white receiver for the National Benefit Life Insurance Company, testified, against the defense's claims, that there was no significant rivalry for the Odd Fellows building. There was competition for the purchase, but it was a competition between friends, who would not have killed

Scott for the privilege of buying a building. *Atlanta Daily World*, 6 February 1935, 1, 5, 7 February 1935, 1, 6, 8 February 1935, 2, 6; and *Baltimore Afro-American*, 9 February 1935, 1, 2, 16 February 1935, 1, 2.

48. *Atlanta Daily World*, 9 February 1935, 1, 5.

49. *Chicago Defender*, 16 February 1935, 1, 8 March 1941, 1; *New York Amsterdam News*, 15 March 1941, 1; *Atlanta Daily World*, 10 February 1935, 1, 6 March 1941, 1, 13 March 1941, 1; and *Baltimore Afro-American*, 15 March 1941, 2.

50. *Baltimore Afro-American*, 16 February 1935, 4.

51. Ibid.

52. Ibid. Matthews continued: "The apathy of the rising generation in the South is deplorable. The argument of those in Atlanta—the city of colleges and universities—a city where a soda-jerker and a bootblack may hold a college degree, a city where what appears to be mere street corner loafers are engaged in discourses on Greek and other classics—is, 'We're getting along all right; why they even segregate you up North.'

"There seems to be a perfect surrender to this diabolical propaganda that the races are different and one is inferior.

"Sitting behind me in the courtroom was a stout old red-faced man, a member of the bar, who as the trial drifted into days, was overheard to remark, 'You know I'm proud to be a white man in Georgia. Just think how much of the taxpayer's money is being spent to solve this n——'s murder. I tell you nobody can say that they don't get fair treatment down here.'"

53. Ibid., 1, 2.

54. *New York Amsterdam News*, 16 February 1935, 1.

55. *Baltimore Afro-American*, 16 February 1935, 2.

56. Ibid.

57. Ibid.

Chapter 4. The SNS, Gender, and the Fight for Teacher Salary Equalization

1. *Mills v. Board of Education of Anne Arundel County*, 30 F.Supp. 245 (1939); Coleman, "Salary Equalization Movement," 236; Jopling, *Life in a Black Community*, 129–143; and Skotnes, *New Deal for All?*, 293–298.

2. Pride, "Register and History," 363.

3. *Galveston Examiner*, 2 December 1939, 1, 2 March 1940, 1, 2, 6.

4. *Baltimore Afro-American*, 24 June 1939, 1, 2; and Farrar, *"Baltimore Afro-American,"* 34.

5. Gilmore, *Gender and Jim Crow*, 33–37; Ware, *Holding Their Own*, 72; Kirk, "NAACP Campaign," 534–535.

6. Gilmore, *Gender and Jim Crow*, 33–37; and Scott Baker, "Pedagogies of Protest," 2783.

7. Gilmore, *Gender and Jim Crow*, 157; Margo, *Race and Schooling*, 52–67; and Kirk, "NAACP Campaign," 533, 535–536.

8. Kirk, "NAACP Campaign," 535.

9. See, for example, Charles H. Thompson, "Progress in the Elimination of Discrimination"; Beezer, "Black Teachers' Salaries"; Scott Baker, "Testing Equality"; and Tushnet, *Making Civil Rights Law*, 116–121.

10. Carby, *Reconstructing Womanhood*; and Karen Anderson, *Changing Woman*.

11. Giddings, *When and Where I Enter*.

12. See Jacqueline Jones, *Labor of Love*.

13. "Scott Newspaper Service [syndicating service], 1935," OBV136, Atlanta Daily World Records, 1931–1996, Manuscript Collection no. 1092, Manuscript, Archives, and Rare Book Library, Emory University, Atlanta, Ga. (hereinafter "Scott Newspaper Service, 1935").

14. Ibid.; and Wade-Gayles, "Black Women Journalists," 139–144, 147. Another teacher was the first black woman to publish a newspaper: Mary Ann Shadd Cary founded the antebellum *Provincial Freeman*, which she published in Canada. Rhodes, *Mary Ann Shadd Cary*, xi–xv.

15. For more on Payne, see James McGrath Morris, *Eye on the Struggle*.

16. *Tademy v. Scott*, 68 F.Supp. 556 (1945).

17. Fifteenth Census of the United States, 1930, Population Schedule, Pensacola City, Fla., sheet no. 22B; *Pensacola City Directory, 1936* (Jacksonville, Fla.: R. L. Polk & Co., 1936) 53; Sixteenth Census of the United States, 1940, Population Schedule, Pensacola, Fla., sheet no. 3B; Florida State Population Census, 1945, Pensacola, Escambia County, Colored Race, precinct 55; and Shofner, "Florida," 110.

18. Brown-Nagin, *Courage to Dissent*, 87–88. Brown-Nagin also makes the case that it was this fight that led to the fight for school equalization, which became a pragmatic alternative to desegregation after *Brown*. See 88–113.

19. *Atlanta Daily World*, 28 April 1941, 5, 26 May 1941, 5, 17 October 1941, 6, 18 October 1941, 1; Shofner, "Florida," 110; and *N. W. Ayer & Son's Directory of Newspapers and Periodicals, 1953* (1953), 173.

20. That ceiling existed even in groups like the WACs and WAVES, demonstrating that there was no escape from patriarchy. Linda Kerber describes the relationship between women and military service, emphasizing the draft (a "preservice" obligation) and military benefits (a "postservice" obligation). Kerber, *No Constitutional Right*, 221–236.

21. *Atlanta Daily World*, 16 June 1942, 1.

22. *Atlanta Daily World*, 29 May 1943, 5; "Federal Aid to General Education," 04-643–04-651; and Advisory Commission on Intergovernmental Relations, *Intergovernmentalizing the Classroom: Federal Involvement in Elementary and Secondary Education* (Washington, D.C.: Advisory Commission on Intergovernmental Relations, 1981), 20.

23. *Atlanta Daily World*, 20 March 1941, 1, 25 August 1941, 2, 30 November 1941, 1, 5 December 1941, 3.

24. Ibid., 9 March 1942, 6.

25. Ibid., 23 April 1942, 6.

26. Ibid., 27 December 1942, 4.

27. Damsel-in-distress scholarship focuses most helpfully on the European literature made possible by the evolution of patriarchal models and their inclusion in the fables and novels of the continent. For more on the damsel in distress in literature, see James Eli Adams, *History of Victorian Literature*, 129; Jackie C. Horne, *History and Construction*, 196–200; and Pleij, "Late Middle Ages," 81–83.

28. *Columbia City Directory, 1943* (Richmond, Va.: Hill Directory Co., 1943), 579; McCray, "World Peace"; McCray, "In Defense of Student Education"; McCray, "Arraignment of Student Inertia"; and "Interview with John McCray." His paper was in the tradition of crusading black presses in Columbia. See Haram, "*Palmetto Leader*'s Mission."

29. Lau, *Democracy Rising*, 136–144; Bedingfield, *Newspaper Wars*, 17–38; Egerton, *Speak Now against the Day*, 227–228, 287–288; Clayton and Salmond, *Southern History*, 68; McGuire, "It Was Like All of Us Had Been Raped," 909, 930; *Atlanta Daily World*, 6 September 1941, 4, 26 December 1941, 6; and J. Thomas Wilson to John H. McCray, 28 September 1941, R1347a, 41–44, John H. McCray Papers, 11294, South Caroliniana Library, University of South Carolina, Columbia (hereinafter McCray Papers).

30. Bedingfield, *Newspaper Wars*, 55–60; R. Scott Baker, *Paradoxes of Desegregation*, 48–53; and M. A. Mouzon to John H. McCray, 30 May 1944; John F. Seignious to Employees of the Charleston Public Schools, 18 May 1944; "Explanations"; "Elementary Schools"; and Alma G. Forrest to John H. McCray, n.d., all in R1347a, 41–45, McCray Papers.

31. *Missouri ex rel. Gaines v. Canada*, 305 U.S. 337 (1938).

32. C. A. Scott and Carter Wesley, NNPA circular letter, 5 March 1945; John H. McCray to C. A. Scott, 10 March 1945; and C. A. Scott, "Combined Report of the Southern and Western Vice-Presidents," in Minutes of the Limited War-Time Conference of the NNPA, 27, 28, and 29 July 1945, R1347a, 45, McCray Papers.

33. Allen Woodrow Jones, "Alabama," 42–43; and *Birmingham Reporter*, 12 March 1921, 1.

34. Alabama newspapers had flourished prior to 1915, but after that, the total number declined, leaving black newspapers only in the urban areas of Birmingham, Mobile, Montgomery, Huntsville, Anniston, Sheffield, and Dothan. The papers that survived emphasized pictures, comics, sports, and society news. Allen Woodrow Jones, "Alabama," 42–43.

35. Allen Woodrow Jones, "Alabama," 43–44; *Montgomery City Directory, 1928* (Richmond, Va.: R. L. Polk & Co., 1928), 276; *Montgomery City Directory, 1929* (Birmingham, Ala.: R. L. Polk & Co., 1929), 258; *Montgomery City Directory, 1931* (Birmingham, Ala.: R. L. Polk & Co., 1931), 287; *Montgomery City Directory, 1933* (Birmingham, Ala.: R. L. Polk & Co., 1933), 217; *Montgomery City Directory, 1935* (Birmingham, Ala.: R. L. Polk & Co., 1935), 250; Fifteenth Census of the United States, 1930, Population Schedule, Montgomery

City, Ala., sheet no. 18A; "Scott Newspaper Service, 1935"; "Scott Newspaper Service [syndicating service], 1936," OBV137, Atlanta Daily World Records, 1931–1996, Manuscript Collection no. 1092, Manuscript, Archives, and Rare Book Library, Emory University, Atlanta, Ga (hereinafter "Scott Newspaper Service, 1936"); and "Scott Newspaper Service [syndicating service], 1937," OBV138, Atlanta Daily World Records (hereinafter cited as "Scott Newspaper Service, 1937").

36. *Atlanta Daily World*, 17 March 1941, 1. Other articles chronicled the fight for salary equalization with straight reporting. *Atlanta Daily World*, 18 March 1941, 2, 19 August 1941, 2.

37. By 1937, when Bradford left the company, circulation was down to 5,632. *N. W. Ayer & Son's Directory of Newspapers and Periodicals* (1933), 38; *N. W. Ayer & Son's Directory of Newspapers and Periodicals* (1934), 36; and *N. W. Ayer & Son's Directory of Newspapers and Periodicals* (1937), 36. Biographical information on Bradford from *Atlanta City Directory, 1927* (Atlanta, Ga.: Atlanta City Directory Company, 1927), 255; Fifteenth Census of the United States, 1930, Population Schedule, Atlanta, Ga., sheet no. 16A; *Atlanta City Directory, 1933* (Atlanta, Ga.: Atlanta City Directory Company, 1933), 197; *Birmingham City Directory, 1934* (Birmingham, Ala.: R. L. Polk & Co., 1934), 100; Sixteenth Census of the United States, 1940, Population Schedule, Omaha, Nebr., sheet no. 6A; and *Omaha City Directory, 1940* (Omaha, Nebr.: R. L. Polk & Co., 1940), 91. Quote from "The *Birmingham World*," *Birmingham-Pittsburgh Traveler: Newspapers*, http://northbysouth.kenyon.edu/2000/Media/Kyle's%20stuff/Birmingham%20World%20page.htm, accessed 4 January 2014.

38. *Birmingham World*, 4 October 1932, 1, 6.

39. Deborah E. McDowell, *Leaving Pipe Shop*, 52. There was competition in the city. The *Birmingham Reporter* was the "Official Organ of the Masons, Eastern Star, Knights of Pythias, and Order of Calanthes of Alabama," but also covered general news. Edited by Oscar W. Adams, the *Reporter* claimed to be an "Exponent of Justice and fair play to all. Special privileges to none." *Birmingham Reporter*, 13 January 1934, 1–8.

40. Quoted in "The *Birmingham World*." See also Roberts and Klibanoff, *Race Beat*, 50.

41. Allen Woodrow Jones, "Alabama," 44; and 1944 Desk Planner, box 7, Emory O. Jackson Papers, A423, Birmingham Civil Rights Institute, Birmingham, Ala.

42. Memorandum: SAC, Birmingham, to Director, FBI, 17 July 1946, FBI Headquarters file 100-HQ-345671; *Birmingham World*, 27 March 1942, 7; and Carter Wesley circular letter, 25 March 1946, 1102.29.2, Birmingham World Office Files, Department of Archives and Manuscripts, Birmingham Public Library, Birmingham, Ala. (hereinafter Birmingham World Office Files).

43. Emory O. Jackson to Hartford Knight and E. W. Taggart, 5 May 1947, 1102.1.1.16, Birmingham World Office Files; and Christopher Brian Davis, "Emory O. Jackson," 83–85.

44. *Birmingham Post*, 14 November 1946, 1; and W. I. Pittman to Emory O. Jackson, 2 December 1946, 1102.29.2, Birmingham World Office Files.

45. *Birmingham News*, 24 January 1947, 4; J. E. Bryan to Ruby Jackson Gainer, 6 May 1947; Cora Mellaney to Ruby Jackson Gainer, 11 May 1947; Emory O. Jackson to E. W. Taggart, 12 May 1947; and Emory O. Jackson to Hartford Knight, 21 May 1947, all in 1102.1.1.16, Birmingham World Office Files; and *Bolden v. School Board of Jefferson County*, No. 5339, Civil Docket, Final Decree, 29 April 1945.

46. "Highlight Dates in the Anti-Salary Discrimination Campaign," and "Teachers Defense Fund Sunday, 19 September 1948," all in box 9 (1940s), Birmingham World Office Files.

47. "Teachers: Know Your Tenure Rights!"; "For Your Information! County School Board Undercuts Democracy in Fight against Court Decree to Equalize Pay of County School Teachers"; National Teachers Division, CIO, Bulletin; and Statement of Sara T. Walsh, Director, National Teachers Division, UPW-CIO, on Intimidation of Birmingham Teachers, all in box 9 (1940s), Birmingham World Office Files.

48. Emory O. Jackson to J. E. Pierce, 12 May 1947, 1102.1.1.21, Birmingham World Office Files.

49. Emory O. Jackson to J. E. Pierce, 1 August 1948, 1102.1.1.21, Birmingham World Office Files; *Birmingham World*, 10 August 1948, 1, 17 August 1948, 1, 27 August 1948, 1; Rutledge, *Emory O. Jackson*, 78–94; and Christopher Brian Davis, "Emory O. Jackson," 85–94.

50. Ruby Jackson Gainer to Birmingham Branch of the NAACP, 27 June 1948; Emory O. Jackson, Birmingham Branch of NAACP, circular letter, 8 September 1948; Emory O. Jackson to the Members of the Program Committee, Jefferson County Progressive Democratic Council, n.d.; and D. S. Stephens to Emory O. Jackson, 6 October 1948, all in 1102.1.1.3, Birmingham World Office Files.

51. *Birmingham World*, 27 August 1948, 1; Edward M. Sneed to W. A. Berry, 5 June 1947; Bernhard J. Stern to J. E. Bryan, 5 June 1947; J. H. Morton to W. A. Berry, 5 June 1947; D. A. Gallimore to W. A. Berry, 6 June 1947; Robert M. Ratcliffe to Sara T. Walsh, 5 June 1947; Elisabeth Christman to Sara T. Walsh, 13 June 1947; Frances Cuahing to Sara T. Walsh, 16 June 1947; Muriel Draper to Sara T. Walsh, 28 June 1947; C. H. Coyle to James E. Folsom, 26 June 1947; Marvin Nichols to James E. Folsom, 27 June 1947; and Muriel Draper to James E. Folsom, 27 June 1947, all in 1102.1.1.16, Birmingham World Office Files; and Christopher Brian Davis, "Emory O. Jackson," 85–94.

52. Publius to Editor, *Birmingham News*, 6 October 1950; and B. A. Jones to Emory O. Jackson, 12 October 1950, both in 1102.1.1.16, Birmingham World Office Files; and *Birmingham World*, 31 October 1950, 1.

53. *Birmingham World*, 26 June 1951, 6.

54. William G. Nunn to Emory O. Jackson, 24 June 1953; C. G. Gomillion to Emory O. Jackson, 6 July 1953; and C. G. Gomillion, "Racial Differentials

in Public Education in Alabama," all in 1102.1.1.16, Birmingham World Office Files.

55. McGuire, *At the Dark End*, 13, 25–38, 55–56, quote 26. There were, unfortunately, plenty of chances for Jackson to do such work for justice in cases of sexual violence. He used his paper to demand action in the rapes of Viola White in 1946 and Gertrude Perkins in 1949.

56. McGuire, *At the Dark End*, 6–39, quote 39; and *Atlanta Daily World*, 19 September 1945, 6.

57. Tushnet, *NAACP's Legal Strategy*, 90–92; and Kirk, "NAACP Campaign," 536–539.

58. Kirk, "NAACP Campaign," 539–541; and *Atlanta Daily World*, 6 May 1940, 6, 29 May 1943, 5.

59. *Atlanta Daily World*, 13 May 1951, 7, 30 May 1951, 6.

60. *Atlanta Daily World*, 1 December 1939, 6, 21 October 1941, 1, 29 December 1942, 1; Hardin, "Kentucky Is More or Less Civilized"; and Luther Adams, *Way Up North in Louisville*, 99–104.

61. *Atlanta Daily World*, 14 November 1940, 1, 30 May 1941, 4, 5 August 1941, 1; Luther Adams, *Way Up North in Louisville*, 90–94; and Hardin, *Fifty Years of Segregation*, 71–72.

62. *Atlanta Daily World*, 7 November 1939, 6.

63. Matthews, *Rise of Public Woman*.

64. Sara Evans, *Personal Politics*; and Cynthia Harrison, *On Account of Sex*.

65. See De Hart, "Second Wave Feminism(s)."

66. Kirk, "NAACP Campaign," 532–534.

Chapter 5. Expansion beyond the South in the Wake of World War II

1. The *Index* lasted until 1942. It was followed by the *Arizona Sun*, edited by Doc Benson, which published from 1942 to 1962. *Arizona Republic*, 20 November 1912, 11, 28 May 1951, 10; Fifteenth Census of the United States, 1930, Population Schedule, Phoenix, Ariz., sheet no. 5A; *Phoenix City Directory, 1941* (Phoenix: Arizona Directory Company, 1941), 193; Matthew C. Whitaker, "Rise of Black Phoenix"; Pride, "Register and History," 53; and Crudup, "African Americans in Arizona," 97–100.

2. The paper here mimicked the Don't Spend Your Money Where You Can't Work campaigns, which began in 1929 and continued through the next several decades. See Hunter, "Don't Buy from Where You Can't Work"; Winston McDowell, "Race and Ethnicity"; Pacifico, "Don't Buy Where You Can't Work"; Skotnes, "Buy Where You Can Work"; and Wye, "Merchants of Tomorrow."

3. *Atlanta Daily World*, 5 August 1938, 2, 21 May 1941, 5, quotes from 24 November 1938, 6, and 30 July 1941, 2.

4. *Phoenix Index*, 20 December 1941, 7, 21 February 1942, 1, 8.

5. Wolseley, *Black Press, USA*, 79–80; and "Publishers." Pegler's column was syndicated throughout the country. See, for example, *San Jose Evening News*, 27 April 1942, 10.

6. Jordan, *Black Newspapers and America's War*, 5. See also Dalfiume, "Forgotten Years," 298–316.

7. American Civil Liberties Union, *Bill of Rights in War*, 8; *Pittsburgh Courier*, 31 January 1942, 3; Fenderson, "Negro Press," 185; and Lambert, *Battle of Ole Miss*, 51. For more on Double V, see Finkle, *Forum for Protest*, 108–128.

8. Field, *Negro Press*, n.p.; Consuelo C. Young, "Study of Reader Attitudes," 148; and Perry, "In Defense," 15–16, 19.

9. Pride, "Register and History," 256; and Syrjamaki, "Negro Press in 1938," 47–48.

10. *Atlanta Daily World*, 16 February 1934, 6.

11. *Atlanta Daily World*, 8 April 1934, A1, 25 May 1934, 1; and *Indianapolis Recorder*, 9 May 1931, 1.

12. Detroit's racialized housing problems stemmed from the early role of black workers in the auto industry. Henry Ford had hired black nonunion workers in the 1920s for his automobile factories, but those opportunities evolved into stagnant jobs that kept black workers at or below the poverty line, turning them ultimately to unionism as a method of organizing against workplace problems, housing problems, and problems with racist groups in the city. See Meier and Rudwick, *Black Detroit*; and Bates, *Making of Black Detroit*.

13. *Atlanta Daily World*, 10 February 1942, 1, 2 March 1942, 1, 17 April 1942, 1, 18 April 1942, 1, 1 May 1942, 1. In May, the paper reported that a letter had been sent to Michigan congressmen by the Civil Rights Federation describing "subversive activity in Detroit" involving Nazi sympathizers and charging the congressional Dies Committee, an early version of the House Un-American Activities Committee chaired by Texas Democrat Martin Dies, with "failure to take action against the Fifth Column." *Atlanta Daily World*, 4 May 1942, 6. For more on the Dies Committee, see Goodman, *The Committee*; and O'Reilly, *Hoover and the Unamericans*.

14. *Atlanta Daily World*, 9 March 1943, 1, 15 June 1943, 2. See Peterson, *Planning the Home Front*.

15. For more on the riot, see Sitkoff, "Detroit Race Riot"; Capeci and Wilkerson, *Layered Violence*; Sugrue, *Origins of the Urban Crisis*; and Shogan and Craig, *Detroit Race Riot*.

16. *Atlanta Daily World*, 23 June 1943, 1, 24 June 1943, 1, 29 June 1943, 1.

17. Fenderson, "Negro Press," 186, 188; Sancton, "Negro Press"; Blakeney, "Sociological Analysis," 12–17; and "Negro Publishers," *Time*, 15 June 1942, 70–72. For more on Pegler, see Pilat, *Pegler*.

18. Fenderson, "Negro Press," 186–188; *Louisville Courier-Journal*, 26 May 1942, 9; and *Pittsburgh Courier*, 14 March 1942, 6. Pegler's attacks were syndicated in his "Fair Enough" column, published throughout the country in papers like the *New York World Telegram*; the five articles were published between April and July. See *New York World Telegram*, 28 April 1942, 13, 13 May 1942, 13, 16 June 1942, 13, 17 June 1942, 13, and 16 July 1942, 13.

19. Fenderson, "Negro Press," 187; and Egerton, *Speak Now against the Day*, 256–257. McGill quoted in Klinkner and Smith, *Unsteady March*, 138.

20. Blackwell, "Black-Controlled Media," 20–22; and Ottley, *"New World A-Coming,"* 281.

21. Simmons, *African American Press*, 74–75; and Washburn, *Question of Sedition*, 84.

22. Simmons, *African American Press*, 75–82, quote 75; and Washburn, *Question of Sedition*, 6–7.

23. Wolseley, *Black Press, USA*, 81, 82.

24. Michaeli, *"Defender,"* 203–207; O'Kelly, "Black Newspapers," 13; Burma, "Analysis of the Present Negro Press," 172; Consuelo C. Young, "Study of Reader Attitudes," 149–152; and *"Fortune* Press Analysis," 233.

25. O'Kelly, "Black Newspapers," 12; and Finkle, *Forum for Protest*, 178–182, quote 179. For examples of how such compromise positions played out in the pages of a fiction publication, see Mullen, "Popular Fronts."

26. Suggs, "Black Strategy and Ideology," 161, 169–172, quote 190; and "South's Greatest Negro Newspaper." See also P. B. Young Jr., "Negro Press—Today and Tomorrow."

27. Suggs, "Black Strategy and Ideology," 185–187; Egerton, *Speak Now against the Day*, 303–312; Aldon D. Morris, *Origins of the Civil Rights Movement*, 67–68; Sancton, "Negro Press," 560; and Gilmore, *Defying Dixie*, 369–372. For more on Young, see Clint C. Wilson II, *Black Journalists in Paradox*, 60–62; and Suggs, "P. B. Young."

28. *Smith v. Allwright*, 321 U.S. 649 (1944).

29. Odum-Hinmon, "Cautious Crusader," 41.

30. Blakeney, "Sociological Analysis," 21–31, 44–50.

31. Ruth Emmeline Scott, "Problem," 28–31.

32. Davis Lee to Carl Murphy, n.d., Marshall:15:07, folder 72, Afro-American Newspapers Archives and Research Center, Baltimore, Md.; Oliver, "History and Development," 14; and *Atlanta Daily World*, 1 December 1941, 6, 2 December 1941, 1. The paper apologized for the smaller size of the *World*, blaming the "labor dispute" for the fewer pages. "It is hoped that the subscribers will bear with the management until a basis of settlement can be reached."

33. *Atlanta Daily World*, 3 December 1941, 1, 7 December 1941, 1, 6, 9 December 1941, 1.

34. *Atlanta Daily World*, 3 December 1941, 1; and *Printing the Dream*.

35. Hornsby, "Georgia," 137–138; Odum-Hinmon, "Cautious Crusader," 45; Henderson, "Heman E. Perry," 240; C. A. Barnett to C. A. Scott, 24 September 1942; and C. A. Barnett to C. A. Scott, 9 January 1943, both in box 148, folder 9; C. A. Scott to C. A. Barnett, 22 July 1943, box 148, folder 10, all in Claude A. Barnett Papers: The Associated Negro Press, 1918–1967, pt. 2, Associated Negro Press Organizational Files, 1920–1966, Chicago Historical Society, Chicago, Ill.

36. "The Negro Daily," 60.

37. Despite this handicap, the *World* succeeded with more than just its Syndicate. As of the early 1940s, the paper produced a sixteen-page national edition every Sunday, with a circulation of roughly six thousand a week. The *World*'s regular edition had a circulation of roughly fifteen thousand in 1942. The paper devoted almost half of its space to advertising (46 percent by Oliver's count), most of it from both black and white local businesses. The paper employed an advertising manager and three ad salesmen to handle the load. Oliver, "History and Development," 13, 17, 18–19, 20.

38. Oliver's cross-section included fifteen teachers, ten businessmen, ten doctors and dentists, ten houseworkers and homemakers, ten high school students, eight beauticians, seven ministers, and five social workers. Oliver, "History and Development," 26, 29.

39. Ingham and Feldman, *African American Business Leaders*, 587; and Egerton, *Speak Now against the Day*, 259–261, quote 260.

Chapter 6. Percy Greene and the Limits of Syndication

1. *Jackson Advocate*, 6 March 1943, 3.

2. The roar of the Roaring Twenties didn't really reach black Mississippi, but the Depression of the 1930s certainly did, further eroding a black press that was already struggling. Only thirty-three black periodicals existed in Mississippi in the decade, and only fifteen of them were commercial presses, most housed in Jackson (the others were six religious, two fraternal, and ten educational). Julius Eric Thompson, *Black Press in Mississippi*, 16; Julius Eric Thompson, "Mississippi," 180–181; Cooper, "Percy Greene," 56–57; and Simmons, *African American Press*, 63. For more on the publications emanating from Mississippi during this period, see the Ayer newspaper directories, which began in 1880 and continued through the civil rights movement, for example, *N. W. Ayer & Son's Directory of Newspapers and Periodicals* (1943).

3. Julius Eric Thompson, "Mississippi," 181–182; and "Oral History with Mr. Percy Greene."

4. Julius Eric Thompson, "Mississippi," 182–183.

5. Julius Eric Thompson, "Mississippi," 182–184; Freda Darlene Lewis, "*Jackson Advocate*," 14–31; and Colleen R. White, "*Jackson Advocate*," 25–28.

6. Julius Eric Thompson, "Mississippi," 184–185. Booker T. Washington did much the same thing. He believed that white southern intransigence was such that there was no fundamental advantage in advocating publicly and dramatically for rights. In such a situation, the only way to fight was to grow stronger within the paradigm, rather than trying to change the paradigm itself, just as a military unit waits for reinforcements when hopelessly outmanned. "I do not favor the Negro's giving up anything which is fundamental and which has been guaranteed to him by the Constitution," he argued. "It is not best for him to relinquish his rights; nor would his doing so be best for the Southern white man." Still, there was a fundamental difference between not relinquish-

ing rights and outright advocacy. Overreach could only set everything back, he believed. But advocacy was something Washington was willing to do. He spoke to Louisiana legislators in 1898, for example, urging them to reconsider the state's grandfather clause. He also organized and raised money for these efforts behind the scenes. He did the same in the fight against Alabama's voting restrictions in 1901. He provided funds for antidiscrimination railroad suits and for suits challenging jury exclusion. He also funded the successful challenge to southern debt peonage. When it came to political participation, Washington considered rights talk fair game, but he stopped at the water's edge of social participation. Harlan, "Secret Life of Booker T. Washington," 393–416.

7. Cooper, "Percy Greene," 60–61; Simmons, *African American Press*, 64–65; and "Oral History with Mr. Percy Greene."

8. Most black people, however, could only read at an elementary school level. Only 4 percent of black Mississippians had completed a year of high school. "Complaint" in Transcript of Record, U.S. Circuit Court of Appeals for the Fifth Circuit, *Tademy v. Scott*, no. 2701, Civil Action, 5–6, Atlanta Daily World Records, 1931–1996, Manuscript Collection no. 1092, box 25, Manuscript, Archives, and Rare Book Library, Emory University, Atlanta, Ga. (hereinafter "Complaint" and hereinafter Atlanta Daily World Records); Sixteenth Census of the United States, 1940: Population, vol. 2, pt. 4, Minnesota–New Mexico, 199–308; Julius Eric Thompson, *Percy Greene*, 27–28; and Transcript of Evidence, Testimony for Plaintiff: Edward Tademy on Direct Examination, in Transcript of Record, U.S. Circuit Court of Appeals for the Fifth Circuit, *Tademy v. Scott*, no. 2701, Civil Action, 68–69, Atlanta Daily World Records.

9. Julius Thompson analyzed two issues of the paper before and after the Tademy event, one in December 1942 and the other in August 1943. In the December 1942 issue, 62 percent of the *Advocate*'s advertisements were from black businesses and 38 percent from white businesses. In August 1943, they were 82 percent and 18 percent. Julius Eric Thompson, *Percy Greene*, 28–30; and Cooper, "Percy Greene," 62.

10. Cooper, "Percy Greene," 62–63; and Julius Eric Thompson, *Black Life in Mississippi*, 23–34.

11. Julius Eric Thompson, *Percy Greene*, 30–32.

12. *Jackson Advocate*, 6 March 1943, 3. The spelling errors, including the two different spellings of the school's name, are original to Greene's editorial.

13. Ibid.

14. *Jackson Advocate*, 13 March 1943, 3. All spelling per original.

15. Ibid.

16. "I had taught school in Hattiesburg for ten years," Tademy testified, "and when I left one of the members of the PTA said they couldn't know whether I was a man or woman because I didn't flirt with the other women around." Transcript of Evidence, Testimony for Plaintiff: Edward Tademy on Direct Examination, 64–65, 70; and Transcript of Evidence, Testimony for

Plaintiff: Rhoda Tademy on Direct Examination, both in Transcript of Record, U.S. Circuit Court of Appeals for the Fifth Circuit, *Tademy v. Scott*, no. 2701, Civil Action, 91–92, Atlanta Daily World Records.

17. The five counties that comprised the Eighth Educational District of the Mississippi Association of Teachers in Colored Schools were Hinds, Yazoo, Warren, Rankin, and Madison. *Atlanta Daily World*, 12 February 1943, 3; *Pittsburgh Courier*, 13 February 1943, 17; Transcript of Evidence, Testimony for Plaintiff: Irma Anderson Norman on Direct Examination, 125; and Transcript of Evidence, Testimony for Plaintiff: Percy Greene on Direct Examination, 110–112, both in Transcript of Record, U.S. Circuit Court of Appeals for the Fifth Circuit, *Tademy v. Scott*, no. 2701, Civil Action, Atlanta Daily World Records.

18. Transcript of Evidence, Testimony for Plaintiff: Percy Greene on Direct Examination, 110–112.

19. Tademy relinquished the presidency of the Eighth Educational District the following year at the group's 1944 meeting at Southern Christian Institute in Edwards, Mississippi. The change in leadership was not the result of the *Advocate* controversy, but rather the normal rotation of power. "Complaint," 4, 6–7; and *Chicago Defender*, 11 March 1944, 5. The Christmas Cheer Club provided food baskets to needy families during the holidays. *Pittsburgh Courier*, 27 November 1943, 14; and *Chicago Defender*, 4 December 1943, 19.

20. The white Barnett often worked for black clients in his practice. See "Oral History with the Honorable Ross Robert Barnett."

21. *Chicago Defender*, 20 November 1943, 8; and Docket 2701, Edward Tademy v. C. A. Scott as Administrator with Will Annexed of the Estate of W. A. Scott, Deceased, et al., Clerk, U.S. District Court, 2501–2750, Civil Actions, vol. 130, RG21, stack area AP, row 19, compartment 27, shelf 6, National Archives and Records Administration, Atlanta, Ga. (hereinafter Docket 2701).

22. For more on the Scott family, see chapter 1. For W. A. Scott's murder, see chapter 3. *Atlanta Daily World*, 8 February 1934, 1, 11 February 1934, 6, 12 February 1934, 6, 13 March 1934, 1; Julius Eric Thompson, *Percy Greene*, 25–26; *New York Amsterdam News*, 14 February 1934, 1; Hornsby, "Georgia," 127–130; Allen Woodrow Jones, "Alabama," 43; and Wolseley, *Black Press, USA*, 73–74.

23. The charges for these services varied, but averaged around fifty dollars per week. *Tademy v. Scott*, 68 F.Supp. 556 (1945).

24. Because of the diversity of their perspectives, instead of one answer to the suit, the Scotts filed five over the course of October and November 1943. The salacious family charges aside, Aurelius and his brothers essentially argued that they could not have had any responsibility because they did not live in Georgia and were barred from participation in the family business. *Chicago Defender*, 20 November 1943, 8; Docket 2701; and Transcript of Record, U.S. Circuit Court of Appeals for the Fifth Circuit, *Tademy v. Scott*, no. 2701, Civil Action, 12–24, Atlanta Daily World Records.

25. Transcript of Evidence, Testimony for Plaintiff: C. A. Scott on Cross-Examination, in Transcript of Record, U.S. Circuit Court of Appeals for the Fifth Circuit, *Tademy v. Scott*, no. 2701, Civil Action, 29–32, Atlanta Daily World Records.

26. Transcript of Evidence, Testimony for Plaintiff: C. A. Scott on Cross-Examination, 33–39; and Transcript of Evidence, Testimony for Plaintiff: C. A. Scott on Direct Examination, 47–48, both in Transcript of Record, U.S. Circuit Court of Appeals for the Fifth Circuit, *Tademy v. Scott*, no. 2701, Civil Action, Atlanta Daily World Records.

27. Transcript of Evidence, Testimony for Plaintiff: Emmeline Scott on Cross-Examination, in Transcript of Record, U.S. Circuit Court of Appeals for the Fifth Circuit, *Tademy v. Scott*, no. 2701, Civil Action, 55–57, Atlanta Daily World Records.

28. Transcript of Evidence, Testimony for Plaintiff: Percy Greene on Direct Examination, 96–100, ibid.

29. Transcript of Evidence, Testimony for Plaintiff: C. A. Scott, Recalled Direct Examination, in Transcript of Record, U.S. Circuit Court of Appeals for the Fifth Circuit, *Tademy v. Scott*, no. 2701, Civil Action, 132–133, 136–140, Atlanta Daily World Records.

30. The Office of Price Administration issued ration books to ensure that the limited resources of the United States would be distributed equitably during wartime. Ration Book No. 2 contained a series of red and blue stamps, the red for meats and dairy products, the blue for fruits and vegetables. *WWII War Ration Book 2* (Washington, D.C.: U.S. Government Printing Office, 1942), L05.156, Memorial Hall Museum, Deerfield, Mass.; and Transcript of Evidence, Testimony for Plaintiff: Edward Tademy on Direct Examination, 68–69.

31. Transcript of Evidence, Testimony for Plaintiff: Irma Anderson Norman on Direct Examination, 119–127.

32. Ibid.

33. Transcript of Evidence, Testimony for Plaintiff: Edward Tademy on Direct Examination, 83–90.

34. Ibid., 67–68.

35. Transcript of Evidence, Testimony for Plaintiff: Percy Greene on Direct Examination, 104, 108–109.

36. Transcript of Evidence, Testimony for Plaintiff: Edward Tademy on Direct Examination, 71–72, 75.

37. The law in question was Georgia Code, §105-712. Russell's opinion rested on the fact that the damages sought by Tademy were merely punitive, which put the claim under the Georgia statute. "A different question might be presented if the plaintiff had proved any actual damage resulting from the libel," wrote Russell. "But as stated, no such damages are shown in this case." Tademy had not lost his job over the scandal, and he had remained in all of his other positions. That apparent lack of harm put his claim under the aegis of the Georgia law requiring notification to potential defendants to give them

a proper opportunity for retraction. *Atlanta Daily World*, 9 October 1945, 6; and *Tademy v. Scott* (1945).

38. The judges were Samuel H. Sibley, Joseph C. Hutcheson, and Leon McCord. McCord wrote the opinion for a unanimous court. *Tademy v. Scott*, 157 F.2d 826 (1946).

39. "Complaint," in Civil Action no. 3161, *Tademy v. Scott*, RG 21, U.S. District Court, Northern District Court of Georgia, Atlanta Division, Cases Other than Bankruptcy (General Index Cases) 1912–1959, case nos. 29176–29189, box 1275, accession no. 29189, National Archives and Records Administration, Atlanta, Ga. (hereinafter NARA).

40. Answer of Defendant Esther Scott, in Civil Action no. 3161, NARA. The decision and the failed attempts at dismissal are also in Civil Action no. 3161, ibid.

41. In early 1948, before the trial, Tademy had another corneal procedure on the left eye. Deposition of Edward Tademy, Plaintiff, 28 February 1948, and Depositions of Kirby Walker and O. B. Cobbins, 12 February 1948, all in Civil Action no. 3161, NARA.

42. Findings of Fact; Judgment; and Statement of Court Costs, all in Civil Action no. 3161, NARA.

43. Cash Receipts, OBV19, Atlanta Daily World Records; and Julius Eric Thompson, *Percy Greene*, 26–27.

44. Cash Receipts, OBV20 through OBV45, Atlanta Daily World Records; and Julius Eric Thompson, *Percy Greene*, 26–27.

45. See Hogan, *Black National News Service*.

Chapter 7. Davis Lee and the Transitory Nature of Syndicate Editors

1. Lee wasn't tried in Bel Air. In a move surprising everyone, his attorneys successfully petitioned for the case to be moved to Towson, twenty-five miles south toward Baltimore. The team also elected to try the case before a judge rather than a jury. It came as no surprise that Lee was convicted. *Aegis* (Bel Air, Md.), 3 June 1927, 1, 4 November 1927, 1; and *Afro-American*, 27 December 1958, 9.

2. Lee was raised by his grandparents Isaac and Caroline Curtis, along with their adopted son Earnest and another grandchild, Edna Clark. Thirteenth Census of the United States, 1910, Population, Harford County, Md., sheet no. 11A; Fourteenth Census of the United States, 1920, Population, Harford County, Md., sheet no. 4B; and "Davis Lee," Social Security number 218-14-8235, U.S. Social Security Death Index, 1935–2014; *State* (Columbia, S.C.), 20 February 1987, 4C; Fifteenth Census of the United States, 1930, Population, Baltimore City, Md., Maryland Penitentiary, sheet no. 7A; *Afro-American*, 21 April 1951, 1, 27 December 1958, 9; and Davis Lee to Carl Murphy, 28 November 1933, Marshall:15:07, folder 72, Afro-American Newspapers Archives and Research Center, Baltimore, Md. (hereinafter Afro-American Archives). See also Farrar, *"Baltimore Afro-American."*

3. Davis Lee to Afro-American Co., 2 May 1931; NAACP to Carl Murphy, 31 October 1931; and Carl Murphy to William T. Andrews, 12 November 1931, all in Marshall:15:07, folder 72, Afro-American Archives; and *Afro-American*, 3 September 1932, 1, 24 December 1932, 3.

4. *Pittsburgh Courier*, 3 June 1933, 10, 17 June 1933, A2. Lee published his early Pan-Africanist ideas in Garvey's *Negro World*, 21 November 1931, 26 March 1932, and 18 June 1932. Tony Martin, *Pan-African Connection*, 108. Lee wasn't the only *Courier* reader frustrated with Schuyler's argument, as demonstrated by letters to the editor, which is surely exactly what Schuyler wanted. *Pittsburgh Courier*, 17 June 1933, A2, 24 June 1933, A2.

5. *Afro-American*, 22 April 1933, 3. On 25 March 1931, after a fight between white and black youths riding a freight car, the nine black passengers were arrested when the train stopped in Paint Rock, Alabama. They were taken to a larger town nearby, Scottsboro. Two white women had been in the freight car as well, and Victoria Price and Ruby Bates accused the black passengers of rape. The case garnered significant attention after eight of the nine boys were sentenced to death by an all-white jury. The subsequent appeals would keep the Scottsboro Boys in the news throughout the decade. They were later proved to be innocent. Dan T. Carter, *Scottsboro*, 3–50; and Norris and Washington, *Last of the Scottsboro Boys*, 17–26, 249.

6. "With the Magazines," *Chicago Defender*, 23 September 1933, 14; and Davis Lee, "Future of the Negro." In October 1933, *Afro-American* columnist Alfred Hendricks recommended Lee's "Future of the Negro" as a strong pamphlet "far away from the beaten path. Nowhere is to be found the average author's hobby horse—'Honey, I'se waitin',' and such stuff." *Afro-American*, 7 October 1933, 17.

7. By September, Lee had returned to his "farm" in Bel Air "for a much needed rest." A report by the Negro Writers Guild wondered "if he will begin that long contemplated novel while in the quiet of rural Maryland." The marriage to Davis was his second; his first wife was Loretta Brooms. *Baltimore Afro-American*, 31 March 1934, 4, 3 November 1934, 9, 24 November 1934, 3; and *Atlanta Daily World*, 28 March 1934, 1, 22 April 1934, 6, 24 September 1934, 6.

8. *Baltimore Afro-American*, 1 December 1934, 4, 8 December 1934, 4, 15 December 1934, 4.

9. Ibid., 24 November 1934, 16, 1 December 1934, 2, 13, 23, 8 December 1934, 23.

10. Ibid., 15 December 1934, 5.

11. Ibid., 15 December 1934, 16, 29 December 1934, 8; and Davis Lee to Carl Murphy, 24 November 1934, Marshall:15:07, folder 72, Afro-American Archives.

12. One of the men who had been paroled with Lee earlier that year was James Davis (no relation to Lucile Davis), who eventually followed his friend Lee to Jacksonville and took over as managing editor of the *Mirror*. In a region

without a preponderance of black collegiate journalism training, employers found newspapermen where they could. *Afro-American*, 10 March 1934, 23, 27 December 1958, 9.

13. *Afro-American*, 10 March 1934, 23, 27 December 1958, 9; *Atlanta Daily World*, 29 April 1935, 2; and Cora L. Bennett, "Henry Houston (Negro Newspaperman)," 29 August 1939, U.S. Works Progress Administration, Federal Writers' Project, Folklore Project, Life Histories, 1936–1939, Manuscript Division, Library of Congress, Washington, D.C., http://www.loc.gov/item/wpalh001755, accessed 30 October 2014.

14. The institution planned to continue the paper's affiliation with the Scott Syndicate, but it did not survive. *Afro-American*, 30 March 1935, 7; Carl Murphy to Porcher L. Taylor, 19 February 1935; Davis Lee to Carl Murphy, 7 January 1935; and "Started Paper with $54; Sells for $2000, May 25, 1935," all in Marshall:15:07, folder 72, Afro-American Archives.

15. *Pittsburgh Courier*, 29 June 1935, 5, 20 July 1935, 1; and Davis Lee, "East Texas Cotton Choppers Don't Know Wages," 20 July 1935; Davis Lee to Carl Murphy, 12 July 1935; Davis Lee to Carl Murphy, 8 August 1935, all in Marshall:15:07, folder 72, Afro-American Archives.

16. *Pittsburgh Courier*, 1 February 1936, 5, 8 February 1936, A6, 15 February 1936, 5, 7 March 1936, 3; *Atlanta Daily World*, 11 February 1936, 5, 15 February 1936, 1, 17 February 1936, 2, 9 March 1936, 2; and *Afro-American*, 29 February 1936, 21.

17. *Atlanta Daily World*, 21 July 1936, 1, 29 July 1936, 1, 30 July 1936, 1; *Afro-American*, 25 July 1936, 6, 1 August 1936, 3; *Chicago Defender*, 1 August 1936, 21; *New York Amsterdam News*, 1 August 1936, 3; *Pittsburgh Courier*, 1 August 1936, 1, 8 August 1936, 24; Thelma Chiles Lee to Carl Murphy, 20 August 1941, Marshall:15:07, folder 72, Afro-American Archives; Davis Lee to Carl Murphy, 16 March 1936; and "Newsman and Kansas School Teacher Wed, July 11, 1936," all in Wheatley:06:04, folder 210, Afro-American Archives.

18. *Afro-American*, 29 February 1936, 21, 11 July 1936, 1; *Atlanta Daily World*, 9 March 1936, 2; and *Pittsburgh Courier*, 7 March 1936, 3.

19. Lee had maintained his connection with the *Afro*, and the group stopped in Baltimore on the way. *Afro-American*, 23 January 1937, 20; and "Stop! Look! Listen!," Marshall:15:07, folder 72, Afro-American Archives.

20. Thelma Chiles Lee to Carl Murphy, 20 August 1941; and Davis Lee to Carl Murphy, 6 September 1937, both in Marshall:15:07, folder 72, Afro-American Archives.

21. *Baltimore Afro-American*, 20 August 1938, 5, 17 September 1938, 8, 24 September 1938, 1, 28 January 1939, 1, 18 March 1939, 1, 6 May 1939, 1, 8; *Chicago Defender*, 29 July 1939, 6; and Mrs. Davis Lee to Carl Murphy, 12 October 1938; "Editor's Action Saves Accused Man from Chair, 7/22/39"; and Davis Lee to Carl Murphy, 17 July 1939, all in Marshall:15:07, folder 72, Afro-American Archives.

22. *Afro-American*, 11 May 1940, 1, 18 May 1940, 11.

23. Davis Lee to Carl Murphy, n.d.; and Davis Lee to Carl Murphy, n.d., both in Marshall:15:07, folder 72, Afro-American Archives.

24. *Afro-American*, 21 December 1940, 12, 17, 19 July 1941, 18; and Carl Murphy to Davis Lee, 28 October 1940, Marshall:15:07, folder 72; and Carl Murphy to Davis Lee, 2 October 1940, Wheatley:06:04, folder 210, both in Afro-American Archives.

25. *New York Amsterdam News*, 27 December 1941, 21; and *Afro-American*, 17 January 1942, 2, 19 September 1942, 10, 19 December 1942, 21. For examples of Lee's relationship with the home office, see *New York Amsterdam News*, 12 July 1941, 9; and *Afro-American*, 19 July 1941, 18, 4 October 1941, 22, 25 October 1941, 4, 20 December 1941, 8.

26. *Afro-American*, 7 March 1942, 14, 28 March 1942, 20, 9 May 1942, 2, 4 July 1942, 3. Lee's coverage of southern migrants continued through the war. See, for example, *Afro-American*, 29 May 1943, 12, 12 June 1943, 12.

27. An earlier report had noted "deep dissatisfaction among the employees" as a result of Lee's "fiery temper and unrestrained use of profanity. Mr. Lee even alleges the existence of a conspiracy to oust him as manager." In the *New Jersey Afro*'s edition of 1 January 1944, Lee was still listed as the paper's managing editor, organizing a benefit for a local drum and bugle corps, which he described as a prevention method for juvenile delinquency. When the benefit's success was reported on 22 January, Lee was not mentioned, an oversight that the editor with a flair for self-aggrandizement would never have allowed had he still been in charge. By 26 February, the paper's advertisements included O. S. McCollum's name as the new managing editor. Lee had been officially relieved of duty at the *New Jersey Afro* on 3 January 1944. McCollum's editorial transition picture in the *Baltimore Afro* appeared on 12 February 1944. *New Jersey Afro-American*, 30 October 1943, 4, 1 January 1944, 1, 14, 22 January 1944, 1, 14, 26 February 1944, 12; and Carl Murphy to Thomas P. MacCarthy, 31 January 1944; Carl Murphy to Davis Lee, 10 January 1944; and "Report on Conference with Messrs. Lee and Henderson, August 9, 1943," all in Marshall:15:07, folder 72, Afro-American Archives; and Furman L. Templeton to H. A. Bergen, 14 January 1944, Wheatley:06:04, folder 210, Afro-American Archives.

28. James H. Murphy to Carl Murphy, 9 May 1945, Marshall:15:07, folder 72, Afro-American Archives. It was a Lee paper in other ways too. In May 1946, he was charged with criminal libel by a local minister of the African Methodist Episcopal Zion Church and released on $500 bail. "Newspaper Editor Faces Grand Jury, N.J., 5-18-46," and *Newark Herald*, 3 May 1946, both in Marshall:15:07, folder 72, Afro-American Archives.

29. *Roanoke Times*, 2 August 1948; and Winner, "Doubtless Sincere," 164–165. Even the conservative *Time* magazine published an excerpt from the piece, noting with satisfaction that in the South Lee could "know the score"

about which restaurant to frequent. "Jim Crow's 'Other Side,'" *Time*, 6 September 1948, 53. So too did the *Congressional Record* years later, when Louisiana congressman F. Edward Hébert included it as part of his remarks in June 1962. *Congressional Record*, 87th Cong., 2nd sess., 1962, vol. 108, appendix, A4421–A4422. The *Dallas Morning News* published it on 21 June 1963, and because of that reprinting, Lee's remarks were again included in the *Congressional Record* by Bruce Alger of Texas. *Congressional Record*, 88th Cong., 1st sess., 1963, vol. 109, appendix, A3992–A3993.

30. *Congressional Record*, 80th Cong., 2nd sess., 1948, vol. 94, pt. 8, 9801, A4947. The following year, South Carolina senator Burnet Maybank also asked that the article be printed in the *Record*, this time reprinted from the *Danville Register*. *Congressional Record*, 81st Cong., 1st sess., 1949, vol. 95 pt. 2, 2676. These inclusions demonstrated the developing ubiquity of Lee's message in the South, with white newspapers across the region reprinting his editorials to demonstrate that black people could agree with them on the subject of integration.

31. *Atlanta Daily World*, 19 August 1948, 6; Behling, "South Carolina Negro Newspapers," 139; and *Carolina Lighthouse*, 14 May 1939, 1, 8. Only one issue of the *Lighthouse* survives. It is housed in Special Collections at the South Caroliniana Library, University of South Carolina, Columbia. Earlier, McCray had a different view of Lee. In June 1946, McCray wrote of him in a complimentary way, agreeing with his 1939 statement that "Hell's going to be so full of preachers that the rest of us won't have a place to go to." *Atlanta Daily World*, 29 June 1946, 3.

32. *Atlanta Daily World*, 26 August 1948, 4, 9 September 1948, 6; *Afro-American*, 28 August 1948, 4, 2 October 1948, C4, 8 January 1949, A2; and *Chicago Defender*, 21 August 1948, 13, 18 September 1948, 15, 25 September 1948, 14. The Syndicate's Emory O. Jackson seconded Young's assessment and encouraged his readers not to give it shrift. *Atlanta Daily World*, 15 October 1948, 2. In September, the white *Montgomery Advertiser* had acknowledged that Lee's newspaper was less than respected, but still supported the editorial as "substantially a re-broadcast of the wisdom of Booker T. Washington." The *Birmingham World* vehemently disagreed, thinking the comparison an insult to Washington. *Montgomery Advertiser*, 22 September 1948; and *Atlanta Daily World*, 2 October 1948, 6. The Lee editorial appeared in papers as far away as Providence, Rhode Island, and Houston, Texas. *Afro-American*, 9 October 1948, 4, 16 October 1948, 4.

33. Davis Lee, "Black Supremacy," *Plain Talk*, Marshall:15:07, folder 72, Afro-American Archives; and Bedingfield, "John H. McCray," 91–92. This was not the first time that Lee had criticized DePriest. In 1936, well before his turn to segregationism, Lee found himself in trouble with Carl Murphy for arguing in the pages of the *Afro* that DePriest "said he would have to lie for [Alf] Landon in order to be elected." The claim left Murphy scrambling to discover

just what proof Lee had of the statement. Carl Murphy to Davis Lee, 6 August 1936, Wheatley:06:04, folder 210, Afro-American Archives.

34. *Congressional Record*, 81st Cong., 1st sess., 1949, vol. 95, pt. 2, 2367. Like so many of Lee's segregationist articles, it was reprinted more than once. It was also read into the record by Alabama congressman Frank Boykin, along with a similar editorial by Lee's former nemesis George Schuyler. "Most of what is said and written about the South is untrue. Today it is not a place of terror and persecution, nor has it been in many decades," wrote Schuyler in his *Pittsburgh Courier* column. "There is little or no evidence that the Negroes anywhere in the South are terrorized and none that I have talked with say so." The two streams of thought had finally coalesced, one traveling from a long history of conservative provocation, the other moving from Garveyism to Washingtonism to what seemed at times to be outright collaboration. *Congressional Record*, 81st Cong., 1st sess., 1949, vol. 95, pt. 12, A652–A654.

35. *Atlanta World*, 28 February 1932, 6, 21 January 1948, 1; Weaver and Page, "Black Press," 23; and Suggs, "Origins of the Black Press," 7. "No unifying central agency directs the opinions expressed in the Negro press," wrote Gunnar Myrdal in 1944. "Like white newspapers, Negro newspapers are in keen competition with one another for circulation." *American Dilemma*, 909.

36. The editorial, originally from the *Telegram*, was reprinted in the *Opelousas Daily World* and probably elsewhere. It was also, like other Lee articles, read into the *Congressional Record* by white southern representatives. This time, both Louisiana's Henry Larcade and Mississippi's John Bell Williams found it worthy of note. *Congressional Record*, 81st Cong., 2nd sess., 1950, vol. 96, pt. 18, A7377, A7466. Lee echoed this message in a letter to Alabama congressman George W. Andrews, claiming that "I want to see my race enjoy every right, every privilege, and every opportunity enjoyed by every other American, but I am convinced by experience and keen observation that he is acquiring these privileges, opportunities, and rights as he is capable of utilizing them, and that to enact such drastic legislation now would precipitate the very thing which we are seeking to avoid, racial conflict." He suggested that Andrews, like himself, emphasize the opportunities available to African Americans in the South and provide "concrete examples of southern racial cooperation and good will." It is significant that Lee assumed by way of introduction that "you no doubt have read some excerpts in your local papers." It was clear that he understood the favor he had earned from white supremacists. The letter was read into the *Congressional Record*, 81st Cong., 2nd sess., 1950, vol. 96, pt. 2, 2236–2237.

37. *Afro-American*, 25 November 1950, 5.

38. There was no evidence of communist ties other than the one informant. Davis Lee, case file NK100-33578, Federal Bureau of Investigation, Newark Field Office, National Archives and Records Administration (hereinafter NARA). File obtained through the Freedom of Information Act.

39. *Afro-American*, 6 January 1951, 19.

40. John White, "Edgar Daniel Nixon," 205–206; and *Atlanta Daily World*, 15 July 1953, 6. The *Afro* listed the total black attendance as only eighteen. *Afro-American*, 25 July 1953, 18.

41. Like so many of Lee's more vituperative commentaries, this one too ended up in the *Congressional Record*, placed there by Clyde Hoey of North Carolina. *Congressional Record*, 82nd Cong., 2nd sess., 1952, vol. 98, pt. 8, A1021–A1022. And again by Senator Spessard Holland of Florida. *Congressional Record*, 82nd Cong., 2nd sess., 1952, vol. 98, pt. 11, A4488. See also *Alabama Journal*, 22 November 1954, 1.

42. *Congressional Record*, 83rd Cong., 2nd sess., 1954, vol. 100, appendix, A4334–A4336.

43. *McComb Enterprise-Journal*, 9 August 1954, 1; Weill, "Mississippi's Daily Press," 28; and *Atlanta Daily World*, 18 February 1953, 4. The editorial was also, unsurprisingly, reprinted in the *Congressional Record*, placed there by John J. Flynt of Georgia. *Congressional Record*, 85th Cong., 1st sess., 1957, vol. 103, pt. 2, 2766–2767.

44. John L. Whalen to H. G. Foster, 25 July 1955, in Davis Lee, case file NK100-33578, Federal Bureau of Investigation, Newark Field Office, NARA. File obtained through the Freedom of Information Act.

45. *Congressional Record*, 85th Cong., 1st sess., 1957, vol. 103, pt. 9, 12136, and pt. 11, 14982–14983. G. A. Rodgers, an Anniston dentist and president of the Alabama NAACP, called Lee "a modern professional carpetbagger [who] is not accepted by Southern Negros." Gordon A. Rodgers to Roy Wilkins, 19 March 1956, reel 33, frames 248–249, pt. 24, Papers of the NAACP, microfilm. In November 1956, the NAACP's director of public relations, Henry Lee Moon, sent letters to publishers across the country who had reprinted the *Newark Telegram* story, berating Lee's work for repeating "many of the hoary clichés used to defend segregation." Most important, while Lee was entitled to his opinion, his writing "reveals that he is either woefully misinformed or is knavishly trying to mislead the public. Certainly, he does not speak for the Negro race either in the South or in the North." The letter refuted Lee's claims point by point, including his statistics. Circular letter of Henry Lee Moon, 13 November 1956, frames 251–253, pt. 24, reel 33, Papers of the NAACP, microfilm.

46. "Lee Publications, Canal 6-1752," Marshall:15:07, folder 72, Afro-American Archives; Lee advertising letter, 6 November 1958, reel 22, frame 405, pt. 24; and Roy Wilkins to W. H. Young, 4 December 1958, reel 22, frame 406, pt. 24, both in Papers of the NAACP, microfilm; and *Anderson Herald*, 9 November 1959, 1.

47. This was a popular argument with southern congressmen. Robert Hemphill of South Carolina first introduced this article by Lee into the *Congressional Record*. *Congressional Record*, 85th Cong., 1st sess., 1957, vol. 103, appendix, A1244–A1245. The following year, his fellow South Carolinian Olin D.

Johnston included it as well. *Congressional Record*, 85th Cong., 2nd sess., 1958, vol. 104, appendix, A7245. The year after that, Alabama's George Huddleston did too. *Congressional Record*, 86th Cong., 1st sess., 1959, vol. 105, appendix, A1293–A1294.

48. That profit was never much, however, particularly for small-time journalists. "Black papers are a miracle in themselves," comments Raymond Boone, a journalism professor at Howard and a former employee of the *Afro-American*, "because they have managed to survive on money so minimal that white publishers wouldn't even consider existing on that level" (quoted in Garland, "Black Press," 47). Fenderson, "Negro Press," 184; O'Kelly, "Black Newspapers," 14; and Brooks, "Content Analysis."

49. *Congressional Record*, 86th Cong., 1st sess., 1959, vol. 105, appendix, A361–A362.

50. Ibid., A4706–A4707. The article was read into the *Congressional Record* again a few years later by Louisiana senator Russell Long. "Where could a more sensible and a more moderate statement be found–anywhere?" Long asked. "Here is the very key to the Negro's quest for a better life. His answer is not agitation. His answer is not the destruction of our property rights. His answer is not the watering down of our free enterprise system or the abandonment of our system of trial by jury." *Congressional Record*, 88th Cong., 2nd sess., 1964, vol. 110, pt. 8, 11233–11234.

51. Roy Wilkins to W. H. Young, 4 December 1958, reel 33, frames 263–264, pt. 24, Papers of the NAACP, microfilm.

52. Lee's suit against the NAACP ultimately reached $5 million, but he lost in state court. *Greenville* (S.C.) *News*, 3 February 1959, 1; *New York Amsterdam News*, 14 February 1959, 1; Sydney C. Orlofsky to Carl Murphy, 8 February 1960, re: Davis Lee v. Phila. Afro-American, Civil Action no. 27480; Davis Lee to Harold R. Boulware, 17 November 1959; Davis Lee v. Philadelphia Afro-American, Civil Action no. 27480, Motion to Dismiss and/or for Summary Judgment; and Davis Lee v. Richmond Afro-American, Civil Action file 3036, Answer to Motion to Dismiss or for Summary Judgment, all in Wheatley:06:04, folder 196, Afro-American Archives; *Afro-American*, 22 December 1962, 17; *Atlanta Daily World*, 15 December 1962, 1; *Lee v. Peek*, 240 S.C. 203 (1962); and *Lee v. Peek*, 371 U.S. 184 (1962).

53. *Anderson Herald*, 15 March 1964, 1, reprinted in Behling, "South Carolina Negro Newspapers," 128–129.

54. *Brown v. Lee*, 331 F.2d 142 (1964); and *Anderson Herald*, 1 June 1964, 5, reprinted in Behling, "South Carolina Negro Newspapers," 136–137.

55. *Los Angeles Sentinel*, 29 December 1960, B6; and "Davis Lee Charges He Was Locked Out of *Savannah Tribune*; Sues for $250,000," ANP press release, 31 May 1961, Tubman:02:02, folder 1167, Afro-American Archives.

56. Lee also met with influential state leaders like cotton magnate Garner Lester, vice president of the National Tax Equality Association and head of the National Ginners Association, and attempted to meet with Walter Sillers,

speaker of the Mississippi House, while in Jackson. His letter listed him as the head of Lee Publications in Anderson, South Carolina, publishing both the *Anderson Herald* and the *Newark Telegram*. Davis Lee to State Sovereignty Commission, 10 April 1962, 7-0-5-55-3-1-1; Albert Jones to Davis Lee, 23 April 1962, 7-0-5-55-3-1-1; Davis Lee to Albert Jones, 29 April 1962, 7-0-5-58-2-1-1; Albert Jones to Davis Lee, 1 May 1962, 7-0-5-59-1-1-1, all in Sovereignty Commission Records, Mississippi Department of Archives and History, Jackson.

57. *South Carolina Herald*, 1 June 1963, 1, as quoted in Behling, "South Carolina Negro Newspapers," 132–135 (Behling misidentifies the *Anderson Herald* as the *South Carolina Herald*).

58. Sarratt, *Ordeal of Desegregation*, 250; Chappell, *Stone of Hope*, 175; and Behling, "South Carolina Negro Newspapers," 101.

59. "Who Is Lee?," reel 39, frames 521–527, pt. 23, Papers of the NAACP, microfilm.

Chapter 8. The Life and Death of the Scott Newspaper Syndicate

1. Hornsby, "Negro in Atlanta Politics," 7; and Baldwin, *Evidence of Things Not Seen*, 36–37.

2. Hornsby, "Negro in Atlanta Politics," 7–8.

3. "Brief History of Atlanta Daily World and Scott Newspaper Syndicate," 1102.8.12, Birmingham World Office Files, Department of Archives and Manuscripts, Birmingham Public Library, Birmingham, Ala. (hereinafter Birmingham World Office Files); and *Chapman v. King*, 154 F.2d 460 (1946).

4. Bacote, "Negro in Atlanta Politics," 343–345, quote 345; and *Atlanta Constitution*, 17 February 1946, 3D.

5. Though he was victorious in this fourth run for Georgia governor, Talmadge died before taking office. Bacote, "Negro in Atlanta Politics," 346–348; *Atlanta Journal*, 8 May 1946, 1; and *Atlanta Daily World*, 2 May 1946, 1. For more on the election, see Elson, "Georgia Three-Governor Controversy"; Sutton, "Talmadge Campaigns"; and William Anderson, *Wild Man from Sugar Creek*.

6. Odum-Hinmon, "Cautious Crusader," 42–43, 67. For more on the Black Shirts, see chapter 1.

7. *Atlanta Daily World*, 12 July 1946, 1; and *Atlanta Constitution*, 12 July 1946, 14.

8. Hornsby, "Negro in Atlanta Politics," 8–9; and Odum-Hinmon, "Cautious Crusader," 44, 77–80.

9. Odum-Hinmon, "Cautious Crusader," 45, 117–122, quote 118; and *Atlanta Daily World*, 2 April 1948, 1, 3 April 1948, 1, 4 April 1948, 1, 7 April 1948, 6.

10. *Atlanta Daily World*, 18 August 1946, 1; and Odum-Hinmon, "Cautious Crusader," 45, 91–112. See also Wexler, *Fire in a Canebrake*; Pitch, *Last Lynching*; and *Printing the Dream*.

11. Odum-Hinmon, "Cautious Crusader," 124–130; Charles H. Martin, "Race, Gender, and Southern Justice"; Lorence, *Hard Journey*, 136–137; Strain, *Pure Fire*, 30; and McGuire, *At the Dark End*, 80–82.

12. Into that milieu came in November 1946 the film premiere of Disney's *Song of the South*, screened in Atlanta because of the success of the Atlanta premiere of *Gone with the Wind* the previous decade. The *World*, however, concerned itself little with the racist fawning over the Lost Cause depicted in the movie, instead emphasizing the need for a federal anti-lynching law, broader voting rights provisions, and more immediate justice for crimes like the Monroe lynchings. It was largely ambivalent about *Song of the South*, though it reprinted wire stories chronicling denunciations of the movie from advocacy groups that saw it as damaging. Bernstein, "Nostalgia, Ambivalence, Irony," 219–220, 223–229; and *Atlanta Daily World* 24 December 1946, 6.

13. *Lighthouse and Informer*, 11 May 1947, 1; *Atlanta Daily World*, 4 May 1947, 1, 6 June 1947, 1, 13 June 1947, 1, 14 June 1947, 1; *Afro-American*, 7 June 1947, 2; and *Pittsburgh Courier*, 10 May 1947, 1.

14. *Atlanta Daily World*, 1 June 1947, 1, 4, 8 June 1947, 4, 1 July 1947, 6, 16 July 1947, 6; *Lighthouse and Informer*, 8 June 1947, 1, 13 July 1947, 1; *Afro-American*, 7 June 1947, 1; and *Chicago Defender*, 14 June 1947, 1, 19 July 1947, 12.

15. Memorandum from C. A. Scott, 9 March 1949, 1102.1.5.1, Birmingham World Office Files; *Atlanta Daily World*, 29 March 1949, 1; and *Chicago Defender*, 5 March 1949, 1.

16. Odum-Hinmon, "Cautious Crusader," 65; and "Atlanta Daily World Newspaper Style Sheet," 1102.8.12, Birmingham World Office Files.

17. *Atlanta Daily World*, 7 October 1954, 1, 8 October 1954, 1.

18. *Mosley v. State*, 211 Ga. 611 (1955); *Atlanta Daily World*, 14 October 1954, 1, 10 November 1954, 1, 14 November 1954, 2, 12 January 1955, 1, 31 May 1955, 1, 3 June 1955, 1, 12 June 1955, 1, 16 June 1955, 1, 22 June 1955, 4, 14 July 1955, 1, 15 July 1955, 1, 21 September 1955, 1, 24 September 1955, 1, 3 December 1955, 1, 4 December 1955, 1, 15 December 1955, 1, 16 December 1955, 1, 23 December 1955, 1, 6 January 1956, 1, 27 January 1956, 1, 1 February 1956, 1, 2 February 1956, 1, 3 February 1956, 1, 5 February 1956, 1, 8 February 1956, 1, 12 February 1956, 1, 29 April 1956, 5, 1 May 1956, 1, 16 May 1956, 1, 14 June 1956, 1, 21 June 1956, 1, 24 June 1956, 1, 27 June 1956, 1, 28 June 1956, 1, 29 June 1956, 4, 30 June 1956, 1; *Afro-American*, 18 February 1956, 8; and *Printing the Dream*.

19. Martindale, *White Press and Black America*, 79–80, 83, 92; Welky, "Viking Girls," 25–27, quote 26; and *Report of the National Advisory Commission on Civil Disorders* (Washington, D.C.: U.S. Government Publishing Office, 1968), 206–208.

20. Doreski, *Writing America Black*, xiii; and Jordan, *Black Newspapers and America's War*, 3–4.

21. "Brief History of Atlanta Daily World and Scott Newspaper Syndicate," Birmingham World Office Files; Blackwell, "Black-Controlled Media," 82; Prattis, "Racial Segregation and Negro Journalism," 313; and Odum-Hinmon, "Cautious Crusader," 45, 66, 115–117.

22. Blackwell, "Black-Controlled Media," 112; Ledger, 1937, 74; and Ledger, 1939, 144, both in box 21, Misc. Ledgers, Atlanta Daily World Records, 1931–1996, Manuscript Collection no. 1092, Manuscript, Archives, and Rare Book Library, Emory University, Atlanta, Ga. (hereinafter Atlanta Daily World Records). The percentages remained the same at the end of 1940. Ledger, 1940, 175, ibid.

23. Odum-Hinmon, "Cautious Crusader," 74–75, 89.

24. Blackwell, "Black-Controlled Media," 121–122; and Odum-Hinmon, "Cautious Crusader," 41, 68.

25. Totals compiled from advertising record, 1948, box 1, Atlanta Daily World Records.

26. Drake and Cayton, *Black Metropolis*, 1:412; Walter White, *A Man Called White*, 208; Poston, "Negro Press"; Blackwell, "Black-Controlled Media," 23; and O'Kelly, "Black Newspapers," 14. See also Brooks, "Content Analysis."

27. Sancton, "Negro Press," 560.

28. Ottley, *"New World A-Coming,"* 281; and Roberts and Klibanoff, *Race Beat*, 76.

29. All totals calculated from the *World*'s 1949 advertising records, box 2, Atlanta Daily World Records.

30. All totals calculated from the *World*'s 1953 advertising records, box 3, Atlanta Daily World Records.

31. All totals calculated from the *World*'s 1954 advertising records, box 4, Atlanta Daily World Records.

32. Atlanta Daily World invoice, 29 December 1958, box 23, Correspondence, 1950s–1960s; Records of Advertising Paid, 1947–1954, box 27, Tax Records, 1940s–1950s, both in Atlanta Daily World Records; and Barnett, "Why Can't We Have Negro Dailies?," reprinted in *Indianapolis Recorder*, 15 January 1938, 13.

33. All totals calculated from Sales Tax, 1951–1955, box 27, Tax Records, 1940s–1950s, Atlanta Daily World Records.

34. Tri-State Printing and Binding to Scott Newspaper Syndicate, n.d.; and Johnson Printery Statement, 29 April 1959, both in box 22, Correspondence, 1950s, Atlanta Daily World Records. All totals calculated from the *Memphis World* weekly financial reports for 1954, box 27, Tax Records, 1940s–1950s, Atlanta Daily World Records.

35. C. A. Scott to C. A. Barnett, 24 November 1951; and Claude A. Barnett, undated note, box 148, folder 10, both in Claude A. Barnett Papers: The Associated Negro Press, 1918–1967, pt. 2, Associated Negro Press Organizational Files, 1920–1966, Chicago Historical Society, Chicago, Ill. (hereinafter Barnett Papers).

36. C. A. Barnett to C. A. Scott, 23 February 1952; Claude A. Barnett to C. A. Scott, 20 February 1955; and C. A. Scott to Claude A. Barnett, 3 March 1955, all in box 148, folder 10, Barnett Papers.

37. Jackson's one available tax return from this period demonstrates that he made $2,524.50 in 1948. See U.S. Individual Income Tax Return, Form

1040, 1948; and Financial Statements, unnumbered box, Emory O. Jackson Papers, A423, Birmingham Civil Rights Institute, Birmingham, Ala.

38. Burma, "Future of the Negro Press," 67.

39. Advertising manager James Russell Simmons was married to Ruth Scott, the youngest of the Scott siblings. When her husband left to fight in World War II, she took his position. Blackwell, "Black-Controlled Media," 110; and Poston, "Negro Press," 16.

40. Brown-Nagin, *Courage to Dissent*, 105–111, quote 106; *Atlanta Daily World*, 18 May 1954, 1, 2, 5, 6; Murphy, "Study of the Editorial Policies," 59–71; and Odum-Hinmon, "Cautious Crusader," 130–150, quote 150.

41. Murphy, "Study of the Editorial Policies," 82, 92.

42. Blackwell, "Black-Controlled Media," 77; Simmons, *African American Press*, 102–103; and Aptheker, *Documentary History*, 7:32–33.

43. Simmons, *African American Press*, 117–118; Aptheker, *Documentary History*, 7:98; and Prattis, "Role of the Negro Press," 274.

44. Alexis Scott interview; and Hornsby, "Georgia," 129–130. The Scotts were not alone. Historian J. Mills Thornton has demonstrated that after the death of Samuel W. Boynton in the early 1960s, for example, black leaders in Selma, Alabama, "were extremely reluctant to assume the very public position as activist that Boynton had held." Thornton, *Dividing Lines*, 493, 540–541, quote 446.

45. Thornton, *Dividing Lines*, 493, 540–541; and Blackwell, "Black-Controlled Media," 77–78.

46. Hornsby, "Georgia," 129–130; and Wolseley, *Black Press, USA*, 73.

47. Lomax, *Negro Revolt*, 201–202.

48. Ibid., 202.

49. Ibid., 202–203.

50. Fenderson, "Negro Press," 181.

51. Ibid., 182–184.

52. Quoted in Simmons, *African American Press*, 118–119; and Aptheker, *Documentary History*, 7:98.

53. C. A. and Portia quoted in Blackwell, "Black-Controlled Media," 102; Hornsby, "Georgia," 130–131; Odum-Hinmon, "Cautious Crusader," 82; and *Printing the Dream*.

54. C. A. Scott to Claude A. Barnett, 25 August 1952; Claude A. Barnett to C. A. Scott, 30 August 1952; and C. A. Scott to Claude A. Barnett, 27 January 1953, all in box 148, folder 10, Barnett Papers.

55. Hornsby, "Georgia," 138–139; *Atlanta Inquirer*, 31 July 1960, 1; *Atlanta Daily World*, 8 February 1970, 2, 7 July 1970, 1; and *Printing the Dream*. See also Wardlaw, "Gatekeeper Analysis."

56. Ingham and Feldman, *African American Business Leaders*, 587–588. For an example of the *World*'s other competitor, see *Atlanta Voice*, 5 January 1969, 1. That paper was founded in 1966, but its first extant editions are from 1969.

57. Blackwell, "Black-Controlled Media," 101, 102; and McPheeters, *Negro Progress in Atlanta*, ii.

58. Frazier, *Black Bourgeoisie*, 50; and Vowels, "Atlanta Negro Business," 48, 55.

59. The *Atlanta Daily World* sold the *Memphis World* in February 1971 and the *Birmingham World* in 1987. Neither survived. Blackwell, "Black-Controlled Media," 85; and Odum-Hinmon, "Cautious Crusader," 39–40.

Conclusion

1. *Atlanta Daily World*, 22 January 1954, 4.

2. Alexander, *New Jim Crow*, 235; Rosenberg, *Hollow Hope*, 52; and Klarman, "*Brown*, Racial Change," 7, 9.

3. Wolseley, *Black Press, USA*, 80, 81.

4. In the 1960s, the SERS was rechristened the Race Relations Information Center; it survived until 1972. Gilpin, "Charles S. Johnson," 197.

5. Odum-Hinmon, "Cautious Crusader," 7–8. Peter Kellogg classifies many people as having an "atrocity orientation," a phenomenon in which individuals or groups notice racism at the onset of carnage or crimes—riots, lynchings, assassinations—but are unable or unwilling to acknowledge the institutional causes of such violent acts or the subtle racism and discrimination that are foundational for those more overt behaviors. That atrocity orientation might help to explain, at least in part, the black southern press's reaction to some civil rights activities. Kellogg, "Northern Liberals and Black America," 109–113.

6. Blackwell, "Black-Controlled Media," v, 1.

7. Loeb, introduction to *The Negro Newspaper*, 28; and Odum-Hinmon, "Cautious Crusader," 14.

8. Thornbrough, "American Negro Newspapers," 467–468.

9. Lambert, *Battle of Ole Miss*, 37–38; and Hodding Carter, *Their Words Were Bullets*, 50.

10. Cruse, *Crisis of the Negro Intellectual*, 65.

11. Doxey A. Wilkerson, "Negro Press," 511; and Singer, "Mass Society," 140–141.

12. Ottley, "*New World A-Coming*," 268; Mims, *Advancing South*, 268; and Gordon, *Georgia Negro*, 265.

13. Roberts and Klibanoff, *Race Beat*, 76.

14. Kreiling, "Making of Racial Identities." As Thomas Sancton wrote in the 1940s, "When a white man first reads a Negro newspaper, it is like getting a bucket of cold water in the face" ("Negro Press," 558). See also Jordan, *Black Newspapers and America's War*, 3.

Bibliography

Newspapers

This book discusses the content of many newspapers that no longer survive by using syndicated stories printed in larger black newspapers like the *Atlanta Daily World*. What follows is a list of newspapers the author actually viewed or cites in the notes. When these papers are only available in archives, their location is listed in the first citation in the notes.

Aegis
Afro-American
Alabama Journal
Alabama Tribune
American Guide
American Progress (Meridian)
American Progress (New Orleans)
Anderson Herald
Arizona Republic
Arkansas Freeman
Arkansas Gazette
Arkansas Survey
Arkansas Survey-Journal
Arkansas Weekly Mansion
Arkansas World
Atlanta Constitution
Atlanta Daily World
Atlanta Independent
Atlanta Inquirer
Atlanta Journal
Atlanta Voice
Atlanta World
Baltimore Afro-American
Baltimore Sun
Banner County Outlook
Baton Rouge Morning Advocate
Baton Rouge Post
Bay View Observer

Birmingham Age-Herald
Birmingham News
Birmingham Post
Birmingham Reporter
Birmingham World
Boston Chronicle
Brownsville Weekly News
Buffalo Star
California Eagle
Cape Fear Journal
Carolina Lighthouse
Carolina Times
Charleston Messenger
Charleston News and Courier
Chattanooga Observer
Chicago Defender
Chicago Tribune
Cincinnati Independent
Cleveland Gazette
Colored Citizen
Columbus Advocate
Connecticut Labor News
Daily Worker
Dallas Express
Dallas Morning News
Des Moines Register
Detroit Echo
Detroit Independent

East Tennessee News
East Texas Times
Evansville Argus
Flint Brownsville News
Florida Sun
Fort Worth Mind
Galveston Examiner
Galveston Guide
Galveston Voice
Greenville Leader
Greenville News
Houston Informer
Illinois Times
Indianapolis Recorder
Indianapolis World
Jackson Advocate
Jacksonville Tribune
Jewish Criterion
Kentucky New Era
Lighthouse and Informer
Los Angeles Sentinel
Louisiana Weekly
Louisville Defender
Louisville Leader
Macon Daily Telegraph
McComb Enterprise-Journal
Memphis Commercial Appeal
Memphis Press Scimitar
Memphis World
Miami Times
Michigan Chronicle
Michigan Tribune
Mississippi Tribune
Mississippi Weekly
Mobile Press Forum Sun
Mobile Press Forum Weekly
Monroe Morning World
Monroe News Star
Montgomery Advertiser
Muskogee Lantern
Nashville Clarion
Nashville Defender
Nashville Globe
Nashville Independent

Nashville Sun
Nashville Tennessean
Nashville World
Negro World
Newark Herald
New Jersey Afro-American
New Jersey Herald News
News-Gazette
New York Age
New York Amsterdam News
New York Herald Tribune
New York Times
New York World Telegram
Nite-Life
Oklahoma Black Dispatch
Oklahoman
Pee Dee Advocate
Philadelphia Tribune
Phoenix Index
Pittsburgh Courier
Progress
Roanoke Times
Ruston Daily Leader
San Jose Evening News
Savannah Journal
Savannah Tribune
South Bend Forum
South Carolina Herald
Southern Broadcast
Southern Enterprise
Southern Liberator
Southern Worker
Southwest Georgian
Spartanburg Herald
St. Louis Argus
St. Louis Post-Dispatch
State
Statesville Record and Landmark
Sunlight
Tri-State Defender
Tropical Dispatch
Tuscaloosa Gazette
Tuscaloosa News
Twin City Herald

Washington Post   *Western Star*
Weekly Echo   *West Virginia Weekly*
Weekly Progress   *Wilmington Journal*
Western Outlook   *World Telegram*

Archival Collections

Abbott-Sengstacke Family Papers, 1847–1997, Carter G. Woodson Regional Library, Vivian G. Harsh Research Collection of Afro-American History and Literature, Chicago Public Library, Chicago, Ill.

Afro-American Newspapers Archives and Research Center, Baltimore, Md.

Atlanta Daily World Records, 1931–1996, Manuscript Collection no. 1092, Manuscript, Archives, and Rare Book Library, Emory University, Atlanta, Ga.

Austin T. Walden Papers, 1915–1965, MSS 614, Atlanta History Center, Atlanta, Ga.

Baltimore County and Baltimore City Equity Papers, Maryland State Archives, Annapolis.

Birmingham World Office Files, Department of Archives and Manuscripts, Birmingham Public Library, Birmingham, Ala.

Black Legion Collection, Clark Historical Library, Central Michigan University, Mount Pleasant.

C. C. [Charles Clinton] Spaulding Papers, 1905–1985, Rare Book, Manuscript, and Special Collections Library, Duke University, Durham, N.C.

Claude A. Barnett Papers: The Associated Negro Press, 1918–1967, pt. 2, Associated Negro Press Organizational Files, 1920–1966, Chicago Historical Society, Chicago, Ill.

Crusader News Agency, Press Releases, 1933–1934, Schomburg Center for Research in Black Culture, New York Public Library.

Donald F. Paine Collection of Hiram Hall, Eugene D. Blanchard, and Stanley Puryear, MS.3204, Special Collections, University of Tennessee Libraries, Knoxville.

Emory O. Jackson Papers, A423, Birmingham Civil Rights Institute, Birmingham, Ala.

George Washington Carver Correspondence, 1932–1939, unprocessed collection, Amistad Research Center, Tulane University, New Orleans, La.

Illinois Times Vertical File, Local History Ephemera Series, Champaign County Historical Archives, Urbana Free Library, Urbana, Ill.

James B. Morris Papers, 1926–1972, R21, Special Collections, State Historical Society of Iowa, Iowa City.

John H. McCray Papers, 11294, South Caroliniana Library, University of South Carolina, Columbia.

Living Atlanta Tapes and Papers, 1914–1985, MSS 637, Kenan Research Center, Atlanta History Center, Atlanta, Ga.

Memphis World Photographs, MS.3181, Special Collections, University of Tennessee Libraries, Knoxville.

National Archives and Records Administration, Atlanta, Ga.

Papers of Governor Fuller Warren, Series 253, State Archives of Florida, Tallahassee.

Papers of the NAACP, Library of Congress, Washington, D.C.

Sadye Harris Powell Family Papers, Manuscript Collection no. 1041, Manuscript, Archives and Rare Book Library, Emory University, Atlanta, Ga.

Sovereignty Commission Records, Mississippi Department of Archives and History, Jackson.

U.S. Works Progress Administration, Federal Writers' Project, Folklore Project, Life Histories, 1936–1939, Manuscript Division, Library of Congress, Washington, D.C.

Works Progress Administration Records, MSS0011, Dr. C. C. and Mabel L. Criss Library Special Collections, University of Nebraska, Omaha.

Legal Decisions

Benton v. Commonwealth, 89 Va. 570 (1893).

Brown v. Lee, 331 F.2d 142 (1964).

Buchanan v. Warley, 245 U.S. 60 (1917).

Chambers v. Florida, 309 U.S. 227 (1940).

Chaney v. Saunders, 3 Munf. 51 (Va. 1811).

Chapman v. King, 154 F.2d 460 (1946).

Davis v. Commonwealth, 99 Va. 868 (1901).

Dean v. Commonwealth, 45 Va. (4 Gratt.) 210 (1847).

Gainer v. School Board of Jefferson County, Alabama, 135 F.Supp 559 (1955).

Henderson v. United States, 339 U.S. 816 (1950).

Herndon v. Lowry, 301 U.S. 242 (1937).

Hey v. Commonwealth, 73 Va. (32 Gratt.) 946 (1879).

Lee v. Peek, 240 S.C. 203 (1962).

Lee v. Peek, 371 U.S. 184 (1962).

McLaurin v. Oklahoma State Regents, 339 U.S. 637 (1950).

Mills v. Board of Education of Anne Arundel County, 30 F.Supp. 245 (1939).

Missouri ex rel. Gaines v. Canada, 305 U.S. 337 (1938).

Mosley v. State, 211 Ga. 611 (1955).

Norris v. Alabama, 294 U.S. 587 (1935)

Parker et al v. State, 194 Miss. 895 (1943).

People v. Hall, 4 Cal. 399 (1854).

Plessy v. Ferguson, 163 U.S. 537 (1896).

Rogers v. Alabama, 192 U.S. 226 (1904).

Shelley v. Kraemer, 334 U.S. 1 (1948).

Sipuel v. Board of Regents of the University of Oklahoma, 332 U.S. 631 (1948).

Smith v. Allwright, 321 U.S. 649 (1944).

State v. Fisher, 1 H. & J. 750 (Md. 1805).

Sweatt v. Painter, 339 U.S. 629 (1950).

Tademy v. Scott, 68 F.Supp. 556 (1945).

Tademy v. Scott, 157 F.2d 826 (1946).

Thomas v. Pile, 3 H. & McH. 241 (Md. 1794).

U.S. v. Classic, 313 U.S. 299 (1941).

U.S. v. Fisher, 25 F.Cas. 1086 (D.C. 1805).

U.S. v. Mullany, 27 F.Cas. 20 (D.C. 1808).

Williams v. Mississippi, 170 U.S. 213 (1898).

Willis v. Walker, 136 F.Supp. 177 (1955).

Other Sources

Adams, James Eli. *A History of Victorian Literature*. New York: Wiley, 2012.

Adams, Luther. *Way Up North in Louisville: African American Migration in the Urban South, 1930–1970*. Chapel Hill: University of North Carolina Press, 2010.

Aiello, Thomas. *The Battle for the Souls of Black Folk: W. E. B. Du Bois, Booker T. Washington, and the Debate That Shaped the Course of Civil Rights*. Westport, Conn.: Praeger, 2016.

——. "Calumny in the House of the Lord: The 1932 Zion Traveler Church Shooting." In *Louisiana beyond Black and White: Recent Interpretations on Race and Race Relations*, ed. Michael Martin, 17–34. Lafayette: University of Louisiana Press, 2011.

——. *The Kings of Casino Park: Race and Race Baseball in the Lost Season of 1932*. Tuscaloosa: University of Alabama Press, 2011.

Alexander, Michelle. *The New Jim Crow: Mass Incarceration in the Age of Colorblindness*. New York: New Press, 2010.

American Civil Liberties Union. *The Bill of Rights in War*. New York: ACLU, 1942.

Anderson, Karen. *Changing Woman: A History of Racial Ethnic Women in Modern America*. New York: Oxford University Press, 1996.

Anderson, William. *The Wild Man from Sugar Creek: The Political Career of Eugene Talmadge*. Baton Rouge: Louisiana State University Press, 1975.

Annotated Code of Tennessee, 1934, vol. 8. Indianapolis, Ind.: Bobbs-Merrill, 1934.

Aptheker, Herbert. *A Documentary History of the Negro People in the United States*, vol. 7. New York: Citadel Press, 1969.

Astor, Gerald. *"... And a Credit to His Race": The Hard Life and Times of Joseph Louis Barrow, a.k.a. Joe Louis*. New York: Saturday Review Press, 1974.

Atlanta—You Ought to Know Your Own! 1937 Directory and Souvenir Program of the National Negro Business League Convention. Atlanta, Ga.: Arnett G. Lindsay, 1937.

Avins, Alfred. "Right to Be a Witness and the Fourteenth Amendment." *Missouri Law Review* 31 (Fall 1966): 471–504.

Bacote, Clarence A. "The Negro in Atlanta Politics." *Phylon* 16 (Fourth Quarter 1955): 333–350.

——. "The Negro in Georgia Politics, 1880–1908." PhD diss., University of Chicago, 1955.

Bailey, Amy Kate, and Stewart E. Tolnay. *Lynched: The Victims of Southern Mob Violence*. Chapel Hill: University of North Carolina Press, 2015.

Bailey, Frankie Y., and Alice P. Green. *"Law Never Here": A Social History of African American Responses to Issues of Crime and Justice*. Westport, Conn.: Praeger, 1999.

Baker, R. Scott. *Paradoxes of Desegregation: African American Struggles for Educational Equity in Charleston, South Carolina, 1926–1972*. Columbia: University of South Carolina Press, 2006.

——. "Pedagogies of Protest: African American Teachers and the Civil Rights Movement." *Teachers College Record* 113 (December 2011): 2777–2803.

——. "Testing Equality: The National Teacher Examination and the NAACP's Legal Campaign to Equalize Teachers' Salaries in the South, 1936–1963." *History of Education Quarterly* 35 (Spring 1995): 49–64.

Baker, Thomas Harrison. *The "Memphis Commercial Appeal": A History of a Southern Newspaper*. Baton Rouge: Louisiana State University Press, 1971.

Baker, William J. *Jesse Owens: An American Life*. New York: Macmillan, 1986.

Baldwin, James. *The Evidence of Things Not Seen*. New York: Henry Holt, 1985.

Barnard, William D. *Dixiecrats and Democrats: Alabama Politics, 1942–1950*. Tuscaloosa: University of Alabama Press, 1974.

Barnett, Albert G. "Why Can't We Have Negro Dailies?," *Afro-American Youth* 1 (December 1937): 4–7.

Bates, Beth Tompkins. *The Making of Black Detroit in the Age of Henry Ford*. Chapel Hill: University of North Carolina Press, 2014.

Bedingfield, Sid. "The Dixiecrat Summer of 1948: Two South Carolina Editors—a Liberal and a Conservative—Foreshadow Modern Political Debate in the South." *American Journalism* 27 (Summer 2010): 91–114.

——. "John H. McCray, Accomodationism, and the Framing of the Civil Rights Struggle in South Carolina, 1940–48." *Journalism History* 37 (Summer 2011): 91–101.

——. *Newspaper Wars: Civil Rights and White Resistance in South Carolina, 1935–1965*. Urbana: University of Illinois Press, 2017.

Beecher, John. "The Sharecroppers Union in Alabama." *Social Forces* 13 (October 1934–May 1935): 124–132.

Beeler, Dorothy. "Race Riot in Columbia, Tennessee, February 25–27, 1946." *Tennessee Historical Quarterly* 39 (Spring 1980): 49–61.

Beezer, Bruce. "Black Teachers' Salaries and the Federal Courts before *Brown v. Board of Education*: One Beginning for Equality." *Journal of Negro Education* 55 (Spring 1986): 200–213.

Behling, Charles H. "South Carolina Negro Newspapers: Their History, Content, and Reception." MA thesis, University of South Carolina, 1964.

Belles, A. Gilbert. "The Black Press in Illinois." *Journal of the Illinois State Historical Society* 68 (September 1975): 344–352.

Berg, A. Scott. *Lindbergh*. New York: Putnam's, 1998.

Bernstein, Matthew. "Nostalgia, Ambivalence, Irony: *Song of the South* and Race Relations in 1946 Atlanta." *Film History* 8, no. 2 (1996): 219–236.

Best's Life Insurance Reports, 17th ed. New York: Alfred M. Best Co., 1922.

Biagi, Shirley, and Marilyn Kern-Foxworth. *Facing Difference: Race, Gender, and Mass Media*. Thousand Oaks, Calif.: Pine Forge Press, 1997.

Bilbo, Theodore G. *Take Your Choice: Separation or Mongrelization*. Poplarville, Miss.: Dream House, 1947.

Bjorn, Lars. *Before Motown: A History of Jazz in Detroit, 1920–60*. Ann Arbor: University of Michigan Press, 2001.

Black, Dan A., Seth G. Sanders, Evan J. Taylor, and Lowell J. Taylor. "The Impact of the Great Migration on Mortality of African Americans: Evidence from the Deep South." *American Economic Review* 105 (February 2015): 477–503.

Blackmon, Douglas. *Slavery by Another Name: The Re-Enslavement of Black Americans from the Civil War to World War II*. New York: Random House, 2008.

Blackwell, Gloria. "Black-Controlled Media in Atlanta, 1960–1970: The Burden of the Message and the Struggle for Survival." PhD diss., Emory University, 1973.

Blakeney, Lincoln Anderson. "A Sociological Analysis of a Negro Newspaper: The *Atlanta Daily World*." MA thesis, Atlanta University, 1949.

Booker, Robert J. *A History of Mechanicsville, 1875–2008: A Glimpse of People, Places, and Events of Knoxville's Elite Black Community and Their Contributions to Society*. Knoxville, Tenn.: Knoxville's Community Development Corporation, 2008.

Borden, Ernest H. *Detroit's Paradise Valley*. Mount Pleasant, S.C.: Arcadia, 2003.

Boston, Michael B. *The Business Strategy of Booker T. Washington: Its Development and Implementation*. Gainesville: University Press of Florida, 2010.

Boyd, Bill. *Blind Obedience: A True Story of Family Loyalty and Murder in South Georgia*. Macon, Ga.: Mercer University Press, 2000.

Boyle, Kevin. *Arc of Justice: A Saga of Race, Civil Rights, and Murder in the Jazz Age*. New York: Henry Holt, 2004.

Brisbane, Robert H. "Davis, Benjamin J[efferson], Sr." In *Dictionary of American Negro Biography*, ed. Rayford W. Logan and Michael R. Winston, 159–160. New York: Norton, 1982.

Brooks, Maxwell. "Content Analysis of Leading Negro Newspapers." PhD diss., Ohio State University, 1953.

———. "A Sociological Interpretation of the Negro Newspaper." MA thesis, Ohio State University, 1937.

Brophy, Alfred L. *Reconstructing the Dreamland: The Tulsa Race Riot of 1921, Race Reparations, and Reconciliation*. New York: Oxford University Press, 2002.

Brown, M. Christopher, II. "Collegiate Desegregation as Progenitor and Progeny of *Brown v. Board of Education*: The Forgotten Role of Postsecondary Litigation, 1908–1990." *Journal of Negro Education* 73 (Summer 2004): 341–349.

Brown-Nagin, Tomiko. *Courage to Dissent: Atlanta and the Long History of the Civil Rights Movement*. New York: Oxford University Press, 2011.

Brundage, W. Fitzhugh. *Lynching in the New South: Georgia and Virginia, 1880–1930*. Urbana: University of Illinois Press, 1993.

Buccellato, James. *Early Organized Crime in Detroit: Vice, Corruption, and the Rise of the Mafia*. Charleston, S.C.: History Press, 2015.

Buchanan, Scott. "The Dixiecrat Rebellion: Long-Term Partisan Implications in the Deep South." *Politics and Policy* 33 (November 2005): 754–769.

Bullock, Penelope L. "Profile of a Periodical: The *Voice of the Negro*." *Atlanta Historical Bulletin* 21 (Spring 1977): 95–114.

Burma, John. "An Analysis of the Present Negro Press." *Social Forces* 26 (December 1947): 172–180.

——. "The Future of the Negro Press." *Negro Digest* 6 (February 1948): 67–70.

Busch, Andrew E. *Truman's Triumphs: The 1948 Election and the Making of Postwar America*. Lawrence: University Press of Kansas, 2012.

Butler, Paul. "Racially Based Jury Nullification: Black Power in the Criminal Justice System." *Yale Law Journal* 105 (December 1995): 677–725.

Campbell, James. *Crime and Punishment in African American History*. New York: Palgrave MacMillan, 2013.

Capeci, Dominic J., and Martha Wilkerson. *Layered Violence: The Detroit Rioters of 1943*. Jackson: University Press of Mississippi, 1991.

Carby, Hazel V. *Reconstructing Womanhood: The Emergence of the Afro-American Woman Novelist*. New York: Oxford University Press, 1987.

Carlin, Amanda. "The Courtroom as White Space: Racial Performance as Noncredibility." *UCLA Law Review* 63 (2016): 450–484.

Carmichael, Stokely, and Charles V. Hamilton. *Black Power: The Politics of Liberation in America*. New York: Knopf, 1967.

Carroll, Brian. *When to Stop the Cheering? The Black Press, the Black Community, and the Integration of Professional Baseball*. New York: Routledge, 2006.

Carter, Dan T. *Scottsboro: A Tragedy of the American South*. New York: Oxford University Press, 1969.

Carter, Hodding. *Their Words Were Bullets: The Southern Press in War, Reconstruction, and Peace*. Athens: University of Georgia Press, 1969.

Chambliss, Rollin. "What Negro Newspapers of Georgia Say about Some Social Problems." MA thesis, University of Georgia, 1933.

——. *What Negro Newspapers of Georgia Say about Some Social Problems*. Athens: University of Georgia Press, 1934.

Chang, Derek. *Citizens of a Christian Nation: Evangelical Missions and the Problem of Race in the Nineteenth Century*. Philadelphia: University of Pennsylvania Press, 2010.

Chappell, David L. *A Stone of Hope: Prophetic Religion and the Death of Jim Crow*. Chapel Hill: University of North Carolina Press, 2004.

Christian, Charles M. *Black Saga: The African American Experience: A Chronology*. New York: Civitas, 1999.

Clark, E. Culpepper. *The Schoolhouse Door: Segregation's Last Stand at the University of Alabama*. New York: Oxford University Press, 1993.

Clayton, Bruce, and John A. Salmond. *Southern History: Ideas and Actions in the Twentieth Century*. New York: Rowman & Littlefield, 1999.

Cobb, Thomas R. R. *A Digest of the Statute Laws of the State of Georgia*. Athens, Ga.: Christy, Kelsea, and Burke, 1851.

Cohen, William. *At Freedom's Edge: Black Mobility and the Southern White Quest for Racial Control, 1861–1915*. Baton Rouge: Louisiana State University Press, 1991.

Cohodas, Nadine. *Strom Thurmond and the Politics of Southern Change*. Macon, Ga.: Mercer University Press, 1995.

Coleman, Ada F. "The Salary Equalization Movement." *Journal of Negro Education* 16 (Spring 1947): 235–241.

Collins, Ernest M. "Cincinnati Negroes and Presidential Politics." In *The Negro in Depression and War: Prelude to Revolution, 1930–1945*, ed. Bernard Sternsher, 258–263. Chicago, Ill.: Quadrangle, 1969.

Connolly, N. D. B. *A World More Concrete: Real Estate and the Remaking of Jim Crow South Florida*. Chicago, Ill.: University of Chicago Press, 2014.

Consumption Habits of the American People. Washington, D.C.: U.S. Bureau of Labor Statistics, 1938.

Cooper, Caryl A. "Percy Greene and the *Jackson Advocate*." In *The Press and Race: Mississippi Journalists Confront the Movement*, ed. David R. Davies, 55–84. Jackson: University Press of Mississippi, 2001.

Covington, Howard E., and Marion A. Ellis, eds. *The North Carolina Century: Tar Heels Who Made a Difference, 1900–2000*. Chapel Hill: University of North Carolina Press, 2002.

Cox, Patrick. *The First Texas News Barons*. Austin: University of Texas Press, 2009.

Crespino, Joseph. *Strom Thurmond's America*. New York: Macmillan, 2012.

Crudup, Keith. "African Americans in Arizona: A Twentieth Century History." PhD diss., Arizona State University, 1998.

Cruse, Harold. *The Crisis of the Negro Intellectual*. 1967; reprint, New York: New York Review of Books, 2005.

Culver, John C., and John Hyde. *American Dreamer: The Life and Times of Henry A. Wallace*. New York: Norton, 2002.

Dalfiume, Richard M. "The 'Forgotten Years' of the Negro Revolution." In *The Negro in Depression and War: Prelude to Revolution, 1930–1945*, ed. Bernard Sternsher, 298–316. Chicago, Ill.: Quadrangle, 1969.

Dann, Martin E., ed. *The Black Press, 1827–1890: The Quest for National Identity*. New York: Capricorn, 1971.

Davis, Benjamin, Jr. *Communist Councilman from Harlem*. New York: International Publishers, 1969.

Davis, Christopher Brian. "Emory O. Jackson: A Traditionalist in the Early Civil Rights Fight in Birmingham, Alabama." MA thesis, University of Alabama, Birmingham, 2006.

Davis, Frank Marshall. *Livin' the Blues: Memoirs of a Black Journalist and Poet.* Madison: University of Wisconsin Press, 1992.

——. "Negro America's First Daily." *Negro Digest* 5 (1946): 86–88.

——. *Writings of Frank Marshall Davis, a Voice of the Black Press*, ed. John Edgar Tidwell. Jackson: University Press of Mississippi, 2007.

Davis, Thomas J. "Louisiana." In *The Black Press in the South, 1865–1979*, ed. Henry Lewis Suggs, 151–176. Westport, Conn.: Greenwood, 1983.

DeCuir, Sharlene Sinegal. "Attacking Jim Crow: Black Activism in New Orleans, 1925–1941." PhD diss., Louisiana State University, 2009.

De Hart, Jane Sherron. "Second Wave Feminism(s) and the South: The Difference That Differences Make." In *Women of the American South: A Multicultural Reader*, ed. Christie Anne Farnham, 273–301. New York: New York University Press, 1997.

Delombard, Jeannine Marie. "Representing the Slave: White Advocacy and Black Testimony in Harriet Beecher Stowe's *Dred.*" *New England Quarterly* 75 (March 2002): 80–106.

deShazo, Richard D., and Lucius Lampton. "The Educational Struggles of African American Physicians in Mississippi: Finding a Path toward Reconciliation." *Journal of the Mississippi State Medical Association* 54 (July 2013): 189–198.

Detweiler, Frederick. *The Negro Press in the United States.* Chicago, Ill.: University of Chicago Press, 1922.

——. "The Negro Press Today." *American Journal of Sociology* 44 (November 1938): 391–400.

Devine, Thomas W. *Henry Wallace's 1948 Presidential Campaign and the Future of Postwar Liberalism.* Chapel Hill: University of North Carolina Press, 2013.

Dillard, Angela D. *Faith in the City: Preaching Radical Social Change in Detroit.* Ann Arbor: University of Michigan Press, 2007.

Dittmer, John. *Black Georgia in the Progressive Era, 1900–1920.* Urbana: University of Illinois Press, 1977.

Divine, Robert A. "The Cold War and the Election of 1948." *Journal of American History* 59 (June 1972): 90–110.

Dolan, Mark K. "Extra! *Chicago Defender* Race Records Ads Show South from Afar." *Southern Cultures* 13 (Fall 2007): 106–124.

Donaldson, Gary A. *Truman Defeats Dewey.* Lexington: University Press of Kentucky, 1999.

Doreski, C. K. *Writing America Black: Race Rhetoric in the Public Sphere.* New York: Cambridge University Press, 1998.

Dorsey, Allison. *To Build Our Lives Together: Community Formation in Black Atlanta, 1875–1906.* Athens: University of Georgia Press, 2004.

Drago, Edmund L. *Black Politicians and Reconstruction in Georgia: A Splendid Failure.* Baton Rouge: Louisiana State University Press, 1982.

Drake, Robert. "Joe Louis, the Southern Press, and the 'Fight of the Century.'" *Sport History Review* 43 (May 2012): 1–17.

Drake, St. Clair, and Horace R. Cayton. *Black Metropolis: A Study of Negro Life in a Northern City*, vol. 1. New York: Harper & Row, 1962.

Dray, Philip. *At the Hands of Persons Unknown: The Lynching of Black America*. New York: Modern Library, 2002.

Du Bois, W. E. B. "The Hampton Strike." *Nation*, 2 November 1927, 471–472.

——. *The Souls of Black Folk*. Chicago, Ill.: A. C. McClurg, 1903.

Dulles, John Foster. "Thoughts on Soviet Foreign Policy and What to Do about It." *Life* 26 (3 June 1946): 113–125.

Duncan, Mae Najiyyah. *A Survey of Cincinnati's Black Press and Its Editors, 1844–2010*. Bloomington, Ind.: Xlibris, 2011.

Duncombe, Stephen. *Notes from Underground: Zines and the Politics of Alternative Culture*. London: Verso, 1997.

Durr, Robert. *The Negro Press: Its Character, Development, and Function*. Jackson: Mississippi Division, Southern Regional Council, 1947.

Dyreson, Mark. "American Ideas about Race and Racism in the Era of Jesse Owens: Shattering Myths or Reinforcing Scientific Racism." *International Journal of the History of Sport* 25, no. 2 (2008): 247–267.

——. "Jesse Owens: Leading Man in Modern American Tales of Racial Progress and Limits." In *Out of the Shadows: A Biographical History of the African American Athlete*, ed. David W. Wiggins, 111–131. Fayetteville: University of Arkansas Press, 2006.

——. "Marketing National Identity: The Olympic Games of 1932 and American Culture." *OLYMPIKA: The International Journal of Olympic Studies* 4 (1995): 23–48.

Egerton, John. *Speak Now against the Day: The Generation before the Civil Rights Movement in the South*. Chapel Hill: University of North Carolina Press, 1995.

Eig, Jonathan. *Opening Day: The Story of Jackie Robinson's First Season*. New York: Simon and Schuster, 2007.

Ellis, William E. *A History of Education in Kentucky*. Lexington: University of Kentucky Press, 2011.

Ellsworth, Scott. *Death in a Promised Land: The Tulsa Race Riot of 1921*. Baton Rouge: Louisiana State University Press, 1992.

Elson, Charles Meyer. "The Georgia Three-Governor Controversy of 1947." *Atlanta Historical Bulletin* 20 (Fall 1976): 72–95.

Erenberg, Lewis A. *The Greatest Fight of Our Generation: Louis v. Schmeling*. New York: Oxford University Press, 2005.

Eskew, Glenn T. *But for Birmingham: The Local and National Movements in the Civil Rights Struggle*. Chapel Hill: University of North Carolina Press, 1997.

Evans, Elizabeth Sandidge. "Atlanta Negro Chamber of Commerce." In *Encyclopedia of African American Business*, vol. 1, ed. Jessie Carney Smith, 152–153. Westport, Conn.: Greenwood, 2006.

Evans, Sara. *Personal Politics: The Roots of Women's Liberation in the Civil Rights Movement and the New Left*. New York: Knopf, 1979.

Fagan, Benjamin. *The Black Newspaper and the Chosen Nation*. Athens: University of Georgia Press, 2016.

Farrar, Hayward. *The "Baltimore Afro-American," 1892–1950*. Westport, Conn.: Greenwood, 1998.

Fassin, Didier. *Enforcing Order: An Ethnography of Urban Policing*. Cambridge: Polity, 2013.

Fassin, Didier, and Richard Rechtman. *The Empire of Trauma: An Inquiry into the Condition of Victimhood*. Princeton, N.J.: Princeton University Press, 2009.

"Federal Aid to General Education." In *CQ Almanac 1946*, 2nd ed. Washington, D.C.: Congressional Quarterly, 1947. http://library.cqpress.com/cqalmanac /cqal46-1410754, accessed 18 August 2016.

"Federal Court Orders Equal Teachers' Salaries in Maryland County." *Crisis* 46 (December 1939): 372.

Feldman, Ruth Elaine. "A Checklist of Atlanta Newspapers, 1846–1948." MA thesis, Emory University, 1949.

Fenderson, Lewis H. "The Negro Press as a Social Instrument." *Journal of Negro Education* 20 (Spring 1951): 181–188.

Ferguson, Karen. *Black Politics in New Deal Atlanta*. Chapel Hill: University of North Carolina Press, 2002.

Fidler, William P. "Academic Freedom in the South Today." *AAUP Bulletin* 51 (Winter 1965): 413–421.

Field, Marshall. *The Negro Press and the Issues of Democracy*. Chicago, Ill.: American Council on Race Relations, 1944.

Finkle, Lee. *Forum for Protest: The Black Press during World War II*. Rutherford, N.J.: Fairleigh Dickinson University Press, 1975.

Fisher, Jim. *The Lindbergh Case*. New Brunswick, N.J.: Rutgers University Press, 1987.

Fleming, G. James. "Emancipation and the Negro." *Crisis* (July 1938): 216.

"Forte, Ormond Adolphus." In *Encyclopedia of Cleveland History*. http://ech .case.edu/cgi/article.pl?id=FOA, accessed 30 October 2014.

"*Fortune* Press Analysis: Negro Press." *Fortune* 31 (May 1945): 233–238.

Foster, Vera Chandler. "Boswellianism: A Technique in the Restriction of Negro Voting." *Phylon* 10 (First Quarter 1949): 26–37.

Fox, Craig. *Everyday Klansfolk: White Protestant Life and the KKK in 1920s Michigan*. East Lansing: Michigan State University Press, 2011.

Frazier, E. Franklin. *Black Bourgeoisie*. New York: Free Press, 1957.

Frederickson, Kari. *The Dixiecrat Revolt and the End of the Solid South, 1932–1968*. Chapel Hill: University of North Carolina Press, 2001.

Friedman, Lawrence J. "Life in the Lion's Mouth: Another Look at Booker T. Washington." *Journal of Negro History* 59 (October 1974): 337–351.

Fultz, Michael. "'The Morning Cometh': African-American Periodicals, Education, and the Black Middle Class, 1900–1930." *Journal of Negro History* 80 (Summer 1995): 97–112.

Gamson, William A., and Gadi Wolfsfeld. "Movements and Media as Interacting Systems." *Annals of the American Academy of Political and Social Science* 528 (July 1993): 114–125.

Garfinkel, Herbert. *When Negroes March: The March on Washington Movement in the Organizational Politics for FEPC.* New York: Atheneum, 1969.

Garland, Phyl. "The Black Press: Down but Not Out." *Columbia Journalism Review* (September–October 1982): 43–50.

Garrett, Franklin M. *Atlanta and Environs: A Chronicle of Its People and Events,* vol. 2. Athens: University of Georgia Press, 1954.

Garrett, Marie. "Charles Clinton Spaulding (1874–1952)." In *Encyclopedia of African-American Business*, vol. 2, ed. Jessie Carney Smith, 741–745. Westport, Conn.: Greenwood, 2006.

Gatch, Thomas L. "The Battle Wagon Fights Back." *Saturday Evening Post,* 1 May 1943, 9–10, 61–62.

Gates, Maurice. "Negro Students Challenge Social Forces." *Crisis* 42 (August 1935): 233.

Gatson, Paul M. *The New South Creed: A Study in Southern Mythmaking.* New York: Knopf, 1970.

Giddings, Paula. *When and Where I Enter: The Impact of Black Women on Race and Sex in America.* New York: William Morrow, 1984.

Gilmore, Glenda Elizabeth. *Defying Dixie: The Radical Roots of Civil Rights, 1919–1950.* New York: Norton, 2008.

——. *Gender and Jim Crow: Women and the Politics of White Supremacy in North Carolina, 1896–1920.* Chapel Hill: University of North Carolina Press, 1996.

Gilpin, Patrick J. "Charles S. Johnson and the Southern Educational Reporting Service." *Journal of Negro History* 63 (July 1978): 197–208.

Glasrud, Bruce A., and Cary D. Wintz. "The Black Renaissance in the Desert Southwest." In *The Harlem Renaissance in the American West: The New Negro's Western Experience*, ed. Bruce A. Glasrud and Cary D. Wintz, 170–182. New York: Routledge, 2012.

Glazier, Jack. *Been Coming through Some Hard Times: Race, History, and Memory in Western Kentucky.* Knoxville: University of Tennessee Press, 2013.

Glick, Josh. "Mixed Messages: D. W. Griffith and the Black Press, 1916–1931." *Film History* 23, no. 2 (2011): 174–195.

Godshalk, David Fort. *Veiled Visions: The 1906 Atlanta Race Riot and the Reshaping of American Race Relations.* Chapel Hill: University of North Carolina Press, 2005.

Goings, Kenneth G., and Gerald L. Smith. "'Unhidden' Transcripts: Memphis and African American Agency, 1862–1920." *Journal of Urban History* 21 (March 1995): 372–394.

Goldfield, David R. *Black, White, and Southern: Race Relations and Southern Culture.* Baton Rouge: Louisiana State University Press, 1990.

Gooden, Amoaba. "Visual Representations of Feminine Beauty in the Black Press: 1915–1950." *Journal of Pan African Studies* 4 (June 2011): 81–96.

Goodman, Walter. *The Committee: The Extraordinary Career of the House Committee on Un-American Activities*. New York: Farrar, Straus & Giroux, 1968.

Gordon, Asa. *The Georgia Negro*. Ann Arbor: University of Michigan Press, 1937.

Gore, George W. *Negro Journalism: An Essay on the History and Present Conditions of the Negro Press*. Greencastle, Ind.: DePauw University, 1922.

Grafton, Carl, and Anne Permaloff. *Big Mules and Branchheads: James E. Folsom and Political Power in Alabama*. Athens: University of Georgia Press, 1985.

Gray-Ray, Phyllis, Melvin C. Ray, Sandra Rutland, and Sharon Turner. "African Americans and the Criminal Justice System." *Humboldt Journal of Social Relations* 21, no. 2 (1995): 105–117.

Green, Ben. *Before His Time: The Untold Story of Harry T. Moore, America's First Civil Rights Martyr*. New York: Free Press, 1999.

Green, Laurie B. *Battling the Plantation Mentality: Memphis and the Black Freedom Struggle*. Chapel Hill: University of North Carolina Press, 2007.

Greene, Melissa Fay. *The Temple Bombing*. 1996; reprint, Cambridge, Mass.: Da Capo Press, 2006.

Griffin, William Wayne. *African Americans and the Color Line in Ohio, 1915–1930*. Columbus: Ohio State University Press, 2005.

Griffin, Willie J. "An Indigenous Civil Rights Movement: Charlotte, North Carolina, 1940–1963." MA thesis, Morgan State University, 2006.

Grillo, Evelio. *Black Cuban, Black American: A Memoir*. Houston, Tex.: Arte Publico Press, 2000.

Grose, Charles. "Black Newspapers in Texas, 1868–1970." PhD diss., University of Texas, 1972.

Grossman, James. *Land of Hope: Chicago, Black Southerners, and the Great Migration*. Chicago, Ill.: University of Chicago Press, 1989.

Hahn, Steven. *A Nation under Our Feet: Black Political Struggles in the Rural South from Slavery to the Great Migration*. Cambridge, Mass.: Harvard University Press, 2003.

Haram, Kerstyn M. "The *Palmetto Leader*'s Mission to End Lynching in South Carolina: Black Agency and the Black Press in Columbia, 1925–1940." *South Carolina Historical Magazine* 107 (October 2006): 310–333.

Hardin, John A. *Fifty Years of Segregation: Black Higher Education in Kentucky, 1904–1954*. Lexington: University Press of Kentucky, 1997.

——. "'Kentucky Is More or Less Civilized': Alfred Carroll, Charles Eubanks, Lyman Johnson, and the Desegregation of Kentucky Higher Education, 1939–1949." *Register of the Kentucky Historical Society* 109 (Summer–Autumn 2011): 327–350.

Harlan, Louis R. *Booker T. Washington: The Making of a Black Leader, 1856–1901*. New York: Oxford University Press, 1972.

——. *Booker T. Washington: The Wizard of Tuskegee, 1901–1915*. New York: Oxford University Press, 1983.

——. "The Secret Life of Booker T. Washington." *Journal of Southern History* 37 (August 1971): 393–416.

Harrison, Cynthia. *On Account of Sex: The Politics of Women's Issues, 1945–1968*. Berkeley: University of California Press, 1988.

Harrison, Lowell Hayes. *A New History of Kentucky*. Lexington: University Press of Kentucky, 1997.

Harvey, William B. "Constitutional Law: Anti-Lynching Legislation." *Michigan Law Review* 47 (January 1949): 369–377.

Hauke, Kathleen A. *Ted Poston: Pioneer American Journalist*. Athens: University of Georgia Press, 1998.

Heitzeg, Nancy A. "'Whiteness,' Criminality, and the Double-Standards of Deviance/Social Control." *Contemporary Justice Review* 18, no. 2 (2015): 197–214.

Hemmingway, Theodore. "South Carolina." In *The Black Press in the South, 1865–1979*, ed. Henry Lewis Suggs, 289–312. Westport, Conn.: Greenwood, 1983.

Henderson, Alexa Benson. *Atlanta Life Insurance Company: Guardian of Black Economic Dignity*. Tuscaloosa: University of Alabama Press, 1990.

——. "Heman E. Perry and Black Enterprise in Atlanta, 1908–1925." *Business History Review* 61 (Summer 1987): 216–242.

Henkin, Louis. "*Shelley v. Kraemer*: Notes for a Revised Opinion." *University of Pennsylvania Law Review* 110 (February 1962): 473–505.

Henri, Florette. *Black Migration: Movement North, 1900–1920*. Garden City, N.Y.: Anchor Press/Doubleday, 1975.

Herndon, Angelo. *Let Me Live*. 1937; reprint, Ann Arbor: University of Michigan Press, 2007.

Higginbotham, A. Leon, Jr. "Race, Sex, Education and Missouri Jurisprudence: *Shelley v. Kraemer* in a Historical Perspective." *Washington University Law Review* 67, no. 3 (1989): 673–708.

——. *Shades of Freedom: Racial Politics and Presumptions of the American Legal Process*. New York: Oxford University Press, 1996.

Hine, Darlene Clark. *Black Victory: The Rise and Fall of the White Primary in Texas*. Millwood, N.Y.: KTO Press, 1979.

Hixson, William B., Jr. "Moorfield Storey and the Defense of the Dyer Anti-Lynching Bill." *New England Quarterly* 42 (March 1969): 65–81.

Hogan, Lawrence D. *A Black National News Service: The Associated Negro Press and Claude Barnett*. Hackensack, N.J.: Fairleigh Dickinson University Press, 1984.

——. *Shades of Glory: The Negro Leagues and the Story of African-American Baseball*. Washington, D.C.: National Geographic, 2006.

Horne, Gerald. *Black Liberation/Red Scare: Ben Davis and the Communist Party*. Newark: University of Delaware Press, 1994.

Horne, Jackie C. *History and Construction of the Child in Early British Children's Literature*. Farnham, England: Ashgate, 2013.

Hornsby, Alton, Jr. "Georgia." In *The Black Press in the South, 1865–1979*, ed. Henry Lewis Suggs, 119–150. Westport, Conn.: Greenwood, 1983.

——. "The Negro in Atlanta Politics, 1961–1973." *Atlanta Historical Bulletin* 21 (Spring 1977): 7–33.

Howard, Victor B. *Black Liberation in Kentucky: Emancipation and Freedom, 1862–1884.* Lexington: University Press of Kentucky, 1983.

——. "The Black Testimony Controversy in Kentucky, 1866–1872." *Journal of Negro History* 58 (April 1973): 140–165.

"Howard, William Schley." In *Biographical Directory of the United States Congress, 1774–Present.* http://bioguide.congress.gov/scripts/biodisplay.pl?index =H000849, accessed 13 May 2014.

Hughes, C. Alvin. "We Demand Our Rights: The Southern Negro Youth Congress, 1937–1949." *Phylon* (First Quarter 1987): 38–50.

Hughes, Langston. "Battle of the Ballot." In *The Collected Works of Langston Hughes,* vol. 10: *"Fight for Freedom" and Other Writings on Civil Rights,* ed. Christopher C. De Santis, 117–122. Columbia: University of Missouri Press, 2001.

Hunter, Gary Jerome. "'Don't Buy from Where You Can't Work': Black Urban Boycott Movements during the Depression, 1929–1941." PhD diss., University of Michigan, 1977.

Hurd, Michael. *"Collie J": Grambling's Man with the Golden Pen.* Haworth, N.J.: St. Johann Press, 2007.

Ingham, John N., and Lynne B. Feldman, *African American Business Leaders: A Biographical Dictionary.* Westport, Conn.: Greenwood, 1994.

"An Interview with Clarence B. Robinson." Tennessee State University, April 1983, http://ww2.tnstate.edu/library/digital/interview2.htm, accessed 13 October 2013.

"Interview with John McCray by Worth Long and Randall Williams." Emory University, http://southernchanges.digitalscholarship.emory.edu/sc19-1_1204 /sc19-1_003, accessed 4 January 2014.

James, Rawn, Jr. *Root and Branch: Charles Hamilton Houston, Thurgood Marshall, and the Struggle to End Segregation.* New York: Bloomsbury, 2010.

Janken, Kenneth Robert. *White: The Biography of Walter White, Mr. NAACP.* New York: Free Press, 2003.

Jencks, Christopher, and David Reisman. "The American Negro College." *Harvard Educational Review* 37 (Winter 1967): 3–60.

"Jervay, T. C." NewStories: An Oral History of North Carolina News Workers and News Makers, University of North Carolina School of Journalism and Mass Communication, http://hallsoffame.jomc.unc.edu/jervay-t-c/, accessed 4 January 2014.

Johnson, Charles S. *Growing Up in the Black Belt: Negro Youth in the Rural South.* Washington, D.C.: American Council on Education, 1941.

Johnson, Guy. "Some Factors in the Development of Negro Social Institutions in the United States." *American Journal of Sociology* 40 (November 1934): 329–337.

Johnson, Marcia Lynn. "Student Protest at Fisk University in the 1920s." *Negro History Bulletin* 33 (October 1970): 137–140.

Jones, Allen Woodrow. "Alabama." In *The Black Press in the South, 1865–1979*, ed. Henry Lewis Suggs, 23–64. Westport, Conn.: Greenwood, 1983.

——. "The Black Press in the 'New South': Jesse C. Duke's Struggle for Justice and Equality." *Journal of Negro History* 64 (Summer 1979): 215–228.

Jones, Edward A. "Morehouse College in Business Ninety Years—Building Men." *Phylon* 18 (Third Quarter 1957): 237.

Jones, Jacqueline. *Labor of Love, Labor of Sorrow: Black Women, Work, and the Family from Slavery to the Present.* New York: Basic, 1985.

Jones-Brown, Delores D. "Race as a Legal Construct: The Implications for American Justice." In *The System in Black and White: Exploring the Connections between Race, Crime, and Justice*, ed. Michael W. Markowitz and Delores D. Jones-Brown, 137–152. Westport, Conn.: Praeger, 2000.

Jones Ross, Felicia G. "Mobilizing the Masses: The *Cleveland Call and Post* and the Scottsboro Incident." *Journal of Negro History* 84 (Winter 1999): 48–60.

Jopling, Hannah. *Life in a Black Community: Striving for Equal Citizenship in Annapolis, Maryland, 1902–1952.* Lanham, Md.: Lexington, 2015.

Jordan, William G. *Black Newspapers and America's War for Democracy, 1914–1920.* Chapel Hill: University of North Carolina Press, 2001.

Junne, George H., Jr. *Blacks in the American West and Beyond—America, Canada, and Mexico: A Selectively Annotated Bibliography.* Westport, Conn.: Greenwood, 2000.

Kelleher, Daniel T. "The Case of Lloyd Lionel Gaines: The Demise of the Separate but Equal Doctrine." *Journal of Negro History* 56 (October 1971): 262–271.

Kellogg, Peter J. "Northern Liberals and Black America: A History of White Attitudes, 1936–1952." PhD diss., Northwestern University, 1971.

Kennedy, William Jesse, Jr. *The North Carolina Mutual Story: A Symbol of Progress, 1898–1970.* Durham, N.C.: North Carolina Mutual Life Insurance Company, 1970.

Kerber, Linda K. *No Constitutional Right to Be Ladies: Women and the Obligations of Citizenship.* New York: Hill and Wang, 1998.

Kerlin, Robert T. *The Voice of the Negro (1919)*, ed. Thomas Aiello. Lewiston, N.Y.: Edwin Mellen Press, 2013.

Kessler, Lauren. *The Dissident Press: Alternative Journalism in American History.* New York: SAGE Publications, 1984.

King, Gilbert. *Devil in the Grove: Thurgood Marshall, the Groveland Boys, and the Dawn of a New America.* New York: Harper, 2012.

Kirby, John B. *Black Americans in the Roosevelt Era: Liberalism and Race.* Knoxville: University of Tennessee Press, 1980.

Kirk, John A. "The NAACP Campaign for Teachers' Salary Equalization: African American Women Educators and the Early Civil Rights Struggle." *Journal of African American History* 94 (Fall 2009): 529–552.

Kirkland, Scotty E. "Mobile and the Boswell Amendment." *Alabama Review* 65 (July 2012): 205–249.

Klarman, Michael J. "*Brown*, Racial Change, and the Civil Rights Movement." *Virginia Law Review* 80 (January 1994): 7–150.

——. "The Racial Origins of Modern Criminal Procedure." *Michigan Law Review* 99 (October 2000): 48–97.

——. "The White Primary Rulings: A Case Study in the Consequences of Supreme Court Decisionmaking." *Florida State University Law Review* 29 (October 2001): 55–107.

Klinkner, Philip A., and Rogers M. Smith. *The Unsteady March: The Rise and Decline of Racial Equality in America*. Chicago, Ill.: University of Chicago Press, 1999.

Kowalski, Greg. *Hamtramck: The Driven City*. Charleston, S.C.: Arcadia, 2002.

——. *Hamtramck: Then and Now*. Charleston, S.C.: Arcadia, 2010.

——. *Wicked Hamtramck: Lust, Liquor, and Lead*. Charleston, S.C.: History Press, 2010.

Kreiling, Albert Lee. "The Making of Racial Identities in the Black Press: A Cultural Analysis of Race Journalism in Chicago, 1878–1929." PhD diss., University of Illinois, 1973.

Krueger, Thomas A. *And Promises to Keep: The Southern Conference for Human Welfare, 1938–1948*. Nashville, Tenn.: Vanderbilt University Press, 1967.

Kuhn, Clifford M., Harlon E. Joye, and E. Bernard West. *Living Atlanta: An Oral History of the City, 1914–1948*. Athens: University of Georgia Press, 1990.

Lamb, Chris. *Blackout: The Untold Story of Jackie Robinson's First Spring Training*. Lincoln: University of Nebraska Press, 2006.

Lambert, Frank. *The Battle of Ole Miss: Civil Rights v. States' Rights*. New York: Oxford University Press, 2010.

Lanctot, Neil. *Negro League Baseball: The Rise and Ruin of a Black Institution*. Philadelphia: University of Pennsylvania Press, 2004.

Lau, Peter F. *Democracy Rising: South Carolina and the Fight for Black Equality since 1865*. Lexington: University Press of Kentucky, 2006.

Lawson, Marjorie MacKenzie. "The Adult Education Aspects of the Negro Press." *Journal of Negro Education* 14 (Summer 1945): 431–436.

LeCour, Joseph B. "The Negro Press as a Business." *Crisis* 48 (April 1941): 108, 141.

Lee, Alfred McClung. *The Daily Newspaper in America: The Evolution of a Social Instrument*. 1937; reprint, New York: Macmillan, 1947.

Lee, Davis. "The Future of the Negro." Manuscript, Archives, and Rare Book Library, Emory University, Atlanta, Georgia.

LeFlouria, Talitha L. *Chained in Silence: Black Women and Convict Labor in the New South*. Chapel Hill: University of North Carolina Press, 2015.

Leonard, Kevin Allen. "'Is That What We Fought For?': Japanese Americans and Racism in California: The Impact of World War II." *Western Historical Quarterly* 21 (November 1990): 463–482.

Lerner, Gerda, and Linda K. Kerber. *The Majority Finds Its Past: Placing Women in History*. Chapel Hill: University of North Carolina Press, 2005.

Lewis, Freda Darlene. "The *Jackson Advocate*: The Rise and Eclipse of a Leading Black Newspaper in Mississippi, 1939–1964." MS thesis, Iowa State University, 1984.

Lewis, Willard "Chuck." *Citizens Trust Bank History*. Atlanta, Ga.: Citizens Trust Bank, 2001.

Lisio, Donald. *Hoover, Blacks, and Lily-Whites: A Study of Southern Strategies*. Chapel Hill: University of North Carolina Press, 1985.

Little, Stuart J. "The Freedom Train: Citizenship and Postwar Political Culture, 1946–1949." *American Studies* 34 (Spring 1993): 35–67.

Loeb, Charles. Introduction to *The Negro Newspaper*, ed. Vishnu V. Oak. 1948; reprint, Westport, Conn.: Negro Universities Press, 1976.

Logan, Rayford W. *Howard University: The First Hundred Years, 1867–1967*. New York: New York University Press, 1968.

Lomax, Louis E. *The Negro Revolt*. New York: Harper, 1962.

Long, Michael G., ed. *First Class Citizenship: The Civil Rights Letters of Jackie Robinson*. New York: Henry Holt, 2007.

Long, Richard A., and Eugenia W. Collier, eds. *Afro-American Writing: An Anthology of Prose and Poetry*. 2nd ed. University Park: Pennsylvania State University Press, 1985.

Lopez, Antonio M. *Unbecoming Blackness: The Diaspora Cultures of Afro-Cuban America*. New York: New York University Press, 2012.

Lorence, James J. *A Hard Journey: The Life of Don West*. Urbana: University of Illinois Press, 2007.

Lucander, David. *Winning the War for Democracy: The March on Washington Movement, 1941–1946*. Urbana: University of Illinois Press, 2014.

Lynchings by States and Race, 1882–1959. Tuskegee, Ala.: Department of Records and Research, Tuskegee Institute, 1959.

Mack, Kenneth W. "Dissent and Authenticity in the History of American Radical Politics." In *Dissenting Voices in American Society: The Role of Judges, Lawyers, and Citizens*, ed. Austin Sarat, 105–143. New York: Cambridge University Press, 2012.

Magliulo, Myrna Colette. "Andrew J. Smitherman: A Pioneer of the African American Press, 1909–1961." *Afro-Americans in New York Life and History* 34 (July 2010): 76–118.

Mancini, Matthew J. *One Dies, Get Another: Convict Leasing in the American South, 1866–1928*. Columbia: University of South Carolina Press, 1996.

Mangum, Charles S., Jr. *The Legal Status of the Negro*. Chapel Hill: University of North Carolina Press, 1940.

Margo, Robert A. *Race and Schooling in the South, 1880–1950: An Economic History*. Chicago, Ill.: University of Chicago Press, 1990.

Margolick, David. *Beyond Glory: Joe Louis vs. Max Schmeling, and a World on the Brink*. New York: Vintage, 2005.

Margot, Louis. "The *Dallas Express*, a Negro Newspaper: Its History, 1892–1971, and Its Point of View." MA thesis, East Texas State University, 1971.

Marquart, James W., Sheldon Ekland-Olson, and Jonathan R. Sorensen. *The Rope, the Chair, and the Needle: Capital Punishment in Texas, 1923–1990*. Austin: University of Texas Press, 1994.

Martin, Charles H. *The Angelo Herndon Case and Southern Justice*. Baton Rouge: Louisiana State Press, 1976.

——. "Race, Gender, and Southern Justice: The Rosa Lee Ingram Case." *American Journal of Legal History* 29 (July 1985): 251–268.

Martin, Tony. *The Pan-African Connection: From Slavery to Garvey and Beyond*. Dover, Mass.: Majority Press, 1983.

Martindale, Carolyn. *The White Press and Black America*. Westport, Conn.: Greenwood, 1986.

Mason, Herman "Skip," Jr. *Black Atlanta in the Roaring Twenties*. Charleston, S.C.: Arcadia, 1997.

"The Masquerade Is Over." *Crisis* 46 (June 1939): 179.

Matthews, Glenna. *The Rise of Public Woman: Woman's Power and Woman's Place in the United States, 1630–1970*. New York: Oxford University Press, 1992.

Maze, John, and Graham White. *Henry A. Wallace: His Search for a New World Order*. Chapel Hill: University of North Carolina Press, 1995.

McCray, John H. "The Arraignment of Student Inertia." *Mule's Ear* 11 (February 1935): 1, 4.

——. "In Defense of Student Education." *Mule's Ear* 8 (March 1932): 2–3.

——. "Talladega Beauties." *Mule's Ear* 8 (March 1932): 3–4.

——. "World Peace." *Mule's Ear* 8 (March 1932): 1.

McDaniel, Karen Cotton. "Elizabeth 'Lizzie' Fouse (1875–1952): Challenging Stereotypes and Building Community." In *Kentucky Women: Their Lives and Times*, ed. Melissa A. McEuen and Thomas H. Appleton Jr., 274–293. Athens: University of Georgia Press, 2015.

McDowell, A. "The Young Men's Progressive Club." *Academy Herald* 1 (May 1909): 25–26.

McDowell, Deborah E. *Leaving Pipe Shop: Memories of Kin*. New York: Scribner, 1997.

McDowell, Winston. "Race and Ethnicity during the Harlem Jobs Campaign, 1932–35." *Journal of Negro History* 69 (Summer–Fall 1984): 134–143.

McGuire, Danielle L. *At the Dark End of the Street: Black Women, Rape, and Resistance*. New York: Knopf, 2010.

——. "'It Was Like All of Us Had Been Raped': Sexual Violence, Community Mobilization, and the African American Freedom Struggle." *Journal of American History* 91 (December 2004): 906–931.

McKenzie, Andre, Kashef Ijaz, Jon D. Tillinghast, Valdis E. Krebs, Lois A. Diem, Beverly Metchock, Theresa Crisp, and Peter D. McElroy. "Transmission Network Analysis to Complement Routine Tuberculosis Contact Investigations." *American Journal of Public Health* 97 (March 2007): 470.

McMillen, Neil. *Dark Journey: Black Mississippians in the Age of Jim Crow.* Urbana: University of Illinois Press, 1989.

McNair, Glenn. *Criminal Injustice: Slaves and Free Blacks in Georgia's Criminal Justice System.* Charlottesville: University of Virginia Press, 2009.

McNeil, Genna Rae. *Groundwork: Charles Hamilton Houston and the Struggle for Civil Rights.* Philadelphia: University of Pennsylvania Press, 1983.

McPheeters, Annie L. *Negro Progress in Atlanta, Georgia, 1950–1960: A Selected Bibliography on Human Relations from Four Atlanta Newspapers.* Atlanta, Ga.: West Hunter Branch, Atlanta Public Library, 1964.

McWhirter, Cameron. *Red Summer: The Summer of 1919 and the Awakening of Black America.* New York: Henry Holt, 2011.

McWhorter, Diane. *Carry Me Home: Birmingham, Alabama: The Climactic Battle of the Civil Rights Revolution.* New York: Simon and Schuster, 2001.

Meeman, Edward J. *The Editorial We: A Posthumous Autobiography*, ed. Edwin Howard. Memphis, Tenn.: Memphis State University Press, 1976.

Meier, August, and Elliot Rudwick. *Black Detroit and the Rise of the UAW.* 1979; reprint, Ann Arbor: University of Michigan, 2007.

Merritt, Carole. *The Herndons: An Atlanta Family.* Athens: University of Georgia Press, 2002.

Michaeli, Ethan. *The "Defender": How the Legendary Black Newspaper Changed America.* Boston: Houghton Mifflin Harcourt, 2016.

Miles, Michael. *The Radical Probe: The Logic of Student Rebellion.* New York: Atheneum, 1971.

Milewski, Melissa. "From Slave to Litigant: African Americans in Court in the Postwar South, 1865–1920." *Law and History Review* 30 (August 2012): 723–769.

——. "From Slave to Litigant: African Americans in Court in the Postwar South, 1865–1920." PhD diss., New York University, 2011.

Milton, Joyce. *Loss of Eden: A Biography of Charles and Anne Morrow Lindbergh.* New York: HarperCollins, 1993.

Mims, Edwin. *The Advancing South: Stories of Progress and Reaction.* New York: Doubleday, 1926.

Mixon, Gregory. *The Atlanta Riot: Race, Class, and Violence in a New South City.* Gainesville: University Press of Florida, 2005.

Moody, Anne. *Coming of Age in Mississippi.* New York: Bantam Dell, 1968.

Moore, John Hammond. "The Angelo Herndon Case, 1932–1937." *Phylon* 32 (Spring 1971): 60–71.

Moore, Joseph E. *Murder on Maryland's Eastern Shore: Race, Politics, and the Case of Orphan Jones.* Mount Pleasant, S.C.: History Press, 2011.

Moran, Robert E., Sr. "Public Relief in Louisiana from 1928 to 1960." *Louisiana History* 14 (Fall 1973): 369–385.

Morris, Aldon D. *The Origins of the Civil Rights Movement: Black Communities Organizing for Change.* New York: Free Press, 1984.

Morris, James McGrath. *Eye on the Struggle: Ethel Payne, the First Lady of the Black Press.* New York: HarperCollins, 2015.

Morris, Robert V. "The Iowa Bystander." Iowa Pathways, Iowa Public Television, http://www.iptv.org/IowaPathways/mypath.cfm?ounid=ob_000289, accessed 4 January 2014.

Morris, Thomas D. "Slaves and the Rules of Evidence in Criminal Trials." *Chicago-Kent Law Review* 68 (June 1993): 1209–1240.

Muhammad, Khalil Gibran. *The Condemnation of Blackness: Race, Crime, and the Making of Modern Urban America.* Cambridge, Mass.: Harvard University Press, 2011.

Mullen, Bill. "Popular Fronts: *Negro Story* Magazine and the African American Literary Response to World War II." *African American Review* 30 (Spring 1996): 5–15.

Murphy, James Buford. "A Study of the Editorial Policies of the *Atlanta Daily World*: 1952–1955." MA thesis, Emory University, 1961.

Murray, Hugh T., Jr. "The NAACP versus the Communist Party: The Scottsboro Rape Cases, 1931–1932." In *The Negro in Depression and War: Prelude to Revolution, 1930–1945,* ed. Bernard Sternsher, 267–281. Chicago, Ill.: Quadrangle, 1969.

Myrdal, Gunnar. *An American Dilemma.* New York: Harper and Brothers, 1944.

N. W. Ayer & Son's Directory of Newspapers and Periodicals, 1928–1955. Philadelphia, Pa.: N. W. Ayer & Son, 1928–1955.

"The Negro Daily: An Analysis of Twenty-Three Issues of the *Atlanta Daily World* during the Period July 4 to August 5, 1945." *Monthly Summary of Events and Trends in Race Relations* (August–September 1945): 59–62.

"Negro Editors on Communism." *Crisis* 41 (April 1932): 17, 119.

Nelson Chesman & Co.'s Newspaper Rate Book. New York: Nelson Chesman & Co., 1921.

Newkirk, Vann Roeshard. "The Development of the National Association for the Advancement of Colored People in Metropolitan Charlotte, North Carolina, 1919–1965." PhD diss., Howard University, 2002.

Newton, Michael. *The FBI and the KKK: A Critical History.* Jefferson, N.C.: McFarland, 2005.

Norrell, Robert J. *Up from History: The Life of Booker T. Washington.* Cambridge, Mass.: Belknap Press of Harvard University Press, 2009.

Norris, Clarence, and Sybil D. Washington. *The Last of the Scottsboro Boys.* New York: Putnam's, 1979.

Norwood, Stephen H. *Strikebreaking and Intimidation: Mercenaries and Masculinity in Twentieth Century America.* Chapel Hill: University of North Carolina Press, 2002.

Oak, Vishnu V. *The Negro Newspaper.* Yellow Springs, Ohio: Antioch University Press, 1948.

O'Brien, Gail Williams. *The Color of the Law: Race, Violence, and Justice in the Post–World War II South.* Chapel Hill: University of North Carolina Press, 1999.

Odum-Hinmon, Maria E. "The Cautious Crusader: How the *Atlanta Daily World* Covered the Struggle for African American Rights from 1945 to 1985." PhD diss., University of Maryland, 2005.

O'Kelly, Charlotte G. "Black Newspapers and the Black Protest Movement: Their Historical Relationship, 1827–1945." *Phylon* 43 (First Quarter 1982): 1–14.

Oliver, Sadie Mae. "The History and Development of the Atlanta Daily World." MA thesis, Hampton Institute, 1942.

"An Oral History with Charles Lemuel Young Sr." Interview by Donald Paul Williams, 1998. Civil Rights Documentation Project, Tougaloo College Archives, Jackson, Miss.

"Oral History with Mr. Percy Greene." University of Southern Mississippi Center for Oral History and Cultural Heritage, http://digilib.usm.edu/cdm /compoundobject/collection/coh/id/15364/rec/1, accessed 30 March 2018.

"Oral History with the Honorable Ross Robert Barnett, Governor of the State of Mississippi." University of Southern Mississippi Center for Oral History and Cultural Heritage, http://digilib.usm.edu/cdm/compoundobject/collection /coh/id/15801, accessed 30 March 2018.

O'Reilly, Kenneth. *Hoover and the Unamericans: The FBI, HUAC, and the Red Menace.* Philadelphia, Pa.: Temple University Press, 1983.

Oshinsky, David M. *Worse than Slavery: Parchman Farm and the Ordeal of Jim Crow Justice.* New York: Free Press, 1997.

Ottley, Roi. *"New World A-Coming": Inside Black America.* New York: Arno Press and the New York Times, 1969.

Pacifico, Michele F. "'Don't Buy Where You Can't Work': The New Negro Alliance of Washington." *Washington History* 61 (Spring–Summer 1994): 66–88.

Painter, Nell Irvin. "Black Journalism: The First Hundred Years." *Harvard Journal of Afro-American Affairs* 2, no. 2 (1971): 30–32.

Perry, Samuel. "In Defense of the Negro Press." *Harvard Guardian* 7 (December 1942): 15–19.

Peterson, Sarah Jo. *Planning the Home Front: Building Bombers and Communities at Willow Run.* Chicago, Ill.: University of Chicago Press, 2013.

Pfaff, Daniel W. "The Press and the Scottsboro Rape Cases, 1931–1932." *Journalism History* 1 (Autumn 1974): 72–76.

Pfeffer, Paula. *A. Philip Randolph, Pioneer of the Civil Rights Movement.* Baton Rouge: Louisiana State University Press, 1990.

Phillips, Osborne. "A Sociological Study of Editorials of the *Atlanta Independent*." MA thesis, Atlanta University, 1948.

Pierce, Richard B. *Polite Protest: The Political Economy of Race in Indianapolis, 1920–1970.* Bloomington: Indiana University Press, 2005.

Pilat, Oliver. *Pegler: Angry Man of the Press.* Boston: Beacon, 1963.

Pinar, William F. "The NAACP and the Struggle for Anti-Lynching Federal Legislation, 1917–1950." *Counterpoints* 163 (2001): 683–752.

Pincus, Samuel R. *The Virginia Supreme Court, Blacks, and the Law, 1870–1902*. New York: Garland, 1990.

Pitch, Anthony S. *The Last Lynching: How a Gruesome Mass Murder Rocked a Small Georgia Town*. New York: Skyhorse, 2016.

Pleasants, Julian M. *Buncombe Bob: The Life and Times of Robert Rice Reynolds*. Chapel Hill: University of North Carolina Press, 2000.

Pleij, Herman. "The Late Middle Ages and the Rhetoricians, 1400–1560." In *A Literary History of the Low Countries*, ed. Theo Hermans, 81–83. Rochester, N.Y.: Camden House, 2009.

Pomerantz, Gary M. *Where Peachtree Meets Sweet Auburn: The Saga of Two Families and the Making of Atlanta*. New York: Scribner, 1996.

Porteous, Clark. "The Two Eds of Memphis—Meeman and Crump." *West Tennessee Historical Society Papers* 45 (1991): 140–152.

Poston, Ted. "The Negro Press." *Reporter*, 6 December 1949, 14–16.

Prattis, Percival L. "Racial Segregation and Negro Journalism." *Phylon* 8 (Fourth Quarter 1947): 305–313.

——. "The Role of the Negro Press in Race Relations." *Phylon* 7 (Third Quarter 1946): 273–283.

Pride, Armistead Scott. "A Register and History of Negro Newspapers in the United States, 1827–1950." PhD diss., Northwestern University, 1950.

Pride, Armistead S., and Clint C. Wilson II. *A History of the Black Press*. Washington, D.C.: Howard University Press, 1997.

Printing the Dream: 75 Years of Atlanta Daily World. Television documentary. Atlanta Interfaith Broadcasters, 2003.

"Publishers: Owners of Negro Newspapers Are Hard-Headed, Farsighted, Race Conscious Businessmen." *Ebony* (November 1949): 47–51.

Rampersad, Arnold. *Jackie Robinson: A Biography*. New York: Knopf, 1997.

Ratzlaff, Aleen J. "Illustrated African American Journalism: Political Cartooning in the *Indianapolis Freedom*." In *Seeking a Voice: Images of Race and Gender in the Nineteenth Century Press*, ed. David B. Sachsman, S. Kittrell Rushing, and Roy Morris Jr., 131–140. West Lafayette, Ind.: Purdue University Press, 2009.

Rhodes, Jane. *Mary Ann Shadd Cary: The Black Press and Protest in the Nineteenth Century*. Bloomington: Indiana University Press, 1998.

Rice, Mitchell F., and Woodrow Jones Jr. *Public Policy and the Black Hospital: From Slavery to Segregation to Integration*. Westport, Conn.: Greenwood, 1994.

Richards, Johnetta Gladys. "The Southern Negro Youth Congress: A History, 1937–1949." PhD diss., University of Cincinnati, 1987.

Roberts, Gene, and Hank Klibanoff. *The Race Beat: The Press, the Civil Rights Struggle, and the Awakening of a Nation*. New York: Vintage, 2007.

Roberts, Randy. *Joe Louis: Hard Times Man*. New Haven, Conn.: Yale University Press, 2010.

Robinson, Stephen Robert. "The Black New South: A Study of Local Black Leadership in Virginia and Alabama, 1874–1897." PhD diss., University of Southampton, 2010.

Rose, Chanelle Nyree. *The Struggle for Black Freedom in Miami: Civil Rights and America's Tourist Paradise, 1896–1968*. Baton Rouge: Louisiana State University Press, 2015.

Rosenberg, Gerald. *The Hollow Hope: Can Courts Bring About Social Change?* Chicago, Ill.: University of Chicago Press, 1991.

Rosenthal, Joel. "Southern Black Student Activism: Assimilation vs. Nationalism." *Journal of Negro Education* 44 (Spring 1975): 113–129.

Rosich, Katherine J. *Race, Ethnicity, and the Criminal Justice System*. Washington, D.C.: American Sociological Association, 2007.

Rothman, Joshua D. *Notorious in the Neighborhood: Sex and Families across the Color Line in Virginia, 1787–1861*. Chapel Hill: University of North Carolina Press, 2003.

Rozier, John Wiley. "A History of the Negro Press in Atlanta." MA thesis, Emory University, 1949.

Rutledge, Anne G. *Emory O. Jackson: Warrior*. self-pub.: CreateSpace, 2014.

Sancton, Thomas. "The Negro Press." *New Republic*, 26 April 1943, 558–560.

Sarratt, Reed. *The Ordeal of Desegregation: The First Decade*. New York: Harper & Row, 1966.

Scott, Alexis. Interview, Family Business Radio, 12 January 2012. In possession of author.

Scott, Ruth Emmeline. "The Problem of Studying Certain Accounting Features of Negro and Foreign Language Weekly Newspapers in the United States, 1938." MA thesis, Atlanta University, 1939.

Secrest, Andrew. "In Black and White: Press Opinion and Race Relations in South Carolina, 1954–1964." PhD diss., Duke University, 1971.

Senna, Carl. *The Black Press and the Struggle for Civil Rights*. London: Franklin Watts, 1993.

Shannon, Samuel. "Tennessee." In *The Black Press in the South, 1865–1979*, ed. Henry Lewis Suggs, 313–356. Westport, Conn.: Greenwood, 1983.

Shofner, Jerrell H. "Florida." In *The Black Press in the South, 1865–1979*, ed. Henry Lewis Suggs, 91–118. Westport, Conn.: Greenwood, 1983.

Shogan, Robert, and Tom Craig. *The Detroit Race Riot: A Study in Violence*. Philadelphia, Pa.: Chilton, 1964.

Simmons, Charles A. *The African American Press: A History of News Coverage during National Crises, with Special Reference to Four Black Newspapers, 1827–1965*. Jefferson, N.C.: McFarland, 1998.

Simons, William. "Jackie Robinson and the American Mind: Journalistic Perceptions of the Reintegration of Baseball." *Journal of Sport History* 12 (Spring 1985): 39–64.

Singer, Benjamin D. "Mass Society, Mass Media and the Transformation of Minority Identity." *British Journal of Sociology* 24 (June 1973): 140–150.

Sitkoff, Harvard. "The Detroit Race Riot, 1943." *Michigan History* 53 (May 1969): 183–206.

——. "Harry Truman and the Election of 1948: The Coming of Age of Civil Rights in American Politics." *Journal of Southern History* 37 (November 1971): 597–616.

——. *A New Deal for Blacks: The Emergence of Civil Rights as a National Issue*, vol. 1: *The Depression Decade*. New York: Oxford University Press, 1978.

Sklaroff, Lauren. *Black Culture and the New Deal: The Quest for Civil Rights in the Roosevelt Era*. Chapel Hill: University of North Carolina Press, 2009.

Skotnes, Andor. "Buy Where You Can Work: Boycotting for Jobs in African-American Baltimore, 1933–1934." *Journal of Social History* 27 (Summer 1994): 735–761.

——. *A New Deal for All? Race and Class Struggles in Depression-Era Baltimore*. Durham, N.C.: Duke University Press, 2013.

Slate, Nico. *Colored Cosmopolitanism: The Shared Struggle for Freedom in the United States and India*. Cambridge, Mass.: Harvard University Press, 2012.

Slavens, George Everett. "Missouri." In *The Black Press in the South, 1865–1979*, ed. Henry Lewis Suggs, 211–256. Westport, Conn.: Greenwood, 1983.

Smallwood, James. "Texas." In *The Black Press in the South, 1865–1979*, ed. Henry Lewis Suggs, 357–378. Westport, Conn.: Greenwood, 1983.

Smith, Gerald L. *A Black Educator in the Segregated South: Kentucky's Rufus B. Atwood*. Lexington: University Press of Kentucky, 1994.

Smock, Raymond. *Booker T. Washington: Black Leadership in the Age of Jim Crow*. Chicago, Ill.: Ivan R. Dee, 2009.

Solomon, Mark. *The Cry Was Unity: Communists and African Americans, 1917–36*. Jackson: University Press of Mississippi, 1998.

"The South's Greatest Negro Newspaper." *Negro Digest* 7 (July 1949): 39.

Standing, Theodore. "A Study of Negro Nationalism." PhD diss., State University of Iowa, 1932.

Staples, Charles R. *The History of Pioneer Lexington, 1779–1806*. 1939; reprint, Lexington: University of Kentucky Press, 1996.

Strain, Christopher B. *Pure Fire: Self-Defense as Activism in the Civil Rights Era*. Athens: University of Georgia Press, 2005.

Strickland, Arvarh E. "Booker T. Washington: The Myth and the Man." *Reviews in American History* (December 1973): 559–564.

Strother, T. Ella. "The Race-Advocacy Function of the Black Press." *Black American Literature Forum* 12 (Autumn 1978): 92–99.

Stuckert, Robert P. "The Negro College—A Pawn of White Domination." *Wisconsin Sociologist* 3 (January 1964): 1–8.

Suggs, Henry Lewis. "Black Strategy and Ideology in the Segregation Era: P. B. Young and the *Norfolk Journal and Guide*, 1910–1954." *Virginia Magazine of History and Biography* 91 (April 1983): 161–190.

——. "Conclusion." In *The Black Press in the South, 1865–1979*, ed. Henry Lewis Suggs, 423–430. Westport, Conn.: Greenwood, 1983.

———. "Origins of the Black Press in the South." In *The Black Press in the South, 1865–1979*, ed. Henry Lewis Suggs, 3–22. Westport, Conn.: Greenwood, 1983.

———. "P. B. Young of the *Norfolk Journal and Guide*: A Booker T. Washington Militant, 1904–1928." *Journal of Negro History* 64 (Autumn 1979): 365–376.

Suggs, Henry Lewis, and Bernadine Moses Duncan. "North Carolina." In *The Black Press in the South, 1865–1979*, ed. Henry Lewis Suggs, 257–288. Westport, Conn.: Greenwood, 1983.

Sugrue, Thomas J. *The Origins of the Urban Crisis*. Princeton, N.J.: Princeton University Press, 1996.

Sullivan, Patricia. *Lift Every Voice: The NAACP and the Making of the Civil Rights Movement*. New York: New Press, 2009.

Sutton, Willis A., Jr. "The Talmadge Campaigns: A Sociological Analysis of Political Power." PhD diss., University of North Carolina, Chapel Hill, 1952.

Sweet, Frank W. *Legal History of the Color Line: The Rise and Triumph of the One Drop Rule*. Palm Coast, Fla.: Backintyme, 2005.

Syrjamaki, John. "The Negro Press in 1938." *Sociology and Social Research* 24 (September–October 1939): 43–52.

Talley, Robert. *One Hundred Years of the "Commercial Appeal": The Story of the Greatest Romance in American Journalism, 1840–1940*. Memphis, Tenn.: Memphis Publishing Co., 1940.

Taylor, George C. L. "The Modern Negro Press." *Southern Workman* 61 (August 1932): 341–346.

Taylor, Jon E. *Freedom to Serve: Truman, Civil Rights, and Executive Order 9981*. New York: Routledge, 2013.

Teel, Leonard Ray. "W. A. Scott and the Atlanta World." *American Journalism* 6, no. 3 (1989): 158–178.

Terkel, Studs. *Hard Times: An Oral History of the Great Depression*. New York: New Press, 1970.

Teske, Steven. *Unvarnished Arkansas: The Naked Truth about Nine Famous Arkansans*. Little Rock, Ark.: Butler Center Books, 2012.

Thomas, Norman. *Human Exploitation in the United States*. New York: Frederick A. Stokes Co., 1934.

Thompson, Charles H. "Progress in the Elimination of Discrimination in White and Negro Teachers' Salaries." *Journal of Negro Education* 9 (January 1940): 1–4.

Thompson, Julius Eric. *Black Life in Mississippi: Essays on Political, Social and Cultural Studies in a Deep South State*. Lanham, Md.: University Press of America, 2001.

———. *The Black Press in Mississippi, 1865–1985*. Gainesville: University Press of Florida, 1993.

———. "Mississippi." In *The Black Press in the South, 1865–1979*, ed. Henry Lewis Suggs, 177–210. Westport, Conn.: Greenwood, 1983.

——. *Percy Greene and the "Jackson Advocate": The Life and Times of a Radical Conservative Black Newspaperman, 1897–1977*. Jefferson, N.C.: McFarland, 1994.

Thornbrough, Emma Lou. "American Negro Newspapers, 1880–1914." *Business History Review* 40 (Winter 1966): 467–490.

Thornton, J. Mills. *Dividing Lines: Municipal Politics and the Struggle for Civil Rights in Montgomery, Birmingham, and Selma*. Tuscaloosa: University of Alabama Press, 2002.

Tindall, George Brown. *South Carolina Negroes, 1877–1900*. Columbia: University of South Carolina Press, 1952.

Tischauser, Leslie V. *The Changing Nature of Racial and Ethnic Conflict in United States History*. Lanham, Md.: University Press of America, 2002.

Tobin, Sidney. "The Early New Deal in Baton Rouge as Viewed by the Daily Press." *Louisiana History* 10 (Fall 1969): 307–337.

Toppin, Edgar A. *A Biographical History of Blacks in America since 1528*. New York: David McKay, 1971.

Tushnet, Mark V. *Making Civil Rights Law: Thurgood Marshall and the Supreme Court, 1936–1961*. New York: Oxford University Press, 1994.

——. *The NAACP's Legal Strategy against Segregated Education, 1925–1950*. Chapel Hill: University of North Carolina Press, 1987.

Tygiel, Jules. *Baseball's Great Experiment: Jackie Robinson and His Legacy*. New York: Oxford University Press, 1983.

U.S. Department of Commerce. *Negro Newspapers and Periodicals in the United States: 1937*. Washington, D.C.: Department of Commerce, 1938.

——. *Negro Newspapers and Periodicals in the United States: 1938*. Washington, D.C.: Department of Commerce, 1939.

Van Auken, Cecilia. "The Negro Press in the 1948 Presidential Election." *Journalism Quarterly* 26 (December 1949): 431–435.

Vogel, Todd, ed. *The Black Press: New Literary and Historical Essays*. New Brunswick, N.J.: Rutgers University Press, 2001.

Vowels, Robert C. "Atlanta Negro Business and the New Black Bourgeoisie." *Atlanta Historical Bulletin* 21 (Spring 1977): 48–63.

Wade-Gayles, Gloria. "Black Women Journalists in the South, 1880–1905: An Approach to the Study of Black Women's History." *Callaloo* 11–13 (February–October 1981): 138–152.

Waller, George. *Kidnap: The Story of the Lindbergh Case*. New York: Dial, 1961.

Wardlaw, Harold Clinton. "A Gatekeeper Analysis of Minority and Majority Newspapers: *Atlanta Inquirer*, *Atlanta World*, and *Atlanta Constitution*." MA thesis, University of Georgia, 1969.

Ware, Susan. *Holding Their Own: American Women in the 1930s*. New York: Twayne, 1982.

Warren, Harris Gaylord. *Herbert Hoover and the Great Depression*. New York: Norton, 1967.

Washburn, Patrick S. *The African American Newspaper: Voice of Freedom*. Evanston, Ill.: Northwestern University Press, 2006.

——. *A Question of Sedition: The Federal Government's Investigation of the Black Press during World War II*. New York: Oxford University Press, 1986.

Washington, Booker T., and W. E. B. Du Bois. *The Negro in the South: His Economic Progress in Relation to His Moral and Religious Development*. Philadelphia, Pa.: George W. Jacobs, 1907.

Wattley, Cheryl Elizabeth Brown. *A Step toward "Brown v. Board of Education": Ada Lois Sipuel Fisher and Her Fight to End Segregation*. Norman: University of Oklahoma Press, 2014.

Weare, Walter B. *Black Business in the New South: A Social History of the North Carolina Mutual Insurance Company*. Durham, N.C.: Duke University Press, 1993.

——. "Charles Clinton Spaulding: Middle Class Leadership in the Age of Segregation." In *Black Leaders of the Twentieth Century*, ed. John Hope Franklin and August Meier, 167–189. Urbana: University of Illinois Press, 1982.

Weaver, Bill, and Oscar C. Page. "The Black Press and the Drive for Integrated Graduate and Professional Schools." *Phylon* 43 (First Quarter 1982): 15–28.

Weill, Susan M. "Mississippi's Daily Press in Three Crises." In *The Press and Race: Mississippi Journalists Confront the Movement*, ed. David R. Davies, 17–54. Jackson: University Press of Mississippi, 2001.

Weiner, Leo. *Africa and the Discovery of America*. 3 vols. Philadelphia, Pa.: Innes & Sons, 1920–1922.

Welky, David B. "Viking Girls, Mermaids, and Little Brown Men: U.S. Journalism and the 1932 Olympics." *Journal of Sport History* 24 (Spring 1997): 24–49.

Wexler, Laura. *Fire in a Canebrake: The Last Mass Lynching in America*. New York: Scribner, 2003.

Whitaker, Matthew C. "The Rise of Black Phoenix: African-American Migration, Settlement and Community Development in Maricopa County, Arizona 1868–1930." *Journal of Negro History* 85 (Summer 2000): 197–209.

Whitaker, Robert. *On the Laps of Gods: The Red Summer of 1919 and the Struggle for Justice That Remade a Nation*. New York: Crown, 2008.

White, Colleen R. "The *Jackson Advocate*, 1938–1995: A Historical Overview." MA thesis, University of Mississippi, 1996.

White, John. "Civil Rights in Conflict: The 'Birmingham Plan' and the Freedom Train, 1947." *Alabama Review* 52 (April 1999): 128–136.

——. "Edgar Daniel Nixon: A Founding Father of the Civil Rights Movement." In *Portraits of African American Life since 1865*, ed. Nina Mjagkij, 199–217. Wilmington, Del.: Scholarly Resources, 2003.

White, Walter. *A Man Called White*. Bloomington: Indiana University Press, 1948.

——. "Portrait of a Communist." *Negro Digest* 9 (February 1951): 84–85.

Wilkerson, Doxey A. "The Negro Press." *Journal of Negro Education* 16 (Autumn 1947): 511–521.

Wilkerson, Isabel. *The Warmth of Other Suns: The Epic Story of America's Great Migration*. New York: Vintage, 2010.

Wilkinson, Christopher. "Big-Band Jazz in Black West Virginia, 1930–1942." *West Virginia History: A Journal of Regional Studies* 1 (Spring 2007): 23–53.

Wilson, Clint C., II. *Black Journalists in Paradox: Historical Perspectives and Current Dilemmas*. Westport, Conn.: Greenwood, 1991.

Wilson, Sunnie, and John Cohassey. *Toast of the Town: The Life and Times of Sunnie Wilson*. Detroit, Mich.: Wayne State University Press, 2005.

Winner, Lauren F. "Doubtless Sincere: New Characters in the Civil Rights Cast." In *The Role of Ideas in the Civil Rights South*, ed. Ted Ownby, 157–169. Jackson: University Press of Mississippi.

Wolseley, Roland E. *The Black Press, USA*. Ames: Iowa State University Press, 1971.

Wolters, Raymond. *Negroes and the Great Depression: The Problem of Economic Recovery*. Westport, Conn.: Greenwood, 1970.

Work, Monroe M., ed. *Annual Encyclopedia of the Negro*. Tuskegee, Ala.: Tuskegee Institute Press, 1937.

WPA Writers' Program. *Texas: A Guide to the Lone Star State*. 1940; rev. ed., New York: Hastings House, 1969.

Wright, George C. "Black Political Insurgency in Louisville, Kentucky: The Lincoln Independent Party of 1921." *Journal of Negro History* 68 (Winter 1983): 8–23.

Wye, Christopher G. "Merchants of Tomorrow: The Other Side of the 'Don't Spend Your Money Where You Can't Work' Movement." *Ohio History* 93 (Winter–Spring 1985): 40–67.

Wynne, Lewis N. "Brownsville: The Reaction of the Negro Press." *Phylon* 33 (Second Quarter 1972): 153–160.

Young, Consuelo. "A Study of Reader Attitudes toward the Negro Press." *Journalism Quarterly* 21 (Summer 1944): 148–152.

Young, P. B., Jr. "The Negro Press—Today and Tomorrow." *Opportunity* 17 (July 1939): 204–205.

Zangrando, Robert L. *The NAACP Crusade against Lynching, 1909–1950*. Philadelphia, Pa.: Temple University Press, 1980.

Ziff, W. B. *The Negro Market: Published in the Interest of the Negro Press*. Atlanta, Ga.: W. B. Ziff, 1932.

"Ziff's List of Negro Papers." In *Nelson Chesman & Co.'s Newspaper Rate Book*, 392–393. New York: Nelson Chesman & Co., 1921.

Zimmerman, Andrew. *Alabama in Africa: Booker T. Washington, the German Empire, and the Globalization of the New South*. Princeton, N.J.: Princeton University Press, 2012.

Index